Understanding VAT on Property

Second Edition

Related titles available from Law Society Publishing:

Commonhold
Gary Cowen, James Driscoll and Laurence Target

Conveyancing Handbook
General Editor: Frances Silverman

Environmental Law Handbook (6th edn)
Trevor Hellawell

Licensing for Conveyancers
Tim Hayden and Jane Hanney

Planning and Compulsory Purchase Act 2004
Stephen Tromans, Martin Edwards, Richard Harwood, Justine Thornton

Profitable Conveyancing
Stephanie Dale

Trust Practitioner's Handbook
Gill Steel with contributions by Robert Mowbray and Charles Christian

Understanding Stamp Duty Land Tax (8th edn)
Reg Nock

All books from Law Society Publishing can be ordered from good bookshops or direct from our distributors, Marston Book Services, by telephone 01235 465656 or email law.society@marston.co.uk. Please confirm the price before ordering.

For further information or a catalogue, please email our editorial and marketing office: publishing@lawsociety.co.uk.

UNDERSTANDING VAT ON PROPERTY

SECOND EDITION

David Jordan

The Law Society

ISBN-10: 1–85328–994–9
ISBN-13: 978–1–85328–994–1

First edition published in 2002

This edition published in 2006 by the Law Society
113 Chancery Lane, London WC2A 1PL
Typeset by J&L Composition, Filey, North Yorkshire

Printed by Antony Rowe Ltd, Chippenham, Wilts

Contents

CONTENTS

Preface

In bringing this book up to date with a second edition, I have again tried to ensure that the complexities of VAT legislation are brought out in a practical way. VAT remains the most complex area of tax legislation in the UK, as recognised by HM Revenue and Customs in deciding that Sched. 10 now requires a complete re-write. I hope that the way this book is set out with its new chapters, and with examples and cross-references in particular, will help practitioners to deal with client matters, whether they have little or no knowledge of VAT and property matters, or are seasoned hands and simply require a reference to confirm issues.

Once again, in view of the constant evolution of VAT and the requirement for a lead time for editorial work and printing, there is a cut-off point after which current changes cannot be dealt with.

In the first edition, I introduced you to my favourite VAT quote: 'Common sense and the law applicable to VAT are not well acquainted', from the *Arbib* (No. 11486) tribunal decision of Miss J. Gort in November 1995. Another of my favourites is: 'Beyond the everyday world, both counsel have explained to us, lies the world of VAT, a kind of fiscal theme park in which factual and legal realities are suspended or inverted', which comes from Sedley L.J., in the *Royal & Sun Alliance Insurance Group plc* Court of Appeal decision from October 2001. If our judiciary has this perception of VAT, how is the ordinary person, into whose hands the government puts the responsibility for accounting correctly for VAT, supposed to stand a chance of getting things right?

Dave Jordan
May 2006

Acknowledgements

The writing of this second edition was a much longer job than writing the initial version. The text itself has been expanded considerably, and ensuring that all the relevant changes since 2002 are put into the correct place has meant that many parts had to be re-written in their entirety.

Once again, Ben Mullane at the Law Society has been of immense help in making sure this work comes into print, and I would also like to thank my wife once again for putting up with the long hours I have spent in the office.

This book remains dedicated to my Dad, James Harold Jordan, who had a thirst for learning, and would have got a real kick out of seeing it.

Table of cases

Table of statutes

Table of statutory instruments and European legislation

EUROPEAN LEGISLATION

CHAPTER 1

General principles

1.1 INTRODUCTION

This book is aimed at the specialist area of VAT and property, but there are of course more general areas of VAT, which may impinge upon property transactions, other than those directly related to the correct treatment of a property transaction. This section of the book attempts to cover these, but should not be taken as an all-exclusive text on, for example, VAT registration matters. It covers those VAT issues which apply to other transactions as well as those in land and property, and the issues raised should really be understood prior to moving on to the rest of the chapters which are specific to certain areas of land and property transactions.

With regard to VAT legislation, we are to a large part governed by European law, and where VAT is concerned the most relevant section of legislation is EC Directive 77/388, the Sixth Directive on VAT, Art. 13B which exempts certain supplies in relation to land, although there are provisions (under Art. 28) for member states to retain exemptions which were in place when the Sixth Directive was introduced in 1977, under which the UK retains the zero rate, which applies to some property transactions. In certain places the European legislation uses the phrase 'Member States shall. . .', such as in providing the exemptions in Art. 13B, and in such cases the UK is obliged to comply strictly to the terms set down in the European legislation – it is not allowed to restrict or widen the exemptions provided for under the European legislation. However, in some cases the word 'shall' is replaced with 'may' and allows member states latitude in the way in which the European legislation is brought into national law. The Sixth Directive is put into effect in the UK by the VAT Act (VATA) 1994, where the exemption for land transactions can be found in Sched. 9, Gp. 1, zero rates can be found in Sched. 8, Gps. 5 and 6 and the lower rates in Sched. 7A, Gps. 6 and 7. The detail of VAT accounting is controlled under the Value Added Tax Regulations 1995, SI 1995/2518 in particular, and many other statutory instruments which will be cited as the need arises.

Judgments from the European Court of Justice (ECJ) take precedence over cases decided in the national courts, regardless of which member state

1

they are in relation to, so that an Italian case decision, for example, can have a direct impact on how VAT should be treated in the UK.

Although the intention of this book is to be comprehensive and user friendly in the way in which it sets out the VAT treatment of land and property transactions, it cannot be emphasised enough that this is a complicated area of VAT law, and in complex cases it is paramount that individual professional advice be taken.

1.1.1 Jargon

In the same way as any specialist area has words which mean specific things in context with their subject matter, so VAT has its own jargon. Probably the first word used in this way for VAT purposes is *supply*. VAT is a tax on the *supply* of goods and services, and a *supplier* is a person who makes supplies of goods or services.

VAT is generally chargeable when the supply is made – not necessarily when it is paid for, although receipt of payment can identify the time at which VAT must be accounted for. This is an important part of the way in which VAT works. For example, a business may supply timber to its customers in return for which it expects payment. If that payment is never made, the VAT is still due to be accounted for as the supply of goods has taken place (unless the Cash Accounting Scheme is being used). In the same way, if money that has been paid over by customers in a shop is stolen, then VAT is due on the supplies made, but if stock is stolen then no VAT is due because no supply has been made. Services provided for no consideration (whether in money or otherwise) are specifically deemed not to be supplies, except in certain specified cases, such as private use of a business asset.

You will also quickly come across the terms *input tax* and *output tax*. These terms refer to the VAT on the flow of goods in or out of the business, not the flow of money, and this is why many people are often confused by them. Input tax is therefore the VAT paid on purchases (expenditure) or goods or services coming into the business; and output tax is the VAT on sales (income) or goods or services flowing out of the business.

The term *taxable person* refers to the registrable legal entity of a business, be it a sole proprietorship, partnership, limited company, co-ownership, trust or other legal entity.

A glossary of terms can be found in **Appendix E**.

1.1.2 Definition of 'land'

For VAT purposes, the definition of *land* includes any building and civil engineering works on it, together with any wall, trees and other plants, or any other structure in, under, on or over the land, whether natural or not, as long as they remain attached to the land.

Under European legislation, the term *building* includes 'any structure fixed to or in the ground' (Sixth Directive, Art. 4(3)).

HM Revenue and Customs (HMRC) accepts that where land and fixtures, such as plant and machinery, are the subject of a single conveyance, there is a single supply for VAT purposes.

1.2 SUPPLY

It is only supplies made by a taxable person 'in the course or furtherance of a business' activity that fall within the scope of VAT (VATA 1994, s.4(1)). The treatment of goods and services for VAT purposes is different – for services there needs to be 'consideration' for a supply to be made, whereas for goods, the simple transfer of ownership is sufficient to comprise a supply (e.g. a gift comprising goods is a supply for VAT purposes, whereas a gift of services is not). Where land and buildings are concerned, a *major interest* (the freehold sale or a lease of over 21 years) is treated as a supply of goods, whereas a *minor interest* (a lease of up to and including 21 years and licences to occupy, etc.) is treated as a supply of services (VATA 1994, s.96(1)). This can be important to recognise when determining the correct VAT treatment, and is of course the reason why they are defined as such – so that the treatment required can be applied.

In cases where assets of a business, including land or buildings, are used for private or other non-business purposes or made available to a third party to use free of charge, there is special provision for a deemed supply to be accounted for (VATA 1994, Sched. 4, para. 5(4)). The value to be applied in such cases is the cost of making the goods available (VATA 1994, Sched. 6, para. 7).

The term 'in the course or furtherance of a business', is not used in the European legislation, which instead refers to an 'economic activity' (VATA 1994, Sched. 4, para. 5(4)) and Sixth Directive on VAT, Art. 4(1)). There is no all-encompassing definition of 'business activity' in the VAT legislation, but VATA 1994, s.94(1) does state that 'business includes any trade, profession or vocation', and VATA 1994, s.94(2) includes memberships to clubs, associations or other organisations and admissions to premises.

Where specific land and property transactions are concerned, the case of *C & E Commrs v. Morrison's Academy Boarding Houses Association* [1978] STC 1, decided that the letting of boarding houses to students constituted a regular activity, conducted on sound and recognised business principles, even where there was no view to commercially making a profit, and the taxable person was therefore 'in the business' of making taxable supplies.

Another important case decision in this area is that of *C & E Commrs v. Lord Fisher* [1981] STC 238, QBD. Lord Fisher organised pheasant shoots on his land and invited friends and relatives to take part, asking them to make a contribution to the costs. The question before the court was whether this constituted a business activity or not. In determining that the activity was not carried on by way of business, the court relied heavily on the guidance set out in *Morrison's* above and set out the following tests, which have been followed ever since:

1. Is the activity a serious undertaking earnestly pursued?
2. Is the activity an occupation or function, which is actively pursued with reasonable or recognisable continuity?
3. Does the activity have a certain measure of substance in terms of the quarterly or annual value of taxable supplies made (bearing in mind that exempt supplies can also be business)?
4. Is the activity conducted in a regular manner and on sound and recognised business principles?
5. Is the activity predominately concerned with the making of taxable supplies for a consideration?
6. Are the taxable supplies that are being made of a kind which, subject to differences of detail, are commonly made by those who seek to profit from them?

European cases on the issue includes *WM van Tiem* v. *Staatssecretaris van Financiën* (ECJ, C-186/89) which determined that the grant of a right over immovable property was an economic activity for VAT purposes. In *DA Rompelman & EA Rompelman-van-Deelen* v. *Minister van Financien* (ECJ, C-268/83) it was determined that input tax incurred before a property was let was a preparatory act to an economic activity and the taxpayer was therefore entitled to registration and recovery of input tax. This would of course depend upon the taxpayer making taxable supplies or intending to do so.

More recently, the issue of 'business' has been looked at by the courts in the cases of *Yarburgh Children's Trust*, [2003] STC 207, ChD and *St Paul's Community Project Ltd* v. *C & E Commrs* [2004] STC 95, ChD. Both cases concerned charities running children's day nurseries and both charged parents for the children's attendance at the day nursery. If the activity were seen as 'non-business' then zero rating would apply to the construction of a new building to accommodate the activity, but if not, standard rating would apply. In both cases the Tribunal and the High Court determined that the activities carried out were not by way of business, essentially on the grounds that the prices charged were at concessionary rates and the service was provided to a district which was socially deprived. After the *Yarburgh* decision by the High Court, HMRC tried to restrict the decision to the individual circumstances of the case, and re-iterated the business tests set out above from the *Lord Fisher* case, but following the *St Paul's* decision it has had to accept that the decisions are of wider application.

1.2.1 Consideration

For VAT purposes, a supply includes: 'all forms of supply, but not anything done otherwise than for consideration' (VATA 1994, s.5(2)(a)). However, nowhere in UK or EU legislation is 'consideration' defined – this has been left to the courts to determine. The European Court's decision in *Staatssecretaris van Financiën* v. *Coöperatieve vereniging "Coöperatieve Aardappelenbewaarplaats GA"* (ECJ, C-154/80) [1981] ECR 445, concerned a cold storage facility for the use of which members paid a charge which was set annually. For two years there was no charge made, but the Dutch government raised an assessment on the basis that the members had received a benefit. The ECJ determined that 'consideration' must be directly linked with the services supplied and must be capable of being expressed in money, therefore the provision of services for no definitive subjective consideration did not constitute the provision of services 'against payment', a term used in the EC Second Directive which has now been replaced with 'for consideration' in the EC Sixth Directive.

In the later case of *Apple & Pear Development Council* v. *C & E Commrs* (ECJ, C-102/86) [1988] STC 221, the question was whether the mandatory charges levied from members constituted consideration for a supply of services. On the grounds that there was no direct link between the level or type of benefits and the level of the mandatory charge which members were obliged to pay, the European Court determined that the mandatory charges were not consideration and the Council was not making supplies for consideration.

1.2.2 Free supplies of land or property/gifts

Where land or property is disposed of free of charge this constitutes a deemed supply for VAT purposes (VATA 1994, Sched. 4, para. 9). In respect of the grant of a major interest (freehold or lease of over 21 years) it is a deemed supply of goods, and in respect of any disposal which does not amount to a major interest it is a deemed supply of services, but treated as a supply of goods under the above legislation, thereby bringing it within the deemed supply rules even if there is no consideration.

The value of the deemed supply is the full cost of making the land or property available, including the cost of any building works carried out. However, the deemed supply rules do not apply if there was no input tax incurred by the person making the supply.

1.2.3 Place of supply

The place of supply is important for determining whether a supply is subject to UK VAT or not. For services relating to land, the place of supply is where the land is situated (VAT (Place of Supply of Services) Order 1992, SI 1992/3121, Art. 5). Services relating to land include:

(a) The grant, assignment or surrender of –

    (i) any interest in land;

    (ii) a personal right to call for or be granted any interest in or right over land; or

    (iii) a licence to occupy land or any other contractual right exercisable over or in relation to land.

(b) Any works of construction, demolition, conversion, reconstruction, alteration, enlargement, repair or maintenance of a building or civil engineering work.

(c) Services such as are supplied by estate agents, auctioneers, architects, surveyors, engineers and others involved in matters relating to land.

This includes conveyancing carried out by solicitors, and the services of loss adjusters in relation to insurance claims for damage to specific land or buildings, and property management, including rent collection.

Therefore, where land is situated in the UK, the supplier of it or of services closely related to it will be required to consider UK VAT, and if supplies are in another member state of the EU it may well be necessary to register for VAT in that member state. The VAT treatment of supplies related to land differ from one member state to another, although the 'place of supply' rules remain the same, and separate advice should therefore be taken in such cases.

Where the land is situated in another member state, in certain cases registration in that member state may be avoided by use of the reverse charge mechanism. This applies where the recipient is registered for VAT and involves the supplier quoting the customer's VAT registration number on the sales invoice (or providing other proof that the customer is 'in business'). The customer then accounts for output tax on the supply and also recovers this as input tax subject to the partial exemption rules. Typically, the reverse charge applies to services listed in VATA 1994, Sched. 5, but its use has been extended in some member states to other services as well. The rules in the member state concerned should be checked before using this procedure for supplies relating to land.

1.2.4 Grants

Grants are outside the scope of VAT provided that they are given at arm's length and there is no supply made to the grantor in return for the funds. The issue was considered by the Court of Appeal in *C & E Commrs* v. *Church Schools Foundation Ltd* [2001] STC 1661, CA. CSF owned and operated seven schools and a company was formed to run the schools whilst CSF concentrated on management of the school properties, and granted a lease in them to the company. The company granted any operating surpluses to CSF and the agreement contemplated that the surpluses would be spent on maintaining and improving the school properties. The High Court decided that there was sufficient reciprocity between them to provide the required nexus between supply and consideration, despite the fact that CSF spent more on improvements than the surpluses granted by the company, and the fact that the grants could not be linked to any specific building works. However, the Court of Appeal overturned this decision on the basis that there was an insufficient link between the consideration and any supply, and certainly no more than there would be considered to be with any other sort of funding.

In the VAT Tribunal, the issue in *Heritage of London Trust Operations Ltd* (No. 18547) was whether a payment of £100,000 negotiated for the appellant by English Heritage for removal of a listed water tower was a 'grant' or 'consideration for a supply'. There was no written contract but the Tribunal examined the individual facts of the case and decided that it was consideration for a standard rated supply.

1.2.5 Sponsorship

Sponsorship is considered to be a supply of advertising services in return for the sponsorship money.

1.2.6 Government subsidies

In *Keeping Newcastle Warm* (ECJ, C-353/00), the European Court of Justice determined that the payment of the subsidy under the Home Energy Efficiency Grants Regulations 1992 did constitute part of the consideration for a supply, being part of the payment received by the claimant in return for the services it supplied to householders, and must therefore be included in the value for VAT purposes, on the basis that the Sixth Directive Art. 11A(1)(a) includes 'subsidies directly linked to the price of such supplies' in the taxable value. There must be a direct link between the funds received and the specific supply of goods or services in order for the funds to be treated as consideration. Setting targets which must be met, for example a common requirement for grants from local authority (service level agreements) and other bodies, does not on its own turn 'funding' into consideration.

1.2.7 Single/multiple supplies

As a result of the decision by the House of Lords (following referral of the case to the European Court of Justice for guidance) in *Card Protection Plan Ltd* (ECJ, C-349/96), HMRC issued *Business Brief 02/2001*, which outlined its policy with regard to single/multiple supplies. In this it stated that all reliance on prior UK case law, trade agreements, statements of practice or simply rulings from the VAT office, are null and void with effect from 1 June 2001, from which date the *Card Protection Plan* tests as laid down by the courts must be applied and the supplies treated accordingly. It also issued *Information Sheet 07/01* to assist businesses in determining whether they are making a number of supplies each chargeable at its own VAT rate or a single supply of different components chargeable at the rate applying to the main element of the supply. The *Card Protection Plan* case concerned whether a package of supplies consisting of mainly insurance, but also other benefits such as discounts on selected purchases, constituted a single supply taxable at one rate of VAT, or a bundle of separate supplies each of which should have its own VAT rate determined as applicable and the consideration therefore apportioned between them. The result was that there was considered to be a single supply, that being the exempt insurance, because this was the main aim of the customer in making the purchase and the other benefits were ancillary to this.

Tests to be applied as a result of the *Card Protection Plan* case

1. Where a transaction consists of a number of features, all of the circumstances in which it takes place must be considered.
2. Every supply must be regarded as distinct and independent but a single supply from an economic point of view should not be artificially split so as to distort the function of the VAT system (application of lower rates, zero rates or exemptions).
3. With the above in mind, it is necessary to consider the essential features of the transaction in order to determine if the customer is being supplied with one supply or several distinct principal supplies.
4. There is a single supply where one element is to be regarded as the principal service to which the others are ancillary.
5. A service must be regarded as ancillary if it does not constitute an aim of the customer in itself, but is simply a means of better enjoying the principal element of the supply.
6. A single price is not decisive, but may indicate there is a single supply.
7. If the circumstances indicate that the customer intended to purchase two or more distinct principal services with different tax liabilities, then the single price must be apportioned.
8. No single factor provides the whole test, they must be applied as a package.

Examples of this issue in VAT and property case law can be found in *Blendhome Ltd (t/a Stanhill Court Hotel)* (No. 16048) in which the tribunal found that the appellant was making a single standard rated supply of hotel accommodation for the purpose of catering rather than a supply of an exempt licence to occupy, and *John Window* (No. 17186) in which the appellant was found to be making a single supply of the exempt right to occupy a stable, rather than separate supplies of the exempt stabling and standard rated livery.

In the more recent decision of the House of Lords in *College of Estate Management* v. *C & E Commrs* [2005] UKHL 62, the issue concerned the provision of a pack of distance learning material (claimed to be zero rated) together with distance learning courses, including some face-to-face teaching and examinations, in the field of property management and construction.

The use of the distance learning pack constituted some 94 per cent of the student's time, with 4.5 per cent face-to-face teaching and 1.5 per cent sitting examinations. The Court determined that it is not the case that in all situations there will be 'principal' and 'ancillary' supplies – such as a restaurant which provides standard rated catering where the food (potentially zero rated) and service element (standard rated) would not be split. In the present case the supply was clearly a single supply of education and therefore wholly exempt, it would have been artificial to split the supply into its component parts.

When the supply of a building includes its fixtures, these are not seen as a separate supply and the fixtures are accorded the same VAT treatment as the supply of the building. Where the fixtures are the subject of a separate supply, then the VAT treatment appropriate to them (usually standard rated) should be applied.

1.3   RATES OF VAT

VAT is a transaction-based tax, rather than a tax based on profits or capital gains. It can therefore apply differently to two or more similar transactions, albeit that the differences are very minor. VAT legislation provides in the first instance that any supply of goods (whether or not for consideration), or services for consideration, is standard rated. It then goes on to provide for other treatments within the Schedules to the VATA 1994 and statutory instruments. The supplier must be sure to fulfil the conditions set down in the legislation (including the sometimes very detailed Notes to the Groups, which often contain exceptions) to gain any treatment other than standard rating. With regard to property-related transactions, the main areas we are concerned with are set out below.

1.3.1   Standard rate

This confers a broadly 'neutral state' for suppliers and applies to freehold sales of new (under three years old) commercial buildings and where the *option to tax* has been exercised. Although VAT at 17.5 per cent must be charged, the supplier is entitled to recover in full any VAT incurred on related expenditure. Standard rate is the liability applied when none of the reliefs to VAT set out below apply.

1.3.2   Reduced rate

The reduced rate is currently charged at 5 per cent. For property purposes it applies only to dwellings and similar buildings in respect of certain conversion and renovation works, and to the installation of insulation and energy saving materials (see VATA 1994, Sched. 7A).

1.3.3 Zero rate

This is the most favourable liability, restricted generally to new or newly converted dwellings and certain other residential/charitable buildings. VAT is charged, but at 0 per cent, and being a taxable supply, the supplier is entitled to recover in full any VAT incurred on related expenditure (see VATA 1994, Sched. 8). The concept behind the zero rates is to relieve completely from VAT certain supplies, usually for social reasons.

1.3.4 Exempt

This is usually the most unfavourable state, unless little or no VAT is incurred by the supplier, in which case it may be favourable. This is the basic VAT treatment for land and property transactions and applies to sales and leases of houses and other residential and charitable buildings (other than new ones which qualify for zero rating in respect of the first grant of a major interest (freehold sale or lease of over 21 years) by the person constructing), leases of commercial property (except where the option to tax has been exercised – see **2.7**) and sales of commercial property over three years old (see VATA 1994, Sched. 9).

1.3.5 Outside the scope

'Outside the scope' generally implies that there is a payment received but there has been either no supply (such as in the case of grants or donations) or the supply has taken place outside the UK. It is also a treatment for special circumstances, such as 'transfer of a business as a going concern' which is statutorily provided for under VATA 1994, s.49 and the VAT (Special Provisions) Order 1995, SI 1995/1268, Art. 5, for protection of HMRC – see **2.15**. Because the supply is outside the scope of VAT, no VAT is charged by the person receiving the funds. Any VAT incurred directly in relation to this non-business income is potentially not recoverable, not being incurred in the course or furtherance of a taxable business activity. However, in the recent High Court decision in *Church of England Children's Society* v. *HMRC Commrs* [2005] EWHC 1692, ChD, it was determined that recovery of input tax on fundraising costs incurred by a charity (employing a third party consultant to generate donations) should be determined in accordance with the VAT treatment of the activity for which the funds raised were used – if this was non-business there would be no entitlement to recovery of VAT on the related costs, etc. Otherwise, if the 'outside the scope' funding is only part of the overall activities, recovery of VAT incurred generally relies on the underlying business activities of the supplier.

The treatment of input tax relating to supplies that are outside the scope because the place of supply is outside the UK is different. If the supply would be taxable if it were made in the UK, then input tax is recoverable.

The treatment of input tax incurred on the transfer of a going concern, such as legal fees relating to the sale of the business, is determined by looking at the overall business activity that is the subject of the transfer. If the business is fully taxable, the input tax is fully recoverable. If the business is wholly exempt, then the input tax is exempt input tax. If the business is partially exempt then the input tax is treated as non-attributable and an apportionment must be calculated (see partial exemption at **1.9**).

There is no list or schedule of 'outside the scope' transactions, because, by their nature, they are either outside the terms of the legislation or are treated as such simply because the place of supply is outside the UK.

1.4 VAT REGISTRATION

1.4.1 Legal entity

For VAT purposes it is the legal entity which registers for VAT, whether that be a sole proprietorship, partnership, limited company, limited partnership, co-ownership, trust, pension fund, etc. Any business activity carried on by that legal entity is covered under the VAT registration, unlike direct tax, where different business activities may be separately taxed. So, for example, a publican who also receives rental income will be taxed on all his activities in the one VAT registration, unless the other activities are carried on with another person to create a separate 'person' for VAT purposes (e.g. a partnership). If an individual has a sole proprietorship business and is also in partnership, therefore, there will be two VAT registrations, one for each legal entity. HMRC has wide powers with regard to the artificial separation of businesses to avoid VAT by splitting business activities so that one or more of them remains under the registration limits (VATA 1994, Sched. 1, para. 1A). A person for VAT purposes is a 'taxable person' when they are or are required to be registered for VAT (VATA 1994, s.3).

The HMRC Statement of Practice on separation of business activities can be found in *VAT Notice 700/1, 'Should I be registered for VAT?'*.

1.4.2 Application for registration

Application for registration is made on form VAT 1, with form VAT 2 being required for partnerships, trustees and co-owners. The form is sent to the appropriate Registration Unit, details of which can be accessed from the

HMRC website at **www.hmrc.gov.uk**. Processing of the registration documents can be assisted by sending a covering letter detailing the business activity being carried out and evidence of intent to make taxable supplies, particularly if none have yet been made, and/or evidence of incurring input tax. With regard to registrations relating to property, HMRC often requires proof of ownership of the property, such as the completion statement or copy of the Land Registry title. In cases where supplies will only be taxable subject to the option to tax being exercised, the option to tax notification should be sent with form VAT 1 (see **2.7.9**). Sending this information with form VAT 1 can avoid the lengthy delays involved when HMRC sends out requests for further information and often a lengthy questionnaire (although this is often sent out in any case – even if the information requested has already been supplied in the covering letter!). Readers should beware of HMRC insisting that a person has to elect to waive exemption prior to being registered. Over the past few years there have been a number of incidents of the Registration Unit insisting that applicants opt to tax – even in cases where the property is residential (where no election is possible) or where the property in question is a commercial property and where HMRC has already been advised there will be the freehold sale of a property under three years old (a mandatory standard rated supply without the election to waive exemption).

1.4.3 Compulsory registration

There are two key tests for compulsory registration for VAT:

1. A business is required to register for VAT when in any period of 12 months, on a rolling basis, it exceeds the registration limit in force – it then has 30 days to notify HMRC of its liability to register and must then register from the first day of the month following the 30-day period. The test is carried out on the turnover on the past 12 months at the end of the month in question, on a rolling basis – see example below (VATA 1994, Sched. 1, para. 1(1b)).
2. For larger businesses there is a requirement that, if at any time it is believed that the turnover in the next 30 days will exceed the annual limit in force, then the business must register with immediate effect although the business still has 30 days in which to notify HMRC of the requirement to register (VATA 1994, Sched. 1, para. 8).

In determining whether the turnover threshold has been exceeded, the sale of capital assets is expressly excluded under VATA 1994, Sched. 1, para. 7, unless it comprises an interest in, right over or licence to occupy land which is a taxable supply at standard rate (VATA 1994, Sched. 1, para. 8).

Example 1

A business exceeds the historic registration limits (item 1 above) at the end of March (turnover in the last 12 months to 31 March). It then has until the end of April to notify HMRC. It must register with effect from 1 May that year. Any income received in respect of supplies made prior to the effective date of registration is free of VAT, but VAT must be accounted for on any income in respect of supplies made from 1 May.

Example 2

A business signs a contract which will generate income over the annual registration limit in the next 30 days (item 2 above). It must register with effect from the date of signing the contract, and account for VAT on any supplies made from that date, although it has 30 days within which to file the application for registration.

1.4.4 Voluntary registration

A business may register for VAT if it is carrying on a business activity which involves the making of taxable supplies, even though the value of those supplies may be minimal (VATA 1994, Sched. 1, para. 9). Most voluntary registrations occur because the business can then claim input tax, although recovery will be limited to the VAT incurred in relation to the taxable supplies it makes only, subject to the partial exemption *de minimis* limits (see **1.9**). For example, a sub-contractor working on new houses will likely be making zero-rated supplies, and by registering will be able to recover any VAT incurred on expenditure.

1.4.5 Intending trader registration

This is for those businesses which are carrying on preparatory works to the making of taxable supplies (e.g. digging ditches in which to put cables to deliver telecommunications services, planting trees in order to grow timber, constructing buildings to be let or sold (VATA 1994, Sched. 1, para. 10). In each case there is likely to be a lead-time until the business will make taxable supplies, but it may nevertheless require registration so that it can recover VAT on its current expenditure. Recovery of input tax is conditional upon taxable supplies being made, although if the business venture fails for some reason there is no requirement to pay back VAT already recovered as long as the intention to make taxable supplies has never changed (see *Intercommunale voor Zeewaterontzilting (INZO)* v. *Belgium* (ECJ, C-110/94, 29 February 1997)).

When applying for registration the evidential requirements tend to be more stringent for an intending trader registration and HMRC will require to see some documentary evidence of intent to make taxable supplies, and with property registrations will often require a copy of the Land Registry title or other evidence of ownership. Providing evidence of having incurred input tax with the intention to make taxable supplies is also useful and a sample of purchase invoices should be sent in with the application for registration, together with a copy of any contract and the election to waive exemption where it is necessary in order for the supplies to be treated as intended taxable supplies. It should also be noted that any person registering on an intending basis with regard to taxable supplies to be made in the future (such as a property developer) but who already has exempt income (such as from letting of houses or commercial property) may wish to negotiate a special partial exemption method (see **1.9.8**), otherwise they may be severely limited in the amount of non-attributable input tax they are entitled to recover.

1.4.6 Group registration

Corporate bodies may register as a group for VAT purposes (VATA 1994, s.43). The main benefits of this is that a single VAT Return is submitted for the group as a whole (which makes the limits for penalties much higher) and that transactions between group companies are not subject to VAT as the group is treated as a single entity for VAT purposes. HMRC has wide powers under VATA 1994, Sched. 9A to counter any avoidance that relies on the grouping provisions to gain a VAT advantage. A group can consist of any companies under common control, in that either one person or a partnership own a controlling interest in the companies, or if one company owns the controlling interest in another (VATA 1994, s.43A). A person controls a company if that person is empowered by statute to control that body's activities (i.e. holds a majority of voting shares) or if a company is that body's holding company within the meaning of the Companies Act 1985, s.736. It is not necessary to include all such companies within the group – one can pick and choose which to include or exclude. The controlling company does not have to be included in the group, and does not have to be established in the UK, but any companies included in the group must be established in the UK (i.e. have a fixed place of business in the UK).

In addition to the control requirements, HMRC has issued *Information Sheet 07/04*, which sets out new eligibility requirements for VAT group registration. The new rules have been introduced to counter a specific VAT avoidance scheme. The key area being addressed is the structure where a supplier to a partly exempt company or group forms a company together with that group, with the group control requirements being met, in order that it can become part of the VAT group and avoid VAT on the charge made for the supplies. The new rules are contained in the VAT (Groups: eligibility) Order 2004, SI 2004/1931 which came into effect on 1 August 2004.

Example

To provide a simple example of the arrangements the new rules are designed to counter, if we have company A which is partially exempt, for example providing standard rated financial advice and receiving exempt financial and insurance commissions, and company B which provides standard rated marketing services to company A, then if company A and company B are under common ownership, they would likely want to form a VAT group so that they remove the VAT cost on the charge from company A to company B. This is normal procedure and is still available under the new rules. However, if company A and company B are not under common control, the arrangements the new conditions were put in place to counter are for company A and company B to set up company C, which is partly owned by each but meets the control requirements to form a VAT group with company A. Once the VAT group is formed, the VAT on the charges previously from company B to company A would be avoided because intra-group supplies between company C and company A would be outside the scope of VAT.

Although the basic definitions and control requirements relating to VAT groups have been retained and continue to apply, from 1 August 2004 there are two new conditions which must be met in order for a VAT group to be formed. Following consultation with interested parties these conditions have been specifically targeted to prevent the type of avoidance arrangements outlined above.

The first of the two conditions that must be met is the 'benefits condition'. This will be satisfied if no more than 50 per cent of the benefits generated by the business activity accrue to third parties. For these purposes 'benefits' include: profits currently being earned by the business activity; charges made by anyone for managing the business activity that involves the making of intra-group supplies or for providing staff for managing it, excluding remuneration or bonuses paid to directors or employees of the body; and any charges made to the body corporate insofar as they exceed open market value.

In addition to the 'specified body' condition, the second condition has been termed as the 'group accounts consolidation condition'. This is met if, under generally accepted accounting practice (GAAP), a person controlling the VAT group consolidates the specified body as a subsidiary in his consolidated group accounts; and there is no third party who under GAAP consolidates the specified body as a subsidiary in his consolidated group accounts. If more than one person controls the group then the first requirement need only be met by one of them. The condition also applies to limited partnerships.

The new rules apply only to a 'specified body', the definition for which is:

1. The VAT group turnover exceeded £10 million in the last year or is expected to exceed £10 million in the coming year. Turnover includes all

supplies made by the group, excluding intra-group supplies. Expected turnover should be estimated on the assumption that the corporate body is included in the VAT group. If the body corporate is the sole general partner of a limited partnership, then the limited partnership's turnover is included.

2. The body corporate concerned is partly owned by a third party (whether directly or through other companies) or the business activity is managed by a third party, or the body corporate is the sole general partner of a limited partnership. A 'third party' is any person or partnership, except anyone who controls the whole group, including direct and indirect holding companies, all the way up to the ultimate controlling person; anyone controlled by a person who controls the whole group (including all subsidiaries); any individual who is a director or employer of the body corporate; a partner in a limited liability partnership.

3. The body corporate or limited partnership has a 'relevant business activity'. 'Relevant business activities' includes: making supplies to other group members which carry VAT (or would carry VAT if the company were not in a VAT group), which are not incidental to the business activity, and where the VAT group cannot recover VAT in full on the supplies (or would not be able to do so if the body corporate were not in the VAT group).

4. The body is not specifically excepted from being a specified body. The specific exceptions are: a body corporate that controls all the other VAT group members; a body corporate whose activities another body corporate is empowered by statute to control; a body corporate whose only activity is acting as a trustee of an occupational pension scheme; charities.

Dormant companies are excluded from the regime because they do not carry out a relevant business activity, but the new rules were also applied with immediate effect to existing groups, which had to examine their circumstances and take action to exclude corporate bodies caught by the new rules from the VAT group, by notifying HMRC within 30 days from their introduction on 1 August 2004.

Application for a new group registration requires a new form VAT 1 to be completed in respect of the representative company (in whose name and to whom all Returns and correspondence will be sent) even in cases where the companies are already registered, together with forms VAT 50 and VAT 51. In all cases, a new VAT registration number will be assigned. HMRC has 90 days to approve or otherwise the creation of a VAT group. Once the group is formed, new companies can be added by use of the form VAT 51 only, even where the new group company is not otherwise registered for VAT. HMRC can refuse to allow a company to leave a VAT group and even in cases where the control requirements cease to exist, HMRC authority to leave the group must be sought and the company will only cease to be a member of the group from the date stipulated by HMRC.

There is also the provision for a self-supply to be accounted for on any assets purchased within the last three years if a company joins a VAT group by way of the transfer of a going concern. The latter measure was introduced to prevent partially exempt groups using the transfer of going concern rules to gain assets free of VAT (VATA 1994, s.44).

1.4.6.1   First grant of a major interest

It should be noted that where a supply comprises of the freehold or lease of over 21 years and is from one group member to another, it is not the first grant of a major interest for zero-rating purposes, because supplies between group members are ignored for VAT purposes. In order to be the first grant of a major interest, the grant must be to a person not in the VAT group. In cases where there is first a grant of a major interest to another group member, and then a grant to a person outside the VAT group, the grant to the person outside the VAT group can be zero rated as the first grant of a major interest, and what went on before within the VAT group is ignored, providing the group member making the grant is the 'person constructing' or converting the building and all the other criteria for zero rating are met. See also *Business Brief 11/03*.

1.4.7   Registration by divisions

A corporate body may register by divisions. However, unlike with group registration there is no choice – if the registration is on a divisional basis, each division must register separately – you cannot group some divisions and have some separate (VATA 1994, s.46).

1.4.8   Flat rate scheme for small businesses

There is a flat rate scheme for businesses with a taxable turnover of less than £150,000, and where total turnover (i.e. taxable plus exempt income) does not exceed £187,500. Set out below are a few of the property related flat rates which apply. In addition, in the first year of registration, the business enjoys a 1 per cent reduction in the rates as set out. The essence of the scheme is that the business charges VAT as normal, but only accounts for output tax to HMRC by applying the flat rate to gross turnover (including VAT, zero-rated income, exempt income, etc.) and also does not claim any input tax unless the purchase is over £2,000 including VAT.

Table 1.1   Flat rate scheme

Main business activity	Flat rate percentage	
	Before 01/01/04	From 01/01/04
Architect, civil and structural engineer or surveyor	13.5	**12.5**
General building or construction services*	9	**8.5**
Hotel or accommodation	10.5	**9.5**
Labour-only building or construction services*	14.5	**13.5**
Lawyer or legal services	13.5	**13**
Mining or quarrying	10	**9**
Real estate activity not listed elsewhere	13	**12**

* Building or construction services, use 'Labour-only' if the value of materials supplied is less than 10 per cent of your turnover. If the value of the materials is more than this, builders use the 'General building' flat rate.
Source: VAT Notice 732.

For further information see *VAT Notice 733, Flat Rate Scheme for Small Businesses*.

1.4.9   Joint ventures

Joint ventures can cause problems for VAT purposes because they involve two or more separate legal entities, usually only one of which has an interest in the land, and the other which usually supplies services to the landowner in return for a share of the profits. In property joint ventures, for example, it is the person holding the interest in the land who will be seen as making the grant of an interest in that land, whereas the other joint venture 'partner' will likely have no interest in the land, and therefore their share of the profits in the arrangement cannot be consideration for the exempt grant of an interest in land. This can lead to positions where the person granting the interest in land makes the exempt supply, and the other person is supplying taxable services, the VAT on which is irrecoverable exempt input tax in the hands of the person granting the interest in the land (see *Strathearn Gordon Associates Ltd* (No. 1884)).

Example

JJ Builders and LL Property Developers have a joint venture agreement regarding the refurbishment of houses. LL Property Developers funds the purchase of the houses and JJ Builders carries out all refurbishment works. The property is then sold and they have an agreement to split the profits on a 50/50 basis. As it is LL Property Developers only who hold an interest in the property, their sale is exempt from VAT. When they pass back half of the profits to JJ Builders, this is consideration for a taxable supply of building services. JJ Builders must account for output tax on the amount received and LL Property Developers (even if it is registered for VAT) will be unable to recover this as it is directly attributable exempt input tax.

In cases where both parties have an interest in the land, they will be treated as co-owners (see **1.4.11**) and a separate VAT registration would be required in joint names if taxable supplies are to be made. If the result of the joint venture (each party having an interest in the land) is an exempt supply, then each joint venture partner would receive his share of the proceeds from the co-ownership registration as outside the scope of VAT.

Structuring of a joint venture in a way that is VAT efficient can be seen in the High Court decision in *Latchmere Properties Ltd* v. *C & E Commrs* [2005] All ER (D) 142. *Latchmere* entered into an agreement with the owner of the land to develop the land in return for a share of the profits. Because funding was difficult to obtain and for Stamp Duty reasons the parties structured the agreement as follows:

1. A minimum sale price for each unit was agreed.
2. A purchase price was also agreed, being the price *Latchmere* would pay the owner of the land when each unit was sold after development, or at the end of a specified period if the unit was not sold.
3. *Latchmere* was to carry out the development at its own cost and risk.
4. The difference between the actual sale price and the agreed minimum sale price would be divided equally between the land owner and *Latchmere*.

As a result of this structuring, *Latchmere* did not have to fund the purchase of the units prior to development and sale and there was a single Stamp Duty charge because there was only one sale, from the original land owner to the eventual purchaser – no units were actually purchased by *Latchmere*, all having been sold to third parties before the specified date. HMRC assessed on the basis that the land owner paid *Latchmere* for the standard rated construction services it had provided in developing the property, with third party payment from the eventual purchasers. *Latchmere* argued that it had acquired an equitable interest in the properties as a result of the agreement with the land owner and that the disposition of this equitable interest was an exempt supply. The VAT tribunal agreed with *Latchmere* that it had gained an interest in the land – it had the right to purchase the units from the land owner and the obligation to purchase them if they were not otherwise sold by the specified date. The consideration received by *Latchmere* was therefore in respect of its interest in land and not in respect of the construction services it had provided – the link with the equitable interest was more direct than the link with the construction services, especially in view of the real risk that *Latchmere* was taking. The tribunal therefore allowed the appeal, and the High Court upheld this decision.

1.4.10 Legal/beneficial owners

A legal interest in land involves its formal ownership, whereas a beneficial ownership of land involves the right to receive the benefit of any supplies made of the land, such as rent or proceeds of sale. In many cases the legal and beneficial ownership of land is in the same hands, but they can be separated and in such cases are treated as separate supplies. However, where the legal and beneficial interests are held by separate persons and a single supply is made in relation to the land (which would normally be seen as made by the legal owner) VAT legislation makes provision for the beneficial owner of a building to be treated as the person making the supply (VATA 1994, Sched. 10, para. 8(1)). The effect is to disregard the legal owner's supply in such cases and treat the supply as being made by the beneficial owner. Input tax is also treated as recoverable by the beneficial owner even if the supply is to the legal owner.

The provisions of VATA 1994, Sched. 10, para. 8(1) were reviewed by the High Court in *Abbey National plc* v. *C & E Commrs* [2005] EWHC 1187 where *Abbey* used the provision to make what has been termed a 'virtual assignment' of its property to a third party in a re-structuring exercise. This comprised an arrangement whereby *Abbey* outsourced its property holdings, including its lease interests, by assigning the right to the income stream for rents to a third party in return for a lump sum. Where the property was leased to *Abbey*, those leases were not legally assigned to the third party because the landlord's permission (required under the terms of the leases) had not or could not be obtained. The intention, nevertheless, was to leave the third party in the same position as if those leases had been legally assigned, so that they could then grant purported leases back to *Abbey* (to occupy them in the course of its business). The High Court accepted that, in these circumstances, a genuine right to occupy the property had been granted by the third party to *Abbey* and accepted that such a supply was exempt subject to the election to waive exemption, but at the time of writing HMRC has been granted leave to appeal to the Court of Appeal. As a result of this decision, HMRC announced a review of 'beneficial ownership' in *Business Brief 23/05*, as its policy prior to this decision was that VATA 1994, Sched. 10, para. 8 only applied in such situations to treat the beneficial owner as the person who made the supply and it considers that the interpretation of the court in this case goes wider than the explanation of its effect given to Parliament when the measure was introduced and that it is wider than EC law permits.

There is also special provision for the transfer of a going concern of property involving beneficial owners – see **2.15.4**.

1.4.11 Co-owners

Where property is owned by a number of people, they are treated as a single VAT registrable entity and registered as a partnership with joint and several liability (VATA 1994, s.51A). Consequently, an option to tax by one co-owner is effective in relation to the whole property. Where a co-owner disposes of his interest in the property there is no supply for VAT purposes by that co-owner. However, where one co-owner acquires the part shares of the other co-owners so that the property is owned by a single person, there is a supply of the property by the co-owners (see **3.8** for details regarding commonhold property).

1.4.12 Development corporations

Development corporations are public bodies but do not qualify for treat-ment under VATA 1994, s.33 (which allows certain government bodies, such as local authorities, to recover all input tax incurred in the course of their non-business statutory activities). They are grant funded, usually by central government, and their supplies may not only consist of the devel-opment of land, but also the improvement of the amenities and infra-structure of the area they are concerned with. Input tax they incur is not seen as related to the grant funding they receive, but rather the use to which the property on which the expenditure is incurred is looked at. There are no special VAT reliefs or treatment for development corpora-tions and it is likely that they will have non-business activities and first have to identify VAT incurred in relation to business activities before deter-mining the amount of VAT which may be recovered subject to the partial exemption rules.

1.4.13 Non-UK resident owners

Overseas owners of land or property in the UK may register for VAT directly at the Overseas Persons Unit at Aberdeen VAT office (HMRC, Overseas Persons Unit, Customs House, 28 Guild Street, Aberdeen AB9 2DY) or by appointing a UK agent and registering at that agent's Registration Unit. For direct registrations at Aberdeen, the taxpayer must undertake either to make the business records available to HMRC in the UK for inspection or to fund the cost of a VAT officer making a trip overseas to the principal place of busi-ness to inspect the records. If a UK agent is appointed, HMRC will require a letter of authority to be submitted with form VAT 1 when applying for regis-tration. The place of supply for supplies of, or closely connected to, land and property is where the land or property is situated, so that non-UK landlords of UK property are subject to the UK VAT system, regardless of where they may have their usual place of business.

An overseas owner of land may also appoint a 'fiscal representative' or 'tax representative' to register for VAT in his place. This is not usually to be recommended as the fiscal representative has personal liability for the overseas land owner, and appointment as an 'agent' is therefore to be preferred, where liability remains with the overseas land owner.

1.4.14 Ownership of property outside the UK

When a person owns property outside the UK, or supplies services closely related to land situated outside the UK, the place of supply rules (VAT (Place of Supply of Services) Order 1992, SI 1992/3121, para. 5) provides that the place of supply is where the land is situated (see **1.2.3**). If the property is in another EU member state, then registration may be required there if, in accordance with the legislation of that member state, any supplies made are taxable.

1.4.15 Transfer of a going concern

There are special rules with regard to registration when a business is purchased as the transfer of a business as a going concern (VATA 1994, Sched. 1, para. 2 and VAT (Special Provisions) Order 1995, SI 1995/1268, Art. 5). In such cases the vendor's turnover in the past 12 months must be identified. If this was over the registration limit, then the registration of the new owner must take place from the date of transfer. This is to prevent a new owner having a 30-day-plus period in which to exceed the limit and then a 30-day notification period, leading to two-plus months of VAT-free turnover before registration would be required under the normal historic turnover rules.

A transfer of a going concern takes place when the business assets are sold, putting the purchaser in the position of being able to carry on the business without a significant break. (For further details regarding the conditions to be met, see **2.15**.)

1.4.16 Deregistration

A business is required to notify HMRC within 30 days of ceasing to make taxable supplies and deregistration will then take place (VATA 1994, Sched. 1, para. 11). A business with a taxable turnover below the deregistration threshold (usually about £2,000 less than the registration threshold) or which can demonstrate to the satisfaction of HMRC that its turnover in the next 12 months will be below the deregistration threshold, is entitled to deregister from VAT (VATA 1994, Sched. 1, para. 13). It is the policy of HMRC not to backdate deregistrations before the date upon which the request is made, in accordance with the legislation (see also *Susan Oldfield* (No. 17352)).

When a business deregisters, there is a deemed supply on the current value of any stock or assets held on that date, on which VAT has been recovered, unless the VAT on the deemed supply would be less than £1,000 (VATA 1994, Sched. 4, para. 8). This includes land and property, for example where the option to tax has been exercised or a new commercial building under three years old (see *Zanex Ltd* (No. 17460)). Therefore, even where rents are under the VAT registration threshold, the landlord may wish to remain VAT registered to avoid this charge upon deregistration.

With regard to land or buildings, it should be noted that where the option to tax has been exercised, there is no deemed supply where the property was acquired without VAT being charged, even if VAT has subsequently been incurred on renovation or refurbishment works. However, the option to tax is still in force and if the rental or other income (such as the freehold sale) means that the registration limit is exceeded, then registration must be re-applied for and VAT accounted for. Where VAT has been recovered in respect of the purchase of an opted property (but not in respect of subsequent works to the building) then VAT output tax will be due on deregistration.

The deemed supply also excludes other goods that were acquired without payment of VAT on the purchase.

In addition, where goods have been incorporated into a building owned by the registered person, and that person deregisters, HMRC states that there is a deemed supply under the VAT (Supply of Services) Order 1993, SI 1993/1507. For example, if a person is registered for holiday letting, and incurs VAT on building repairs, and then deregisters, HMRC would require a deemed supply to be accounted for. However, there is doubt as to whether this is absolutely correct. The legislation actually states:

3.   Subject to articles 6, 6A and 7 below, where a person carrying on a business puts services which have been supplied to him to any private use or uses them, or makes them available to any person for use, for a purpose other than a purpose of the business he shall be treated for the purposes of the Act as supplying those services in the course or furtherance of the business, except for the purposes of determining whether tax on the supply of the services to him is input tax of his under section 24 of the Act.

3A. For the purposes of this Order, references to services supplied to a person include references to supplies of–

   (a)   a major interest in land,
   (b)   any building or part of a building,
   (c)   any civil engineering work or part of such a work, or
   (d)   any goods incorporated or to be incorporated in a building or civil engineering work (whether by being installed as fixtures or fittings or otherwise).

The wording of para. 3 of the Order requires VAT output tax to be accounted for where services (including the items in para. 3A) are put to use 'privately' or used for other than 'business' purposes. A correct reading would therefore only require output tax to be accounted for on deregistration if the business ceased, not, for example, if it fell below the deregistration limits and continued after deregistration took place.

The deemed supply also does not apply in cases where: the assets are disposed of by way of a transfer of a going concern; the business is carried on by a person after the death, incapacity or bankruptcy of the registered person; or the person deregisters due to joining the flat rate scheme for farmers.

Where a capital item is retained at deregistration and is still within its adjustment period, a final adjustment must be made (see **1.10**). This can be an expensive trap, with 10 per cent of the VAT on the purchase price of the asset at stake for every year left in the 10-year adjustment period.

1.4.17 Pre-registration input tax

When registering for VAT, it is important to remember to take action on a timely basis with regard to input tax incurred before the date of registration (VAT Regulations 1995, SI 1995/2518, reg. 111). Input tax incurred prior to the date of registration on services is restricted to that incurred in the six months prior to the registration date (including construction services and materials supplied in conjunction with them). The six-month rule for services is based on the reasoning that any services provided prior to this will have been 'used up' prior to the registration and will not therefore be used in the making of taxable supplies. There is therefore no apportionment required for any services which have been used partly before and partly after registration, a claim for the full amount of input tax paid on the purchase can be made (see *Denise Jerzynek* (No. 18767)).

For goods, recovery is limited to those on hand at the date of registration and purchased within three years of the date of registration, and it is necessary to provide a list of stock and assets on hand at the date of registration to be kept with records for inspection as required.

Recovery of input tax on pre-registration purchases is excluded for any goods which have been supplied on or consumed prior to the date of registration, and any services such as work on goods where the goods have been supplied on or prior to the registration date. If input tax has been incurred earlier than these time limits allow, then it may be possible to register from an earlier date (see **1.4.19**).

Example

A new property development company may incur costs of obtaining planning permission, negotiating land purchase, construction costs, etc. long before making a taxable supply and being required to be registered for VAT. The company should preferably apply to register as an intending trader (see **1.4.5**) when it commences its activities, but if for any reason this does not happen, it can apply for registration retrospectively to a date within six months of first incurring input tax on services, thus securing recovery of this VAT, but the application for a retrospective date must be made with the initial application for registration or the availability of this facility will be lost. The strict policy of HMRC is to refuse retrospective registration once the person is registered. If the company applied for registration at a current date more than six months after VAT on services was incurred, it would be unable to recover that VAT.

With regard to building materials supplied with construction services more than six months prior to the date of registration, see *Park Avenue Methodist Church Trustees* (No. 17443), where the tribunal decided that it would be wholly artificial to separate any goods supplied with construction services and dismissed the appeal, so that the six-month rule only applied. However, where shop fitting is concerned and the goods are more discernible than just building materials, such as service counters, cabinets, mirrors and other display items fixed to the building, see *G, J and B Miller* (No. 18630) in which the VAT tribunal held that there was a supply of goods to be fitted and substantially allowed the appeal.

1.4.18 Pre-incorporation input tax

Input tax incurred before the date of incorporation may be recovered providing that it was incurred by a person who became a member, officer, or employee of the company and they are reimbursed or have received an undertaking that they will be reimbursed for the whole of the amount paid, providing that person was not at the time a taxable person in their own right – subject of course to the above timing rules for recovery of pre-registration input tax (VAT Regulations 1995, SI 1995/2518, reg. 111).

1.4.19 Retrospective registration

Once the date for registration has been chosen, HMRC will not allow retrospection, but a retrospective registration date may be granted if it is asked for at the time of the initial application for registration. In this way a date can be chosen within six months of first incurring input tax on services or within the three-year rule for goods. HMRC has discretion on whether or not to allow retrospection and it is necessary to show that it would have allowed registration on the date requested had it been asked for at that time. Incurring input tax with the intent to make taxable supplies is a sufficient reason for registering and copies of the earliest invoices should be sent with the registration application to evidence this.

It can sometimes be necessary to notify the option to tax as a precondition to registering for VAT. Strictly, this should only be required if the option to tax would need to be exercised to achieve the taxable supplies intended by the developer, and if the intention is to make a standard rated freehold sale of a new commercial building, for example, then no option to tax should be required. As the option to tax cannot be exercised retrospectively, a retrospective registration is not available in cases where it is necessary to opt to tax in order for taxable supplies to have been made, especially in cases where the prior written permission of HMRC is required, but it may be possible to opt to tax from a current date and obtain an agreed apportioned recovery of some of the input tax (see also option to tax at **2.7** and *Notice 742A Opting to Tax Land and Buildings*).

1.5 TAX POINTS

1.5.1 Basic tax point

The term 'tax point' refers to the time at which VAT is required to be accounted for. For VAT accounting purposes, services are treated differently to goods, because they tend to be intangible and it can be difficult to determine exactly when they are carried out. There are 'basic' tax point rules for both goods and services, which may be superseded by 'actual' tax points. The basic tax point for a supply of goods is the date that the goods are removed, made available or delivered to the customer. For services, the basic tax point is the date when the service is performed, and is usually taken as the time when the service is complete, apart from the invoicing (VATA 1994, s.6; VAT Regulations 1995, SI 1995/2518, regs. 81–95).

1.5.2 Actual tax point

For both goods and services an 'actual' tax point occurs at the earliest of the basic tax point, the date of issue of a tax invoice, or the date of receipt of payment, unless any of the special rules set out below apply.

1.5.3 14-day rule

There is a further accounting simplification to the tax point rules which provides that if an invoice is raised within 14 days of the basic tax point, then the invoice date becomes the tax point for the supply, providing that payment has not already been received. In certain cases the 14-day rule can be extended, but authority from HMRC must be obtained in writing. For example, if a business invoices once a month the 14-day rule may be extended to 30 days. It can be beneficial to defer the tax point by using this mechanism, particularly if doing so means that the VAT on a large transaction does not have to be accounted for until the next VAT period.

For solicitors, the 14-day rule is extended, by agreement of HMRC with the Law Society, to three months after the performance of the services in cases where the consideration is not ascertainable at or before the time of when the services are supplied (e.g. legal aid cases).

For local authorities, the 14-day rule has been extended to two months from the date of performance of the services.

It should be remembered in all cases that if a VAT invoice is not issued within the 14 days (or whatever extension to this applies) then the tax point becomes the date of performance of the services.

1.5.4 Continuous supplies of services

Where there is a continuous supply of services, for example management services, so that the date of completion of the service is never reached, the tax point becomes the earliest of the date of issue of a VAT invoice or the date of receipt of payment.

However, in cases where the supplier and recipient are connected, and the recipient is unable to recover all of the VAT charged as input tax, special anti-avoidance tax point rules come into play, requiring that there is a tax point at the end of a period of 12 months from the date the services commenced (VAT Regulations 1995, SI 1995/2518, reg. 94B).

1.5.5 Construction services

Where services are supplied in the course of construction, demolition, repair or maintenance of a building, or civil engineering work, under a contract which provides for payments to be made periodically or from time to time, the tax point is treated as being the earliest of the date of issue of a tax invoice or receipt of payment.

However, in cases where it is the intention or expectation of the supplier or a person responsible for financing the cost of the supplies, that the land on which construction is taking place will be put to non-taxable use (such as for educational, health, financial or insurance businesses) by either the supplier, a person financing the cost of construction or a person connected with either of them, then there is a tax point on the date of performance of the construction works. This is to prevent abuse of the special tax point rules for construction services where the VAT cannot be recovered by the recipient, and was introduced to combat the arrangement where a wholly owned company was set up to buy in construction services from a third party contractor, but would then supply them on to the connected exempt business over a lengthy period of time, thus delaying the VAT loss to the exempt business over a number of years, instead of immediately on the receipt of services from the third party contractor.

Essentially, if a person connected to you or a sub-contractor working on the project, or a person who financed you or a sub-contractor working on the project (excluding normal payment for construction services) will occupy the building and that person is unable to recover at least 80 per cent of their input tax under the partial exemption rules (see **1.9**) then the tax point is the performance date rather than the earliest of the date of receipt of payment or issue of a tax invoice.

1.5.6 Cash Accounting Scheme

Use of the Cash Accounting Scheme, which businesses may join if their turnover is under £660,000 per annum (from 1 April 2004), and remain in until their turnover exceeds £825,000 per annum (from 1 April 2004), over-rides the normal VAT accounting rules so that VAT is accounted for on sales when payment is received and VAT is claimed on purchases when payment is made. However, the tax point rules themselves remain unchanged for all other purposes. For further information see *VAT Notice 731, Cash Accounting*.

1.5.7 Deposits

Because a deposit is part payment (in advance) for the supply it creates a tax point and VAT must be accounted for on the date of receipt, to the extent of the amount received. Deposits received by solicitors in relation to property transactions create a tax point if they are held by the solicitor as agent for the vendor. However, in cases where the solicitor holds the deposit as stakeholder (as is usual in commercial property transactions) no tax point is created because 'payment' has not been received by the vendor. This difference can be vital when purchasing/selling a property as a transfer of a business as a going concern.

If a deposit is later refunded in whole or in part, then the VAT accounted for on receipt of the deposit can be adjusted accordingly.

Deposits paid at auction can often cause problems, by creating a tax point in cases where the auctioneer receives the payment as agent for the vendor. For further information see **2.15.11** under 'transfer of a going concern' in relation to this point.

Deposits taken for security purposes, which are refundable when, for example, the goods hired are returned in good condition, are outside the scope of VAT because they do not represent payment for any supply.

1.5.8 Self-billing

Self-billing is an arrangement often used in the construction industry, or for payments of royalties, for example. It refers to the arrangements where the recipient of the supply issues the accounting document, a self-billed invoice, instead of a tax invoice which would of course usually be issued by the supplier. Since 1 January 2004, there is no longer a requirement to obtain approval in writing from HMRC prior to using self-billing. However, there are regulations which must be adhered to, such as making the following statement on each self-billed invoice: 'THE VAT SHOWN IS YOUR OUTPUT TAX DUE TO HM REVENUE AND CUSTOMS'. Details of the requirements can be found in *VAT Notice 700/62, Self Billing*. When self-billing is being used both the supplier and the recipient must agree to its use and the supplier must not issue a tax invoice as well as the self-billed invoice raised by the recipient of the supply.

1.5.9 Authenticated receipts

This system is often used in the construction industry (VAT Regulations 1995, SI 1995/2518, reg. 13(4)) and the tax point is the date of receipt of payment by the supplier. It works in a similar fashion to self-billing (see **1.5.8**) by the customer/main contractor preparing the authenticated receipt document and sending it with payment to the sub-contractor (sometimes the supplier prepares this document as a 'request for payment'). When the sub-contractor receives the payment he authenticates the document by signing it and returns it to the customer/main contractor. The document should show the date on which payment was received and all the other details normally shown on a proper tax invoice. Under these procedures the customer/main contractor is allowed to recover input tax as soon as the sub-contractor receives the payment and is not obliged to wait until the authenticated receipt is received – although it must subsequently ensure one is held for evidence of the claim to input tax. A VAT invoice must not be issued if authenticated receipts are being used. In order to use authenticated receipts the supplier and customer must agree its use.

1.5.10 Compulsory purchase of land

On compulsory purchase of land, if the amount of consideration is not known, then the supply is treated as taking place each time a payment is received (VAT Regulations 1995, SI 1995/2518, reg. 84(1)). The disposition of land subject to a compulsory purchase order is an exempt supply, subject to the option to tax (see **1.9**).

1.5.11 Freehold sales where consideration is not known

When the amount of consideration is not known, the supply is treated as taking place either under the normal tax point rules, or by the direction of HMRC at any other time specified, or each time any part of the consideration is received, or each time the supplier issues a VAT invoice. However, where the land is standard rated as the sale of a new commercial building or civil engineering work and is to be occupied by a person who is either connected to the grantor, has provided finance for the development project whether directly or indirectly, and is not eligible to recover all of their input tax, then the above tax point is disapplied for tax avoidance reasons, and the tax point becomes the date of supply. This prevents connected parties, where the purchaser cannot recover input tax, from gaining a cash flow advantage by not determining the consideration to be paid (see also **1.6.4**).

1.5.12 Other cases where consideration is not known

In cases other than the sale of a new commercial building or civil engineering work (see **1.5.11**) where land or property is sold and the value or full value is not known at the time of sale, then the normal tax point rules apply to the amount which can be identified at the time of sale. In respect of the balance, the tax point will be the date of receipt of payment or issue of a tax invoice, whichever is earlier.

1.5.13 Leases of over 21 years

When payments under a lease of over 21 years are due periodically or from time to time, then the supply is treated as taking place at the earliest of each time part of the consideration is received by the supplier, or each time the supplier issues a VAT invoice. A landlord can also issue a scheduled tax invoice, for a period not exceeding one year, which must show the dates that payments are due and the amount payable on each date, together with the rate of VAT applicable at the time of issue of the invoice. In such cases the tax point is treated as the date the amount is payable or receipt of payment, whichever is the earlier. If there is a change in tax rate, the invoice ceases to be a tax invoice for payments not yet due or made and a replacement is required.

In cases where the supplier and recipient are connected, and the recipient is unable to recover all of the VAT charged as input tax, special anti-avoidance tax point rules come into play, requiring that there is a tax point at the end of a period of 12 months from the date the services commenced (VAT Regulations 1995, SI 1995/2518, reg. 94B.

1.5.14 Retentions

The tax point for retentions in relation to construction services is treated as the earliest of the date the retention payment is received by the supplier or the date of issue of a tax invoice (VAT Regulations 1995, SI 1995/2158, reg. 89).

In the event that the supply to which the retention refers involves a supply of goods, the normal tax point rules apply.

1.6 VALUE

It is important to recognise that VAT is accountable on the supply, rather than by reference to the payment, although the latter may denote when the VAT due is accountable. Generally, a supply of goods takes place whenever the ownership of the goods is transferred, even if this is free, for example by way of a gift (unless the gift is under £50 in value, in which case there is special provision for no output tax to be chargeable). For services, it is necessary for there to be consideration, whether it is in money or in another form – there is no VAT to account for on a free supply of services (VATA 1994, s.19).

Where the consideration is wholly in money, then its value is taken as the amount that, with the addition of VAT, is equal to the consideration.

Example

If the consideration for a supply is £100, then the £100 includes the value of the supply, plus the VAT. With VAT at 17.5 per cent, the £100 is therefore 117.5 per cent of the value and the VAT may be extracted from the consideration by multiplying by 17.5 per cent/117.5 per cent, or 7/47 in its simplest form (by dividing both 17.5 and 117.5 by 2.5). This is known as the 'VAT fraction'.

Where the consideration is not in money terms, the value is taken to be the cost of goods identical in age and condition, or where this cannot be ascertained the value of goods similar to the goods concerned, or if neither of these can be ascertained the cost of producing the goods if they were produced at that time.

The golden rule is the vendor must always ensure the consideration provided for in the agreement is VAT exclusive. In the case of *Hostgilt Ltd* v. *Megahart Ltd* [1998] STC 141, ChD, a High Court judge commented that the term 'exclusive of VAT' on its own is not necessarily conclusive – the price should be stated as 'plus VAT at the appropriate rate' or similar wording. The case concerned the contract for the option on a sale of land, followed by its sale, which was subject to VAT. The contract specified that the supply was 'exclusive of VAT' and the purchase price was stated as £400,000. Megahart Ltd refused to pay the VAT on the grounds that the contract did not specify VAT as being payable. The case was approached on the basis that the possibility of the transaction being subject to VAT was commonly known in the construction industry, and would not therefore generally take either party by surprise. Hostgilt Ltd contended that it was common for prices to be quoted as either 'VAT exclusive' or 'VAT inclusive' and that it was understood that 'VAT exclusive' meant that the purchaser would pay VAT in addition to the purchase price. The High Court considered that the clause was intended to have some meaning, but that Megahart Ltd's interpretation would result in the clause having no meaning – it would merely be a statement of fact. It was plain that the clause was intended to have more effect than that and if it was not to be deprived of all effect it must mean that VAT was to be added to the purchase price. This meaning was clear enough in the context of commercial property transactions.

In *Wynn Realisations Ltd* v. *Vogue Holdings Inc.* [1999] STC 524, CA, the parties agreed a price 'exclusive of VAT'. The vendor had warranted not to opt to tax and the parties believed VAT would only be chargeable subject to the option to tax. It was later determined that part of the property sold consisted of a commercial building under three years old, so that part, amounting to some £715,000, was a mandatory standard rated supply. The High Court decided that 'exclusive of VAT' meant that if VAT was payable the vendor would fund this. However, the Court of Appeal overturned this decision and ruled that the phrase 'exclusive of VAT' meant that if VAT was payable, the purchaser was to pay this in addition to the contract price quoted.

1.6.1 Open market value

In cases where a supply is made at less than open market value and the supplier is connected to the recipient (under the terms set out in the Income and Corporation Taxes Act (ICTA) 1988, s.839) and the recipient is not entitled to fully recover VAT incurred, then HMRC may direct that the value shall be taken as open-market value. Such a direction must be given in writing within three years of the date of the supply (VATA 1994, Sched. 6, para. 1).

1.6.2 Change of rate (including on exercise of the option to tax)

Where there is a change of rate, including cases where the option to tax is exercised, the legislation provides that VAT may be added to the contract price, unless the contract specifically provides otherwise (i.e. if the contract stipulates that the contract price is inclusive of VAT, then VAT must be extracted from the existing price, but if the contract is silent on VAT, or as is more usual, stipulates that the price is exclusive of VAT, then the additional VAT payable may be added to the value (VATA 1994, s.89)).

1.6.3 Barter transactions

Land swaps would typically fall within this category, which includes any transaction where the consideration is not paid wholly in money. In such cases, there are two supplies, one comprising of land A in consideration for land B, and one for land B in consideration for land A. The value for VAT purposes is the money equivalent of the transaction in each case (VATA 1994, s.19(3)). If VAT is chargeable on either transaction, its recovery will depend upon the use to which that party puts the land or intends to put the land.

1.6.4 Consideration deferred/not known at time of sale – connected parties

In cases where the value of the consideration for the sale of the freehold of land or buildings cannot be determined at the time of sale (the usual tax point for the transaction) there are special rules allowing VAT on the unde-termined part of the consideration to be accounted for at the time it is received (VAT Regulations 1995, SI 1995/2518, reg. 84(2), see **1.5.11**). However, from 28 November 2002, due to the use of this facilitation measure in avoidance schemes (see *RBS Property Development Ltd and The Royal Bank of Scotland Group plc* (No. 17789)) an amendment was made for trans-actions between related parties so that the supplier had to exercise the elec-tion to waive exemption, and all such additional consideration was therefore standard rated. Prior to this amendment, consideration received within the three-year period from completion would be standard rated, but any consid-eration received after the three-year period would have been exempt from VAT.

From 10 April 2003, further amendments were made to this provision under VATA 1994, s.96(10A) and (10B) so that the deferred part of the consideration has the same treatment as the initial part, and applies to all grants of an interest in land or buildings, not just to freehold sales. Therefore, for any grant on or after 10 April 2003, deferred consideration is treated in the same way as the initial grant. The regulations continue to block use of the facilitation measure between connected parties to prevent the VAT cost of a building being spread over a number of years.

1.6.5 Deductions

Where deductions are made from the consideration paid over, such as income tax under the construction industry special scheme, or Construction Industry Training Board levies, it is the gross value which must be used for VAT purposes.

1.7 VAT PENALTIES

There are penalties for non-compliance with the VAT legislation. The most common of these are the penalties for late notification of a liability to register for VAT, Default Surcharge for where the payment due on any Return is late, and Misdeclaration Penalty where the amount declared on any Return is substantially in error. All of the penalties were originally introduced at much harsher levels than they are today, typically with a top-level penalty of 30 per cent of the tax involved. Due to weight of public opinion they have been reduced over the years to the current levels.

1.7.1 Criminal charges

In most cases, HMRC deals with VAT fraud under the civil procedures, but there is provision for criminal action to be taken which can lead to imprisonment for a period of up to seven years, and/or substantial fines. The burden of proof is 'beyond reasonable doubt' in criminal cases, rather than 'on balance of probability' as for civil cases, and therefore criminal action tends to take more resources to pursue, and is therefore generally reserved for novel cases, cases involving professional advisers or large value cases (VATA 1994, s.72).

1.7.2 Civil fraud

The majority of VAT fraud cases are dealt with on a civil rather than criminal basis (VATA 1994, s.60). The penalty is 100 per cent of the tax involved, although this can be mitigated, usually by up to 80 per cent in cases where the taxpayer cooperates with the investigation and helps to identify the tax due (VATA 1994, s.70). With effect from 1 September 2005, HMRC has adopted a procedure which does not involve taped interviews under caution, as was the case with the old Customs' 'VAT Notice 730 procedure' and is now more like the old Inland Revenue Hansard procedure. Existing cases will continue to be dealt with under the old procedures and initially only the HMRC Special Civil Investigation staff will use the new procedures. Under this procedure, it is left to the taxpayer and his professional advisers to prepare a short report detailing the offence and the tax due, although HMRC does review this.

1.7.3 Late registration penalty

The penalty applies if a taxpayer is late in notifying his liability to register for VAT and is levied at a minimum of £50, or if greater, 5 per cent of the tax calculated from the date registration should have been notified to the date it actually was, for a lateness of up to nine months. The rate increases to 10 per cent for a lateness of nine to 18 months, and 15 per cent for any lateness over 18 months. In practice, HMRC does not generally apply the penalty if the lateness is under two months. It is the receipt of the VAT 1 form by HMRC which stops the penalty from running – no other form of notification will do for these purposes. This penalty can also be mitigated if there are exculpatory circumstances, and may be removed if there is a reasonable excuse (see **1.7.8** and VATA 1994, s.67).

1.7.4 Default Surcharge

If a taxpayer is late with the payment due on a Return, on the first occasion a Default Surcharge Liability Notice is sent. This warns the taxpayer that any lateness in the next 12-month period will be subject to a surcharge. The next lateness is subject to a 2 per cent surcharge and the liability period is extended to 12 months from the last lateness. For any further lateness in the liability period the surcharge is increased to 5 per cent, then 10 per cent with a maximum of 15 per cent for any subsequent lateness. To become clear of a liability to a Default Surcharge the taxpayer must ensure payments are made on a timely basis until the Surcharge Liability Notice expires, usually 12 months after the last lateness. The surcharge may be removed if there is a reasonable excuse (see **1.7.8** and VATA 1994, s.59).

1.7.5 Misdeclaration Penalty

This penalty is levied when major errors occur in the tax declared due on a VAT Return, or when a centrally issued assessment understates the amount of VAT due and the taxpayer does not advise HMRC within 30 days of this. It does not imply dishonesty or any intent to evade tax, but is simply a mechanism to encourage the correct accounting for VAT by the taxpayer, VAT being a self-assessed tax. For the error to be subject to a Misdeclaration Penalty (MP), it must exceed either £1 million or 30 per cent of the 'gross amount of tax' (output tax plus input tax) in respect of the Return in question. Liability to an MP may be avoided by making a voluntary disclosure of the error to HMRC. This must be made prior to an officer booking an assurance visit or otherwise requiring an inspection of the records. The penalty is levied at 15 per cent of the amount of the error. The reasonable excuse rules also apply to this penalty (see **1.7.8** and VATA 1994, s.63).

1.7.6 Repeated Misdeclaration Penalty

As its name suggests, this penalty is designed to catch repeated errors, but with a much lower threshold than MP, applying to errors where the VAT which would have been lost is the lesser of £500,000 or 10 per cent of the gross amount of tax (output tax plus input tax) due on the Return. To be liable to a Repeated Misdeclaration Penalty (RMP), the taxpayer must have been served with a penalty liability notice (which must be served by the end of the fifth accounting period commencing with the one in which the inaccuracy first occurred). The period covered by penalty notice is eight consecutive

accounting periods. The penalty is levied at 15 per cent of the error(s) identified. The reasonable excuse rules also apply to this penalty (see **1.7.8** and
VATA 1994, s.64).

1.7.7 Other penalties

There are other penalties, for example for issuing a wrong certificate of zero
rating in respect of a relevant residential or relevant charitable building
(VATA 1994, s.62) or for issuing an invoice purporting to show VAT when not
registered (VATA 1994, s.67), the penalty is 100 per cent of the tax involved.
For general breaches of regulatory provisions, the penalties are £5 per day for
a first offence, rising to £10 per day for second offences and £15 per day for
subsequent offences. These would apply where, for example, HMRC required
that the taxpayer keep or produce certain records (usually in writing) and he
has failed to do so.

1.7.8 Reasonable excuse

A penalty will not be applied where the taxpayer has a reasonable excuse for
the error, be it late notification, Default Surcharge or Misdeclaration Penalty.
'Reliance on a third party' and 'lack of funds' are statutorily barred from
being a reasonable excuse (VATA 1994, s.70(4)). For example, a taxpayer
cannot rely upon his accountant (a third party) as a reasonable excuse in
respect of an error or lateness, but there have been cases where the
accountant has been guilty of gross negligence or malfeasance and a reasonable excuse has been allowed. With lack of funds, the tribunal will consider
the underlying reason for the lack of funds (VATA 1994, s.70).

1.7.9 Mitigation

All of the penalties may be mitigated, depending upon the circumstances. In
particular, the penalty for civil fraud can be mitigated down to 20 per cent in
the event that the person concerned fully co-operates with the investigation
and discloses the correct tax due, etc.

Other penalties, such a 'misdeclaration' and 'late registration' (with a
maximum penalty of 15 per cent of the tax due) can also be mitigated by
varying degrees. For example, in *A W Smith* (No. 19113), the misdeclaration
penalty was mitigated from 15 per cent to 5 per cent in a case where the
taxpayer made incorrect partial exemption calculations. Mitigation was
granted by the tribunal on the grounds that he was conscious of the need to
make partial exemption calculations, he kept proper records which could
enable him to do so, he made an effort to produce proper calculations, and he
sought some advice.

It is usually necessary to request mitigation in order for it to be considered.

1.7.10   Default interest

Default interest is seen as commercial restitution for underpayment of VAT and is levied on all assessments and voluntary disclosures (unless in the case of a voluntary disclosure it is under £2,000) and there is no appeal against the charge to interest on grounds of reasonable excuse, although an appeal can be made as to the amount charged. It is not an allowable expense for direct taxes (ICTA 1988, s.827(1)). If the assessment is not paid within the time limit, usually 30 days, then additional interest is calculated (VATA 1994, s.74).

Historically, there have been problems in calculating interest if there are already credits due to the taxpayer which have not been paid, and for this reason any charge to interest should be checked. It is calculated on a simple interest basis (i.e. X days at the applicable prevailing rate). The Treasury sets the rate to be charged, which is amended from time to time.

In *VAT Notice 700/43 Default Interest*, HMRC states that it will not normally charge interest in cases where the unpaid VAT would have been recoverable by the recipient of the supply – only in cases where they are out of pocket as a result of output tax not being declared, etc.

Interest is chargeable back to the date the tax should have been paid, but where any assessment or voluntary disclosure goes back more than three years, default interest is capped to the latest three years of that period.

1.7.11   Interest due to official error

In cases where HMRC has given an incorrect ruling, leading to the taxpayer being out of pocket, there is provision for interest to be paid by it. Interest is payable from the date when the VAT was overpaid or underclaimed to the date on which repayment is authorised (often repayment and payment of the interest can take a few days after this due to processing). The rates are set by the Treasury and are varied from time to time, but are much lower than the rates for Default Interest (see **1.7.10** and VATA 1994, s.78).

1.7.12   Repayment supplement

Repayment supplement becomes payable by HMRC if it has delayed the refund of a repayment return for more than 30 days after the date it is received, excluding any days when it is making enquiries as to whether the claim is correct. If the amount is incorrect by more than the greater of £250 or 5 per cent of the claim, the supplement is not payable. The rate is the greater of £50 or 5 per cent of the repayment claim (VATA 1994, s.79).

1.8 RECOVERY OF INPUT TAX

In order to be recoverable, VAT on purchases must have been incurred in the course or furtherance of a taxable business activity. The requirements for recoverability of input tax in relation to property development are set out clearly in the decision in *C & E Commrs* v. *Southern Primary Housing Ltd* [2003] EWCA Civ 1662, in which the taxpayer bought standard rated land which had been subject to the election to waive exemption by the vendor. The taxpayer then sold the land to a housing association without opting to tax, but also entered into a contract with the housing association to construct new housing on the land. The issue was whether the input tax on the land purchase was recoverable by the taxpayer, who argued that the construction contract was dependent upon the land purchase and re-sale, and that the input tax on the land purchase was therefore non-attributable for partial exemption purposes (or attributable to both the taxable building contract and the exempt land sale). The Court, however, ruled that the land purchase and VAT thereon was a cost component of the land sale only, not the construction contract, and that there was nothing in the construction contract which provided a direct and immediate link to the land purchase – the input tax was therefore wholly exempt and non-recoverable being over the *de minimis* limits for partial exemption (see **1.9.2**).

To be recoverable as input tax, therefore, the input tax must be a cost component of a taxable business supply to which there is a direct and immediate link.

In addition, it is only the person to whom the supply is made that is entitled to recover the VAT as input tax. For example, in a case where a tenant defaults on rental payments, and a sub-tenant makes payment of the rent due by the tenant direct to the landlord, the sub-tenant has no right to recover any VAT on the rent which is a supply by the landlord to the tenant, not to the sub-tenant. The lead case in this area is *C & E Commrs* v. *Redrow Group plc* [1999] STC 161, HL, in which Redrow operated a sales incentive scheme in which they paid the estate agents' fees for the houses sold by purchasers of their new houses. The House of Lords determined that because Redrow instructed the estate agents, and the estate agents invoiced them, even though the supply was to the owners of the houses, Redrow received/obtained something of benefit in return for the payment made which was for the purpose of Redrow's business and as party to the arrangements they were therefore entitled to recover the VAT charged. As a result of this decision, HMRC issued *Business Brief 27/99* which sets out its policy in this area, in which it stated:

> Our view is that the decision only applies where the circumstances are similar to the Redrow case. That is, where there is a claim to input tax credit by a taxable person who has commissioned the goods or services and contracted with the supplier for them. The claim would then be allowed to the extent that the goods or

services provided by the supplier on which input tax is incurred are used by the taxable person in making taxable supplies.

Specifically, Customs do not consider that the *Redrow* decision supports a broad principle of 'anyone that pays for a supply is its recipient and can deduct the tax on it' or, alternatively, that 'anyone who pays must always be receiving a supply of something in return for the payment'. For example, we consider that it has no relevance to circumstances where a third party is simply meeting the costs of another. Neither do we accept that a taxable person must have paid for a supply in order to be entitled to recover the input tax.

These principles were applied in the case of *Lester Aldridge* (No. 18864), where a partnership of solicitors took a lease of their office premises in the name of a nominee company (because a lease cannot be granted to more than four partners so that it is common practice for a larger partnership to be the beneficiary of a nominee company) and the partnership recovered VAT input tax on the rental payment. HMRC argued that the partnership has no right to recover input tax on the supply which was by the landlord to the nominee company, but the tribunal, on grounds that the partnership occupied the property, had paid the rent, guaranteed the rent and had agreed to enter into a lease in the event that the nominee defaulted, held that the supplies were made to the partnership under *Redrow* principles.

Often, at the time of making the claim, the expenditure may have been incurred without the taxable supply having been made. In such cases the recovery of the input tax relies on the *intention* of the taxpayer. A classic example would be incurring input tax on the purchase of building materials to construct a building which will eventually be sold as standard or zero rated when it is completed (VATA 1994, ss.25–26).

The legislation also provides, under the VAT Regulations 1995, regs. 108 and 109, for cases where the intention changes and instead of making taxable supplies, the supplies made are exempt, or vice versa. A classic example of this can be found in the case of *Tremerton Ltd* v. *C & E Commrs* (1999) STC 1039, in which the court determined that the VAT incurred by the company was actually used in making an exempt sale of the option to purchase a site that it had originally intended to develop itself (and would have led to the making of taxable supplies). As such, HMRC was correct in assessing the input tax previously recovered because although the intended use at the time of claim was taxable, the actual use to which the purchases were first 'used' was exempt.

HMRC has issued *Business Brief 14/04* (which replaces *Information Sheet 08/01 Speculative Property Developers – Input Tax*) which states that a speculative property developer should deal with VAT on costs, when they have no clear intention as to what supplies they will make, such as those on potential or abortive projects, as residual input tax until such time as the clear intentions in relation to the project are known. In the event that the project is abortive then no further adjustment is required, the costs are treated as a general overhead of the business, but if the project becomes wholly taxable or wholly exempt then an additional claim or pay back will be required. The *Business Brief* was issued as a result of the tribunal's decision in *Beaverbank Properties Ltd* (No. 18099), which determined that a business did not have to actually exercise the option to tax in order to intend to make taxable supplies where the supply would be exempt but for the option to tax. In such cases, HMRC would expect to see alternative written evidence, such as acceptance of a bank loan on the premise that the VAT incurred would be fully recoverable.

In the case of *C & E Commrs* v. *Briararch Ltd* [1992] STC 732, QBD, the company carried out works to a listed building with the intention of granting a 25-year lease which would have been zero rated. Instead, however, because of market conditions, it granted a four-year lease which was exempt from VAT, although it retained the intention to grant a long lease when it was able to. The court determined that as the intention to grant the long lease had been retained, the company should be entitled to recover 25 (intended long lease)/29 (intended long lease plus four-year lease granted) of the VAT incurred. This case was heard together with the case of *C & E Commrs* v. *Curtis Henderson* [1992] STC 732, QBD, in which a house which was intended for sale (zero rated) was let for a period of nine months prior to the freehold sale (exempt) and in this case the court's decision was that the VAT incurred should also be apportioned.

For information regarding the specific rules for pre-registration input tax, see **1.4.17**.

1.8.1   Evidence for input tax recovery

The correct evidence is required before a claim to input tax can be made. In most cases this is a proper tax invoice (VAT Regulations 1995, SI 1995/2518, reg. 14) and for purchases under £250 in value, a less-detailed tax invoice (reg.16). (Prior to 1 January 2004, the limit for a less-detailed tax invoice was £100). For purchases from vending machines, no tax invoice is required if the purchase is under £25 in value (*Notice 700, The VAT Guide, para. 8.6(e)*). For imports the evidence required is the certificate of VAT paid, which must be in the name of the importer and claimant of the input tax. At a VAT inspection, an officer is likely to carry out checks to ensure that the correct evidence is held, particularly in relation to large or unusual purchases.

1.8.2   Tax invoices

A proper tax invoice must contain the items of information set down in the VAT Regulations 1995, SI 1995/2518, reg. 14(1), which were amended with effect from 1 January 2004 for European harmonisation purposes:

(a) an identifying number;
(b) the time of supply;
(c) the date of issue of the document;
(d) the name, address and registration number of the supplier;
(e) the name and address of the person to whom the goods or services are supplied;
(f) (revoked with effect from 1 January 2004);
(g) a description sufficient to identify the goods or services supplied;
(h) for each description, the quantity of the goods or the extent of the services, and the rate of VAT and the amount payable, excluding VAT, expressed in any currency;
(i) the gross amount payable, excluding VAT, expressed in any currency;
(j) the rate of any cash discount offered;
(k) (revoked with effect from 1 January 2004);
(l) the total amount of VAT chargeable, expressed in sterling;
(m) the unit price.

1.8.3 Less detailed tax invoice

If a purchase is under £250 (£100 prior to 1 January 2004) in value, a less detailed tax invoice is satisfactory evidence for input tax recovery. This still requires certain items of information and a simple shop receipt will not necessarily contain this, although many have been adapted to do so. A less detailed tax invoice must contain the following items of information (VAT Regulations 1995, SI 1995/2518, reg. 16(1)):

(a) the name, address and registration number of the retailer;
(b) the time of the supply;
(c) a description sufficient to identify the goods or services supplied;
(d) the total amount payable including VAT; and
(e) for each rate of VAT chargeable, the gross amount payable including VAT and the VAT rate applicable.

A less detailed tax invoice does not specify the value of VAT included in the supply and, interestingly, there is no requirement that the currency is sterling. To calculate this you should apply the VAT fraction to the gross value of the supply. With VAT at 17.5 per cent the VAT fraction is 7/47 (this is the simplest form of the fraction 17.5/117.5) so that where the gross value of an invoice is £100 there will be £14.89 VAT included in this if the supply is standard rated ($100 \times 7/47 = 14.89$). With VAT at the reduced rate of 5 per cent, the VAT fraction is 5/105 or 1/21.

1.8.4   Invoicing in a foreign currency

If you are invoicing in a foreign currency (including euros) and need to charge UK VAT, then you must enter the VAT value in sterling on the invoice at the time of supply. This is so that there is no doubt how much output tax is accountable by the supplier and how much input tax is recoverable by the purchaser, regardless of the effect of exchange rates. The exchange rate used can be the period rate of exchange published monthly by HMRC, alternatively, the rate published in the national newspapers is acceptable. If you have problems in using these rates then discussion with HMRC may result in you being permitted to use another method.

1.8.5   Non-deductible input tax

Even when VAT has been charged on a supply to you, there are certain occasions when this VAT is statutorily blocked for recovery purposes (VAT (Input Tax) Order 1992, SI 1992/3222). The most common examples of this are:

- purchase of a car which is not used/to be used wholly for business purposes;
- purchases of goods within the margin scheme for second-hand goods – you will not receive a VAT invoice for a supply purchased as a second-hand item and recovery of input tax on an item to be sold under a margin scheme is blocked because you are only required to account for VAT on the profit you make when selling the item;
- purchases for the purposes of business entertainment;
- purchases of goods or services to be sold under the tour operator's margin scheme – as for second-hand items above, VAT is only required to be accounted for on the profit margin on goods or services sold under the tour operator's margin scheme;
- purchases by builders of certain items to be installed in dwellings and relevant residential/charitable buildings.

VAT incurred in relation to exempt or non-business activities is also restricted (see also **1.9** on partial exemption).

1.8.6   Purchases for both business and non-business purposes

When an item is purchased for both business and non-business purposes, the taxpayer has a choice of how to deal with the input tax. The preferred route of HMRC is that an apportionment should be made so that only the appropriate proportion for business use should be claimed. For example, if a building is purchased by a charity which will be partly used for business purposes such as a retail shop, and partly used for non-business charitable purposes, such as the offices over the shop for running the charitable non-business activities, and the proportion of the building being used as a shop is 50 per cent (whether by value, floor area, or other fair means) then 50 per cent should be recovered.

However, this changed as a result of the decision in *Lennartz* v. *Finanzamt München III* (ECJ, C-97/90). This was a German case in which the good Doctor Lennartz had recovered VAT in full on a car, and the German tax authorities had argued that as the car was used for private as well as business purposes, full recovery was not allowable. The European Court, however, ruled that input tax was recoverable in full, but that an output tax charge for the private use must be made in each VAT period, and in *News Release 1/92* HMRC announced that this treatment would be available for goods only in the UK also, but that businesses could continue to apportion the recovery in such cases if they wished to do so instead.

HMRC has therefore had to allow taxpayers to recover all of the input tax on the VAT Return covering the period in which the item is purchased, but then account for output tax on the non-business use each period. This has become known as the '*Lennartz* mechanism'.

Example

A VAT registered person purchases a yacht for £1 million plus VAT of £175,000. The yacht is used for the business of chartering and also by the owner for private cruising. Under the initial apportionment method the owner would determine the business use as a percentage of the total use and recover this proportion of the input tax only. If this is determined as, say, 50 per cent, based on time available for use, then the owner would recover £87,500 and £87,500 would be irrecoverable, and that would be an end to it (providing HMRC was satisfied at any later inspection that the apportionment was reasonable).

Under the *Lennartz* mechanism, the owner would recover the whole of the £175,000, but each VAT quarter would have to account for output tax on the private use element under the deemed supply provisions in VATA 1994, Sched. 4, para. 5. HMRC has stated that, in order to calculate this, private usage must be accounted for over a five-year period (20 years for buildings) and a straight-line depreciation means that each quarter VAT of £8750.00 is at stake (£175,000/20 quarters). If the private use is 50 per cent in the quarter, then the output tax charge is £4,375 (£8,750 × 50 per cent). This calculation must be carried out for each period in the 5 years (20 years for buildings) and then ceases.

Where an asset is not in use for the whole of the period, the private use must be calculated as the number of days used privately as a percentage of the number of days the yacht or other asset is used (not as a percentage of the number of days in the period including days when it is not used). This basis of the calculation comes from the European Court decision in *Enkler* v. *Finanzamt Homburg* (ECJ, C-230/94) which concerned the recovery of input tax on a camper van.

Therefore, in the event that in each of the 20 quarters in the five-year period the non-business use is calculated as being exactly 50 per cent, over the whole five years the business would have paid deemed supplies totalling £87,500

(20 × £4,375). Businesses are required to keep records to evidence the business/private use arrived at.

This obviously appears very attractive from a cash flow point of view. However, there is a downside to using the *Lennartz* mechanism. Because the goods are treated as business assets and all of the input tax on their purchase has been recovered, VAT is accountable in full when the goods are sold or in the event that the owner deregisters, whereas if the apportionment method is used then output tax is only due on the proportion treated as a business expense. Therefore, using the above examples, although in both cases the actual cost to the owner is £87,500 (although with the *Lennartz* mechanism it is spread over the whole five-year period rather than an 'up-front' cost) when the asset is sold the owner using the *Lennartz* mechanism must pay output tax on the full selling value, whereas the owner using the apportionment method only has to account for output tax on 50 per cent (the business element) of the selling price. Thought should therefore be given to the long-term use of the asset when considering which method to use when purchasing the asset.

There have been several attempts by HMRC to limit the application of the *Lennartz* mechanism. In the 2003 Budget, HMRC introduced an anti-avoidance measure to prevent taxpayers using the *Lennartz* mechanism for buildings and land. The measure, introduced as VATA 1994, Sched. 4, para. 5(4A), prevented the *Lennartz* mechanism being used for land, buildings, civil engineering works, refurbishments and fixtures and fittings. When the European Court decision in *Seeling* v. *Finanzamt Starnberg* (ECJ, C-269/00) (another German case but involving a businessman who had recovered VAT in full on a house for use as a home and for his business) was released later that year, it resulted in HMRC having to amend their recently announced policy change. This change involved recognising that certain services (such as construction services) result in 'goods' and that the input tax may therefore be treated under the *Lennartz* mechanism rather than an initial apportionment being required. However, the Sixth Directive does allow member states to withhold use of the *Lennartz* mechanism where it is for the purposes of preventing tax avoidance under the Sixth Directive, Art. 6(2), subject to a derogation being granted to do so, and HMRC relied on this to continue the block on the use of the *Lennartz* mechanism for land and buildings after 9 April 2003, the date from which the Budget announcement had effect. Therefore, for construction services incurred prior to 9 April 2003, when the restriction was introduced, HMRC had to allow use of the *Lennartz* mechanism where taxpayers preferred its use, but for construction services where no entitlement to input tax recovery arose before 9 April 2003, the anti-avoidance legislation announced in the Budget remained in place. In addition, HMRC accepted that in the case of goods other than land and buildings use for business and private/non-business purposes, where services were purchased which increased the value of goods, such as work to a yacht or computer system, then these services could be subject to the *Lennartz* mechanism.

In *Charles (P), T S Charles-Tijmens* v. *Staatssecretaris van Financiën* (ECJ, C-434/03) it was determined that member states cannot use the derogation under Art. 6(2) of the Sixth Directive to prevent taxpayers claiming input tax incurred on capital goods used for both business and private/non-business purposes under the *Lennartz* mechanism. As a result of this, HMRC have had to accept that the legislation it introduced in the 2003 Budget is *ultra vires* and they now accept that businesses can recover input tax on land and buildings using the *Lennartz* mechanism and can apply it retrospectively where they were prevented from doing so as a result of the 2003 policy. This was announced in *Business Brief 15/05*.

HMRC has also tempered this change with the announcement that it will challenge any attempts to exploit the use of the *Lennartz* mechanism to obtain an unfair Revenue advantage by introducing artificial arrangements. It is difficult to see, however, where the artificial arrangements issue might come into force in such circumstances – a charity or college purchases a building which it will use for both business and non-business purposes and under the current rules can either use an initial apportionment method to recover that part of the input tax that relates to its business use of the asset, or it can quite legitimately use the *Lennartz* mechanism to recover all of the VAT on the purchase price and pay a deemed supply on non-business use each quarter – nothing artificial about that.

For land and property, HMRC states that it considers a 20-year period (instead of the five years for other assets) to be reasonable, unless a shorter period can be specifically identified – such as the remainder of the term of a lease. This was the period identified by the European Court in the *Wolfgang Seeling* (ECJ, C-269/00) decision as being appropriate as representing the 'economic life' of the asset.

Input tax incurred on services which are to be used for both business and private/non-business purposes continues to be subject to the initial apportionment method only and this applies to repairs and maintenance of goods which does not significantly affect their value, although HMRC has invited any business which considers it should be entitled to use the *Lennartz* mechanism with regard to such services to apply to them for a ruling, indicating that providing VAT avoidance is not identified then this should be allowed.

It should also be noted that, in the case of a disagreement with HMRC over the apportionment on the recovery of input tax in these cases, an appeal to the VAT tribunal is limited to considering whether the determination made by HMRC is unreasonable, although the tribunal is entitled to look at any additional information provided to it when considering the case.

1.8.7   The three-year cap

Prior to 18 July 1996, a taxpayer was entitled to claim overpaid VAT for a period of six years retrospectively (VATA 1994, s.80). However, with effect from this date, and having immediate effect, the three-year cap was implemented, initially only for amounts of overpaid VAT claimed by taxpayers and then also for amounts assessed by HMRC.

The European Court determined that the three-year cap was fair, but commented adversely on its immediate effect in the case of *Marks & Spencer plc* v. *C & E Commrs* (ECJ, C-62/00), as a result of which a retrospective transitional period was introduced, allowing taxpayers to make a claim for overpaid output tax under the old rules provided that they could convince HMRC that they were aware of their ability to make a claim prior to 1 June 1997. Such claims were required to be made by 30 June 2003 (extended from 31 March due to the *Grundig Italiana SpA* (ECJ, C-255/00) decision of the European Court of Justice). The validity of the retrospective transitional relief has been further challenged in the cases of *Michael Fleming (t/a Bodycraft)* v. *C & E Commrs* [2006] EWCA Civ 70 and *Conde Nast Publications Ltd* v. *Customs & Excise* [2005] EWHC 1167, ChD, with the former having been heard in the Court of Appeal in October 2005 and the latter in January 2006. In the Fleming decision, the Court determined that it could not read into the legislation a transitional period which simply was not there, unlike in the *Grundig Italiana* case where the legislation had provided a transitional period, although one which was too short and the ECJ ruled that it should be extended. At the time of writing, the *Conde Nast* decision has not been released, but it is expected to essentially follow that of *Fleming*. It is also understood that HMRC intends to appeal the decision to the House of Lords. Also, in the case of *EMI Group* (No. 19417), the question of the validity of the retrospective transitional period has now been referred to the European Court.

Essentially, under the VATA 1994, s.80, claims for overpaid VAT output tax are limited to three years from the end of the VAT period in which the overpaid VAT was accounted for, or from the date legal proceedings commenced in relation to the claim.

For underclaimed VAT input tax, under the VAT Regulations 1995, SI 1995/2518, reg. 29, the three-year cap has effect from 1 May 1997 (due to an error in the way the cap was initially implemented).

A claim is only valid if it stipulates the amount claimable, taking into account any necessary partial exemption calculations.

1.9 PARTIAL EXEMPTION

Where a business makes taxable supplies only, it is entitled to recover all of the VAT incurred on its expenditure, unless that VAT is statutorily blocked (see **1.8.5**). Where a business makes exempt supplies only, it is not entitled to register for VAT, let alone recover any of the VAT it incurs. Many businesses, however, make both taxable and exempt supplies – they are partially exempt

– and the partial exemption rules simply govern their right to recover input tax. These rules are contained at Part XIV of the VAT Regulations 1995, SI 1995/2518, regs. 99–107.

1.9.1 Standard method

There is a standard method for determining the amount of VAT that may be recovered. Using the standard method, input tax must first be directly attributed as far as possible to the supplies that it was, or is to be used, to provide.

Example

A landlord charges an exempt rent to his tenant and incurs VAT on refurbishment costs. The VAT on these costs would be directly attributable to the exempt supplies of rent and would not be eligible for recovery (subject to the *de minimis* limits – see **1.9.2**). However, if the landlord is charging a standard rated rent (e.g. if the option to tax has been exercised in respect of a commercial building) the VAT on the refurbishment costs would be directly attributable to taxable supplies and would be fully recoverable.

In carrying out this attribution of input tax, the concept of 'direct and immediate link' and 'cost component' have been derived from European law and case law. For input tax to be treated as 'taxable input tax' and therefore be recoverable (in whole or in part) it must generally have or be intended to have a direct and immediate link to one or more supplies on which output tax is or will be payable – whether at standard, reduced or zero rate (*BLP Group plc* v. *C & E Commrs* (ECJ, C-4/94)). The concept of 'cost component' derives from Art. 2 of the First VAT Directive (Dir. 67/227) which provides that: 'On each transaction, value added tax, calculated on the price of the goods or services at the rate applicable to such goods or services, shall be chargeable *after deduction of the amount of value added tax borne directly by the various cost components*' [italics added for emphasis].

These concepts are clearly set out in the Court of Appeal's decision in the case of *C & E Commrs* v. *Southern Primary Housing Ltd* [2004] STC 209, CA. The case concerned the treatment of input tax on land purchased and sold on as exempt from VAT, but with a separate building contract with the housing association to construct houses on the land. The High Court had found that there was a direct link between the land purchase and the building contract, as well as the onward sale of the land, so that the input tax should be treated as residual, rather than directly attributable to the onward exempt sale of the land. The Court of Appeal, however, determined that the only direct and immediate link of the land purchase was to the land sale and the input tax on the land purchase was therefore exempt input tax, the sale of the land being

47

exempt. Although there is clearly a link between the land purchase and the building contract (which could not have been entered into but for the land purchase), there is no 'direct and immediate link' – the 'direct and immediate link' is with the land sale which was exempt and the input tax on the land purchase was therefore directly attributable exempt input tax. By the same token there was no direct and immediate link between the building materials, etc., purchased for the building contract and the land sale. The building materials were a cost component of the building contract only and were therefore directly attributable to the taxable building contract.

For any VAT which cannot be directly attributed, typically VAT on overhead items, or items which are used on both taxable and exempt activities, a 'standard method' calculation is made:

$$\frac{Taxable\ turnover\ (ex\ VAT)}{Total\ turnover\ (ex\ VAT)} \times 100 = recoverable\ percentage\ (rounded\ up)$$

(Note that in cases where the business incurs more than £400,000 non-attributable input tax, with effect from 1 April 2005, rounding up may not be applied.)

$$Non\text{-}attributable\ input\ tax \times recoverable\ percentage\ = \frac{recoverable}{input\ tax}$$

In carrying out this calculation, supplies consisting of the sale of any capital assets must be excluded on the basis that they would distort the calculation.

The following supplies are also excluded, but only where they are incidental to the business activities of the trader:

- the grant of a major interest in any property – whether exempt, zero rated or standard rated;
- the grant of a lease, tenancy or licence to occupy where VAT of less than £1,000 p.a. is incurred in relation to the property;
- finance-related income under Gp. 5 of Sched. 9 to the VATA 1994 such as interest on monies on deposit, hire purchase commission, commission on arranging mortgages and sale of financial instruments;
- the sale of any items where recovery of input tax was statutorily blocked;
- the value of any self-supplies.

This provision exists because it is recognised that many otherwise fully taxable businesses receive interest from money held on deposit, for example. The exclusion would not apply to supplies related, for example, to buildings made by a property developer. The concept of 'incidental' was considered by the European Court in *Regie Dauphinoise – Cabinet A Forest Sarl* (ECJ, C-306/04) in which the business was engaged in property management, but invested sums received as advances and received interest. The same staff that dealt with property management dealt with the investments. The ECJ ruled that the investment activities were not 'incidental' because the receipt of interest was a 'direct, permanent and necessary extension of the taxable activity of property management companies' and, as such, the interest should be included in partial exemption calculations.

1.9.2 *De minimis* limits

The directly attributable exempt input tax plus the proportion of the non-attributable input tax left after this calculation is the 'total exempt input tax' incurred by the business. If this total exempt input tax is under certain limits, known as the *de minimis* limits, then the fact that the business has potentially irrecoverable input tax is ignored and the business may recover all of its VAT.

At the present time (and since 1995) the limit is that exempt input tax must not exceed both £625 per month and 50 per cent of the total input tax incurred by the business. In other words, if the taxpayer is making quarterly Returns and the exempt input tax is under £1,875 *and* the taxpayer has incurred as much or more input tax on taxable activities (after carrying out the calculations above) then the taxpayer may recover all of his input tax. There is no question of recovering the first £1,875 and not claiming anything over the limit – if the limit is exceeded, none of the exempt input tax is claimable.

In carrying out these calculations a business must include all VAT incurred on its business activities, it cannot simply choose to exclude some from the calculation, or by not claiming it at all.

If there is non-business activity, then separate calculations must be carried out to determine the amount of VAT relating to business activities only before the above calculations are carried out.

1.9.3 Annual adjustment

The partial exemption calculation must be carried out for every VAT period, and an annual adjustment is required on an annual basis. The tax year runs to 31 March, 30 April or 31 May, depending on when the business' tax periods end. The annual adjustment is carried out at the end of a tax year and any adjustment is entered in the VAT Return for the period following the end of the tax year, so for a VAT year end of 31 March the annual adjustment is calculated to 31 March and entered in the June quarter Return for quarterly periods, and the April Return for monthly periods. In carrying out the annual adjustment, the same principles are used as for the monthly/quarterly calculations, but using the total figures for the year (e.g. total taxable income, total exempt income, total non-attributable input tax). The result of this calculation is then compared with the amounts actually claimed, and an adjustment is made accordingly. The percentage calculated for the annual adjustment is rounded up, unless the business has in excess of £400,000 non-attributable input tax when it must be calculated to two decimal places. The *de minimis* limit for the whole year is, of course, 12 × £625, or £7,500, and the 50 per cent rule also still applies. It is possible to apply for a different VAT year, such as the calendar year, but approval is required in writing from HMRC. HMRC may also stipulate special VAT periods for the protection of the Revenue.

The first time a business becomes partially exempt, the annual adjustment period starts from the beginning of the VAT period in which exempt input tax is first incurred and runs to the end of the VAT year. The *de minimis* limits apply accordingly, so that if the first 'year' is only six months long, then for the annual adjustment the monetary limit is $6 \times £625 - £3,750$, with the 50 per cent rule applying. Similar treatment applies to the deregistration of the business.

The effect of the annual adjustment is to even out the recovery percentage over the whole of the year, so that in some quarters a business may be under the *de minimis* limit and for other quarters it may be over, but the quarterly recovery is provisional depending on the annual position.

1.9.4 Standard method override

With effect from 18 April 2002 a further complication to the standard method was introduced for businesses with non-attributable input tax exceeding £50,000, or where non-attributable input tax exceeds £25,000 and comprises 50 per cent or more of total input tax. In the case of groups of companies (not necessarily VAT groups) the override applies where non-attributable input tax exceeds £25,000. The measure is intended to prevent the avoidance of VAT in cases where, for example, input tax is incurred and recovered in one VAT year where the partial exemption recovery percentage under the standard method is very favourable, whereas the actual use of the goods or services in the following year is predominantly exempt. The rules (VAT Regulations 1995, SI 1995/2518, reg. 107A–E) also apply when the use of the goods or services is by the transferee subsequent to the transfer of a going concern. HMRC states that it will rarely apply, except in cases of abuse.

There is, however, no precise definition of how to determine the 'use' to which goods or services are put. In some cases this will be clear, for example where a care home is constructed and used for a couple of weeks for taxable purposes before being put to wholly exempt use in the following tax year. HMRC states that the override will be likely to apply where inputs are incurred in one period but used in another, where high values in one period distort the recovery rate or if purchases are not used in proportion to supplies made, or where input tax is non-attributable but is incurred in relation to a predominantly exempt part of the business.

Where the override applies, any required adjustment is made on an annual basis and adjustments are made in the same VAT Return as for the annual adjustment itself (see **1.9.3**) or on the final Return in respect of a business which is deregistering.

See *VAT Information Sheet 04/02* and *VAT Notice 706, Partial Exemption* for further information and examples of calculations.

1.9.5 Share issue costs

Recovery of input tax on the issue of shares must also be dealt with as a separate item, in accordance with the VAT treatment of the shares only (VAT Regulations 1995, SI 1995/2518, reg. 103(2)).

In *Easyjet plc* (No. 18230), the company had claimed input tax amounting to £325,000, incurred on work carried out on the annual audit and on work relating to the issue of shares charged by an accountancy firm and a single invoice was raised for both the audit work and the work on the share issue. The issue of shares was global, and 23.65 per cent of them were issued to non-EU parties. They argued on the basis of the *Southampton Leisure Holdings plc* (No. 17716) decision, that full deduction should be allowed. However, the tribunal chairman determined that as some of the shares had been issued to non-EU parties, reg. 103(2) of the VAT Regulations 1995 came into play, and required that the input tax on the issue of the shares be treated under this regulation rather than under the terms of reg. 101 as general non-attributable input tax. The tribunal therefore decided that the company was entitled to full recovery on the value of work carried out for the audit, but was restricted to 23.65 per cent recovery on the work for the issue of shares. The chairman drew a distinction from the *Southampton Leisure* case because in that case there were no shares issued to non-EU parties. The case provides an excellent summary on the position of input tax recovery on share issues as it currently stands.

As a result of the decision in this case and following the decisions in *Halladale Group plc* (No. 18218) and *Actinic plc* (No. 18044), HMRC announced a change in the treatment of input tax incurred on a Stock Exchange Listing:

- Where a Stock Exchange Listing takes place with no issue of shares, the input tax will be treated as for general overheads.
- Where a Stock Exchange listing takes place with an issue of shares or intention to issue shares, then the VAT incurred is seen as wholly related to the share issue for partial exemption purposes (exempt or outside the scope for shares sold to a customer outside the EU).
- Where the share issue is not done to raise capital, then the input tax may be treated as residual.

However, in May 2005 the ECJ released its decision in *Kretztechnik AG* v. *Finanzamt Linz* (ECJ, C-465/03) which determined that a first issue of shares was not a supply and that input tax incurred in relation to the share issue should therefore be recoverable in accordance with the underlying activities of the business, i.e. as non-attributable input tax. HMRC has issued *Business*

Brief 12/05 which sets out its revised policy in this area to bring it into line with this decision, but strictly in relation to a first issue of shares. In this it states:

> There are a number of other situations in which a company may issue shares where the circumstances will differ greatly from those which existed in Kretztechnik. In particular, a share issue may take place as part of a company merger, demerger or other restructuring. HM Revenue & Customs are taking legal advice on the extent to which Kretztechnik applies to these other share issue situations and further guidance will be issued to businesses after this advice has been received.

1.9.6 Timing of input tax

The tribunal decision in *Little Bradley Farm Partnership* (No. 18429) concerned the timing of input tax for partial exemption purposes. Some of the expenditure involved had been paid for by one of the partners, on their personal credit card, in the VAT partial exemption year, but the partner had not been reimbursed for this expenditure prior to the year-end, and it had been put into the partial exemption calculations in the period of reimbursement. The inclusion of the input tax on this expenditure in the partial exemption year in question (when it was paid for by the partner on the credit card) would have taken the business over the *de minimis* limits for partial exemption purposes, but if it was not included, then the business was *de minimis* and able to recover all of its VAT. The tribunal determined that when the partner had made the purchases she had been acting in her capacity as a partner of the business, notwithstanding that the liability for payment for the goods in question fell upon her personally. The debt from the partnership to her arose immediately upon purchase of the goods, and therefore the tribunal considered that the partnership had made the purchase through one of its partners at the time of purchase, rather than at the time of reimbursement of the partner, and dismissed the appeal. Interestingly, the tribunal also found that if the partner had instead been a director or employee of a company, the company would have found itself in parallel circumstances, since they too would be acting on behalf of the company.

1.9.7 VAT groups and partial exemption

When dealing with a VAT group and partial exemption, it is important to remember that although intra-group supplies are outside the scope of VAT, the treatment of input tax incurred by one company in the group may depend upon the use made of the purchase by another group company if the benefit of the purchase is passed on. For example, if one company in the group purchases materials to manufacture an item that is then installed in goods which are sold by another company in the group, the treatment of input tax incurred by the first company will depend upon the VAT liability of the sale by the second company – if this is taxable the input tax is directly attributable to taxable supplies and fully recoverable. In practice, such input tax is often treated by groups as non-attributable or, worse, non-recoverable, due to lack of information passing back down the line.

See also **1.4.6** regarding control requirements and the special measures brought in to counter VAT avoidance using VAT groups.

1.9.8 Special methods

A method other than the standard method (a 'special method') may be agreed with HMRC if it believes that the method in current use gives an unfair result, and with effect from 1 April 2005 must be in writing whether negotiated by agreement or directed by HMRC. Prior to this, when a business changed its method without written approval and HMRC accepted it without comment (such as during the course of an inspection), the new method had been deemed by the courts to be a valid *de facto* special method. Special methods commonly used include use of floor area (although in recent years HMRC has been reluctant to allow this following the tribunal decision in *Optika Ltd* (No. 18627), staff salaries or head count, and cost/profit centre based methods. Any basis of calculation may be used as long as it is easy to evidence and is agreed with HMRC. Many trade organisations have agreed special methods with HMRC. A special method cannot usually be agreed retrospectively unless there has been no special method put in place in the business, but once agreed, applies to the whole of the partial exemption year in which it was agreed.

Property developers often use a special method, because they often incur input tax far in advance of the supplies they will make using the purchases on which input tax is claimable. For example, a new business carrying on the construction of new houses may register for VAT and in the first period incur VAT on purchasing building materials which are a cost component of the intended future taxable supplies (at zero rate) of the sale of new houses, and this VAT is therefore fully recoverable. Also, the builder will undoubtedly incur overheads. If the builder owns another property which is let exempt from VAT, then the only income in the first period would be exempt income, leading to nil recovery of VAT on overheads under the standard method, even though the majority of the overheads would have been used in connection with the making of taxable supplies. A special method would enable the builder to recover the VAT on the overheads to the extent they could be shown to be used for taxable purposes. For example, an input tax-based calculation (directly attributable taxable input tax over directly attributable taxable input tax plus directly attributable exempt input tax) would be fairer than an output based one. Methods based on attribution of input tax to specific projects and recovery based upon the VAT liabilities appropriate to that project are also often used by developers.

In the event that input tax is not covered by the special method, leaving a gap in the method, the input tax must, from 1 April 2005, be attributed according to the use to which it is put.

1.9.9 Special method override

From 1 January 2004 the special method override was introduced in order for HMRC to be able to override a special method where it results in an unfair recovery of input tax (VAT Regulations 1995, SI 1995/2518, reg. 102A–C). It is also open to the taxpayer to apply for the override to have effect where the special method results in a lower recovery than is fair and reasonable. Before applying the override, HMRC must have grounds as to why they believe the method used does not 'fairly and reasonably represent the extent to which goods or services are used in making taxable supplies', and they are then required to issue a Notice setting this out and requiring the business to recover input tax according to 'use' in the same way as the standard method override requires. Originally, HMRC also had to show that they have attempted, unsuccessfully, to persuade a business to comply, before issuing a Notice, but with effect from 1 April 2005 this is no longer a requirement.

Unlike the standard method override, in which the adjustments are made on an annual basis, any adjustments required under the special method override apply to the VAT period commencing after the service of the Notice or such later date as may be specified by HMRC, and must be made to the input tax in the accounting period covered by the Return. For the annual adjustment the override applies to that part of the longer period falling after the date of the Notice.

A business wishing to invoke the special method override, for example in a case where the special method agreed no longer suits the activities, must also issue a Notice to HMRC, setting out the reasons why the special method is no longer fair and reasonable. There appears to be no requirement for HMRC to agree to a change and the business is then entitled to adjust the input tax recovered according to the use that the input tax is put to, for periods commencing after the Notice is served. For the annual adjustment, recovery by use, rather than the special method, applies for that part of the annual adjustment period falling after service of the Notice.

1.10 CAPITAL GOODS SCHEME

The Capital Goods Scheme is an extension to the partial exemption rules and applies to certain items of computer equipment and land and buildings (VAT Regulations 1995, SI 1995/2518, Part XV; Sixth Directive on VAT, Art. 20(2)). It recognises that these items are not simply used up in the year of acquiring them and therefore requires an adjustment of the recovery of input tax over a longer period. The provisions do not apply to any capital items acquired or brought into use before 1 April 1990, when the scheme was first introduced. When a capital item is acquired, the normal rules for claiming input tax under the partial exemption regulations apply in the VAT Return in which the tax point for the purchase falls. When there is a change in the extent of the taxable use of that item in a period of adjustment, an input tax adjustment has to be made either paying additional VAT back, or claiming additional input tax from HMRC. It is also vital to be aware of the Capital Goods Scheme in relation to the option to tax blocking rules.

Categories of land and property regarded as capital items

1. Land, buildings or parts of buildings (or civil engineering works or parts thereof brought into use on or after 3 July 1997) where the value of the interest supplied to the owner, by means of a standard rated supply, is £250,000 or over.
2. A building where the owner's interest was, on or before 1 March 1997, treated as self-supplied to him, and the value of the supply is £250,000 or more.
3. A building constructed by the owner where the value of the taxable grants relating to the land and the standard rated supplies made in connection with the construction of the building are £250,000 or more.
4. An extension of a building where additional floor area is created which is 10 per cent or more of the original floor area and the value of the standard rated supplies if £250,000 or more.
5. On or after 3 July 1997, a building which the owner refurbishes or fits out where the value of capital expenditure on taxable supplies of services or goods affixed to the building (other than those which are zero rated) is not less than £250,000.

In addition to land and buildings, the scheme also covers computers and computer equipment costing £50,000 or more.

The scheme does not apply to goods acquired or expenditure on goods held *solely* for resale, so would not in the normal course of events apply to a property developer, except to the building they occupy themselves in the course of their business. It is the VAT exclusive value of the building/land which counts for measuring against the £250,000 limit – other fees such as legal fees or estate agent's fees should not be included.

When the value of the interest in the land/building supplies is by way of rent, it is not included in the value unless it is payable more than 12 months in advance or is invoiced by the supplier for a period of more than 12 months. (Where the adjustment period commenced before 3 July 1997, rent is excluded from the value.)

In respect of constructed buildings, the value must include any taxable land, and any taxable goods or services supplied for, or in connection with, the construction of the building, including:

- professional and managerial services including architects, surveyors and site management;
- demolition and site clearance;
- building and civil engineering contractors' services;
- materials used in the construction;
- security;
- equipment hire;
- haulage;
- landscaping; and
- fitting out, including the value of any fixtures.

In respect of fitting out or refurbishment, it is the value of any capital expenditure affixed to the building which become part of the fabric of the building. HMRC generally accepts that if an item of expenditure is a 'Profit and Loss' item, it is not 'capital expenditure' for the purposes of the scheme. Depending upon the individual project, phased works could be a single item or a number of items for the purpose of the scheme. For example, where there are separate contracts for each phase and one phase is completed before the next starts, then the different phases would be treated as separate items for Capital Goods Scheme purposes. However, if there is a single building and work is done in phases merely to facilitate occupation of the building whilst the works are carried out, this will be a single building/refurbishment for the purposes of the scheme.

The Capital Goods Scheme applies to the item from the date of first occupation or use. For example, in *Witney Golf Club* (No. 17706) a new extension was constructed to the golf clubhouse costing £1.9 million. It first came into use in March 1999 and so the first Capital Goods Scheme adjustment period was to 31 March 1999, during which period the Club made taxable supplies only and the input tax incurred in this period on the capital item was therefore fully recoverable, with adjustments being required in future intervals according to use. In this case the builder rendered the final invoice of £600,000 plus VAT of £105,000 in April 1999 and the issue at tribunal was the treatment of this input tax. The Club argued that it should be recovered in accordance with the recovery in the March 1999 year end, in accordance with the rest of the input tax on the capital item, but HMRC argued and the tribunal agreed, that as the input tax was incurred in the year commencing 1 April 1999 it must be recovered in accordance to the use in that period and not the earlier one. Therefore, any capital item where the costs are split over more than one partial exemption year may well be subject to different initial recovery rates.

1.10.1 Period of adjustment

The period of adjustment for land and buildings is 10 intervals (usually years) unless the interest held in the land is less, for example a leasehold building with less than 10 years remaining where the adjustment period would be to the end of the lease. The adjustment percentage to be applied at the end of each interval is the difference (if any) between the extent to which the capital item was used in making taxable supplies in the first interval and the extent to which it is so used in the subsequent interval in question. Under European legislation, there is provision for the adjustment period to be extended to 20 years.

The period of adjustment for computers is 5 years.

1.10.2 When to make the adjustment

The adjustment is made on the VAT Return for the second prescribed accounting period following the end of the interval. The intervals will normally be the same as those used for partial exemption annual adjustment purposes, so for a VAT year-end of 31 March, any Capital Goods Scheme adjustments will be entered in the Return for the period ending 30 September. From 3 July 1997 there are special rules regarding the timing of intervals on the transfer of a going concern and when a company joins or leaves a VAT group, to ensure that a tax advantage is not gained by using these occurrences to shorten the application of the period over which intervals apply (see **1.10.4**).

With effect from 10 March 1999, HMRC introduced amendments to thwart the use of the Capital Goods Scheme for VAT avoidance (see *East Kent Medical Services* (No 16095)). The schemes in question relied on pre-letting the land prior to the capital item in question being constructed (so that the statutory block to the option to tax would not apply – see **2.7.2**) and the amendments now provide that where it is expected or intended that the item in question will become a Capital Goods Scheme item, then the block to the option to tax will apply.

The effect of the Capital Goods Scheme is to adjust the initial recovery of VAT made under the partial exemption rules in the initial year of purchase over the next 10 years for property, or less if it is a lease of a shorter period. Particular care must be taken when disposing of a property because the remainder of the 10 adjustments required are treated as the same VAT liability as the disposal, so that if the disposal is a taxable event the remainder of the adjustments are 100 per cent taxable, if an exempt disposal the remainder of the adjustments is 100 per cent exempt (see example under **1.10.5**).

In addition, from 3 July 1997, the amount of the VAT claimed on a capital item cannot exceed the VAT charged on its disposal during the period of the Capital Goods Scheme. This was introduced to prevent the avoidance of VAT by extracting the value of a capital item through an exempt grant of a lease. HMRC states that in cases where a building is disposed of for less than its purchase value due to market forces, the vendor may apply by concession for this rule not to apply. This mechanism works by making the difference in VAT claimed to that chargeable being subject to clawback by HMRC.

1.10.3 Expiry of lease

If a lease expires whilst the item is subject to the Capital Goods Scheme, then no adjustments are required for any remaining complete intervals. The same applies if the item is destroyed, lost or stolen.

1.10.4 Transfer of a going concern/VAT groups

If the capital item is disposed of as part of the transfer of a going concern, the purchaser takes over the remaining adjustments under the scheme and will therefore require details of any prior adjustments.

Example

The owner of a business manufacturing washers purchases a new industrial unit costing over £250,000 from which the business is operated and incurs VAT on the purchase price. The industrial unit is used solely for the purpose of manufacturing washers for the following five years. As the business is fully taxable the owner has recovered all of the VAT on the purchase price and as the use has not changed during the five years there have been no adjustments required under the Capital Goods Scheme. The owner of the business decides to retire and sells the business, including the industrial unit. The new owner takes over the remaining five adjustments under the Capital Goods Scheme. If, for example, he decides that the business needs more space and moves the business to a new industrial unit, the use of the old industrial unit may change or it may be sold. If the building is let or sold, without opting to tax, the rent will be exempt and the new owner will be required to pay back 10 per cent of the VAT claimed by the original owner for each of the remaining intervals, the use having changed to wholly exempt. If the new owner sells the industrial unit without opting to tax, the final adjustment under the Capital Goods Scheme will be due and he must pay back the VAT on all the remaining adjustments on the date of sale. The requirement to pay back the VAT can be avoided by use of the option to tax (see **2.7**).

In respect of a transfer of a going concern, the treatment of the interval end date changes depending upon whether the purchaser takes over the vendor's VAT registration number. If the vendor's VAT registration number is not taken over, from 3 July 1997, the current interval ends on the date of transfer and each subsequent interval ends on the anniversary of that date. The vendor is therefore required to make an adjustment on the date of disposal. This special treatment of intervals also applies if a company owning a capital item moves in or out of a VAT group. The anniversary date remains the adjustment date regardless of any further movements in or out of the group.

Example

The existing owner of a building which was purchased four years ago sells the building as part of a transfer of a going concern of the sale of the business. The existing owner's VAT periods ends at calendar quarters, so that the interval end date is 31 March. The new owner of the business (and building) does not take over the VAT registration number of the vendor. The building is sold on 22 July. The current interval ends on 22 July and the vendor makes an adjustment to that date. The new owner takes over the remaining adjustments under the Capital Goods Scheme with the intervals remaining at 22 July, the first being on the anniversary of the purchase.

If the vendor's VAT registration number is taken over then the new owner takes over responsibility for the remaining adjustments under the Capital Goods Scheme with no change in the interval end dates.

Example

The existing owner of a building which was purchased four years ago sells the building as part of a transfer of a going concern of the sale of the business. The existing owner's VAT periods ends at calendar quarters, so that the interval end date is 31 March. The new owner of the business (and building) takes over the VAT registration number of the vendor. The new owner takes over the remaining adjustments under the Capital Goods Scheme with the intervals remaining at 31 March.

1.10.5 How to determine 'use'

The use of the item is usually determined under the partial exemption rules (see **1.9**) in cases where the capital item is used generally for the purposes of the business. For example, if a partially exempt business wholly occupies a building in the course of its business, the use will be taxable to the extent of the recovery percentage under the partial exemption method. However, if the building is partly used for the purposes of a taxable business activity, and partly let out, for example, without the option to tax having been exercised, then the use might be more correctly determined by a floor area apportionment as well, prior to looking at the rate of recovery for that part of the building occupied by the business. There is no set method for determining use in the legislation, and this is therefore an area that can be negotiated with HMRC and any fair and reasonable method can be used. Provided the method used is fair and reasonable there is no requirement to obtain permission from HMRC prior to its use, unlike with a special method for partial exemption. However, in view of the potential VAT at stake, a business would be prudent to gain the agreement of HMRC for the method used.

If the business is *de minimis* for partial exemption purposes, it is treated as fully taxable and may recover all of the VAT incurred for Capital Goods Scheme purposes as well. The Capital Goods Scheme adjustment does not form part of the exempt or taxable input tax for partial exemption purposes. If the business is using a special partial exemption method, the *de minimis* rules are ignored for the purposes of the Capital Goods Scheme unless the special method specifically includes this.

Example

The calculation is carried out as follows, assuming the property in question was purchased for £1 million plus VAT of £175,000. This situation below may well apply to a members' golf club, for example. The formula used to calculate adjustments under the Capital Goods Scheme is as follows:

$$\frac{\text{VAT on item} \times (\text{initial \% – current \%})}{\text{Period of adjustment}} = \begin{array}{c}\text{Amount repayable}\\ \text{to/claimable}\\ \text{from HMRC}\end{array}$$

(a) **Year 1** – VAT incurred £175,000
   Taxable use 60% (under partial exemption method)
   Calculation: £175,000 × 60% = £105,000 recoverable

(b) **Year 2** – Taxable use 75%

   Capital Goods Scheme adjustment:

   $$\frac{£175,000 \times (60 - 75)\%}{10} = -£2,625$$

   Claim £2,625 from HMRC

(c) **Year 3** – Taxable use 50%

   Capital Goods Scheme adjustment:

   $$\frac{£175,000 \times (60 - 50)\%}{10} = £1,750$$

   Pay £1,750 to HMRC

(d) **Year 4** – Taxable use 65%

   Capital Goods Scheme adjustment:

   $$\frac{£175,000 \times (60 - 65)\%}{10} = -£875$$

   Claim £875 from HMRC

(e) If the property were to be sold after four years, the remaining adjustments are treated at the liability of the sale of the building, except when the building is sold as (or as part of) a transfer of a going concern, where the purchaser takes over the adjustments:

(i) **Sale standard rated**

Remaining adjustments $10 - 4 = 6$

$$\frac{£175,000 \times (60 - 100)\%}{10} \times 6 = -£42,000$$

Claim £42,000 from HMRC

(ii) **Sale exempt**

Remaining adjustments $10 - 4 = 6$

$$\frac{£175,000 \times (60 - 0)\%}{10} \times 6 = £63,000$$

Pay £63,000 to HMRC

From the above example it is clear to see the potential pitfall in making an exempt sale of a property subject to the Capital Goods Scheme, although the example is of course simplified, assuming that the sale takes place at the end of an interval. In practice, an apportionment would probably be required depending upon the time of the sale. Use of the option to tax would avoid the clawback of the £63,000 in the above example and turn the adjustment into an additional claim of £42,000. It can be seen that asking the right questions when a property is being sold becomes vital in the light of this – simply enquiring whether the option to tax has been exercised and fixing the VAT treatment accordingly is not sufficient. If the option to tax has not been exercised then the correct VAT treatment of the sale will be exempt from VAT, assuming the property is more than three years old. However, not opting to tax may leave the vendor with a potentially huge VAT debt under the Capital Goods Scheme.

See also **1.13.3** in respect of 'use' where property is disposed of subject to two inextricably linked transactions.

1.10.6 Interaction with capital allowances

Capital allowances for income and corporation tax purposes are based on cost, including irrecoverable VAT. Adjustments under the Capital Goods Scheme, therefore, clearly impact on the value of capital allowances.

1.11 BAD DEBT RELIEF

When a VAT registered business has accounted for VAT on a supply, but payment has not been received from the customer within six months from the date payment was due, then the supplier can make a claim for bad debt relief (VATA 1994, s.36 and VAT Regulations 1995, SI 1995/2518, Part XIX). In order to make a claim the supplier must have 'written off' the debt, which has a particular definition for these purposes and simply requires the supplier to make a posting to a 'refunds for bad debt' account, rather than formally writing off the debt for accounting purposes. Prior to 1 January 2003, the supplier was also required to send the customer a Notice detailing the date of issue of the Notice, the date of the claim, the date and number of any VAT invoice issued in relation to the supply, the amount written off as a bad debt for each supply, and the amount of the claim. The effect of receipt of the Notice on the customer was that the customer had to repay any input tax which he may have claimed in respect of the supply. For invoices raised since 1 January 2003 it is no longer a requirement to send the Notice, but the customer must automatically adjust any input tax claimed on the debt when the date six months after payment is due is reached, by reducing the input tax claimed on their VAT Return for the period covering that date. This has become a fertile area for assessments on VAT inspections as it is an area often overlooked by the customer and easy for officers to review aged creditors.

The actual claim for bad debt relief is entered in Box 4 on the VAT Return, and if any payments are subsequently received, then an adjustment to the claim must be made. The claimant must ensure that records relating to the claim are preserved for inspection as necessary for a period of four years from the date of making the claim. A claim can be made at any time after the six months from the date payment was due for a period of three years after that date.

Any payment received from the customer is generally seen as applying to the oldest debt, unless it is specifically allocated to a later one. In cases where part payment is received the part payment is always treated as inclusive of VAT.

Example

For a case of a supply for £1,000 plus £175, the customer pays the £1,000 only, the £1,000 is treated as being £851.06 net, plus £148.94 VAT. The bad debt relief that can be claimed is therefore £175 $\times$ 7/47 = £26.06, even if the customer stipulates that it is the VAT of £175 he is refusing to pay.

There are also other detailed conditions regarding supplies which qualify for bad debt relief. For example, the value of the supply must not be more than the customary selling price and the debt must not have been paid, sold or factored under a valid legal assignment. Also, if the business owes the debtor, the amount must be set off reducing the amount which can be claimed under the bad debt relief rules. For further information see *VAT Notice 700/18, Relief from VAT on Bad Debts*.

1.12 TAX AVOIDANCE DISCLOSURE REGULATIONS

HMRC introduced legislation to require the disclosure of use of certain avoidance schemes with effect from 1 August 2004 (VATA 1994, Sched. 11A and VAT (Disclosure of Avoidance Schemes) (Designations) Order 2004, SI 2004/1933). These measures are designed to counter what HMRC perceives to be 'abusive avoidance' and the legislation specifies 'designated schemes', 'provisions within schemes' and 'provisions associated with schemes', where disclosure to HMRC is required within 30 days of the due date for the first VAT Return in which the scheme is used (VAT (Disclosure of Avoidance Schemes) Regulations 2004, SI 2004/1929, reg. 2). It should be noted that the rules apply to schemes where use commenced prior to 1 August 2004 as well as those commenced after this date.

The requirement to disclose schemes does not mean that the scheme cannot be used, it simply provides HMRC with notice that it is being used so that they are able to challenge it if they wish to do so. There is also a voluntary register for businesses that devise and market VAT schemes, and a business using a scheme registered by a promoter will not have to register the scheme separately.

Notification should be made by post to: HM Revenue & Customs, VAT Avoidance Disclosures Unit, 4th Floor West, New King's Beam House, 22 Upper Ground, London, SE1 9PJ, or by e-mail to: vat.avoidance.disclosures. bst@hmce.gsi.gov.uk. For further details please refer to *VAT Notice 700/8, Disclosure of VAT Avoidance Schemes*.

1.12.1 Designated Schemes

The list of schemes that must be disclosed has been published by HMRC as the VAT (Disclosure of Avoidance Schemes) (Designations) Order 2004, SI 2004/1933 and applies to any business with a turnover exceeding £600,000. There is a penalty of 15 per cent of the tax avoided for non-disclosure. The main schemes which impact on property are as follows.

1. First grant of a major interest in a building

Any scheme comprising or including the first grant of a major interest in any building of a description falling within Item 1(a) of Gp. 5 of Sched. 8 (new dwellings, relevant residential, relevant charitable buildings, etc.) where:

63

(a)   the grant is made to a person connected with the grantor; and

(b)   the grantor, or any body corporate treated as a member of a VAT group under VATA 1994, s.43 of which the grantor is a member, attributes to that grant input tax incurred by him:

  (i)   in respect of a service charge relating to the building; or

  (ii)   in connection with any extension, enlargement, repair, mainten-ance or refurbishment of the building, other than for remedying defects in the original construction.

2.   *Leaseback agreement*

Any scheme comprising or including the supply of goods, or the leasing or letting on hire of goods ('the relevant supply') by a taxable person to a connected relevant person where:

(a)   the taxable person or another taxable person connected with him, including the relevant person, is entitled to credit for all the input tax arising on the purchase of the goods;

(b)   the relevant person uses the goods in the course or furtherance of a business carried on by him, and for the purpose of that business, other-wise than for the purpose of selling, or leasing or letting on hire, the goods; and

(c)   the relevant person or a person connected with him has directly or indi-rectly provided funds for meeting more than 90 per cent of the cost of the goods.

Notes

  1.   'Relevant person' means any person who, in respect of the relevant supply, is not entitled to credit for all the input tax wholly attributable to the supplies he makes.

  2.   The provision of funds includes:

  (a)   the making of a loan of funds; and

  (b)   the provision of any consideration for the issue of any shares or other securities issued wholly or partly for raising the funds.

  3.   The grant, assignment or surrender of a major interest in land is not a supply of goods for the purposes of this scheme, the relevant person uses those goods in the course or furtherance of any business carried on by him.

3.   *Surrender of relevant lease (added with effect from 1 August 2005) (The VAT (Disclosure of Avoidance Schemes) (Designations) (Amendment) Order 2005, SI 2005/1724)*

Any scheme comprising or including the surrender by an occupier of a building of a relevant lease, tenancy or licence to occupy where:

(a) the occupier or any person connected to him is a relevant person;
(b) the building is a capital item for the purposes of reg. 113 of the VAT Regulations 1995;
(c) before the surrender the occupier paid relevant VAT and was not entitled to full credit for, or refund of, that VAT under any provision of the Act or regulations;
(d) following the surrender the occupier continues to occupy at least 80 per cent of the area previously occupied; and
(e) following the surrender the occupier pays no relevant VAT or pays less than 50 per cent of the relevant VAT paid before the surrender.

Notes

1. Relevant lease, tenancy or licence to occupy means any lease of, tenancy of or licence to occupy the building granted or assigned to the occupier where –

    (a) an election under paragraph 2 of Schedule 10 (election to waive exemption) has been made in relation to the building; and
    (b) that election has not been revoked in accordance with paragraph 3(5) of Schedule 10.

2. Relevant person means any person who –

    (a) is a lessor of the building;
    (b) is an owner of the building for the purposes of regulation 113 of the VAT Regulations 1995; and
    (c) has made an election under paragraph 2 of Schedule 10 in relation to the building.

3. Relevant VAT means VAT on rent paid or payable by the occupier in relation to the building.
4. Surrender includes any termination by the occupier of the relevant lease, tenancy or licence to occupy where he has entered into any agreement, arrangement or understanding (whether legally binding or not) with the lessor regarding that termination.
5. Building includes any part of that building.

1.12.2 Provisions associated/included with schemes

Businesses with a turnover in excess of £10 million per year must disclose the use of schemes which have certain 'provisions associated or included with schemes', again within 30 days of the due date for the first return affected by the scheme.

Provisions associated with schemes are as follows.

1. Confidentiality condition

An agreement preventing or limiting the disclosure of how a scheme gives rise to a tax advantage. (HMRC has stated that a standard engagement letter confidentiality clause will not trigger this condition – what it is concerned with is conditions put in place to keep schemes confidential – see *Business Brief 14/05*.)

2. *The sharing of the tax advantage with another party to the scheme or with the promoter*

1. An agreement that the tax advantage to a person accruing from the operation of the scheme be shared to any extent with another party to it or another person promoting it.
2. A person is a promoter of a scheme if, in the course of a trade, profession or business which involves the provision to other persons of services relating to taxation:

    (a) he is to any extent responsible for the design of the proposed arrangements; or
    (b) he invites persons to enter into contracts for the implementation of the proposed arrangements.

3. *Fee payable to a promoter which is in whole or in part contingent on tax savings from the scheme*

1. An agreement that payment to a promoter of the scheme be contingent in whole or in part on the tax advantage accruing from the operation of the scheme.
2. A person is a promoter of a scheme if, in the course of a trade, profession or business which involves the provision to other persons of services relating to taxation:

    (a) he is to any extent responsible for the design of the proposed arrangements; or
    (b) he invites persons to enter into contracts for the implementation of the proposed arrangements.

1.12.3 Provisions included in schemes

1. *Prepayment between connected parties*

1. A payment for a supply of goods or services between connected persons:

    (a) before the time applicable under VATA 1994, s.6(2) or (3); or
    (b) where the supply is a continuous supply and the payment is before the goods or services are provided.

2. A supply is a continuous supply if it is a supply to which regs. 85 (leases treated as supplies of goods), 86 (supplies of water, gas or any

form of power, heat, refrigeration or ventilation), 90 (continuous supply of services), 91 (royalties and similar payments) or 93 (supplies in the construction industry) of the VAT Regulations 1995 applies.

For the purposes of para. (1)(b) of the VAT Regulations 1995 goods or services are provided at the time when, and to the extent that, the recipient receives the benefit of them.

2. Funding by loan, share subscription or subscription in securities

The funding in whole or in part of a supply of goods or services between connected persons by means of a loan between connected persons or the subscription for shares in, or securities issued by, a connected person.

3. Off-shore loops

A supply of a relevant service which is used or intended to be used, in whole or in part, directly or indirectly, in making to a person belonging in the UK, a supply which is zero rated, exempt or treated as made in another country (and not in the UK) by virtue of VATA 1994, s.7(10) (place of supply of services).

A 'relevant service' is a service of a description falling within:

(a) Art. 3(a) of the VAT (Input Tax) (Specified Supplies) Order 1999, SI 1999/3121 (services supplied to a person who belongs outside the member states);
(b) Art. 3(b) of that Order (services directly linked to the export of goods to a place outside the member states), insofar as they are supplies of a description falling within Item 2 of Gp. 5 of Sched. 9 (the making of any advance or any credit); or
(c) Art. 3(c) of that Order (the provision of intermediary insurance or financial services);

or is a supply of a description specified in any of paras. 1 to 8 of Sched. 5 to VATA 1994 (services supplied where received), and the recipient of that supply belongs in a country, other than the Isle of Man, which is not a member state.

4. Property transactions between connected persons

1. A relevant grant where:

(a) the grantor or grantee of the interest or right is a person who is not entitled to credit for all the input tax wholly attributable to the supplies he makes;
(b) any work of construction, alteration, demolition, repair, maintenance or civil engineering has been or is to be carried out on the land; and

67

(c)   the grant is made to a person connected with the grantor.

2.   'Relevant grant' means the grant of any interest in or right over land or of any licence to occupy land or, in relation to land in Scotland, any personal right to call for or be granted any such interest or right, other than a grant of a description falling within Item 1 of Gp. 5 (first grant of a major interest by a person constructing a building designed for dwelling, or intended for use solely for residential or charitable purposes; or by a person converting a non-residential building to residential use) or Item 1 of Gp. 6 (first grant of a major interest in a protected building by a person reconstructing it) of VATA 1994, Sched. 8.

3.   'Grant' includes an assignment or surrender and the supply made by the person to whom an interest is surrendered when there is a reverse surrender.

5.   *Issue of face-value vouchers*

1.   The issue of face-value vouchers for consideration.

2.   Paragraph 1 does not apply where:

(a)   the issuer expects, on reasonable grounds, that at least 75 per cent of the face-value of the vouchers will be redeemed within three years of the date on which the vouchers were issued; and

(b)   the vouchers were issued to relevant persons.

3.   A relevant person is:

(a)   any person who is not connected with the issuer; or

(b)   any body corporate:

(i)   which is a member of the same VAT group as the issuer for the purposes of VATA 1994, s.43; and

(ii)   which does not intend to supply the vouchers, directly or indirectly, to any person connected with the issuer outside that VAT group.

4.   'Face-value vouchers' means tokens, stamps or vouchers of a description falling within para. 1(1) of Sched. 10A to VATA 1994 (face-value vouchers) and 'face-value' has the meaning given by para. 1(2) of that Schedule.

1.13   VAT PLANNING

In recent years HMRC has mounted a successful campaign to prevent many of the planning schemes which were widely used by exempt and partially exempt organisations to enhance their input tax recovery. Use of the option to tax is the key area for VAT planning with commercial property (see **2.7**). In the event that use of the option to tax is prevented by the statutory block, it is a 'grant of facilities' which is often used – a means of creating a taxable supply without using the option to tax. Whilst this means that output tax is due on income (as would be the case with the option to tax), it does allow recovery of input tax. Many of the schemes are also now subject to the disclosure rules (see **1.12**) and whilst this does not mean that they cannot be used, it does allow HMRC the opportunity of challenging them, and the uncertainty created by this is often sufficient to put off taxpayers. The simplest of schemes using a grant of facilities has been in existence for many years and is known as the 'library scheme'. Essentially, any school, college or university requiring a new library building can gain full VAT recovery by carrying out construction through a wholly owned company, stocking with books, and making a zero-rated supply of the hire of books to the school. (Although the VAT may be restricted if the library is used for other purposes as well as the hire of books, e.g. exempt educational purposes.) Other schemes may use a standard rated facilities hire charge to achieve at least a cash flow saving. For example, the author is aware of a crematorium constructed in a wholly owned company by a funeral director, which grants standard rated rights to use the facilities to the funeral director and others. What is key to such schemes is that the facilities must be the prime reason for the person wanting to use the building, rather than occupation of the building itself. Other areas of use could be in sports, for example, but care must be taken here because of the exemption for a series of grants of sporting facilities in certain cases. A classic example of this type of arrangement using 'facilities' which fall short of a licence to occupy is found in the case of *Mount Edgcumbe Hospice Ltd* (No. 14807), and the VAT tribunal provided guidance on the difference between a 'licence to occupy' and the 'grant of facilities' in *Abbotsley Golf & Squash Club Ltd* (No. 15042).

The tribunal's decision in *Halifax plc and Others* v. *C & E Commrs* [2002] STC 402, ChD was somewhat of a landmark for VAT – on the basis that the transactions carried out had no commercial basis, they were deemed not to have been carried out in the course or furtherance of any business activity, and therefore input tax was not recoverable. The case concerned the construction of three call centres, but if Halifax had simply contracted with a building company to provide the construction services it would have been unable to recover much of the VAT incurred due to its partially exempt status.

Instead, Halifax first let the site to a separately VAT registered company (LPDS) on a lease of 20 years, with an option to extend this for 99 years, and LPDS agreed to carry out certain minor works for Halifax. As well as these minor works, LPDS contracted with CWPI for them to carry out the construction of the call centres, and made sure a record was kept of its intention to assign the lease once a suitable tenant could be found. This aspect was important so that the works would not fall under the Capital Goods Scheme, and would be 'trading', rather than 'capital' expenditure. It appears from the decision that HMRC did not attack the scheme on this aspect. In the VAT year in which the minor works were carried out, LPDS invoiced Halifax with a taxable supply, and also prepaid CWPI for most of the construction works for the call centres. Because LPDS had only made taxable supplies in this VAT year it was entitled to recover all of the VAT it incurred on non-attributable purchases (the supplies from CWPI were to be used for the minor taxable supply to Halifax and the exempt assignment of the lease and were therefore residual). CWPI bought in the building services from a third party contractor and recovered all of the VAT incurred against the onward taxable supply to LPDS.

In the following VAT year LPDS assigned the lease to HPIL, exempt from VAT, there being no option to tax in force. HPIL in turn sub-let the call centres to Halifax, and thus Halifax received the use of the call centres virtually VAT-free, assuming the arrangements worked.

HMRC argued that a transaction entered into purely to avoid VAT did not constitute a 'supply' and was not an 'economic activity', or that in the alternative, a transaction entered into solely for VAT avoidance purposes was an abuse of rights under the terms of EC law and should be ignored. Halifax of course argued that each of the transactions was genuine and the supplies had actually been made, resulting in profits for the companies involved, and therefore had genuine commercial consequences.

The tribunal, however, could not discern any commercial or business rationale for the transactions apart from to make the VAT avoidance scheme work. If the scheme did work, it would cause distortion of competition in both the UK and EC sense. It found on this basis that neither LPDS or CWPI made 'supplies' of construction services. It also found that the destination of the supplies should not be determined simply under the terms of the contract, but taking into account all the surrounding circumstances. It did not find that there was an abuse of rights, the appellant not having obtained any rights as a result of the transactions.

The case was appealed and was remitted from the High Court to the tribunal to reconsider its decision on the basis that it may have only looked at 'commerciality' from the perspective of Halifax plc rather than the other companies involved. The issue was referred by the VAT tribunal to the ECJ, (C-255/02) together with other similar cases (*BUPA Hospitals Ltd* (C-419/02) and *University of Huddersfield Higher Education Corporation* (C-233/03)) and the ECJ's decision was released on 21 February 2005. The Court followed the Advocate General's Opinion that each of the transactions must be considered objectively and the fact that the supply was made with the sole intention of obtaining a tax advantage does not disqualify it from being a supply of goods or services for VAT purposes. However, the Court also determined that where the essential aim of the transactions is to gain a tax advantage, this would be an abuse of the formal workings of the legal provisions and that the member state was entitled in such circumstances to deny input tax recovery and to look through the offending transactions, so that in this case Halifax was deemed to have received the supplies direct from the third party contractors. It also stipulated that when assessing input tax the member state should also offset any output tax that had been accounted for in relation to the transactions. The *University of Huddersfield* decision was made on a similar basis to *Halifax*.

In the *BUPA* case, which involved prepayment for unspecified medical goods etc., it determined that a payment should not be considered to be made where the goods or services to be supplied had not been specifically identified.

Although HMRC will see these decisions as victories, and on the basis of the facts of each individual case and the way the decisions went they are, it must be remembered that each of the parties admitted that the sole purpose of the arrangements, which were wholly artificial, were to avoid VAT. The decision has, however, brought a good deal of common sense to the issue of VAT avoidance, and whilst making artificial arrangements for a tax advantage may no longer be feasible, the ECJ made some specific comments regarding the validity of tax planning generally which should assist in any challenges by HMRC against arrangements which utilise the legislation to gain a tax relief without the use of artificial structures.

The VAT tribunal has also ruled in other cases, for example *J E and H L Laurie (t/a the Peacock Montessori Nursery)* (No. 17219) on the same basis as in *Halifax*. This concerned a sub-lease and under-lease on a barn being converted for use as a day nursery for children, which is of course exempt from VAT. The standard rated lease was entered into for 'a small tin of baked beans, if demanded', and the transactions were deemed to have been entered into solely to recover the VAT incurred, and were not in the course or furtherance of a business.

1.13.1 Interposed lease scheme

If a building is tenanted partly by partially exempt persons and partly by fully taxable persons, and that part of the building occupied by the fully taxable tenant is to be refurbished at the landlord's expense, then forming a wholly owned company and granting it a lease, with the wholly owned company then granting a lease to the fully taxable tenant only, will allow the wholly owned company to opt to tax the lease and thus gain full input tax recovery on the refurbishment costs, without the option to tax applying to the exempt or partially exempt tenants. The fully taxable tenant will of course be able to recover the VAT on the lease.

The arrangements can be put in place to limit the effect of the option to tax generally, but the wholly owned company must not be part of the VAT group because the effect would be to opt to tax the whole building.

1.13.2 Lease-leaseback scheme

This scheme received notoriety in the case of *Robert Gordon's College* v. *C & E Commrs* [1995] STC 1093, HL, and is now of course a 'designated scheme' for disclosure purposes (see **1.12**). It involves setting up a wholly owned company to which a lease is granted with the option to tax being exercised, thus allowing recovery of VAT on construction costs. The wholly owned company then leases the building back to the trading company, having also opted to tax, thus placing the use of the property in the hands required, but changing the VAT cost from one on capital expenditure to a revenue cost over the term of the lease. HMRC states that the worst of these schemes left it recovering the VAT cost on the capital expenditure over a period of 1,000 years, due to the value on the leaseback arrangements. The scheme is now blocked for capital items under the Capital Goods Scheme, but can still be used for smaller developments with a value of under £250,000, such as dental surgeries, doctor's surgeries, day nurseries for children, and other small buildings constructed for non-taxable use, where circumstances allow, and providing that VAT saving is not the only reason for undertaking the project using a wholly owned company and leaseback arrangements. It is common, for example, for buildings and building projects to be held in separate companies in order to ring-fence the potential liability should things go wrong. The arrangements may even be put in place for extensions, for example, to nursing homes, as long as the appropriate ground lease, etc., is put in place. HMRC does challenge such schemes, but having put the £250,000 limit in place and linked the statutory block on the option to tax to this limit, it might be said to have almost invited such arrangements (at the time of writing the author is unaware of any cases which have tested these principles through the courts on *Halifax*, etc., grounds for arrangements under £250,000).

A similar scheme involving lease/leaseback with the intent of collapsing the leases and turning the cash flow advantage into a permanent VAT saving, was challenged in *University of Huddersfield Higher Education Corporation* (No. 17854), and this case was joined with the *Halifax* case in referral to the European Court of Justice (see **1.13** above).

1.13.3 Sale of taxable freehold followed by exempt lease of 999 years

The case of *Centralan Property Ltd* (ECJ, C-63/04), is a company wholly owned by the University of Central Lancashire Higher Education Corporation. The university constructed a new building and sold it to Centralan for £6.4 million plus VAT of £1,137,500. Centralan granted a lease of 20.5 years to the university on the same day at a rent of £300,000 p.a. and having elected to waive exemption, this was also standard rated, and it therefore recovered the VAT paid on the purchase of the building. Two years later, Centralan granted a 999-year lease to a subsidiary company for £6.37

million, and three days later it sold the freehold reversion to the university for £1,000 plus VAT. The 999-year lease was exempt from VAT as Centralan and the subsidiary were connected persons. Centralan then deregistered and on its final Return entered a Capital Goods Scheme adjustment of £934, being the £1,137,500/10 × 3/365 (the three days exempt use). HMRC raised an assessment on the basis that on the grant of the 999-year lease there were seven out of the 10 adjustment periods left in the Capital Goods Scheme period – £1,137,500/10 × 7 = £796,250. The tribunal found that as both supplies (the 999-year lease and the freehold reversion) were made in the same period, both should be taken account of for the purposes of the final adjustment under the Capital Goods Scheme, and the assessment was reduced to £796,090. Centralan appealed the decision to the High Court, which made a referral to the European Court of Justice. The ECJ released its decision on 15 December 2005, that:

> ... where a 999-year lease over capital goods is granted to a person against the payment of a substantial premium and the freehold reversion in that property is transferred three days later to another person at a much lower price, and where those two transactions are inextricably linked, and consist of a first transaction which is exempt and a second transaction which is taxable, and if those transac-tions, owing to the transfer of the right to dispose of those capital goods as owner, constitute supplies within the meaning of Article 5(1) of that directive, the goods in question are regarded, until the expiry of the period of adjustment, as having been used in business activities which are presumed to be partly taxable and partly exempt in proportion to the respective values of the two transactions.

At the time of writing, the High Court has not released its decision based on the ECJ answer to the referred question, but it is clear that the tribunal decision will in effect stand.

1.13.4 Golden brick scheme

This scheme is one used by housing associations in particular, or other organ-isations constructing residential property and relies on the legislation at VATA 1994, Sched. 8, Gp. 5, Item 1 including in the zero rating a partly completed dwelling, etc. Therefore, rather than purchasing opted land, the housing association contracts with the land supplier to start construction, and to complete the build to one brick/course of bricks above foundation level. The purchase of the land and partly completed building is then zero rather than standard rated, and the construction can be completed as a zero-rated contract by the same or another contractor.

The scheme is also useful where a property owner who has opted to tax is selling the building to be converted into dwellings, etc. and the purchaser does not wish to be charged VAT (e.g. if the dwellings will be subject to short-term lets). If the property owner commences the construction/conversion of the dwellings the sale to the purchaser becomes zero rated, still allowing the property owner to make a taxable supply and retain input tax recovery, but without charging VAT to the purchaser.

1.13.5 Delayed purchase of freehold by exempt business

In cases where the purchaser of the property is exempt (or partially exempt) and wants to minimise the VAT cost of purchase of a new building, it might be possible to enter into an arrangement whereby the purchaser rents the building for three years and then purchases it. The letting of the building would be exempt from VAT and once the building is more than three years old (from the date of completion or first occupation) the freehold sale would also be exempt from VAT. The effect of this would be that the developer/ vendor would be unable to recover the VAT incurred in construction/ purchase of the building, but this could be considerably less than the VAT on the sale by the developer/vendor. The VAT cost would of course have to be factored in to the selling price, as would the cost to the developer/vendor of the delayed purchase.

1.14 DISPUTES WITH HMRC

In cases of dispute with HMRC there are two main routes for resolving disagreements of a technical nature, such as the VAT treatment of a supply. First, a request for 'review and reconsideration' can be made. The is an internal HMRC procedure and application is made to the officer who initially supplied the ruling and should be referred by him/her to the Review and Reconsiderations Officer in order to gain a second opinion on whether the officer's decision/assessment is correct.

The other route for dealing with disputes is via the VAT and Duties Tribunals, which is administered by the Department for Constitutional Affairs, a separate and independent government body. Application for a formal appeal of this nature is made on form TRIB 1.

Many professional advisers advocate entering a formal appeal at the same time as requesting a 'review and reconsideration' because, if successful, costs of and incidental to the appeal may be claimed from HMRC. Costs cannot be 'of and incidental to an appeal' if it has not been formally lodged. If the matter is settled before hearing, then the formal appeal can always be withdrawn upon settling the matter of costs.

HMRC does have a fund to pay costs outside the formal appeal process, but this is generally a much smaller contribution and is only payable in the event that it can be shown the decision was unreasonable, etc.

CHAPTER 2

Commercial property

2.1 INTRODUCTION

The legislation with regard to land and property works by providing exemption for all grants of interests in, rights over or licences to occupy land, or in Scotland, any personal right to call for or be granted any such interest or right (VATA 1994, Sched. 9, Gp. 1, Item 1). This specifically includes assignments, surrenders and reverse surrenders, under Note 1 to the Group. However, in addition to providing an overall exemption, the legislation then goes on to provide for certain supplies which are excluded from the exemption (these are mainly short-term rights over land).

2.2 LAND TRANSACTIONS

A supply of bare land is exempt from VAT subject to the option to tax. There are occasions when the option to tax is not available (see **2.7.1**). Where the sale of land includes minor civil engineering works the supply must be apportioned between the exempt bare land (subject to the option to tax) and the standard rated new civil engineering works.

Example

Building land is developed to the extent that groundworks such as a road or sewage pipes/utilities have been constructed. The supply falls short of a work of civil engineering, but the supply must be apportioned on a fair and reasonable basis between the value of the exempt bare land and the new standard rated civil engineering works.

2.3 FREEHOLD SALE OF COMMERCIAL PROPERTY

The freehold sale (in Scotland the *dominium utile*) of a commercial property or work of civil engineering (which includes any property which is not 'designed as a dwelling' (see **3.2**), intended solely for 'relevant residential' use (see **3.3**) or intended for 'relevant charitable' use (see **5.2.1**) is standard rated if it was completed less than three years before the freehold sale. Standard rating also applies to partly completed commercial buildings or partly completed civil engineering works. The standard rated treatment applies to any number of freehold sales during the three-year period (VATA 1994, Sched. 9, Gp. 1, Item 1(a) and Note 4).

If the freehold sale of a new or partly completed building or civil engineering work includes the sale of bare land which is ancillary to it, then the VAT treatment of the bare land follows the liability of the main supply and is also standard rated.

The date of completion of a building is taken for these purposes as the date the architect issues the certificate of practical completion or the date on which it is first fully occupied, whichever comes first. For civil engineering, it is the date the engineer issues the certificate of completion or the date it is first used, whichever comes first (VATA 1994, Sched. 9, Gp. 1, Note 2). In cases where a building is occupied prior to completion, the question will be whether it is *fully occupied* for these purposes. There is no definition given of *fully occupied*, but it would presumably involve all parts of the building being occupied to some extent (e.g. all the separate offices in an office block having some occupation). HMRC has stated that it will challenge any artificial arrangements to leave a building only partially occupied for these purposes.

Where there is the freehold sale of a building after three years or more have elapsed from the date of completion or first occupation, the transaction is exempt from VAT (VATA 1994, Sched. 9, Gp. 1, Item 1) subject to the option to tax (see **2.7**). This sudden change of treatment after the three-year cut off period can create a trap for the unwary.

Example

If a building is purchased whilst still under three years old, VAT will be charged on a mandatory basis (without the election to waive exemption having been exercised). If the purchaser then disposes of the building when it is more than three years old, then the supply is exempt from VAT, subject to the election to waive exemption. This can create a situation where the input tax on the original purchase must be adjusted under the Capital Goods Scheme (see **1.10**) and a clawback is due to HMRC.

Because the supply of a major interest in land (lease of over 21 years or freehold sale) is a supply of goods for VAT purposes, the above treatment applies even when there is no consideration. So, for example, where a new farm building has been erected and the land, including that on which the building stands, is gifted or is transferred as an inheritance, VAT will apply to the transaction if the building is under three years old (unless the transaction can be treated as the transfer of a business as a going concern (see **2.15**)).

Article 4(3) of the Sixth Directive on VAT provides a definition of a building for VAT purposes: 'A building shall be taken to mean any structure fixed to or in the ground'. Although this has not been transposed into UK law and legal definitions (e.g. UK law would not consider a 'monument' to necessarily be a 'building' unless one could enter into it, etc.), the taxpayer can directly rely on it. In the case of *Rudolf Maierhofer* v. *Finanzamt Augsburg-Land* (ECJ, C-315/00), the European Court determined that the exemption for letting of buildings applied to pre-fabricated buildings. Mr Maierhofer had constructed single-storey and two-storey buildings similar to prefabricated houses using prefabricated components. The buildings stood on a concrete base erected on concrete foundations sunk into the ground. The walls, which were made of panels, were secured to the foundations by bolts. The roof framework was covered with tiles. The floors and walls of the bathrooms and kitchens were tiled. The construction system was such that the buildings could be dismantled at any time by eight persons in ten days and subsequently re-used. Some of the buildings were on land which a local authority had let to Mr Maierhofer and others were on land which the lessee of the buildings, the Free State of Bavaria, had rented itself. In both cases the sites were to be fully restored to their original condition once the lease came to an end. The national authority had assessed tax at standard rate on the grounds that the buildings being let were not 'immovable property' but the Court determined that they fit within the description laid down in Art. 4, despite the fact that Mr Maierhofer did not own an interest in the land in certain cases.

There may be instances where it would be useful to rely on this in the UK. For example, a business letting pre-fabricated classrooms to a school to put on their own land could qualify for exemption. As the school would be unlikely to be able to recover the VAT, it may be beneficial for exemption to apply. In other cases where pre-fabricated buildings are used temporarily, such as on building sites, where the contractor is entitled to recover VAT, exemption would not be the preferred route.

In 2002 the government introduced the commonhold system of property ownership (Commonhold and Leasehold Reform Act 2002) in which each owner owns the freehold interest in their unit and the common parts of the property are owned by the commonhold association, usually a limited company, of which each resident is a 'unit holder'. The commonhold association looks after repairs and maintenance of the properties as a whole, usually making a monthly service charge to fund these. This service charge is exempt from VAT, subject to the option to tax (see **2.6** and **2.7**). Purchases of units in the commonhold are treated in the same way as a freehold interest for VAT purposes.

2.3.1 Supplies made pursuant to developmental tenancies, leases or licences

This provision relates to the developer's self-supply, under VATA 1994, Sched. 10, para. 5, which was repealed in respect of developments that commenced on or after 1 March 1995 and was completely abolished with effect from 1 March 1997. It essentially provided that if the tenant, lessee or licensee became liable to account for a developer's self-supply, then the rent became taxable at standard rate. This provision still applies to leases caught in the period up to 1 March 1997 (i.e. the leases remain standard rated without the option to tax having been exercised) but is ineffective after that date (VATA 1994, Sched. 9, Gp. 1, Item 1(b)).

2.3.2 The right to take game or fish

Standard rating applies where the right to take game or fish is supplied on its own (VATA 1994, Sched. 9, Gp. 1, Item 1(c)). In cases where the free-hold interest in land includes the right to take game or fish, then the supply is seen as a single supply of land and is exempt, unless of course the option to tax has been exercised. Where an interest in the land is granted which falls short of the freehold, then the legislation provides for apportionment of the consideration if the right to take game or fish is a valuable right (VATA 1994, Sched. 9, Gp. 1, Note 8). HMRC allows that if the value of the right to take game or fish is under 10 per cent of the total consideration, then an apportionment need not be made (*Notice 742, Land and Property*).

The case of *Carter* (No. 17288), involved a pheasant breeder who sold live pheasants to his customers out of the shooting season. Mr Carter released the pheasants on his land and then allowed the customers to come onto his land free of charge during the shooting season, to shoot the pheasants. The price charged per pheasant was more than that paid by commercial buyers who took the pheasants away. The decision was made on the basis that the sale comprised zero-rated food for human consumption rather than standard rated shooting rights. This appears to be a reliance on form over substance, and following the *Halifax plc* case the decision seems somewhat surprising, in that there would seem to be no commercial basis for the free right of entering the land to shoot the pheasants.

2.3.2.1   Shooting syndicates

Where a number of individuals contribute towards the cost of the shooting, there is no supply to the members of the syndicate and the funds received from them are outside the scope of VAT. However, if the syndicate charges third parties (not members of the syndicate) for the right to shoot, or supplies other goods or services, it invalidates the treatment as a syndicate and it must register for VAT and account for VAT on all its supplies, including those to syndicate members.

If you are registered for VAT and grant shooting rights to a syndicate of which you are a member for less than their normal value, VAT must be accounted for on the open market value of those rights. VAT is also chargeable if other goods or services, such as the services of a gamekeeper or beater, are also supplied.

In cases where a landowner accepts contributions towards the cost of maintaining a shoot ('shooting in hand') there is a supply of standard rated services unless the following conditions are met:

- it is only friends or relatives who shoot with the landowner;
- the shoot is not publicly advertised;
- the shooting accounts show an annual loss at least equal to the usual contribution made by a 'gun' over a year – effectively the landowner in his personal capacity makes a contribution of at least the same amount as any other 'gun';
- the loss is not borne by any business but by the landowner personally.

2.3.2.2   Fishing rights

If you operate a still-water fishery and allow a person to choose whether to return caught fish to the water or to take them away, making a separate charge for the fish which are taken away in addition to the right to fish, and the fish are of a type normally used as food in the UK, then the separate charge for the fish taken away qualifies for zero rating as food, under VATA 1994, Sched. 8, Gp. 1. The right to fish is standard rated.

Rod licences supplied by the National Rivers Authority are outside the scope of VAT.

2.3.3   Accommodation in hotels, inns, boarding houses or similar establishments

Where sleeping accommodation, accommodation in rooms in conjunction with sleeping accommodation, or rooms for the purpose of a supply of catering, are provided in a hotel, inn, boarding house or similar establishment, the supply is standard rated (VATA 1994, Sched. 9, Gp. 1, Item 1(d); also see **7.7**).

Note (9) to the Group defines 'similar establishment' as any premises in which furnished sleeping accommodation is provided, whether board or facilities for the preparation of food are provided or not, which is used by or held out as being suitable for visitors or travellers. A good résumé of the issues involved here can be found in the tribunal decision of *Acorn Management Services* (No. 17388), which decided against the taxpayer in regard to serviced student accommodation.

Where a hotel or guest house only provides accommodation for long-term guests, who have no other place of residence, this does not prevent standard rating from applying, see *McGrath (RI)* v. *C & E Commrs* [1992] STC 371, QBD and also *Namecourt Ltd* (No. 1560), which determined that a 'similar establishment' normally provides accommodation for a transient class of resident.

Rooms let for wedding receptions, dinner-dances, etc., where the primary use is for the purposes of a supply of catering, are always standard rated. However, rooms let for conferences organised by third parties, or other purposes where the primary use is not catering, are exempt from VAT subject to the option to tax. Hotels usually use a 'delegate rate' in charging for such supplies, the rate depending upon the individual needs of the delegates. Where the rate includes a meal, for a single inclusive price, HMRC has confirmed that each element of the supply should be treated separately and the consideration apportioned accordingly. Where the 24-hour delegate rate is charged (including sleeping accommodation), the charge should also be apportioned according to the separate elements of the supply – conference room hire exempt (subject to the option to tax), meals standard rated, sleeping accommodation standard rated.

In cases where a hotel lets a room for a conference and supplies morning coffee and afternoon tea only of minimal value, this is incidental to the main supply and if a single charge is made, the whole would be exempt from VAT, subject of course to the option to tax. If the charges are separate, then standard rating would apply to the provision of the refreshments.

In cases where the hotel organises and runs its own conference or a similar event, the charge for entry is standard rated.

HMRC announced its change in policy in this area in *Business Brief 01/06* dated 18 January 2006. Prior to this they had viewed any conference including sleeping accommodation as a single standard rated supply.

2.3.3.1   Long-stay guests

There is provision within VATA 1994, Sched. 6, para. 9 with regard to the supply of accommodation to an individual in a hotel, etc., for reduction of the value of the supply where the stay is in excess of four weeks. The value is reduced to the value of the supply which is attributable to facilities, which must be treated as at least 20 per cent.

Example

If a person stays in a guest house for six weeks, the final period of two weeks is subject to VAT on (at least) 20 per cent of the value of the supply. Food must be dealt with separately, so that if the charges made are £25 per night, including evening meal and breakfast, with the food being £10 of the value, VAT would be chargeable on (at least) the reduced amount of £25 – £10.00 = £15.00 × 20% = £3. VAT is therefore due on the food element of £10 plus at least £3, total £13.00; VAT calculated at £13.00 × 7 / 47 = £1.94 as opposed to the £3.72 VAT that would be due on the whole £25. The requirement to account for VAT on at least 20 per cent of the value is to take account of other facilities offered by this type of accommodation.

In the case of *Afro Caribbean Housing Association Ltd* (No. 19450), the appellant had entered into an agreement with the British Refugee Council (BRC) to supply accommodation for asylum seekers and refugees for which BRC would pay. The agreement specified that the supply of accommodation was by way of a licence to occupy to the individual occupant of the room. HMRC argued that the supply was to BRC and that therefore the reduced value for stays of over four weeks did not apply (because this applies only where the supply is to the individual). The tribunal found that there was a tripartite relationship with accommodation being supplied to BRC but the actual accommodation in the room being supplied to the individual (and payment being made by BRC) and that there is no requirement in the legislation that the person who receives the taxable supply of accommodation and the person physically occupying the room be the same person. Therefore the conditions for the reduced value were met and the appeal was allowed. (Note, at the time of writing this decision has only just been released, and in view of the number of other similar cases where HMRC has assessed tax in similar circumstances, it is quite possible that this decision will be appealed.)

In the case of *Look Ahead Housing and Care Ltd* (No. 17613), the Commissioners argued that the appellant was supplying exempt welfare services rather than standard rated and long stay reduced rate accommodation. The appellant successfully argued that it did not supply welfare services, although the accommodation was supplied to 'distressed' persons and assistance was provided in claiming housing benefits etc., staff were not qualified to and did not provide welfare services.

2.3.3.2 Supplies of food and accommodation to employees

Where food or accommodation are supplied to employees by the owner of a hotel, etc., the value of the supply is taken as 'nil' under VATA 1994, Sched. 6, para. 10.

2.3.4 Holiday accommodation (see also 7.8)

Any grant of an interest in, right over or licence to occupy holiday accommodation is standard rated (VATA 1994, Sched. 9, Gp. 1, Item 1(e)). Under Note 13 to the Group, 'holiday accommodation' includes any accommodation in a building, including a beach hut or chalet, caravan, houseboat or tent, which is advertised or held out as holiday accommodation, or as suitable for holiday or leisure use, excluding accommodation in a hotel, inn, boarding house or similar accommodation. It also includes the supply of land for the development of holiday accommodation.

The freehold sale of holiday accommodation which is over three years old is specifically excepted from standard rating under Note 12 to the Group. In the case of a lease, tenancy or licence in holiday accommodation which is over three years old, the exception to standard rating applies only to the extent that any consideration is in the form of a premium. Therefore, these supplies of holiday accommodation which are over three years old are exempt from VAT.

2.3.4.1 Seasonal pitches for caravans

Standard rating applies to the provision of seasonal pitches for caravans and the provision of facilities to persons to whom pitches are provided at caravan parks (VATA 1994, Sched. 9, Gp. 1, Item 1(f)).

A seasonal pitch includes one that is provided for less than one year, or one where occupation throughout the year, or period of rental, is prevented under the terms of any covenant, planning consent or similar permission (Note 14 to the Group). Standard rating applies to seasonal pitches, even if the use of the pitch is for residential purposes (see also *Colaingrove Ltd* v. *C & E Commrs* [2004] EWCA Civ 143).

Any reservation fee or premium is considered to be payment for the right to a pitch and is consequently also standard rated. Winter storage of caravans is also standard rated (see *A E House & Son* (No. 2620)).

2.3.4.2 Pitches for tents

The provision of pitches for tents or of camping facilities is standard rated (VATA 1994, Sched. 9, Gp. 1, Item 1(g)).

2.3.5 Parking facilities

The grant of facilities for parking a vehicle (including cars, commercial vehicles, motorcycles, bicycles, caravans, etc.) is standard rated (VATA 1994, Sched. 9, Gp. 1, Item 1(h)). This includes the letting, leasing or licensing of such facilities, but not the freehold sale, which remains exempt with the option to tax (unless the garage is under three years old, in which case it is a mandatory standard rated supply). In cases where an exempt grant includes a supply of car parking facilities, for example the lease of office premises with car parking facilities, there is a single exempt supply and no need to apportion the consideration in relation to the car parking facilities included (see *Skattenministeriet* v. *Morten Henriksen* (ECJ, C-173/88) and **3.2.3** for hire of a garage in conjunction with a dwelling). Where there is a separate charge for the provision of car parking space together with an exempt charge for the rent of office accommodation, for example, the treatment will depend upon the application of the 'composite supply' rules (see **1.2.7**). If the car parking charge is a minor amount and incidental to the overall supply, then exemption may apply to the overall charge made. In such cases it is recommended that clearance is sought from HMRC for the proposed treatment.

The hire of a garage will be standard rated even if it is not intended for use as parking, but for example, for storage. The standard rating also includes the letting of land specifically for the construction of a garage.

It is also important to differentiate between the hire of a field, for example, which may be used by the hirer for parking cars but is not specifically a car parking facility, which remains exempt from VAT with the option to tax. However, if land is specifically let to a person to use as a car park or to construct a garage then it is standard rated. See also *Venuebest Ltd* v. *C & E Commrs* [2003] STC 433, ChD, in which land had been used for a long period for car parking and was subject to a lease which the court therefore held to be standard rated.

The freehold sale of a car park is standard rated if it is under three years old, and otherwise is exempt, subject to the option to tax.

'Parking facilities' includes the letting of a taxi rank, as well as the right to park or store vehicles of any description, but does not include the letting of land or buildings to a motor retailer for storing stock in trade, or to a vehicle distributor for use in their trade.

2.3.6 Right to fell and remove standing timber

The right to fell and remove standing timber is standard rated (VATA 1994, Sched. 9, Gp. 1, Item 1(j)).

2.3.7 Moorings for boats and storage of aircraft

The grant of facilities for mooring or storage of a ship, boat or other vessel and for the housing or storage of an aircraft, is standard rated. This does not include houseboats where the mooring fee is exempt from VAT (VATA 1994, Sched. 9, Gp. 1, Item 1(k) (see also *Fonden Marselisborg Lystbadehavn* v. *Skatteministeriet* (ECJ, C-428/02)), as is the hire of a garage together with a houseboat, provided the garage is reasonably close to the mooring. There is also the exemption for eligible sports bodies where the moorings supplied are closely related to sports, such as to a member of a sailing club (VATA 1994, Sched. 9, Gp. 10, Item 3).

2.3.8 Entrance to sports grounds or places of entertainment

The grant of any right to occupy a box, seat or other accommodation at a sports ground, theatre, concert hall or other place of entertainment is standard rated (VATA 1994, Sched. 9, Gp. 1, Item 1(l)). However, if a box at a sports ground for example, is let when a sports event is not being held, for use by the hirer as an office, then the supply may be treated as exempt from VAT, subject to the option to tax. HMRC states in *VAT Notice 742, Land and Property* that this supply is standard rated regardless of whether the entertainment is actually in progress when the accommodation is used, but see *Southend United Football Club Ltd* (No. 15109), where the tribunal said that the purpose of exception in Item 1(l) was to tax entertainment, and that in principle it should be interpreted as operating only when a box was actually available to view a football match.

Hire of an entire sports ground, theatre or other place of entertainment is exempt from VAT, subject to the option to tax.

2.3.9 Letting of sports facilities

The grant of any facilities for the playing of sport or participating in any physical recreation is standard rated (VATA 1994, Sched. 9, Gp. 1, Item 1(m)), unless the grant is for a series of lets and the following conditions are met:

(a) if the grant of facilities is for a period of 24 hours or more; or

(b) if the grant of facilities is for a series of 10 or more periods, whether or not exceeding 24 hours; and

 (i) each period is in respect of the same activity carried on in the same place;

 (ii) the interval between each period is not less than one day and not more than 14 days;

 (iii) consideration is payable by reference to the whole series and is evidenced by written agreement, including evidence that payment is due in full for the series, regardless of whether they are used or not. (A written agreement can consist of an exchange of letters or an invoice for the single amount, as well as a formal written agreement. If there is a clause in the agreement allowing a rebate if the facilities are not used by the lessee for, say, one week, then this invalidates the condition. However, a clause allowing a refund in the event that the facilities are not available will not invalidate the exemption);

(iv) the grantee has exclusive use of the facilities;

(v) the grantee is a school, club, association, or an organisation representing affiliated clubs or constituent associations.

Example

A football club hires the football ground to a school, with a written agreement stipulating a single payment of £650 for two hours each Tuesday afternoon during the winter term (11 weeks) during which time they will have sole use of the facilities. The hire charge is exempt from VAT provided that the football club has not elected to waive exemption.

If a sale of land includes sporting rights, then the sale is exempt from VAT subject to the option to tax (see **2.7**). If you lease land which includes sporting rights, then provided the value of the sporting rights is less than 10 per cent of the total value of the supply, the supply is exempt from VAT. In the event that the value of sporting rights exceeds 10 per cent of the total, the value must be apportioned on a fair and reasonable basis.

There is also an exemption available, in VATA 1994, Sched. 9, Gp. 10, for the grant of facilities to participate in sports supplied by a non-profit-making organisation to an individual.

2.4   OPTIONS AND OTHER RIGHTS

Also excluded from exemption are the right to call for or be granted an interest or right within any of the Items in VATA 1994, Sched. 9, Gp. 1, Items (a) or (c)–(m) including an equitable right, a right under an option or pre-emption (the right of first refusal), or in relation to land in Scotland, a personal right (VATA 1994, Sched. 9, Gp. 1, Item 1(n)).

For example, the grant of an option to purchase a new freehold building (one which is under three years old) is standard rated. This applies even in cases where the option may not be exercised until the building is over three years old, i.e. the VAT treatment is fixed at the tax point for the particular transaction.

In cases where the option is purchased, and between the granting of the option and it being exercised the supplier exercises the election to waive exemption (see **2.7**), the VAT treatment of the grant of the option is fixed at the tax point of the transaction, and the VAT treatment of the supply under the exercising of the option is fixed at the tax point of that supply. It is therefore possible to have an exempt grant of an option, and a standard rated supply when that option is exercised, although it has been known for HMRC to argue that the exercising of the election to waive exemption retrospectively affects the treatment of the original grant of the option, so a clearance from them would be advisable.

2.5   MIXED USE

Where there is a 'mixed use' development the legislation provides for apportionment of values, in either the case of construction work at different rates of VAT or of disposal of the completed development (VATA 1994, Sched. 5, Gp. 5, Note 10).

2.6   LETTING OF COMMERCIAL PROPERTY

The grant of a lease in a commercial building is exempt from VAT, regardless of the term of the lease or age of the building, subject to the election to waive exemption (VATA 1994, Sched. 9, Gp. 1, Item 1 and Sched. 10, para. 2).

2.7   THE ELECTION TO WAIVE EXEMPTION

The 'election to waive exemption', or 'option to tax' as it has become commonly known (and is in fact properly known under European legislation) applies to land and commercial property only and was introduced with effect from August 1989 (although elections made prior to 1 November 1989 could have effect from 1 April 1989). The essence of the election to waive exemption is to provide a mechanism to prevent the creation of otherwise irrecoverable input tax relating to an exempt supply of land or a commercial building. Input tax which is attributable to an exempt supply is in principle irrecoverable (see **1.9**) but the option to tax converts the exempt supply to a standard rated one thus allowing for full recovery of related input tax, for example on the construction or refurbishment of a building (see also *Notice 742A, Opting to Tax Land and Buildings*). The option to tax is probably the single most important area in commercial land and property VAT matters because it provides a mechanism for VAT planning, structuring of transactions, and allows for the minimising of irrecoverable VAT. Having said that, it has been the subject of considerable anti-avoidance legislation over the past few years due to its perceived abuse and certain aspects of its application are therefore quite complicated (VATA 1994, Sched. 10, para. 2; Sixth Directive on VAT, Art. 13C). At the time of writing, this section of the legislation is facing a complete re-write, with HMRC admitting that it is the most complex piece of VAT legislation.

The option to tax is separate from registration for VAT – it is a common misconception that VAT is chargeable on commercial rent if a person is VAT registered. This is not so, for VAT to be chargeable the person must be VAT registered *and* have opted to tax (although charging VAT on what would otherwise be an exempt rent, for example, could be taken as an indication that the property owner had in fact elected (see *Fencing Supplies Ltd* (No. 10451), and **2.7.6**). If supplies under the option to tax will be the only taxable supplies made, then a copy of the option to tax should be sent to the Registration Unit when application is made to register for VAT, as it will require evidence that taxable supplies will be/are being made. The Registration Unit is also likely to require proof of ownership of the building before the registration application will be processed.

The option to tax applies to the building and its curtilage (VATA 1994, Sched. 10, para. 3(3)). There is no definition of curtilage but it is generally taken as the area around the building which comprises its grounds. If a building is opted, and the land surrounding a building is extensive, then the interpretation of HMRC is that the option to tax extends to the land that enjoys the benefits of the services provided by the building.

There is no provision under UK law for opting part of a building only, but this position is relatively easy to attain by granting a lease or licence on that part to be opted to a wholly owned company which can then opt to tax its interest in that part of the property only (although the arrangement could have other potential tax implications, such as Stamp Duty, and may be challenged by HMRC as being artificial (see **1.13**)).

Exercising the option to tax does not make input tax incurred prior to the election recoverable unless the person electing has not previously received any exempt income in relation to the property (VATA 1994, Sched. 10, para. 5). In cases where exempt income has previously been received in respect of the building to be opted, permission must be sought from HMRC prior to the election being exercised and agreement reached on how much of the previously incurred VAT can be recovered, although there is provision for automatic permission in certain circumstances (see **2.7.4**).

In the case of an abortive project where input tax is incurred, and recovery depends upon the option to tax, it is not necessary to have actually elected to waive exemption and notified this to HMRC. All that is required is for the person to have intended to elect to waive exemption (see *Beaverbank Properties Ltd* (No. 18099)).

2.7.1 When can't the option to tax be exercised?

In certain cases the option to tax will have no effect, even if it has been exercised:

1. A building or part of a building intended for use as a 'dwelling' or a number of dwellings or solely for 'use for a relevant residential purpose' or intended solely for 'use for a relevant charitable purpose' other than as

an office (VATA 1994, Sched. 10, para. 2(2)(a) and (b)). However, in the case of *SEH Holdings Ltd* (No. 16771), SEH had purchased a former public house and re-sold it to two purchasers, entering into a contract with them to convert the building into flats and to build new flats on the site. The vendor of the public house had opted to tax, but VAT was not charged in accordance with the above. The tribunal decided, on grounds that it would provide more certainty in determining the correct VAT treatment of transactions, that it was the immediate purchaser's use that mattered for these purposes, and as SEH had not used the building for qualifying purposes or carried out the conversion themselves the option to tax stood, and was therefore not disapplied (it is understood that the result of this case was never in fact enforced by HMRC). The result of this decision is that in order for the option to tax to be disapplied the purchaser must either carry out the conversion or have the building converted themselves rather than selling it on. This leaves the vendor in the invidious position of a potential retrospective charge to VAT in the event that the purchaser changes their mind and, for example, sells the building on. Therefore, far from creating certainty, the decision caused considerable confusion.

In a later case, *PJG Developments Ltd* (No. 19097), the appellant sought a ruling from HMRC that the option to tax should be disapplied on a former public house it had purchased, but HMRC refused, citing *SEH Holdings Ltd*, above. The use of the building as a public house had ceased at the time of the purchase and the vendor had gained planning permission to turn it back into two semi-detached houses, as it had been prior to use as a public house. The tribunal distinguished *SEH Holdings Ltd* on the facts of the case and allowed the company's appeal, holding that both parties were aware of PJG's intention to convert the building back into houses at the time of the sale (and there was no possibility of PJG making a zero-rated supply of the converted houses as part had always been used for residential purposes, so that VATA 1994, Sched. 10, paras. 2(2A) and (2B) were not in point). The tribunal also found that there was no requirement for the purchaser's intention to be directly and explicitly communicated to the vendor, nor was there a requirement that the residential use had to be by the purchaser or some other person to whom the purchaser would sell the property on to.

It is clear, therefore, that provided the vendor is aware of the purchaser's intentions as to use of the building after the sale, the option to tax should be disapplied. This should be brought to the vendor's attention as soon as possible, and despite the comments of the Tribunal in *PJG* above, it would be prudent for the terms of the disapplication of the option to tax to form part of the contract so that it is clear what both parties intend. It should be noted that an 'intention' must be firmly based and amounts to more than a 'hope' (see *D S Menzies* (No. 15733)) and it would be expected that an application for planning permission has been submitted with an expectation of it being granted.

2. There is also provision in cases where the purchaser intends to convert a non-residential building which has been elected, and will be granting a zero-rated major interest in the converted property, for the option not to be disapplied as in (1) above and for VAT at standard rate to therefore be charged. This allows the person selling the non-residential building to avoid suffering irrecoverable exempt input tax, the VAT chargeable on the sale being recoverable by the person making the zero-rated grant. Both parties to the transaction must agree for the VAT to remain chargeable and the agreement must be evidenced in writing (VATA 1994, Sched. 10, para. 2(2)(a) and (b)).

3. Pitches for residential caravans (VATA 1994, Sched. 10, para. 2(2)(c)).

4. Facilities for mooring a residential houseboat (VATA 1994, Sched. 10, para. 2(2)(d)). A houseboat is defined as a floating decked structure designed or adapted for use solely as a place of permanent habitation, which does not have the means of or is not capable of being readily adapted for self-propulsion, and where residence is permitted throughout the year, not being restricted by any planning consent, covenant or similar provision.

5. A grant of land to a registered housing association if the housing association has given to the grantor a certificate stating that the land is to be used (after any necessary demolition work) for the construction of a building or buildings intended for residential or qualifying use (VATA 1994, Sched. 10, para. 2(3)(a)). In the tribunal case of *Langstane Housing Association Ltd* (No. 19111), the tribunal confirmed HMRC's insistence that the certificate had to be issued prior to the grant – the wording of the legislation: 'a grant *is* made' and '*has* given . . . a certificate' make this clear. It should be noted that for these purposes 'land' includes any buildings on the land. In the *Langstane Housing Association* case, the purchase was of a commercial building that the housing association intended to convert into dwellings.

6. A grant of land to an individual if the land is to be used for the construction, otherwise than in the course or furtherance of the business carried on by him, of a building intended for use by him as a dwelling, i.e. a DIY housebuilder (VATA 1994, Sched. 10, para. 2(3)(b)).

7. In cases where the building is of mixed use, only part of which qualifies for the option to tax, there is provision for apportionment of the supply between the taxable and exempt elements (VATA 1994, Sched. 10, para. 2(1)).

2.7.2   The anti-avoidance block

Where the grant is made by a *developer* of the building and either the developer or a person responsible for financing the grantor's development of the land for exempt use, intended or expected that the land would become *exempt land*, the option to tax is disapplied (VATA 1994, Sched. 10, para. 2(3AA)). This exclusion to the option to tax applies to any building acquired or constructed or reconstructed by the developer, including any other works, such as fitting out or refurbishment costs, which fall to be treated as a capital item under the Capital Goods Scheme (see **1.10**). It was introduced as an anti-avoidance measure to prevent businesses which would normally be unable to recover VAT, due to being exempt, from recovering input tax on buildings by putting artificial structures in place. A typical scheme involved the lease of the property to an associated/wholly owned company and the lease back of the property, using the option to tax to make the rental charges standard rated. This allowed recovery of VAT in full on the capital costs of construction, whilst the VAT on the leaseback was irrecoverable. The leaseback would, however, be spread over a number of years, in some cases as many as 1,000, at a low market rent. These sort of arrangements are now a designated scheme and subject to the disclosure rules (see **1.12.1**).

The current version of the anti-avoidance block was introduced on 19 March 1997. It applies to grants made after 26 November 1996, except in the case of grants made between 26 November 1996 up until 30 November 1999, if the terms of the grant were agreed in writing before 26 November 1996. From 10 March 1999 the block also applies to grants where it is intended or expected in the future that the item will become a capital item for the purposes of the Capital Goods Scheme, whereas prior to that date it only applied if the building was a capital item at the time of the grant. Part of this latter measure required developers to treat grants made between 19 March 1997 and 10 March 1999 as made on 10 March 1999.

In cases where the supply which gives rise to the statutory block having force is subsequently changed, the option to tax would reactivate and become effective once again, for example if a property let to a connected exempt/partially exempt company is subsequently let to an unconnected party.

2.7.2.1   Meaning of 'exempt land'

The legal definition of *exempt land* is contained in VATA 1994, Sched. 10, para. 3A(7) and applies where the grantor, a person responsible for financing the grantor's development, or a person connected with either of them, is in occupation of the land (whether in occupation of all or part of the land) and the land is not being used 'wholly or mainly for eligible purposes'. The rule of thumb test used by HMRC for 'wholly or mainly for eligible purposes' is that the building must be used for at least 80 per cent taxable use. In *VAT Notice 742A, Opting to Tax Land and Buildings*, HMRC states:

For someone to be in occupation of the development for eligible purposes they must be occupying it for the purpose of making mainly taxable supplies, or for other supplies which entitle them to credit for their input tax. 'Mainly' means substantially more than half.

There is therefore grounds for arguing that businesses marginally missing the 80 per cent rule of thumb test should still qualify as 'mainly'.

The definition of a *connected person* is determined in accordance with ICTA 1988, s.839, and includes a spouse or other relative and spouse's relatives, business partners and their spouses or relatives, any company under common control or the trustees of a settlement of which you are a settlor.

If the person occupying the land is not making any supplies, but intends to make supplies which will be taxable, then the above provisions do not apply.

2.7.2.2   Meaning of 'developer'

A grant is made by a *developer* of the land if:

(a)   the land or building concerned is a capital item for the purposes of the Capital Goods Scheme (e.g. a non-residential building or extension or fitting out costs, in excess of £250,000); or

(b)   the person granting the interest or a person financing his development of the land for exempt use, intended or expected that the land, building or building to be constructed on the land, would become an asset subject to the Capital Goods Scheme, in the hands of the grantor or a person to whom the grantor transfers it as a going concern

unless the grant is made at a time after which adjustments are required under the Capital Goods Scheme (VATA 1994, Sched. 10, para. 3A(2)).

Part (b) above was added to para. 3A(2) as a result of a VAT planning scheme which purported to grant a lease over the land only, before the building was constructed, hence potentially the land was not a Capital Goods Scheme item (see *East Kent Medical Services* (No. 16095) below).

A person responsible for financing the grantor's development of the land is any person with the intention or expectation that the land will become exempt land, who:

• directly or indirectly provides finance for the development, whether wholly or partly;

• enters into any agreement, arrangement or understanding to procure finance for the development, whether wholly or partly;

• directly or indirectly provides funds to discharge any liability incurred by any person for or in connection with the raising of funds to meet the grantor's development of the land, whether in whole or in part;

91

- directly or indirectly procuring that any such liability will be discharged by another.

The above includes:

- making a loan;
- providing a guarantee or security;
- providing the consideration for the issue of any shares or other securities for raising such funds;
- the transfer of any assets or value as a consequence of which the funds are made available;
- a tenant paying a premium which funds construction costs.

This block to the option to tax does not apply when the grant is made to a local authority (or to a government department or National Health Service Trust) to the extent that it occupies the property for the purposes of its outside-the-scope statutory activities (VATA 1994, Sched. 10, para. 10).

A key example of this block in force is the case of *Winterthur Life UK Ltd* (No. 15785), where the appellant was the representative member of a VAT group which included the personal pension schemes of the three partners carrying on the business of insurance broking in partnership – an exempt or substantially exempt business activity. Contributions to the pension schemes were used to acquire new business premises (in addition to bank funds which covered more than 70 per cent of the acquisition cost) which were to be partly occupied by and leased to the partnership. The appellant notified HMRC of its option to tax but HMRC ruled that the blocking applied because the partners were to occupy the premises and were connected persons who had financed the acquisition and were not wholly taxable (VATA 1994, Sched. 10, para. 2(3AA)(b)(ii) and 3A(7)). The partners argued that the contributions did not amount to the financing or part financing of the acquisition by the trustees of the pension funds – they were paid for benefits under the personal pension schemes, not to provide finance for the acquisition of the property. They further argued that this was a legitimate commercial transaction and not VAT avoidance, which the legislative measure was designed to protect HMRC from. The tribunal found that at the time the lease was granted the three individuals expected to occupy the premises together for otherwise than eligible purposes. Finance included a transfer of assets or value as a consequence of which the funds were made available to wholly or partly finance the acquisition (VATA 1994, Sched. 10, para. 3(5A)(d)). Furthermore, an EU member state was not limited to measures to prevent possible evasion, avoidance or abuse in restricting the scope of the option to tax (Sixth Directive on VAT, Art. 13C). The appeal was dismissed.

A further similar decision was reached by the tribunal in *Brambletye School Trust Ltd* (No. 17688), where the anti-avoidance provisions in VATA 1994, Sched. 10, para. 2(3AA) and 3A(7) and (13) were determined to apply.

The school constructed a new sports hall and opted to tax, letting it to a subsidiary which ran a sports club consisting mainly of pupils of the school, but also for employees and families of students and the public, and claimed the input tax on the construction costs. The claim was rejected by HMRC because the land on which the hall was built was exempt land (VATA 1994, Sched. 10, para. 2(3AA)(b) and 3A(7)); and the *school* was 'in occupation of the land' due to its pupils using the hall. The tribunal decided that there were four issues which decided whether the school occupied the hall:

1. Priority was given to the use of the hall by pupils during the school day until 6 p.m. and when the pupils used the hall they were supervised by school staff.
2. School staff supervised use of the hall by the pupils and that use was mainly for school purposes.
3. The school continued to be responsible for pupils using the hall.
4. At all times when the hall was used by the pupils, control of the hall through the supervision of the staff rested with the school, which employed the staff. Therefore, the school had a physical presence through the members of staff and the pupils and it occupied the hall.

Another similar decision was arrived at by the tribunal in *East Kent Medical Services* (No. 16095). The issue at stake was whether a building in the course of construction was a 'building' for the purposes of the Capital Goods Scheme. If so, the block to the option to tax would apply. If not, this provided a loophole in the legislation so that VAT could be recovered on the capital cost of constructing the building – the scenario encompassed a lease/leaseback arrangement and much hinged upon when the building was first brought into use. The tribunal ruled that in the context of the Capital Goods Scheme the use of the building was not limited to physical use or occupation of the building. An underlease granted on 16 March 1998 was a grant of the land with the building and constituted use of the land including the building, as a capital item for the purpose of the appellant's business. There was no test of a building's fitness for habitation or physical completion for these purposes and its uncompleted state did not prevent it from being considered as a building. HMRC has since changed the legislation to ensure this type of planning cannot succeed, so that where an item is intended to be a capital item for the purposes of the Capital Goods Scheme, the block to the option to tax is effective.

It should be remembered that the block to the option to tax only applies to buildings which are capital items for the purposes of the 'Capital Goods Scheme'. This means that lease and leaseback arrangements (common prior to the statutory block) are possible if the building costs less than £250,000 (purchase or construction) in standard rated taxable expenditure, although HMRC may challenge such arrangements on the grounds that they are artificial, and disclosure may be required (see also **1.12**). It should be remembered, however, that it was HMRC which set the threshold of the Capital Goods Scheme at £250,000 and linked the block on the option to tax to this. If they had intended that schemes below this limit should not be successful, it would have been a simple matter to set the threshold to nil for these purposes (although as far as the author is aware, this argument has not yet been tested through the courts). Such schemes might apply, for example, to doctor's or dentist's surgeries, or an optician's, insurance broker's, or children's nursery premises, etc. An example of one scheme, which failed due to timing of the option to tax, can be found in *Fforestfach Medical Centre* (No 16587).

In *Belgocodex SA* v. *Belgium* (ECJ, C-381/97) the Court held that a member state is not precluded from abolishing the right of option and reintroducing exemption, and that a member state has a wide discretion as to the detailed provisions relating to the option to tax (Art. 2, First Directive on VAT (Dir. 67/227) and Art. 13C, Sixth Directive on VAT (Dir. 77/388)).

2.7.3 Other conditions to the option to tax

1. The option has effect from the day of the election or such later day as may be specified in the election notification (VATA 1994, Sched. 10, para. 3(1)). In other words, the election to waive exemption cannot be applied retrospectively.
2. From 1 March 1995, it is possible to opt to tax buildings selectively except those forming complexes consisting of a number of units grouped around a fully enclosed concourse or those connected by internal links or covered walkways (prior to March 1995 parades of shops, precincts and complexes of buildings such as industrial estates were considered to be a single building for the purposes of the option to tax). For these purposes a car park (above or below ground), a public thoroughfare, and any statutory requirement such as a fire escape does not constitute a link. HMRC states that if there is a group of buildings which have been treated as separate for the purposes of the option to tax, with some opted and some not, and the buildings are subsequently enclosed, the option to tax will not spread to the un-opted units (*Notice 742A, Opting to Tax Land and Buildings*, paras. 2.2 and 2.3). In *Charterhouse Mercantile Properties Ltd* (No. 17835) the taxpayer purchased an industrial estate consisting of 68 units in February 1988, and in 1992 opted to tax. In August 1998 the taxpayer was granted planning permission in respect of a triangular piece of land in the centre of the industrial estate, which had been staked off to prevent it being used for car parking. The taxpayer sought to let this land without charging VAT, which HMRC opposed. The tribunal reviewed the facts and decided that the industrial estate was a 'complex', so that the 1992 election covered at least the estate as developed at that time, and concluded that by staking off the triangular area

of land the taxpayer intended to keep their options open in respect of it and had not intended to include it in the option to tax.

3. Discrete areas of agricultural land may also be opted to tax selectively (prior to March 1995 in relation to agricultural land the option to tax affected 'adjacent' agricultural land in the same ownership – a discrete area could not be opted). This could cause problems if only part of a farm, for example, was going to be developed as, say, a golf course. Before this change, if the option to tax was exercised on part of the farmland, the remaining parts of the farm also fell under the option (VATA 1994, Sched. 10, para. 3(3)). Where the option to tax was exercised prior to March 1995 it remains in force for any group of buildings or land upon which it then had effect.

4. The option to tax is at the sole discretion of the landlord. It is not necessary to consult the tenant before exercising the option to tax, although commercial reality sometimes comes into play, for example, if the buildings are intended for occupation by small, unregistered businesses such as market stalls, or exempt businesses such as banks, building societies or insurance companies, etc., which cannot recover VAT.

5. Once the option to tax has been exercised on a building or land it governs all the supplies made by that person (or anyone else bound by the option because of any VAT grouping) unless the block mentioned above has effect or the option to tax is otherwise statutorily disapplied, by converting the premises into a dwelling for example. It is therefore necessary for the person exercising the option to apply VAT on the rents to the tenant and on the final disposal of the building to a third party. With regard to rents, for the avoidance of doubt the option to tax covers the rent, service charge rent, and insurance rent.

6. From 1 March 1995 the option to tax may be revoked within three months (in *Business Brief 23/05* it was announced that this would be increased to 12 months) with prior written permission of HMRC, provided that no input tax has been claimed in relation to the property and no output tax has been charged in relation to the property and the property has not, since the date of the election, been part of a transfer of a going concern under VAT (Special Provisions) Order 1995, SI 1995/1268, Art. 5. The option to tax may also be revoked after being in force for 20 years, again with the written permission of HMRC. The revocation conditions (VATA 1994, Sched. 10, para. 3(5) are currently under review by HMRC which has set out initial guidance in *Business Brief 23/05*.

This sets out two potential routes for permission:

(a) *Automatic permission.* This will be available in cases where:

- there has been no pre-payment covering any supply of goods or services for more than the next six months following the date of revocation;
- no capital item is held (HMRC recognises that many properties will be capital items, so are exploring this condition further);
- any rents charged have not been undervalued, and no balloon payments fall due at any time after the proposed revocation;
- the taxpayer held an interest in the property at least 20 years prior to revocation and that property was subject to the election to waive exemption at that time.

(b)   Permission consent. HMRC states that it will grant permission in other cases where one of the above conditions is not met, providing the taxpayer does not obtain a tax advantage other than future supplies of the property being tax-free.

7. It is necessary in order for the option to be effective for the person exercising the option to notify HMRC within 30 days of exercising the election, or such later time as the Commissioners may in their discretion allow. Such notification must be in writing, preferably using HMRC form VAT 1614. This is a separate issue from the actual election itself (VATA 1994, Sched. 10, para. 3(6)) – see *Blythe Limited Partnership* (No. 16011) and **2.7.9** on how to opt to tax.

8. Following the case of *Chalegrove Properties Ltd* (No. 17151) the option to tax is treated as being made when the notification is put into the post, assuming that it is notified by post, rather than the day on which the notification is received by HMRC, provided that prior permission of HMRC is not required.

9. Where the building which is to be opted is used both for non-residential and residential/qualifying purposes, for example a single lease of a shop with a flat above the shop, there must be apportionment between the standard rated element for the commercial premises and the exempt element for the residential accommodation.

10. The option to tax does not automatically pass on from one owner of a building to another. If a person purchases or rents a building which is opted, then he must decide whether or not to exercise the option to tax himself and notify HMRC within the 30-day time limit, if necessary, to avoid non-recovery of VAT on the purchase price.

11. If the option to tax is exercised by one company in a VAT group, then the option effectively applies to all the companies in the VAT group at that time (VATA 1994, Sched. 10, para. 3(7)). This applies to any company joining the group after the date of election whilst the elected property is still within a group company. This is to prevent a company holding an opted property from joining a VAT group and then transferring the property to another group member (supplies between group members being

outside the scope of VAT) and then the recipient company leaving the VAT group with an 'un-opted' property.

12. Where the legal title and beneficial ownership of a property are separately held, it is the beneficial owner of the building who is seen as making the supply in relation to the land or building, and therefore the beneficial owner who should be registered for VAT, opt to tax and claim any input tax incurred (VATA 1994, Sched. 10, para. 8). In cases where there are numerous beneficiaries, such as with a pension fund, the trustees of the pension fund are seen as making the supply and it is therefore the trustees who should register and opt to tax.

13. Where there are joint owners, this is seen as a separate legal entity for VAT purposes and there should be a single VAT registration and therefore a single option to tax. Co-owners of a single property cannot separately opt to tax.

14. If the opted property is demolished, then HMRC states that the option to tax ceases to have effect (see *Notice 742A, Opting to Tax Land and Buildings*). This can work in favour of the developer who can then choose whether or not to opt to tax in respect of subsequent disposal or development of the site. However, in the German case of *Finanzamt Goslar* v. *Breitsohl* (ECJ, C-400/98) the European Court's decision released on 8 June 2000 determined that the option to tax affected both the building and the underlying land. In *Business Brief 23/05*, HMRC announced that it will be legislating to bring its policy in line with this decision. However, it has stated that if a building is demolished and a new building constructed, the taxpayer will have the opportunity to revoke the option to tax in respect of the new building and land, provided no supplies have yet been made in respect of that building. The new rules will also only apply to elections made after the change in legislation becomes effective.

HMRC also currently states that if you have opted to tax land, and subsequently construct a building on the land, then the option to tax will not apply to the building (see *Notice 742A*, para. 2.4). This also contradicts the above case decision by the European Court, but is again to be the subject of a change in legislation as set out above.

2.7.4 Automatic permission

Restrictions were introduced from the 1 January 1992 on the ability of persons to exercise the option to tax without first obtaining the written permission HMRC. If an exempt grant has been made or is to be made in relation to the land at any time after 31 July 1989 and before the day on which the election is to have effect, prior written permission must be obtained from HMRC. HMRC is empowered to seek a fair and reasonable attribution of input tax relating to the property before agreeing to the exercise of the option to tax (VATA 1994, Sched. 10, para. 3(9)). In *Notice 742A, Opting to Tax*

Land and Buildings, para. 5.2, HMRC allows that automatic permission is granted in the following circumstances:

1. It is a mixed-use development and the only exempt supplies have been in relation to the dwellings.
2. You do not wish to recover any input tax in relation to the land or building incurred before your option to tax has effect; and

   (a) the consideration for your exempt supplies has, up to the date when your option to tax is to take effect, been solely by way of rents or service charges and excludes any premiums or payments in respect of occupation after the date on which the option takes effect. Regular rental and/or service charge payments can be ignored for the purposes of this condition. Payments are considered regular where the intervals between them are no more than one year and where each represents a commercial or genuine arm's length value; and

   (b) the only input tax relating to the land or building that you expect to recover after the option to tax takes effect will be on overheads, such as regular rental payments, service charges, repairs and maintenance costs. If you expect to claim input tax in relation to refurbishment or redevelopment of the building you will not meet this condition.

   Notes

   When deciding whether you meet this condition you should disregard:
   - any input tax you can otherwise recover by virtue of the partial exemption *de minimis* rules (VAT Regulations 1995, reg. 106);
   - any input tax you are entitled to recover on general business overheads not specifically related to the land or building, such as audit fees.

3. The only input tax you wish to recover in relation to the land or building incurred before your option to tax takes effect relates solely to tax charged by your tenant or tenants upon surrender of a lease; and

   (a) the building or relevant part of the building has been unoccupied between the date of the surrender and the date the option to tax is to take effect; and

   (b) there will be no further exempt supplies of the land or building; and

   (c) you do not intend or expect that you will occupy the land or building other than for taxable purposes.

4. The exempt supplies have been incidental to the main use of the land or building. For example, where you have occupied a building for taxable purposes the following would be seen as incidental to the main use and the condition would be met:

(a) allowing an advertising hoarding to be displayed;
(b) granting space for the erection of a radio mast;
(c) receiving income from an electricity sub-station.

The letting of space to an occupying tenant, however minor, is not incidental.

The need to seek permission prior to the option to tax being effective can cause delays and, in such cases, sufficient time for permission to be granted must be budgeted for. It is unlikely that HMRC will refuse permission, but possible that it may dispute the amount of input tax which becomes recoverable as a result of exercising the option to tax, and this may of itself exacerbate the amount of irrecoverable VAT due to the delay in the option to tax taking effect. HMRC has also set out the information it requires in order to consider the permission at para. 5.5 of *VAT Notice 742A, Opting to Tax Land and Buildings* (see **2.7.9**).

2.7.5 Dangers of not opting on time

The European Court held that member states were entitled to introduce restrictions regarding the retroactivity of the option to tax in the Luxembourg case of *Luxembourg* v. *Vermietungsgesellschaft Objekt Kirchberg Sarl* (ECJ, C-269/03). The dangers of not opting to tax on time are best looked at by the example of case law.

Norbury Developments Ltd (ECJ, C-136/97). Norbury purchased some building land and were charged VAT, the option to tax having been exercised. They subsequently sold the land without themselves opting to tax and HMRC assessed the VAT they had recovered on the purchase price. Norbury argued that under European legislation there should be no exemption for 'building land' and the supply should be automatically standard rated. The European Court ruled that in the transitional period member states were allowed to retain exemptions already in place and that the exemption in UK land was therefore valid. The assessment was upheld.

C & E Commrs v. *Trustees for R & R Pension Fund* [1996] STC 889, QB. The trustees purchased a property on which VAT was paid, and then let it without themselves opting to tax. The trustees subsequently opted, once the oversight had been brought to their attention. HMRC assessed all of the VAT on the purchase price, arguing that as the value of the property was over £250,000 it was subject to the Capital Goods Scheme. This allows initial recovery on the basis of use in the first period with subsequent adjustments on an annual basis. The court agreed with HMRC.

Royal & Sun Alliance Insurance Group plc v. *C & E Commrs* [2003] UKHL 29. The appellant opted to tax five buildings which had been empty for some time and made a claim for input tax in respect of rents paid to the landlord prior to the option having been exercised. HMRC refused any recovery and the tribunal upheld the decision on the grounds that simply because the next supply made in respect of the buildings was taxable did not mean that the input tax was attributable to these supplies – the group had originally taken on the properties with a view to self-occupation and it was substantively exempt from VAT. The input tax had been incurred prior to the option being exercised and was exempt input tax. The High Court, however, overturned this decision on the grounds that there was a direct and immediate link between the group obtaining the superior leases and meeting its obligations under them and it considered that the rent paid to the superior landlord was a 'cost component' of the taxable rent later charged to its tenants. The Court of Appeal upheld the decision of the High Court by a majority decision. The House of Lords, however, allowed the appeal by the Commissioners, holding that where a landlord grants a time-limited interest in land he is treated as making supplies in successive units of time (each time a payment is due) and that the grants prior to the election being exercised were different to the grants after the election had been exercised. A change of plan about how the leases were to be used in the future was not a change of intention to which reg. 109 of the VAT Regulations 1995 would apply, and therefore the input tax incurred prior to the election having been exercised did not become taxable input tax once it was so exercised.

Classic Furniture (Newport) Ltd (No. 16977). This appeal concerned the sale of a property by the appellant to its 100 per cent shareholder director, who would then let the property to the appellant company. It appears that the director had opted to tax in order to recover the VAT of £475,000 charged on the selling price, but HMRC contended that the appellant had not, and that the VAT was not therefore properly chargeable. A belated notification was sent by the appellant's advisers some five months after the transaction, which the Commissioners took as a belated election, rather than a belated notification (see **2.7.6**) which they rejected. The tribunal considered on the evidence that the appellant had opted to tax prior to the transaction taking place, and that the letter of some five months later was a belated notification and should be accepted. The Commissioners had carried out an inspection on the director, on receipt of the repayment claim and had accepted at that time that the director's option to tax was valid, but had not taken any action at that time regarding the apparent lack of notification by the appellant – the tribunal commented that they found this strange.

2.7.6   What if VAT has been charged but no election has been notified?

In cases where VAT has been charged but either the election has not been notified or the position is not known, HMRC will usually accept that the election has been exercised and the position can be formalised by submitting a belated notification (see *Fencing Supplies Ltd* (No. 10451). Since 1 March 1995, it has only been necessary for an option to be notified within 30 days (or such later period as the Commissioners may allow) in order to be valid. Therefore, it may be unclear whether a valid election has been made prior to that date, especially as in cases where the total letting income was under £20,000 p.a. there was no requirement to notify the election prior to 1 March 1995 at all. In such cases it can be difficult to determine the correct VAT status of the building. However, if VAT has been charged but there is no record of the election having been exercised with the local VAT office, and the total rent received is over £20,000 p.a. then it can be assumed that the building has been opted and appropriate corrective action of a belated notification taken, or if it is more beneficial to the client it could be argued that the VAT was charged in error and that the election has not been made, in which case the VAT overcharged should strictly be repaid to the tenant.

HMRC has set out its policy regarding belated notifications of the option to tax in *Business Brief 13/05*. In this it states that it will usually accept a belated notification:

> if the trader can provide evidence, such as the minutes of a Board or management meeting, or correspondence referring to the decision. However, we accept that this is sometimes not available, so in its absence we would normally accept a statement from the responsible person, plus evidence that:
>
> - all the relevant facts have been given;
> - output tax has been properly charged and accounted for from the date of the supposed election; and
> - input tax recovery in respect of the land or building is consistent with the trader having made taxable supplies of it.
>
> There may be other circumstances where we would accept a belated notification, but this would depend on the individual circumstances of the case.
>
> Conversely, HMRC may not accept that a decision to opt to tax was taken, even when the above conditions are met, if for example:
>
> - there has been correspondence concerning or investigation into the liability of supplies of the property in question since the supposed date of the option, and no mention of the option to tax was made;
> - the trader or his representative has previously put forward an alternative explanation for the charging of output tax (for example, that the supply was not of land and buildings, or was of a sports facility).
>
> Moreover, HMRC reserves the right to refuse to accept the belated notification if to do so would produce an unfair result, or if the exercise of the discretion was sought in connection with a tax avoidance scheme.

Where VAT has been charged it is therefore likely that both HMRC, and the tribunal, would see this as an indication that the election to waive exemption has been exercised on the grounds that exercising the election is the only legal way in which VAT could be charged, and if input tax has also been claimed this would reinforce that indication (see *Fencing Supplies Ltd* (No. 10451) cited above).

2.7.7 Central register

There is now a central office dealing with all options to tax:

Option To Tax, UK Central Office,
HM Revenue and Customs,
Portcullis House,
21 India Street,
Glasgow G2 4PZ

Tel: 0141 308 3548/3599
Fax: 0141 308 3367
E-mail: optiontotaxnationalunit@hmce.gsi.gov.uk.

HMRC was supposed to be compiling a central register of the option to tax, but the size of the operation required to sift taxpayers' files to provide the necessary information is considerable, and therefore the information from local offices has not in many cases been forwarded. However, the Option to Tax Unit has access to all taxpayer's electronic folders and evidence of a prior election should be noted in this. Written authority from the person who owns the interest in the land or buildings will be required.

2.7.8 Interaction with Stamp Duty

Stamp Duty is chargeable on the VAT inclusive value of the transaction being stamped. The Stamp Duty Office operates on the principle that if it is possible for the option to tax to be exercised then the stampable value should include any VAT which would be payable, whether or not it has been exercised at the time the document is stamped. Therefore, in cases where the option to tax has not been exercised, but it is still possible for the vendor to do so, the Stamp Office will levy Stamp Duty on the consideration as if VAT were chargeable in addition to the price. In cases where it is the parties' intention that the option to tax should not be exercised, therefore, it is worth including a clause in the contract that the vendor will not opt to tax.

2.7.9 How to opt to tax

Exercising the option to tax is a two-stage operation. First, there is the decision to opt to tax. This should preferably be evidenced in writing, such as board meeting minutes. Secondly, there is the notification of the option to tax. This is made in writing to:

Option To Tax, UK Central Office,
HM Revenue and Customs,
Portcullis House,
21 India Street,
Glasgow G2 4PZ

Tel: 0141 308 3548/3599
Fax: 0141 308 3367
E-mail: optiontotaxnationalunit@hmce.gsi.gov.uk.

HMRC provides a form which has space for all of the information required – form VAT 1614 which is also available from their website (**www.hmrc.gov.uk**). A map or plan of the opted property should also be included wherever possible, with the property subject to the election outlined in red. The written notification should be sent in within 30 days of taking the decision to elect to waive exemption.

In practice, if the decision has been made to opt to tax (evidenced, for example, by the charging of VAT on rent from a certain date) but notification has not been made, then HMRC is generally prepared to accept a belated notification and accept that the election has effect from the date the owner started to charge VAT.

Permission from HMRC is required if the person electing has previously received exempt income in respect of the property (see **2.7.4** for further details). Where the conditions for automatic permission are met, you should advise HMRC when making notification of the option to tax, by ticking the appropriate box on form VAT 1614. If you do not meet the conditions for automatic permission, you should write to HMRC, allowing time for its consideration and granting of permission, prior to opting to tax. The following information will be required:

1. Details of future plans for the building.
2. Details of input tax incurred in the 10 years prior to opting which you wish to recover, including amounts and how they have been calculated, what the input tax relates to, and when it was incurred. Also provide information on input tax expected to be incurred between the time of applying for permission and the time the option to tax is intended to have effect.
3. Details of the value of input tax you expect to incur in the future if permission is granted, and what this income will relate to (e.g. rents, etc.).

103

4.   The total value of exempt supplies in relation to the building in the 10 years prior to your request for permission, the value of any supplies which will fall between the request for permission and opting to tax and details of any grants made for prepayments of rent.
5.   The expected value of taxable supplies you intend to make in the future after the date of the option to tax, should permission be granted. Also, supply details of any exempt grants expected to be made where the option to tax would be disapplied (see **2.7.2**).

If permission is not requested it cannot be granted retrospectively and the option to tax will not have effect. Any VAT charged prior to the grant of permission will be VAT charged in error and due as a debt to the Crown, unless it is refunded, and any input tax claimed will be treated as exempt input tax and non-recoverable subject to the partial exemption *de minimis* limits.

   The notice of election must be signed by a responsible person. In the case of a sole proprietor it must be the sole proprietor who signs the notification, in the case of a partnership it must be a partner, and in the case of a company it must be an officer of the company. In *Hammersmith and West London College* (No. 17540), the tribunal determined that an election to waive exemption, notified by an assistant principal, was a valid election, despite the college arguing that the assistant principal (who had by the time of the hearing left the college's employ) did not have authority to do so. If you request a third party, such as a professional adviser, to notify the option to tax for you, HMRC will require a letter of authority from you, or it will not accept the notification. You should also notify HMRC if you subsequently revoke that authority.

2.8   LICENCE TO OCCUPY

The grant of any 'interest in or right over land' or any 'licence to occupy land' is exempt from VAT (VATA 1994, Sched. 9, Gp. 1, Item 1). A grant of an interest in land includes the grant of mineral rights (*profits a prendre*) over the land and also of easement. There are a number of recognised examples of a licence to occupy land but the principle to retain exemption is that the grantee is given exclusive occupation of a clearly defined site to the exclusion of other people not within his control. In view of the uncertainty provided by case law on the subject, HMRC carried out a review and published a report on 21 July 1999. HMRC found that case law was not too helpful in providing set guidance on what constituted a 'licence to occupy' – each was considered and decided on its individual facts, and lacked any consistent theme. As no legal definition was found possible, HMRC has issued clearer guidance in *VAT Notice 742, Land and Property*, ss.2.5–2.7:

2.5 What is a licence to occupy land?

A licence is an authority to do something that would otherwise be a trespass. A licence to occupy land is created when the following criteria are met:

(a) the licence is granted in return for a consideration paid for by the licensee;
(b) the licence to occupy must be for a specified piece of land, even if the licence allows the licensor to change the exact area occupied, such as to move the licensee from the third to fourth floor;
(c) the licence is for the occupation of the land by the licensee;
(d) another person's right to enter the specified land does not impinge upon the occupational rights of the licensee; and either:
(e) the licence allows the licensee to physically enjoy the land for the purposes of the grant, such as to hold a party in a hall; or
(f) the licence allows the licensee to economically exploit the land for the purpose of its business, such as to run a nightclub.

2.6 Examples of supplies that are licences to occupy land

- the provision of office accommodation, such as a specified bay, room or floor, together with the right to use shared areas such as reception, lifts, restaurant, rest rooms, leisure facilities and so on;
- the provision of a serviced office that includes use of telephones, computer system, fax machine, photocopiers and so on;
- granting a concession to operate a shop within a shop, where the concessionaire is granted an area from which to sell their goods or services;
- granting space to erect advertising hoardings;
- granting space to place a fixed kiosk on a specified site, such as a newspaper kiosk or flower stand at a railway station;
- hiring out a hall or other accommodation for meetings or parties and so on. The use of a kitchen area, lighting and furniture can be included;
- granting a catering concession, where the caterer is granted a licence to occupy a specific kitchen and restaurant area, even if the grant includes use of kitchen or catering equipment; or
- granting traders a pitch in a market or at a car boot sale.

2.7 Examples of supplies that are not licences to occupy land

- sharing business premises where more than one business has use of the same parts of the premises without having their own specified areas;
- providing another person with access to office premises to make use of facilities, such as remote sales staff away from home having access to photocopiers and the like at another office;
- allowing the public to tip rubbish on your land;
- storing someone's goods in a warehouse without allocating any specific area for them;
- granting of an ambulatory concession, such as an ice cream van on the sea front or a hamburger van at a football match;
- allowing the public admission to premises or events, such as theatres, historic houses, swimming pools and spectator sports events. This includes admission to a series of events, such as a season ticket; or
- any grant of land clearly incidental to the use of the facilities on it, such as hiring out safes to store valuables or the right to use facilities in a hairdressing

105

salon or granting someone the right to place a free standing or wall mounted vending or gaming machine on your premises.

C & E Commrs v. *Sinclair Collis Ltd* (ECJ, C-275/01). This case concerned whether the profit sharing arrangements between an owner of vending machines and a public house constituted an exempt licence to occupy land or a standard rated supply of services. A previous case, *Wolverhampton and Dudley Breweries plc* (No. 5351), had been decided on the basis of the 'substance and reality' test of what had been provided – the court went beyond the terms of the contract between the parties to see what had in substance and reality been provided, and determined this was not, or not just, a licence to occupy land. In *Sinclair Collis Ltd* the Court of Appeal ruled that the tribunal had in each case been distracted by the substance and reality test – the substance and reality test should only be brought into use when the contract itself did not make clear what was being supplied, or the substance and reality differed considerably from the terms of the contract. In this case it was quite clear that what was being provided was a licence to occupy land in return for a share in the profits. The case was appealed to the House of Lords who made a referral to the ECJ as to whether the right to install, operate and maintain cigarette machines in the premises, in a place nominated by the owner of the premises, is capable of amounting to the letting of immovable property under Art.13B(b) of the Sixth Directive on VAT. The ECJ held that as there was no particular area provided for the machines in the agreements (the owner could place them where he wished) and Sinclair Collis Ltd's (the machine owner) occupation of the site-owners' space was merely therefore a means of effecting the service – the exclusive right to sell cigarettes on the premises in return for a share of the profits – which was standard rated, not amounting to the letting of immovable property. Also, access to the machine was controlled by the site owner and not by Sinclair Collis Ltd, the machine owner.

It should be noted that where the agreement does stipulate the placement of the machine in a specific area, and access is controlled by the machine owner, this could amount to the letting of immovable property and thus qualify for exemption. See also *Business Brief 18/03* for HMRC guidance on this area.

Blendhome Ltd (t/a Stanhill Court Hotel) (No. 16048). The hotel was licensed as a venue for civil marriage services and, when it was so used, the reception was often held there as well. Specific rooms were used for the marriage services and the reception respectively, and an exclusivity fee was paid for which the party was given exclusive use of the public rooms and grounds of the hotel. Where that included an evening the appellant would not let bedrooms to other guests and part of the charge made was to cover this. VAT was accounted for on this charge and on the bar and catering charge. HMRC argued that there was a single composite supply of the provision of hotel accommodation for sleeping or catering and this was excluded from exemption (VATA 1994, Sched. 9, Gp.1, Item 1(d)) – the quality of exclusivity merely enhanced this package. The tribunal found that the reception facilities were the primary consideration for which the appellant paid and the exclusivity merely enhanced that supply – applying *Card Protection Plan Ltd* v. *C & E Commrs* (ECJ, C-349/96), [1999] STC 270 (para.30) – the supply was standard rated. See also *Leez Priory* (No. 18185), where a similar decision was reached.

Holmwood House School Developments (No. 18130). This case concerned arrangements set up to attempt to recover input tax on the construction of school buildings where the block to the option to tax would have applied. The arrangements purported to create two licences over land neither of which was for the exclusive use of any one licensee, thus making the licence standard rated. The appellant granted the licences of 'educational facilities' to the school and to another separate but associated business providing education to assisted places students. The tribunal determined that the true subject of the supply was the buildings, as all the students were being taught together, and ruled that the licences conferred joint rights of occupation as if the licensees were joint owners, and there was thus one exempt supply of letting or leasing the buildings.

John Window (No. 17186). This case involved the supply of livery, and the appellant successfully argued that there was a single supply of a licence to occupy the stable, the livery services being ancillary to the main supply. Prior to this decision, HMRC had always treated livery services as a single standard rated supply. However, following the *Card Protection Plan Ltd* principles (see **1.2.7**), it is clear that if the predominant nature of the supply is letting, it will be a single exempt supply – but this may not always be the case, depending upon the value of the livery services provided.

2.8.1 Hairdressers and chair rental

Many hairdressing salons have in the past structured their business so that the stylists are self-employed and a licence to occupy the chair is granted to them, exempt from VAT. There will usually also be an additional charge for use of other facilities or for supply of shampoo and other goods – standard rated. HMRC has vigorously opposed such schemes on the basis that there cannot be a licence to occupy if the self-employed stylist has free rein of the premises and is not restricted to his/her own defined space under the terms of the licence to occupy. They have been quite successful with cases through the VAT tribunal. For example, in *Simon Harris Hair Design Ltd* (No. 13939) the tribunal agreed with HMRC that there was a single supply of standard rated facilities:

We consider that the licences are economically useless without the other elements, the most important of which are services of the juniors and the use of the wash basins and the dryers. Put another way, we consider that as a matter of common sense there were single supplies.

Following this decision, agreement was reached between the National Federation of Hairdressers and HMRC that such arrangements do not result in an exempt licence to occupy land – the whole of the charge to the self-employed stylists is standard rated as a right to carry on business. However, the arrangements are still worthwhile if the salon owner's taxable turnover is below the VAT registration limits.

The more recent joined decision in *W E Mallinson & M Woodbridge (t/a The Hair Team); L J Mould (t/a Leon Jaimes Hair Fashions)* (No. 19807) followed the above in determining that there was a single standard rated supply, the predominant part being taxable goods and services, and that the supply of a fixed space in the salon was incidental to this.

2.8.2 Grazing rights

A supply of grazing rights is treated as a supply of animal feedstuff and is zero rated under VATA 1994, Sched. 8, Gp. 1, Item 2. However, see *J A King* (No. 933), regarding casual grazing licences, which were held not to qualify for either zero rating or exemption.

2.9 RENT-FREE PERIODS

Rent-free periods have traditionally caused problems. HMRC originally took the view that a rent-free period represented consideration for a supply by the tenant to the landlord and should be taxed. It has now refined this and its stated current position is that if the rent-free period is granted as a result of the tenant doing something or agreeing to do something in return for it (i.e. there has got to be a specific nexus) the value of the rent-free period will represent non-monetary consideration for the tenant's action and therefore be subject to VAT. HMRC has now accepted the position that where a rent-free period is granted simply as a reflection of the current state of the market (e.g. to allow a higher initial rent level to be set for the purpose of the next rent review) there is not consideration for a supply.

The *Ridgeons Bulk Ltd* v. *C & E Commrs* [1994] STC 427, QBD, decision illustrates how the rent-free period is seen as consideration for a supply of services by the tenant to the landlord. In this case the landlord granted a lease to the tenant, the tenant agreed to refurbish the building for £400,000 and was granted a three-year rent-free period, specifically in consideration for the agreement to refurbish. The tenant had to account for VAT on the supply of refurbishment services to the landlord, the value of the supply being the value of the rent-free period. The landlord could not recover this VAT as input tax unless it in turn exercised the option to tax on the property. This case illustrates that we are dealing here with two supplies in VAT terms, a taxable supply from the tenant to the landlord and an exempt supply by the landlord to the tenant (subject to the option to tax). It is important to recognise the possibility that HMRC may come knocking on the door of either party demanding VAT due on the transactions as appropriate, so it is important to get the correct contract terms in place. In the *Ridgeon's Bulk* case above, the VAT chargeable by the tenant was exempt input tax in the hands of the landlord and therefore non-recoverable.

2.10 INDUCEMENTS/AGREEMENT TO ENTER INTO A LEASE

Where an inducement payment is made to a tenant to enter into a lease, HMRC accepts that this is outside the scope of VAT provided that the tenant does no more than simply agree to be bound by the terms of the lease in paying the rent and carrying out periodic redecoration, etc. A taxable supply will only arise if the tenant agrees to provide benefits outside the terms of a normal lease. In *Business Brief 12/05* HMRC provides examples of circumstances where it would consider there to be a taxable supply:

- undertaking building works to improve the property by carrying out necessary repairs or upgrading the property;
- carrying out fitting out or refurbishment works for which the landlord has responsibility and is paying the tenant to undertake;
- acting as anchor tenant.

It also states:

> HM Revenue & Customs accept that this is a difficult area where the undertakings of landlords and tenants can change a number of times in the course of negotiating a tenancy. HM Revenue & Customs will therefore seek as much documentation as possible before reaching a decision. HM Revenue & Customs will not assume that there has been a supply and agree that less specific indicators do not determine the issue. For example, publicity indicating that Company X is to take a lease in a development does not, in itself, determine that the company is an anchor tenant. Equally, undertakings to use improved materials as part of continuous repairs under a tenant repairing lease would not constitute a taxable benefit to the landlord under the first example above.

2.11 LANDLORD'S CONTRIBUTIONS

It is common for a landlord to make a monetary contribution when tenants make improvements to the property. Such payments are standard rated being consideration for the tenant's providing valuable benefits under the lease, and the ability of the landlord to recover the VAT which must be charged/ accounted for by the tenant depends upon the VAT liability of the rent (see *Gleneagles Hotel plc* (No. 2152) and *Neville Russell* (No. 2484)).

2.12 EXHIBITIONS

The supply of space or a stand at an exhibition comprises the right to occupy land and is exempt from VAT subject to the option to tax (see **7.6**). The right to occupy covers the supply of lighting and power and insurance if provided by the same supplier. Most owners of exhibition venues elect to waive exemption because of the standard rated costs incurred, and most businesses exhibiting are in a position to recover the VAT charged. Supplies of organising an exhibition are, however, treated as taxable where the services are performed under the VAT (Place of Supply of Services) Order 1992, SI 1992/3121 (see also **1.2.3**).

2.13 ASSIGNMENT AND TERMINATION OF LEASES

The assignment of a lease is treated for VAT purposes at the same VAT liability for the underlying lease, as a result of the decision in the case of *Lubbock Fine & Co* v. *C & E Commrs* (ECJ, C-63/92), [1994] STC 101. Following the *Lubbock Fine* case, HMRC also issued guidance accepting that the liability of variations to a lease between the landlord and existing tenant also follow the VAT liability of the underlying rent.

2.13.1 Reverse surrenders

VATA 1994, Sched. 10, Gp. 1, Note 1(A) defines a reverse surrender as a transaction 'in which the person to whom the interest is surrendered is paid by the person by whom the interest is being surrendered to accept the surrender'. In other words where payment is made by the tenant to the landlord.

Reverse surrenders were included in the exemption under Gp. 1 from 1 March 1995, subject to the election to waive exemption. Prior to this date HMRC had argued that reverse surrenders were taxable at standard rate, until the tribunal's decision in *Central Capital Corp Ltd* (No. 13319) where it was decided that a landlord made a supply when he agreed in return for payment to accept the surrender of his tenant's lease, and that the supply was exempt by virtue of Art. 13B(b) of the Sixth Directive on VAT (Dir. 77/388).

2.13.2 Assignment to a third party/reverse premiums

In *Cantor Fitzgerald International* (ECJ, C-108/99) Cantor took an assignment of a lease from Wako, the current tenant of a property, in return for a payment for agreeing to accept the assignment. Wako remained liable for rent if Cantor defaulted, but Cantor also covenanted to meet these obligations and an associated company joined as guarantor for Cantor's performance of its obligations.

While accepting that the supply of an assignment of an interest in land, such as a lease, is in principle an exempt supply, HMRC argued that Cantor was not making such a supply. Before the assignment it had no interest in the land, so could scarcely have supplied one. The service of accepting the assignment was separate from the assignment itself, and was therefore taxable at standard rate, not being the grant of an interest in land.

Cantor maintained that the supply was based entirely on the original lease and changed the relationship between the original parties. The landlord was involved in the transaction, as the landlord's licence was needed for the assignment to be carried out. The transaction was no more outside the contractual relationship than an assignment where the assignee paid the assignor, and this was admitted to involve an exempt supply by the assignor. It was not logical for a surrender paid for by the tenant to be exempt (as in *Central Capital Corp Ltd* above) but for an assignment paid for by the tenant to be taxable.

The tribunal considered that a conventional letting was not usually the mere grant of a term of years for a sum, but involved a number of mutual contractual obligations between landlord and tenant, covering such matters as repairs, rents, service charges, insurance, etc. and this appeared to have formed the basis of *Lubbock Fine*. The *Cantor* case, like *Lubbock Fine*, involved a variation of these mutual obligations. Additional contractual parties were added to the relationship, without the original tenant being released. The fact that the monetary consideration moved from assignor to assignee rather than the other way around seemed immaterial to the question of VAT liability. The tribunal concluded that the assignment fell within the reasoning in *Lubbock Fine*, and that Cantor's supply of accepting the assignment was exempt. The case went to appeal at the High Court and a question was submitted to the ECJ (C-108/99) requesting clarification of the decision in the *Lubbock Fine* case as it applies to these circumstances. The European Court determined that as the tenant had no prior interest in the lease concerned, the reverse premium could not be said to be exempt from VAT. This went against the Advocate General's Opinion which supported Cantor's stance.

The service of accepting the assignment of a lease is therefore standard rated.

The *Mirror Group plc* (ECJ, C-409/98) case, which was heard at the European Court in conjunction with the *Cantor Fitzgerald* case, concerned a reverse premium paid by a landlord to a prospective tenant to enter into an agreement for a new lease, to accept the grant of a new lease or to take an option on a new lease. A similar decision was reached to that in *Cantor*, that the reverse premium fell outside the exemption, as there was no interest in land in place at the time the supply was made, but see **2.10** regarding HMRC current guidance.

2.13.3 Variations of leases

HMRC has issued a policy statement in *The Law Society's Gazette* (1 May 1991) with regard to the VAT implications upon variation of a lease where there is a surrender and re-grant by operation of law:

1. Where there is a payment to the tenant this will be treated as payment for the surrender of a lease and exempt with the option to tax.
2. Where there is a payment to the landlord this will be treated as payment for the new lease and exempt with the option to tax.
3. Where there is no payment it will be treated as though there were no supply with no VAT implications, provided that:

    (a) the new lease is for the same building for an extended term; or
    (b) the new lease is for a larger part of the same building for the same or an extended term; or
    (c) the new lease is for bare land for an extended term; or
    (d) if the variation obliges the tenant to carry out building works it will be treated as if there is no supply provided there is no direct benefit (such as a rent-free or rent reduction period). If there is a direct benefit then the supply will be treated as exempt with the option to tax. The danger here is that if the option to tax has not been exercised then the VAT on the supply of the building works to the landlord would carry non-recoverable VAT in the hands of the landlord.

Where the variation of the lease involves the removal of a restrictive covenant, this is generally dealt with as the surrender of the existing lease with the re-grant of a new lease without the restrictive covenant which previously applied, as is dealt with above.

2.13.4 Third party costs (indemnities)

In the case of *Poladon Ltd* (No. 16825) the tribunal ruled in favour of HMRC on the matter of the recovery of legal and other fees paid by the company. A condition of the loan facilities supplied by the bank was that the company would pay the cost of surveyor's reports, valuation of the property and a solicitor's report on the title. The bank instructed its own solicitors and appointed the surveyor and valuers suggested by the company. The tribunal found that the agreement clearly stated that the costs were incurred by the bank and that the solicitors, surveyors and valuers were acting on their behalf. The services were therefore supplied to the bank and not to the company and the company was not therefore entitled to recover the VAT on them. The company did not incur any liability to the suppliers, although the arrangement did result in the company obtaining the benefit of the loan facilities.

Where a tenant is required to pay legal costs of a landlord in order to obtain the grant of the lease, the payment of the costs is seen as part of the consideration for the grant of the lease and is therefore exempt from VAT, subject to the option to tax. If the lease is exempt therefore, the costs will be payable inclusive of the VAT charged, and such VAT will not be recoverable by the tenant, as above.

2.13.5 Compensation

The general position on compensation is that when a sum is paid by the landlord to a tenant under the terms of the Landlord and Tenant Act 1954 or the Agricultural Tenancies Act 1995, that payment is outside the scope of VAT provided a notice to quit under statutory procedure is served by the landlord and complied with by the tenant. Such payments may be made, for example, for manurial values, standing crops or milk quotas left behind – see, for example, *Mohr* v. *Finanzamt Bad Segeberg* (ECJ, C-215/94) in which the Court ruled that the compensation paid to a farmer to discontinue milk production was not consideration for a taxable supply by the farmer, and was therefore outside the scope of VAT. But any additional payments by the landlord, for example in recognition that the tenant is to quit earlier than is statutorily necessary, or compensation paid under purely voluntary negotiations, even if the amount is based on the statutory provisions, will be exempt from VAT as a surrender, subject to the option to tax.

In cases where a court settlement is paid, one must look to the issue involved to determine if the amount paid in settlement is consideration for a supply. For example, where a building contactor invoices for £100,000 of standard rated building work and the property owner disputes the amount due, perhaps because he considers the work to be sub-standard in some way, the amount paid in settlement of the proceedings is likely to be seen as consideration for the supply of services. In this case a credit note should be raised by the builder in respect of the agreed reduction in the value of supplies.

However, where a defendant in proceedings settles out of court without agreeing that any supply at all has been made, the amount of the settlement is seen as payment for the defendant dropping the proceedings and no VAT is due (see *Reich* (No. 9648)).

In *Financial & General Print Ltd* (No. 13795), the company claimed input tax in respect of a lease termination payment on a printing machine after going into receivership. HMRC assessed the input tax on the grounds that there had been no supply by the owner of the machine in respect of the termination. The tribunal found that the payment was due under the terms of the breach of contract and there was no supply for VAT purposes – it was damages and therefore outside the scope of VAT and the company had no right to claim input tax.

2.13.6 Dilapidations

It has in practice been accepted by HMRC that a dilapidation payment made by an outgoing tenant to a landlord is outside the scope of VAT where it is essentially compensatory for failure to undertake required repairs and maintenance. The contract (lease) defines the tenant's obligations in this regard and, in essence, the sum paid by the tenant represents payment to the landlord in recompense for a breach of covenant. Where there are additional claims for consequential damages because of default by the tenant, the question is more complicated. HMRC has accepted that where legal action is initiated and a settlement is made between the parties (out of court) then such a payment will be outside the scope of VAT unless it specifically relates to standard rated supplies.

When a landlord uses a dilapidation payment to refurbish a property, then the recovery of input tax incurred is determined by the intended use of the property.

2.13.7 Mortgage capping

This is where the developer or vendor of a property agrees to meet the additional costs of mortgage payments in the case of an interest rate rise, etc. Following the case of *N Iliffe & D C Holloway* (No. 10922) these are not seen as payments for any supply by the purchaser and are outside the scope of VAT.

2.14 SERVICE CHARGES

When service charges are supplied by the landlord to tenants in respect of the upkeep of common areas or repairs to the fabric of the building, then the VAT treatment is the same as for the lease – exempt if the option to tax has not been exercised and standard rated if it has – because the service charge is seen as additional consideration for the right to occupy the land. Service charges covering items such as insurance, rates, electricity, security, maintenance of lifts, receptionist, etc., all fall within the treatment as a right to occupy or to better enjoy the land occupied.

Service charges supplied by a third party are always standard rated because they are not supplied with a right to occupy land. Similarly, service charges made in respect of freehold property will usually be standard rated.

Where services are supplied to the demised area occupied by the tenant, such as office cleaning, the charge made is usually standard rated.

2.14.1 Serviced office accommodation

Serviced office accommodation is primarily seen as an exempt licence to occupy land, subject to the option to tax, providing that there is a degree of exclusivity in the rights of the occupier to use the accommodation provided (see also **7.12** for further details).

2.14.2 Shared offices

The provision of space in an office falls short of a licence to occupy because it does not provide exclusivity of use, the space being shared with others. In cases where an office is shared but the occupant has exclusive use for the period they are using it, this will fall within the treatment as the right to occupy and be exempt, subject to the option to tax.

2.14.3 Joint occupation

Where you and other parties have entered into an agreement with the landlord to jointly occupy premises, and one of the occupants collects the rent and service charge from each of the occupants to pass over to the landlord, these contributions are outside the scope of VAT, because the person collecting has not made a supply to the other occupants.

2.14.4 Managing agents

Services supplied by managing agents to the landlord of managing the property are always standard rated. However, in cases where managing agents are responsible for providing services to the tenants, the position will depend upon the terms agreed. Often a managing agent will be put in funds by the landlord and will pay for services provided to the tenant on their behalf. In such cases the VAT incurred on such services is the input tax of the landlord. In other cases the managing agent will act as principal in the transactions and in such cases will recover the VAT on such services, recharging the costs, plus VAT as appropriate, to the landlord.

2.14.5　Interest on arrears of rent

Interest on arrears of rent is exempt from VAT under VATA 1994, Sched. 9, Gp. 5, Item 2, whether or not the option to tax has been exercised. HMRC stipulates that in order to qualify for exemption under this heading the interest charge must be separately shown on the invoice.

2.14.6　Collecting rent from third parties

In cases where a tenant has sub-let a property and defaulted on the rent, the rent is often collectable from the sub-tenant. In cases where the option to tax has been exercised, this will include the VAT due on the rent. Although the sub-tenant is liable to pay this VAT it is not their input tax to recover, because the supply remains to the tenant and not to them, and invoices should continue to be made out to the tenant. The sub-tenant may, however, negotiate a lease direct with the landlord to resolve this.

The position remains the same if, on default by the tenant, the rent is payable by a guarantor. Invoices should remain made out to the tenant and the guarantor has no right to recovery of input tax.

2.14.7　Insurance for loss of rental income

In cases where loss of rental income has been insured and the landlord receives a payment from the insurance company, this is not consideration for a supply and is treated as outside the scope of VAT. Therefore, even in cases where the option to tax has been exercised, there is no VAT to account for on the insurance receipt.

2.14.8　*Mesne* profits

Mesne profits are damages awarded where the occupant continues to occupy the property after their right to occupy has expired. There is therefore no supply by the landlord in the case of *mesne* profits which are treated as 'outside the scope of VAT' and no output tax is due.

2.14.9　Rent adjustments on disposal of properties

In cases where a contract for sale of a property provides for an adjustment on the completion statement to reflect rent paid in advance, the adjustment is treated as outside the scope of VAT.

2.15 TRANSFER OF A GOING CONCERN

Where business assets are sold as a transfer of a going concern (TOGC) the transaction is deemed not to be a supply for VAT purposes and is therefore treated as 'outside the scope of VAT' (VATA 1994, s.49; VAT (Special Provisions) Order 1995, SI 1995/1268, Art. 5; Sixth Directive on VAT, Art. 5(8)).

If the conditions of a TOGC are fulfilled, this treatment is mandatory and if VAT has been charged on such a supply HMRC may disallow the input tax recovered by the purchaser. Of course, if VAT is not charged when it should be, HMRC will raise an assessment. In view of the high value often involved, it is therefore vital that the correct treatment is applied. The purpose of the legislation is to prevent situations arising where VAT is charged by the vendor of a business and not paid over to HMRC but HMRC fall liable to repay the VAT to the purchaser of the business. In view of the potentially large values involved this was seen as a danger area by HMRC, but by treating the transaction as outside the scope of VAT this danger is removed. The conditions that must be satisfied to establish a TOGC are as follows:

1. The assets are to be used by the transferee in carrying on the same kind of business as that carried on by the transferor, whether or not as part of an existing business.
2. The transferee is already, or immediately becomes as a result of the transfer, a taxable person (see **1.4.15**).
3. In relation to a part transfer of assets, that part is capable of separate operation.
4. With particular regard to the transfer of let property or a transfer of a business including property, if the property is 'new' or if the transferor has opted to tax the property, the purchaser must also elect to waive exemption, and notify HMRC of this option prior to a tax point being reached (date of completion or payment, whichever is earlier – beware deposits, if they are held by the vendor's solicitor as agent rather than as stakeholder).
5. The purchaser must also, with effect from 18 March 2004, provide written notification to the vendor that their election to waive exemption is not subject to the statutory block under VATA 1994, Sched. 10, para. 2(3AA) (see **2.7.2**). There was a transitional period with this condition which was effective until 30 June 2004 (originally to 31 May 2004) in that, providing the statutory block did not apply, the notification did not have to be provided. HMRC has also stated (*Business Brief 12/04*) that in the event that a notification is provided but is subsequently found to be incorrect, it will 'not seek to recover any uncharged output tax from the transferor and the supply will remain a TOGC' (VAT (Special Provisions) Order 1995, SI 1995/1268, Art. 5(2A)).

6. There must be no significant break in trading of the business to be transferred. A significant break would be one sufficient for the trade of the
business to wane away. A break simply for refurbishment would be
considered insufficient.

With regard to condition (1) above, the European Court determined in the
case of *Zita Modes Sarl* v. *Administration de l'enregistrement et des domaines*
(ECJ, C-497/01) that:

- the undertaking (or part) transferred must be capable of carrying on an
independent activity, rather than being the simple transfer of assets, such
as the sale of stock; and
- the buyer does not need to pursue the same type of business as the seller
prior to the transfer, and must intend to continue the business transferred
rather than liquidating the assets.

There is no guidance laid down on the length of time that the purchaser must
intend to continue the business, but clearly an immediate onward sale of the
assets in question (such as an immediate sub-sale of a property) would deny
use of the provision. For let property the prudent measure would be to ensure
that at least one quarterly rent payment is received.

It is essential that if TOGC treatment is being considered the agreement is
drafted so that the vendor has warranties to ensure that the above conditions
are satisfied so as to allow the transaction to be VAT-free. If VAT is to be
charged on the transaction, the purchaser will wish to be satisfied that the
above conditions are not met and therefore the transaction is not a TOGC
and the VAT charged may be recovered as input tax. If VAT is not properly
chargeable on a transaction, it is not input tax and may not be recovered by
the purchaser (see *Genius Holdings BV* v. *Staatssecretaris van Financiën* (ECJ,
342/87)). HMRC nevertheless has the right to collect any amount charged as
VAT as a debt due to the Crown under VATA 1994, Sched. 11, para. 5. It
should also be borne in mind that stamp duty is payable on the VAT inclusive
value of the transaction. For a draft VAT clause regarding transfer of a going
concern see **Appendix C**.

2.15.1   HMRC POLICY ON CLEARANCES

The policy of HMRC is not to supply a specific written clearance if the TOGC
clearly falls within the parameters set down in its *VAT Notice 700/9, Transfer
of a Business as a Going Concern*. For this reason, contracts should not provide
for the VAT to be paid by the purchaser and held in escrow until such time as
a clearance from HMRC has been obtained – it may never be. However, if the
provisions of any unusual contract are put to HMRC, it should be willing to
provide a clearance, if only on the specific point not covered in the leaflet. It is

usually in the interests of both parties to obtain a ruling from HMRC where necessary prior to the transaction taking place if this is possible. To ensure that all the relevant factors are put before HMRC, both parties should agree the contents of any letter requesting a ruling, but application should be made by the seller, as the VAT treatment of a transaction is the responsibility of the supplier to determine.

Due to this policy some property TOGC transactions have been structured to ensure that the 'going concern' provisions do not apply. This is simply done in the case of new or opted property by the purchaser opting to tax with effect from the day of completion but not notifying this to HMRC until after the transaction is complete (within the usual 30 days allowed – see **2.7**). Appropriate clauses are of course required in the contract. This is a particularly useful ploy when either a charity or an insolvency practitioner is involved, as certainty of treatment is paramount due to the potential of personal liability, etc. The purchaser will be able to recover the VAT charged, and permission of HMRC is not required because the purchaser has received no exempt income prior to electing to waive exemption.

2.15.2 HMRC guidance on rented property as a TOGC

The following is an extract from section 7 of *VAT Notice 700/9, Transfer of a Business as a Going Concern* (March 2002)

Examples of when a business can be transferred as a going concern
If you:

- own the freehold of a property which you let to a tenant and sell the freehold with the benefit of the existing lease, a business of property rental is transferred to the purchaser. This is a business transferred as a going concern even if the property is only partly tenanted. Similarly, if you own the lease of a property (which is subject to a sub-lease) and you assign your lease with the benefit of the sub-lease, this is a business transferred as a going concern
- own a building which is being let out where there is an initial rent-free period, even if the building is sold during the rent-free period, you are carrying on a business of property rental
- granted a lease in respect of a building but the tenants are not yet in occupation, you are carrying on a property rental business
- own a property and have found a tenant but not actually entered into a lease agreement when you transfer the property to a third party (with the benefit of the prospective tenancy but before a lease has been signed), there is sufficient evidence of intended economic activity for there to be a property rental business capable of being transferred
- are a property developer selling a site as a package (to a single buyer) which is a mixture of let and unlet, finished or unfinished properties, and the sale of the site would otherwise have been standard rated, then subject to the purchaser electing to waive exemption for the whole site, the whole site can be regarded as a business transferred as a going concern

119

Examples where there is not a transfer of a going concern

If you:

- are a property developer and have built a building and you allow someone to occupy temporarily (without any right to occupy after any proposed sale) or you are 'actively marketing' it in search of a tenant, there is no property rental business being carried on
- own the freehold of a property and grant a lease, even a 999-year lease, you are not transferring a business as a going concern – you are retaining your asset (the freehold) and creating a new asset (a lease). Similarly, if you own a headlease and grant a sub-lease you are not transferring your business as a going concern
- sell a property where the lease you granted is surrendered immediately before the sale, your property rental business ceases and so cannot be transferred as a going concern – even if tenants under a sub-lease remain in occupation
- sell a property to the existing tenant who leases the whole premises from you, this cannot be a transfer of a going concern because the tenant cannot carry on the same business of property rental
- have granted a lease in respect of a building and the tenant is running a business from the premises. The tenant then sells the assets of his business as a going concern and surrenders his lease to you. You grant the new owner of the business a lease in respect of the building. This is not a transfer by you of a property rental business.

2.15.3 Purchase by directors or pension fund of trading company

The TOGC rules may be used in cases where the directors of a company, or a company pension fund, wish to purchase a property to be let to the trading company. In order for this to work the trading company has to agree to enter into a lease with the vendor of the building (see bullet point (4) at **2.15.2** above), subject of course to the building being purchased by the directors or pension fund, as required. Providing the other conditions for TOGC treatment are met, this structure avoids the purchaser having to fund VAT on the transaction and avoids Stamp Duty Land Tax (SDLT) on the VAT which would otherwise be chargeable. It is particularly effective in cases where the property value is such that VAT added would take the value to a higher SDLT band.

2.15.3.1 *Action required*

1. In order for the arrangement to work, there must be a 'property letting business' in the terms of *VAT Notice 700/9* above and the tenant business must therefore provide the vendor with a letter of intent to take a lease on the property. For the protection of both the vendor and the purchaser this can be subject to the sale to the purchaser going through.
2. The purchaser (pension scheme or directors as co-owners) must register for VAT. This is best achieved prior to the transaction taking place but

does not have to be as long as it is effective from the date of purchase. Forms VAT 1 and, potentially, VAT 2 required.

3. The purchaser must elect to waive exemption (form VAT 1614) and notify this to HMRC prior to a tax point (it is best if the deposit on exchange is held by the vendor's solicitors as stakeholder so no tax point is created at this stage). This should preferably be sent with the application for registration.

4. The purchaser must notify the vendor/vendor's solicitors by letter that the statutory block does not apply. This is usually dealt with as a covering letter when a copy of the election and acknowledgement from HMRC is provided to the vendor's solicitors.

2.15.4 Beneficial owners

HMRC has issued a Statement of Practice effective from 1 June 1996, as to the treatment of transfers of an interest in land to a nominee for a named beneficial owner (see *VAT Notice 700/9, Transfer of a Business as a Going Concern*, section 9). The treatment under the Statement is optional. From this date, HMRC will consider the named beneficial owner of the land, and not the nominee, to be the transferee for the purpose of establishing the transfer of a property letting business as a going concern provided, of course, that both parties agree to this treatment. HMRC sees the beneficial owner as being the person carrying on the business and this would prevent the TOGC rules applying but for the Statement. It is particularly relevant to land held in a nominee company for a pension fund.

The following 'Notice of Agreement' example is taken from *VAT Notice 700/9*. It does not have to be used and any other written evidence would suffice, such as an exchange of letters:

Notice of Agreement to adopt Statement of Practice
Property: (Address)
Transferor/vendor: (X)
Nominee/purchaser: (Y)
Future Beneficial Owner: (Z)
X, Y and Z confirm that they have agreed to adopt the optional practice set out in HM Revenue and Customs Business Brief 10/96 in relation to the purchase of the Property pursuant to an agreement dated ( ) between X and Y.
Following the transfer of the Property Y will hold the legal title as nominee for Z, the beneficial owner.
SIGNED for and on behalf of X:
SIGNED for and on behalf of Y:
SIGNED for and on behalf of Z:
DATE:

2.15.5 Sub-sales

Where there is an immediate sub-sale or series of sub-sales there cannot be a TOGC, because the intermediate parties cannot carry on the same business as the initial and ultimate parties.

The *Kwik Save Group plc* (No. 12749) case involved the purchase of supermarkets by Kwik Save, some of the contracts allowing Kwik Save to nominate a third party (an associated company) to take a conveyance instead of Kwik Save. All payments were made by Kwik Save which debited the associate through inter-company accounts as necessary. The tribunal decided that as the contract had not been novated (so that the ultimate purchaser stepped into the shoes of the initial purchaser) then a TOGC could not take place.

Therefore, to enable a TOGC there must be a novation of the whole contract. Alternatively, in the Kwik Save example, if they had been members of the same VAT group, the transactions would have been treated as a TOGC.

2.15.6 Capital Goods Scheme

Where a property purchased as a TOGC or included in a TOGC is subject to the Capital Goods Scheme, then the purchaser takes over the remaining adjustments under the scheme. It is therefore vital that the purchaser ask questions relating to the initial purchase of the building and the VAT incurred on it, any refurbishments, extensions or fitting out which may be an item for the purposes of the Capital Goods Scheme, together with details of any adjustments made under the Capital Goods Scheme to date (see also **1.10**).

2.15.7 Transfer of records

The records of the business must be passed to the purchaser by the transferor, unless permission in writing is obtained for the transferor to retain them. This process is usually just a formality, particularly where it is part only of the business that is sold and the records for this are inseparable (VATA 1994, s.49(1)(b)).

2.15.8 Transfer of VAT registration number

The purchaser may request the transfer of the vendor's VAT registration number (assuming the vendor is to cease in business and no longer requires it). This may seem a good way to save costs on stationery, etc., but the transfer of the registration number makes the purchaser liable for VAT liabilities arising prior to the transfer. It also qualifies the purchaser to claim bad debt relief in respect of supplies made prior to the transfer, and this may make transfer of the registration number worthwhile, but care should be taken that the liabilities potentially taken on do not exceed the benefit of the bad debt relief claimable. Application for transfer of the registration number is made on form VAT 68 (this form may be downloaded from **www.hmrc.gov.uk**). As a result of the transfer, the purchaser will be responsible for completing the VAT return which covers the period in which the transfer falls, and must make sure he has possession of the necessary information (VATA 1994, s.49(2)).

Transferring the VAT registration number can also leave the seller of the business in the position of having no VAT registration number under which to recover VAT on costs relating to the sale of the business and subsequent costs of winding up the accounts, etc., which must then all be dealt with via the purchaser who has taken on the VAT registration number. This is all very well if the transfer is simply a change of legal entity from sole proprietorship to limited company with the same owner, for example, but not if the purchaser is a third party.

2.15.9 VAT groups and TOGCs

In cases where the purchaser of a business as the TOGC is a group of companies which is partially exempt, then the representative member must account for a self-supply on the value of any assets purchased in the three years prior to the date of transfer (VATA 1994, s.44). This concept was introduced to prevent the avoidance of VAT by use of the TOGC rules and group provisions for companies to acquire assets in a fully taxable company which then joins the VAT group having recovered all of the VAT incurred on purchase of the assets. It works by output tax being accounted for on the value of the assets, and then the group is able to recover input tax on the self-supply in accordance with its partial exemption position. Assets which are subject to the Capital Goods Scheme are not included in the self-supply as the future adjustments are taken over by the purchaser in any case. In cases where the VAT on the original purchase of the assets has already been subject to restriction under the partial exemption rules, this may be taken account of when applying the self-supply. The value to be applied is the open market value.

2.15.10 Recovery of VAT on fees relating to sale of a business

Where a person sells their business as a going concern, VAT on the costs of that sale are treated as residual input tax of the business transferred. Therefore, if the business is fully taxable (able to recover all of its input tax) then the seller can recover all of the VAT on costs relating to the sale. However, if the business is only able to recover part of its input tax under the partial exemption rules (see **1.9**) then the seller must restrict recovery of input tax accordingly, and if the business transferred is wholly exempt, then the seller is unable to recover any of the costs (see *Abbey National plc* (ECJ, C-408/98).

The same procedure applies from the purchaser's perspective, with input tax recovery being in accordance with the extent to which the business acquired will be used to make taxable supplies.

2.15.11 Purchase of a property at auction

Where a property is purchased at auction it may be treated as a TOGC if it is over three years old and there has been no election to waive exemption in respect of the property. If the property is under three years old or there has been an election to waive exemption in respect of the property, then the rule at **2.15(4)** comes into force and the purchaser must ensure the election to waive exemption is notified prior to paying the deposit on the day of auction, otherwise the auction house will have no alternative but to charge VAT (see **2.7.3(8)** on timing of the option to tax). In cases where VAT is charged, the purchaser will be able to recover the VAT providing he opts to tax with effect from the date of acquisition and notifies this to HMRC within the 30 days allowed, but for a TOGC to be effective the option to tax must be notified before a tax point is reached.

2.15.12 Review of TOGC rules by HMRC

HMRC announced a review of the rules applying to TOGCs in September 2000. The aim of the review was to try to clarify the law by identifying and simplifying administrative difficulties and, bearing in mind the importance of the transaction to both parties, to consider changes which may lead to more certainty. The results of the review were published by HMRC in August 2005 in the paper *Summary of Responses: VAT – Transfer of a Going Concern (TOGC)* which is available on their website at **www.hmrc.gov.uk**. At the time of writing, there have been no changes to the legislation as a result of this consultation.

Practice points on a TOGC

1. Is the purchaser to use the assets for the same purposes as the vendor?
2. Is the purchaser able to continue to run the business, despite perhaps requiring assets from elsewhere to do so (e.g. intellectual property)?
3. Is the vendor registered for VAT (special rules for registration of the purchaser if the vendor's turnover is over the registration limit)?
4. Is the purchaser registered for VAT (or required to be because of the vendor's turnover exceeding the registration limits in the past 12 months)?
5. Has VAT been charged by the vendor when it should not have been?
6. Have assets subject to the Capital Goods Scheme been transferred? (Transfer of remaining adjustments.)
7. Is new or opted land or property included in the transfer? If so, the purchaser must opt to tax and notify HMRC prior to a tax point being reached, and provide a written notification to the vendor that the option to tax is not subject to the statutory block. (Watch deposits held by solicitor as agent, rather than as stakeholder.)
8. Who is responsible for keeping the records of the business. If not being transferred has permission of HMRC been obtained?
9. Is the VAT number to be transferred (form VAT 68)? It is not usually recommended that the VAT registration number is taken on by the purchaser, where the purchaser is a third party to the vendor, as this involves taking on liabilities for any potential VAT errors in the registration. It does, however, also allow recovery of VAT on bad debts for invoices raised prior to the transfer. Where the transfer is of a partnership to a limited company, with the ownership remaining the same, there should be no problem with taking on the existing VAT registration number, but the new legal entity may in any case want a fresh start.
10. Does the transfer involve a group? If so, a self-supply may be accountable on assets purchased in the last two years.

CHAPTER 3

Residential property

3.1 EXISTING RESIDENTIAL PROPERTY

The freehold sale or letting of existing dwellings and other residential property is generally exempt from VAT (VATA 1994, Sched. 9, Gp. 1, Item 1) unless it has not been used as a dwelling for 10 or more years (see **3.1.1**). This means that businesses involved in the sale of existing housing cannot register for VAT and cannot recover VAT on their costs. For example, a business purchasing existing houses, refurbishing them and selling or letting them, is unable to recover VAT incurred on the work (although the reduced rates for a 'changed number of dwellings conversion' or for the renovation of a dwelling which has been empty for three years or more may apply, reducing the VAT costs to 5 per cent on qualifying works (see **4.6** and **4.7**).

It is also possible to carry out this type of activity on a small scale together with other taxable activities, such as new build housing, or general building services and use the partial exemption *de minimis* limits in order to recover VAT on related costs (see **1.9.2**).

3.1.1 Renovations

The grant of a major interest (freehold sale or lease of over 21 years) in a renovated dwelling or relevant residential use building (see **3.3.1**) is zero rated, provided that it has not been used as a dwelling, number of dwellings or for a relevant residential purpose for a period of 10 years or more prior to sale (VATA 1994, Sched. 8, Gp. 5, Item 1(b), Note 7(b)). Prior to 1 August 2001 this Note restricted the zero rating to dwellings, etc., which had not been used as such since 1 April 1973. The reduced rate of 5 per cent also applies to qualifying works (see **4.7**). If work starts prior to the 10-year point being reached, the VAT on costs will still be recoverable providing that the sale is made after the 10-year point is reached. It is obviously recommended that evidence is obtained to prove the 10-year point has passed, such as from the local authority (Empty Property Officer/Council Tax Office/Electoral Roll). Occupation by squatters and for non-residential purposes (such as storage for a business) can be ignored.

In the case of *Beverley Properties Ltd* (No. 18232), HMRC produced evidence from the Council Tax Office that an occupant had been paying council tax at the full rate during the 10-year period, which invalidated the zero rating claimed by the appellant.

The zero rate also applies to the grant of a major interest in a partly completed project. There is no case law on what 'partly completed' means, but HMRC states that a real and meaningful start on the conversion must have been made and that the work must have been more than securing or maintaining the existing structure.

The freehold sale or lease (for whatever term) in other renovated dwellings or relevant residential use buildings is exempt from VAT.

3.2 NEW DWELLINGS

The first grant of a major interest (freehold sale or lease of over 21 years) by the 'person constructing' in a building 'designed as a dwelling or number of dwellings' or a building for use for relevant residential or relevant charitable purposes is zero rated for VAT (VATA 1994, Sched. 8, Gp. 5, Item 1). In the case of a lease this applies to the first payment of rent or any premium paid. Zero rating is 'taxable' and the supplier is therefore able to recover VAT on his expenditure in full.

However, where the person constructing (or any other person) grants a lease of up to 21 years, this is exempt from VAT (VATA 1994, Sched. 9, Gp. 1, Item 1), leading to non-recovery of any VAT incurred (although the construction work itself should be zero rated – see **Chapter 4**).

Only the 'first grant of a major interest' (i.e. freehold sale or lease in excess of 21 years (VATA 1994, s.96)) in the qualifying categories of dwellings, relevant residential and relevant charitable buildings, attracts zero rating. Any future grants are exempt from VAT. For these purposes, therefore, any subsequent rent received is exempt from VAT and ongoing input tax is not recoverable, subject to the partial exemption rules (see **1.9**). Where a lease contains break clauses, which may be exercised prior to the expiry of 21 years, this does not invalidate the zero rating from applying. To be a major interest, however, the grant must be of the legal interest, not the beneficial or equitable interest.

In respect of VAT groups, only a grant to a person which is not a member of the VAT group counts as the first grant of a major interest, with any grants to other group members not counting as such (see *Business Brief 11/03*).

If, due to an oversight, the term of the lease granted is less than the required 'over 21 years' for zero rating to apply, this can be subsequently corrected by obtaining a Deed of Rectification (see *CS & JM Isaacs* (No. 14656), see also **1.8** regarding input tax recovery where the intention is to grant a major interest but market forces result in short-term letting instead).

There are a number of conditions imposed on this zero rating:

1. The person granting the major interest must qualify as the 'person constructing' the building. This will normally be the person carrying out the building work or commissioning it. In any case, the person constructing will have a direct involvement in the ordering or construction of the building. In order to grant a major interest, the person constructing must also own sufficient interest in the land in order to do so. Furthermore, HMRC has limited the status of 'person constructing' by restricting it to the first supply of a major interest in the newly constructed building. This interpretation denies zero rating to a person constructing who grants a major interest of, for example, a freehold sale, after having granted a lease of over 21 years. The lease of over 21 years would be zero rated but the freehold sale would be exempt. This change was made from 1 March 1995 subsequent to HMRC losing *Link Housing Association Ltd* v. *C & E Commrs* [1992] STC 718, CS.

2. In the case of a grant of a major interest by virtue of a lease over 21 years, the zero rating applies only to the premium or first rent received (VATA 1994, Sched. 8, Gp. 5, Note 14) and subsequent payments, for example future rent and service charges are exempt rather than zero rated. This can have an effect on the recovery of related input tax, but VAT incurred in the course of construction of the building is generally seen as being attributable to the first rent payment or premium only.

3. The building must be of a type which may be zero rated, i.e. a dwelling, relevant residential or relevant charitable building.

4. The building must be completely new. A person may only zero rate the grant of a major interest in a building he is constructing if that building is new rather than the reconstruction, alteration or enlargement of an existing building. Partly completed buildings also qualify for the relief, provided they have progressed beyond the foundation stage.

3.2.1 Definition of a dwelling

A building is 'designed as a dwelling' (from 1 March 1995) for the purposes of the first grant of a major interest and new construction, provided the following conditions are met (VATA 1994, Sched. 8, Gp. 5, Note 2):

1. The dwelling consists of self-contained living accommodation.
2. There is no provision for direct internal access from the dwelling to any other dwelling or part of a dwelling.
3. The separate use or disposal of the dwelling is not prohibited by the terms of any covenant, statutory planning consent or similar provision. This was tested by the tribunal in its application to a DIY housebuilder in the case of *P H Wiseman* (No. 17374). In a previous case, *Hopewell-Smith* (No. 16725), the tribunal had determined that zero rating did not

apply only if both the separate use or disposal was prohibited – if one of them was not, then zero rating applied. However, this recent case looked into the historical provision of the legislation and determined that both the separate use and disposal must not be prohibited in order for zero rating to apply, specifically rejecting the *Hopewell-Smith* reasoning. It is interesting to note that in Sched. 7A, for the 5 per cent rates, the Commissioners have used the wording 'separate use *and* disposal'. An argument pointing this difference out might lead a court to determine that by using a different word, the legislators intended a different meaning.

4. Statutory planning consent has been granted in respect of that dwelling and its construction or conversion has been carried out in accordance with that consent.

The meaning of 'designed as a dwelling' was also tested in the case of *Turner Stroud and Burley Construction Ltd* (No. 15454), in which the company constructed a riverside dwelling house, raised and supported on stilts, with a boat dock beneath and a staircase from this to the living accommodation above. There was a swimming pool away from the river at the end of the building. The dock included sheet piling to support the riverbank and this was attached to the stilts supporting the house. HMRC argued that the building was partly designed as a boat store and that part was not construction of a dwelling, did not qualify as a garage, and was standard rated. The tribunal found that although the boat dock was not structurally part of the building it was part of the design of the building and was integral to it. It was not a garage. The whole building was designed as a dwelling and the construction services of the boat dock were therefore zero rated and the appeal was allowed.

Where only part of a new building qualifies as a dwelling and part does not, for example a flat over a shop, then only the dwelling part qualifies for zero rating (VATA 1994, Sched. 8, Gp. 5, Note 10) and an apportionment must be made to determine the value of the zero-rated supply. There is no fixed method for determining the apportionment, but it must be a fair and reasonable calculation. Commonly, either the selling value of the different parts or the floor area of the dwelling divided by the floor area of the shop plus dwelling (omitting common parts) is used.

3.2.2 Reconstruction, alteration, enlargement or extension

Zero rating applies only to newly constructed buildings and not to reconstruction, alteration or enlargement or extension of an existing building, except to the extent that any enlargement or extension creates an additional dwelling (VATA 1994, Sched. 8, Gp. 5, Note 16). There is also an exception in the case of charitable annexes (see **5.3**).

For example, the construction of a new floor on an existing block of flats, to provide a number of new flats, will qualify for zero rating under this heading in addition to houses or blocks of flats constructed from ground level as completely new buildings. However, if any of the new flats include part of the existing accommodation, then zero rating will not apply to that dwelling.

From 1 March 1995 a building only ceases to be an existing building when it is demolished completely to ground level or, if required by planning consent, a single façade is retained (double façade for a corner plot) (see VATA 1994, Sched. 8, Gp. 5, Notes 16 and 18). Therefore, if any of the existing building is left above ground level, except as above, the resultant completed 'new' building will not qualify for zero rating.

This was tested in the case of *R & SL Midgley* (No. 15379), in which the appellants gained planning permission for an extension to their house in December 1995. The builders subsequently found that all the walls except one were unstable and demolished them to ground floor level, the remaining wall being retained up to first floor level. In January 1997, when the work was nearing completion, the appellants applied for planning permission for a replacement dwelling and in March 1997 retrospective permission for a 'replacement dwelling incorporating part of an existing wall' was granted. The Commissioners argued that it was work to an existing building, the original house having remained in existence throughout the work. The appellants argued that it was a new building, the retained wall being required as a condition of planning permission. The tribunal held that as the planning permission was granted on the basis that a wall should be retained, that was a requirement of the permission even if it was not a condition, and that the building ceased to be an existing building when all except one of the walls was demolished. To that extent the appeal was allowed, with costs.

The above decision can be contrasted to that in *Mark Tinker* (No. 18033) where the appellant inherited a house in a poor state of repair, and devised a two-stage demolition of the original building and construction of a replacement. First the existing kitchen was demolished and a new kitchen and bathroom constructed, and then five years later the rest of the house was demolished and new accommodation constructed. The tribunal agreed with HMRC that because of the two-stage demolition and time gap the building at no time ceased to be an 'existing building' (effectively the kitchen/bathroom was an extension to the remaining building after the first stage and the new accommodation constructed after the second stage was an extension to the new kitchen/bathroom) so that none of the work was zero rated.

3.2.3 Garages

The supply of a garage with a dwelling is specifically included within the terms of the zero rating for the grant of a major interest (freehold sale or lease of over 21 years) in a new dwelling (VATA 1994, Sched. 8, Gp. 5, Note 3).

In cases where a garage is let with a dwelling which is not new, the supply will be exempt from VAT providing that the garage is reasonably near the dwelling and the lease of the dwelling includes the garage or the tenant takes up the lease of the garage from the same landlord at the same time as taking up the lease on the dwelling.

If a garage is leased separately from a dwelling, then the supply is standard rated (VATA 1994, Sched. 9, Gp. 1, Item 1(h)).

3.3 OTHER RESIDENTIAL PROPERTY

The grant of a major interest (freehold sale or lease of over 21 years) in a building to be used for relevant residential purposes is zero rated for VAT if it is made by the 'person constructing' (see **3.2(1)**) and supported by a certificate from the purchaser that they will be using the property for the qualifying purpose (VATA 1994, Sched. 8, Gp. 5, Item 1).

3.3.1 Use for a relevant residential purpose

The legislation (VATA 1994, Sched. 8, Gp. 5, Item 1, Note 4) defines 'use for a relevant residential purpose' as meaning:

(a) a home or other institution providing residential accommodation for children;
(b) a home or other institution providing residential accommodation with personal care for persons in need of personal care by reason of old age, disablement, past or present dependence on alcohol or drugs, or past or present mental disorder;
(c) a hospice;
(d) residential accommodation for students or school pupils;
(e) residential accommodation for members of any of the armed forces;
(f) a monastery, nunnery or similar establishment; or
(g) an institution which is the sole or main residence of at least 90 per cent of its residents.

Specifically excluded from the above are uses as a hospital, a prison or similar institution, or a hotel, inn or similar establishment.

The legislation indicates that the building or part of the building must be designed 'solely' for a relevant residential purpose before zero rating may be allowed. It has been accepted by HMRC, however, that an office in a residential home for the use of a warden, matron or similar person may be ignored. Where only part of the building qualifies for zero rating, a 'reasonable apportionment' must be made between zero-rated work and standard-rated work (see also *University Court of the University of St Andrews* v. *C & E Commrs* (No. 19054)).

131

3.3.2 Certificates

A condition of zero rating in respect of 'relevant residential buildings' is that the customer must be in a position to provide a certificate that they will use the building for qualifying purposes. This certificate must be provided before the transaction takes place (VATA 1994, Sched. 8, Gp. 5, Note 12). In cases where the sale is not to the person who will use the building for qualifying purposes, for example a sale by the developer to a person who will let the building on (whether to a qualifying person or not), the zero rating does not apply, and the sale will be standard rated as a new building. Providing that the person who will let the building to the qualifying user supplying the certificate has 'person constructing' status (he has commissioned or ordered the construction of the building) his supply may qualify for zero rating (assuming it will be a lease of over 21 years) (see also *Notice 708, Buildings and Construction*, Appendix A).

It is therefore the main contractor or developer working/selling directly to the person who will use the building for qualifying purposes who qualifies for zero rating upon the production of a certificate. The certificate must be produced to HMRC on demand by the vendor to support the zero rating of his sale of the building. There is a penalty of 100 per cent of the tax involved for the wrong issue of a certificate (VATA 1994, s.62).

3.3.3 Student accommodation

The case of *Denman College* (No. 15513) looked at the term 'relevant residential' building for VAT purposes. The college is owned by a charity affiliated to the National Federation of Women's Institutes and provided 3–6-day courses in improving the knowledge and skills of Women's Institute members. In 1997 it built two residential blocks to provide accommodation for course attendees, containing study bedrooms with bed, desk, armchair and shower or bathroom. Meals were provided elsewhere but hot drinks could be made in the rooms. HMRC decided that the new buildings did not qualify for zero rating as residential accommodation for students as they did not have all the facilities to make them inhabitable as a residence or place of abode. HMRC argued that the exemptions must be applied in the narrow construction and 'residential' must connote something in the nature of housing for the zero rating to apply and fall within the social reasons required under the EU law. The tribunal accepted that the 'exemptions' must be construed narrowly, but thought there was no reason why residential accommodation had to be a person's residence. The ECJ had not ruled that only housing could qualify for relief under social reasons and it was clear from other buildings qualifying as 'relevant residential' under the legislation that a building need not be housing or a person's residence to qualify. The ordinary meaning of residential accommodation included students' accommodation, regardless of the lack of catering or kitchen facilities in the blocks. A garage or dining hall on its own might not qualify as residential but living accommodation did not have to be self-contained to qualify as residential accommodation.

Vacation letting of student accommodation for purposes other than for a supply for qualifying purposes (e.g. to a commercial organisation for a conference) can lead to the building not being eligible for zero rating (but see *R on the application of Greenwich Property Ltd* [2001] STC 618, AC, in respect of university/higher education student accommodation where the Concordat applies – see also **7.5.1**) either on the original construction or through the self-supply on change of use during a period for 10 years after construction, accountable under VATA 1994, Sched. 10, para. 1 (see **3.3.7**).

3.3.4 Care homes

Nursing/rest homes qualify as relevant residential buildings for VAT purposes and the grant of a major interest in a new nursing/rest home by the person constructing is therefore zero rated, as is its construction, providing in either case that the recipient of the supply issues a certificate to the supplier that they will be using the building for the qualifying purpose (see also **7.3**).

In the VAT tribunal case of *Hill Ash Developments* (No. 16747), the partnership carried out works to a house and outbuildings which had been purchased by one of the partners for use as a nursing home and sheltered accommodation, and treated these works as zero rated. The house was a listed building, but the listing did not include the outbuildings, for which planning permission had been gained to convert them into an extension for care flats and an administration block for the nursing home, providing a staff room, general office, storage and a kitchen. The taxpayer argued that this was the conversion of a non-residential building into a dwelling/relevant residential use and also qualified for zero rating as an approved alteration to a listed building. The tribunal found that the use of the administration block was so tied up with the main residential building that it constituted use for relevant residential purposes.

Another tribunal case involving nursing homes is *John Michael Barrie Strowbridge* (No. 16521), in which the appellant purchased a nursing home (13 beds) and contracted with a builder to carry out alterations and refurbishment of the existing building, and also to construct a new building to provide rooms for about 27 additional patients. When the builder queried the issue of a zero-rate certificate the plans were changed so that the new works became a separate home, with no internal access as had previously been provided for. There were already separate supplies of water, gas and electricity. The existing house and the new 'lodge' were registered as nursing homes separately. Due to the sudden death of five patients, and the requirement for staff/patient ratio the homes became unviable to run as separate units and the internal access was re-instated. The appellant ran the home as a single unit for about six months before selling it. HMRC assessed the builder for VAT on the construction. Evidence was available from the local planning authority that in its view the creation of two autonomous units did not require planning consent as no material change of use had occurred. The tribunal found that in replacing the internal access the appellant had genuinely changed his original intentions, regardless of the fact that the amendment to the original plans had occurred in order to avoid VAT. His subsequent decision to revert to the original plan did not alter the fact that upon completion of the work there was a separate nursing home. The construction of the lodge was therefore zero rated.

3.3.5   Internal access provided at a later date

The same rules apply to relevant residential buildings in respect of reconstructions, enlargements and extensions as for new dwellings (see **3.2.2**). The case of *D S Menzies* (No. 15733) concerned the construction of a relevant residential building, adjacent to an existing building, which in itself qualified for zero rating under VATA 1994, Sched. 8, Gp. 5, Item 1. However, 28 days after construction was completed an internal link to the existing building was formed and the Commissioners ruled that this turned the 'construction' into an extension or annexation of an existing building (VATA 1994, Sched. 8, Gp. 5, Note 9(b)) which was standard rated. The works were carried out under different contracts and were separately accounted for and certified by the architect. At the time of completion of the construction there was a gap of one metre between the buildings and no common wall – no preparations for an internal link had been made. HMRC saw the work as a single project and argued that an ordinary man would construe the work as an extension, enlargement or annexation of the existing building, and that it had always been the intention to link the buildings. The tribunal ruled that there was no evidence that it had always been the intention to link the buildings – it required further construction work as well as demolition. Until this work was carried out the buildings were physically separate and the work could not be carried out until the additional funding was obtained – any intention was a hope rather than a decided course of action. The appeal was allowed.

3.3.6   Partially qualifying buildings

In cases where only part of the building qualifies for zero rating as being a dwelling or relevant residential, there is provision for the value of the supplies to be apportioned (VATA 1994, Sched. 8, Gp. 5, Note 10, see also **3.2.1**). Note that in order for apportionment to apply it must be part of the building which is wholly used for qualifying purposes. Apportionment is not available where any part of the building is used for only some of the time for qualifying purposes and for other times for non-qualifying purposes.

3.3.7 Change of use of a qualifying building

Where a person who acquires a building or part of a building (whether by purchase, lease or construction) which qualifies for zero rating on relevant residential grounds, changes the use of the building so that it would no longer qualify for zero rating, within 10 years from the date of completion, then the legislation (VATA 1994, Sched. 10, para. 1) provides that a self-supply must be accounted for by that person. The value of the self-supply with effect from 1 June 2002, is 10 per cent of the value of the zero-rated works for each year or part year left in the 10 years since completion, for which non-qualifying use will apply (i.e. after one complete year of qualifying use only 90 per cent of the self-supply has to be repaid, after two years this reduces to 80 per cent and so on until after nine years only 10 per cent has to be repaid and after 10 years, no self-supply is required). Prior to 1 June 2002 the whole of the VAT benefit of the zero rating was clawed back by HMRC, regardless of the time the building had been used for qualifying purposes in the 10 years after construction/completion.

In the event that the property owner is not registered for VAT, the self-supply counts towards the registration limits and therefore if the value of the self-supply is over the registration limits in force, registration will be required, if only to account for the self-supply.

The self-supply is also recoverable as input tax if the non-qualifying use is wholly taxable, otherwise in accordance with the partial exemption rules (see **1.9**). For example, if the non-qualifying use is as a hotel and supplies are fully taxable, or if the supplies are of letting the building and the option to tax is exercised.

Note that the self-supply may be subject to the Capital Goods Scheme (see **1.10**).

Example

A care home operator purchases a new building for £500,000 to use for relevant residential purposes, providing a certificate to the developer, but after four complete years of use for qualifying purposes, changes the use of the building in its entirety to a hotel (a business activity). The care home operator must account for the self-supply.

If the care home operator had not provided the certificate, VAT of £87,500 would have been payable on the purchase price. As the care home operator has used the building for four complete years for qualifying purposes and there are six complete or partly complete years remaining in the 10-year period the self-supply is reduced by 40 per cent to 60 per cent. £87,500 × 60% = £52,500 and the care home operator has to pay this amount to HMRC. If the care home operator is not VAT registered it would still have to account for VAT to HMRC and would be required to register for VAT to do so, because the deemed supply value (£300,000) is over the VAT registration limits. The self-supply is declared in Box 1 of the VAT Return.

However, the output tax on the self-supply may then also be recovered as input tax in accordance with the partial exemption rules. If the hotel is not partially exempt, it would be able to recover this VAT on the self-supply in full.

In the event that the building is sold to a person who will not use it for qualifying purposes, then VAT at standard rate must be charged. If the purchaser will continue to use the property for qualifying purposes, then the transaction may qualify as a transfer of a going concern (see **2.15**). If not, the sale will be zero rated if this is the first grant of a major interest and the purchaser provides the requisite certificate, or if it is not the first grant of a major interest the supply will be exempt from VAT.

3.4 BUILDINGS CONVERTED FROM NON-RESIDENTIAL

Zero rating is available from 1 March 1995 (and since 21 July 1994 by concession) for the first grant of a major interest in a non-residential building converted into a building 'designed as a dwelling' or a relevant residential use building, for example a barn conversion (VATA 1994, Sched. 8, Gp. 5, Item 1(b)) (see **3.2.1**, **3.3.1** and **Appendix E** for definitions) in exactly the same way as for new housing. The sale of a building 'in the course of conversion' is also eligible for the relief, although there is no guidance available on the extent of the work required for the building to be considered as being 'in the course of conversion'. It is a safe assumption that planning permission must have been granted and the work of conversion (not simply repairs to the existing structure) must have at least commenced.

The definition of 'non-residential' for these purposes is set out in Note 7 to the Group as being a building which is:

(a) neither designed nor adapted for use as a dwelling or as a number of dwellings nor for a relevant residential purpose; or

(b) if it is designed, or adapted, for such use but it was constructed more than 10 years before the grant of the major interest; and no part of it has, in the period of 10 years immediately preceding the grant, been used as a dwelling or for a relevant residential purpose.

This precise wording is vital to the application of the relief. A building is 'designed as a dwelling' if the conditions in Note 2 to the Group (see **3.2.1**) are met. However, 'adapted as a dwelling' has a much wider application and includes living accommodation which falls outside the closely worded definition in VATA 1994, Sched. 8, Gp. 5, Note 2.

Even if the building is designed or has been adapted for use as a dwelling, the resultant dwelling, after the completion of the work, may still qualify for zero rating on conversion if the building has not been used as a dwelling for at least 10 years (see **3.1.1**).

Example

DJ Properties acquires a three-storey house with a barn in the grounds. The planning permission is for the conversion of the house into three flats, and the conversion of the barn into two semi-detached dwellings. The works, plus any materials used in the provision of those works, to both the house (see **4.6.3**) and the barn (see **4.6.2**) will be chargeable at 5 per cent. The sale of the three flats (or the lease of them, regardless of the term) will be exempt from VAT, whilst the sale of the two semi-detached houses will qualify for zero rating under the above rules. DJ Properties will therefore be able to recover the VAT charged in respect of the barn, but unable to recover the VAT in respect of the flats, subject to the partial exemption de minimis limits (see **1.9.2**).

3.4.1 Conversion of public houses

A particular danger area for conversions is that of public houses, where pre-existing living accommodation may prevent the zero rate from applying. In the early case of *Temple House Developments Ltd* (No. 15583) the tribunal ruled in favour of the appellant, but would be unlikely to do so on similar circumstances today. The lead case is this area is that of *C & E Commrs* v. *Lady Blom-Cooper* [2003] STC 669, CA, in which a couple purchased a building which had previously been used as a public house and obtained planning permission to convert it into a family dwelling. The Commissioners rejected the DIY Housebuilder's claim on the grounds that the first and second floors had been used by the publican as residential accommodation. The Court of Appeal upheld the rejection of the claim on the grounds that the purpose of VATA 1994, Sched. 8, Gp. 5, Note 9 was to remove the zero rate in cases where the building already contained a residential part unless the result of the conversion was to create an additional dwelling or dwellings.

In the case of *Calam Vale* (No. 16869) the VAT tribunal, albeit 'entirely unwillingly', dismissed the appeal regarding the conversion of a public house into a single dwelling. HMRC argued that the definition of a building 'designed as a dwelling' at Note 2 of the legislation is meant to apply to a dwelling after construction or conversion, whereas Note 7, which defines a 'non-residential' building, is meant to refer to a building before its conversion. The term 'dwelling' should otherwise be given its ordinary meaning and includes living accommodation outside the ambit of Note 2. The existence of pre-existing living accommodation for the landlord therefore prevented the 'conversion' from qualifying for zero rating. A similar decision was reached in *Tobell* (No. 16646).

3.5 RESTRICTION OF INPUT TAX RECOVERY FOR DEVELOPERS

Under the terms of the VAT (Input Tax) Order 1992, SI 1992/3222, Art. 6 developers are prevented from recovering input tax incurred on goods incorporated or fitted into the building other than building materials (much in the same way as builders are prevented from charging VAT on such items at the lower or zero rate). A list of the items can be found at **4.5**.

However, in the case of *Rialto Homes plc* (No. 16340) the tribunal determined that trees and shrubs included on the plans at the stage of planning permission were materials ordinarily installed by builders. For further information see **4.5**. In earlier cases (*Tilbury* (No. 1102, June 1981) and *McClean Homes (East Anglia) Ltd* (No. 7748, June 1992)) the tribunals had decided that trees and shrubs were not ordinarily installed by builders.

Prior to 1 March 1995 the restriction only applied to dwellings and not to relevant residential and relevant charitable buildings, so the latter could be fitted out without a VAT cost arising. It should also be noted that the restriction only applies to the goods incorporated in the building and not to the services of fitting them. Developers should therefore be sure to obtain separate invoices in relation to fitting costs.

3.5.1 Show houses

Where the input tax recovery is blocked (see list of items at **4.5**) the sale of the show house, complete with these items, will be zero rated. However, if other furnishings are also included in the sale (such as curtains and furniture) then standard rate VAT must be charged. Where the block applies and the items are removed before sale, the block still applies to the recovery of input tax but the separate sale, if any, is exempt from VAT (VATA 1994, Sched. 9, Gp. 14). If there is no sale and the items are simply discarded, there is no output tax to account for, but if the items are taken to be used for non-business purposes a deemed supply at their value in their current condition is required.

3.6 MANAGEMENT OF DWELLINGS, RELEVANT RESIDENTIAL AND RELEVANT CHARITABLE PROPERTIES

Generally the VAT treatment of service charges in relation to common areas follows the same VAT treatment as the lease, so for dwellings, relevant residential and relevant charitable properties, where the option to tax is not available, the service charge by the owner of the building will be exempt from VAT.

Where services in respect of common areas are supplied by a person who is not the landlord or lessor, however, the services cannot qualify for exemption, because they are not part of the consideration for a right over land. However, in respect of domestic property there is an Extra-Statutory Concession (No. 3.18) effective from 1 April 1994 (see *VAT Notice 48, Extra-Statutory Concessions*) which allows for the exemption to apply, provided that each resident is obliged to accept the service because it is supplied to the estate or block of flats as a whole. The Extra-Statutory Concession does not apply to service charges in respect of holiday accommodation or hotels, etc.

Where a developer transfers the common areas of a private housing or industrial estate to a management company which will maintain them, then this is not a supply for VAT purposes if the transfer is effected for nominal consideration. (This includes roads, footpaths, communal parking and open space, etc.) Input tax incurred on the provision of such amenities is recoverable in accordance with the VAT treatment of the disposal of the buildings.

3.6.1 Managing agents

The services of a managing agent supplied to the landlord are always standard rated, and are typically charged as a commission on the value of rents charged and collected on the landlord's behalf. In many cases the costs relating to the property are invoiced direct to the managing agent, but the VAT on such costs is not the input tax of the managing agent (unless he is incurring the costs as principal and re-invoicing them to the landlord (e.g. under s.47(3) VATA 1994, which provides for agents of undisclosed principals to be treated as a principal). Where a managing agent acts on behalf of a landlord in making mandatory service charges to occupants the supply is exempt from VAT. VAT incurred by the managing agent on the supply of such services in such cases will be exempt input tax and therefore non-recoverable.

The above rules also apply to tenant controlled management companies.

3.7 HOLIDAY ACCOMMODATION

The short-term letting of holiday accommodation is specifically standard rated, being excluded from exemption under VATA 1994, Sched. 9, Gp. 1, Item 1(e) and from zero rating under VATA 1994, Sched. 8, Gp. 5, Note 13 (see also **7.8**). In addition, the freehold sale or the premium for a lease is standard rated if the property in question is under three years old. The freehold sale or the premium for a lease in holiday accommodation which is over three years old is exempt from VAT.

139

Holiday accommodation includes beach huts and chalets, caravans, house-boats or tents, any accommodation held out or advertised as holiday accommodation or as suitable for holiday or leisure use, and any building designed as a dwelling and its site where residence throughout the year is restricted by the terms of any statutory covenant, planning consent or similar permission (see *Poole Borough Council* (No. 7180) and *Haven Leisure Ltd* (No. 5269)). It also includes sites for erection of holiday accommodation.

A planning opportunity often used by developers of holiday accommodation is to sell the land to the purchaser separately from the construction of the holiday home. Although the sale of the land will be standard rated, because the planning permission provides for the erection of holiday accommodation, provided that the accommodation being constructed qualifies as 'designed as a dwelling' (see **3.1.1**) the construction costs will be zero rated. This makes the property cheaper for the purchaser and therefore more attractive. In setting up such arrangements it is best to have the land and construction supplied by separate legal entities. Care must be taken to ensure that the construction is not commenced prior to the sale, otherwise it could be argued that in substance and reality the sale is that of constructed holiday accommodation and the whole amount received from the purchaser would be standard rated.

3.7.1 Off-peak letting of holiday accommodation

In areas where the holiday period is seasonal, HMRC allows the treatment of the letting of accommodation for residential purposes to be exempt from VAT, providing that the letting is for a period of over four weeks. HMRC states that in areas such as London, Brighton and Blackpool where there are conferences all year round there is clearly no defined holiday season, but otherwise construe the holiday season as lasting at least from Easter to September.

3.7.2 Time-shares

A premium received for time-share accommodation is standard rated if the accommodation is under three years old, and exempt if the property is more than three years old (see *Cottage Holiday Associates Ltd* [1983] STC 278, QB). Any periodic payments or service charges are always standard rated.

3.7.3 Residential caravan parks

Whilst seasonal caravan parks are standard rated, the letting of pitches in permanent residential caravan parks is exempt from VAT. If there is a restriction on occupation of the site throughout the year, this will be seen as not residential and standard rating will apply.

140

Where VAT is incurred in the development of a residential caravan site (such as provision of utilities and hardstanding) this is seen as attributable to the letting of pitches (see *Stonecliff Caravan Park* (No. 11097)) and is therefore exempt input tax and non-recoverable subject to the partial exemption *de minimis* limits (see **1.9.2**). However, the provision of brick skirtings was seen as integral to the sale of the caravan and thus also qualifies for zero rating and input tax recovery on related costs. The civil engineering work involved in construction of a new residential caravan park will be zero rated (see **4.8.1**).

The sale of residential caravans themselves are zero rated under VATA 1994, Sched. 8, Gp. 9, Item 1 provided they are 'caravans exceeding the limits of size for the time being permitted for the use on roads of a trailer drawn by a motor vehicle having an unladen weight of less than 2,030 kilograms'. The zero rating does not extend to removable contents which may be sold with a caravan, such as mattresses, tables, chairs, televisions, etc., on which VAT at standard rate must be accounted for.

3.8 COMMONHOLD

Under the commonhold system (Commonhold and Leasehold Reform Act 2002, Part 1) each owner owns the freehold interest in their unit and the common parts of the property are owned by the commonhold association, usually a limited company, of which each resident is a 'unit holder'. The commonhold association looks after repairs and maintenance of the properties as a whole, usually making a monthly service charge to fund these. This service charge is exempt from VAT.

The sale of the units by the developer to the owners is treated in the same way as a freehold sale or first grant of a long lease and is zero rated (VATA 1994, Sched. 8, Gp. 5, Item 1) as is the transfer of the common parts to the commonhold association. Future supplies in relation to the units are exempt (VATA 1994, Sched. 9, Gp. 1, Item 1).

A commonhold may also be set up where existing freeholders or leaseholders group together because they have shared roads, paths or services. This could mean some freeholders transferring part of their freehold to the commonhold association and this supply is likely to be exempt from VAT in the majority of cases (VATA 1994, Sched. 9, Gp. 1, Item 1) although a building constructed by the current owner which has not been the subject of the first grant of a major interest could qualify for zero rating under VATA 1994, Sched. 8, Gp. 5, Item 1.

The Commonhold and Leasehold Reform Act 2002, Part 2, permits leaseholders to acquire the freehold interest in a property through collective enfranchisement and to extend the length of their individual leases. The freehold title of the property is held by a nominee that must be a qualifying Right to Enfranchisement company. There is also provision for leaseholders who do not wish to buy the freehold of a property to enable them to form a 'Right to Manage' Company to undertake the landlord's or service provider's duties. Once again, the service charges by a Right to Enfranchisement company or a Right to Manage company are exempt from VAT.

CHAPTER 4

Construction services

4.1 INTRODUCTION

The supply of construction services can be either:

- *standard rated* (typically commercial buildings or repairs and maintenance works to any buildings);
- *reduced rated* (typically works in relation to conversion into or of domestic or relevant residential buildings); or
- *zero rated* (typically new construction of dwellings or relevant residential and relevant charitable buildings, and works of approved alterations to protected buildings).

See **Appendix E** and **Chapter 1** for definitions.

The legislation in this area is highly complicated and there are always conditions to be adhered to before the reliefs from VAT can be benefited from.

Prior to 1984, all alterations were zero rated, but after this date it is only approved alterations to listed buildings and scheduled monuments which retain zero rating (see **Chapter 6**). In 1989 VAT was introduced on the construction of new commercial buildings, and in 1994/5 certain additions to the zero rates for supplies to housing associations and construction of charitable annexes were announced. In 2001 the reduced rate of 5 per cent was introduced for qualifying conversions and renovations of empty buildings. The legislation has therefore been amended and added to on many occasions, and combined with case law the issues involved can become complex.

One must, of course, always start with the premise that supplies are standard rated, unless there is specific provision for exemption, or a reduced or zero rate.

As the supply of construction services is never exempt from VAT, and therefore all VAT incurred should be recoverable (subject to specific statutory blocks), the main issue for a contractor is to ensure that the VAT treatment of his supplies is correct, whilst taking advantage of any reliefs which are available, especially if the customer is unable to recover VAT where it has to be charged.

4.2   COMMERCIAL BUILDINGS

The supply of construction services in relation to commercial buildings is always standard rated.

4.3   SELF-SUPPLY OF CONSTRUCTION SERVICES

The self-supply of construction services applies in cases where own labour (whether employed rather than self-employed or from another company in a VAT group) is used to provide construction services which would have been taxable at a rate other than zero rate (i.e. construction of commercial rather than residential buildings) if they were bought in from a third party (VAT (Self-Supply of Construction Services) Order 1989, SI 1989/472). The concept of the self-supply is to prevent the avoidance of VAT by partially or wholly exempt businesses by employing labour and therefore avoiding the VAT cost of bought-in services. It applies in cases where the value of such services (whether within a single company or a VAT group of companies) is over £100,000 and used for:

(a)   construction of a building;
(b)   extensions, alterations or annexations which create not less than a 10 per cent increase in floor area;
(c)   construction of any civil engineering work.

The value of any demolition work preparatory to or contemporaneous with the construction work and professional services must also be included in the self-supply.

The value of goods and materials is not included in the self-supply because, where these are bought in, a VAT cost will already arise, which will be recovered in accordance with the partial exemption position of the taxpayer.

The self-supply operates by calculating the VAT on the value of the construction services, etc., and accounting for this as output tax, to be declared in Box 1 of the VAT Return. This figure can also be recovered as input tax (part of the entry to Box 4 on the VAT Return) subject to the partial exemption rules (see **1.9**). Therefore, the self-supply only has any real effect when the business is unable to recover all of its input tax.

Example

An optician's business constructs a new branch, using employed labour amounting to £120,000. The optician must account for VAT of £120,000 × 17.5% = £21,000 in Box 1 of its VAT Return. Its ability to recover the VAT of £21,000 depends upon its partial exemption position. On the assumption that it has a recovery of 65 per cent of non-attributable input tax, £13,650 (£21,000 × 65%) may be recovered in Box 4 of its VAT Return. The balance of £7,350 is exempt input tax and non-recoverable subject to the partial exemption *de minimis* limits.

If the value of the self-supply is over £250,000 it will also be subject to the Capital Goods Scheme (see **1.10**).

In cases where the developer is not registered for VAT, triggering the self-supply in itself creates a liability to register and account for the VAT due. Notification to HMRC is required within 30 days.

4.4 DWELLINGS AND OTHER RESIDENTIAL BUILDINGS

Zero rating of construction services in relation to dwellings is restricted to new build, conversion from non-residential when supplied to a housing association only, approved alterations to protected buildings (see **Chapter 6**) and civil engineering works to provide residential caravan parks. There are also some services which qualify at the lower rate of VAT in connection with the renovation of dwellings which have been empty for three years or more and for a 'changed number of dwellings conversion' (e.g. where a house is converted into flats). Other construction services are standard rated, such as extensions, as are the services of professionals such as architects, surveyors or consultants and other persons acting in a supervisory capacity.

4.4.1 Construction of new dwellings

Zero rating is provided for the 'supply in the course of construction' of a building 'designed as a dwelling' or number of dwellings – essentially houses or apartments/flats (VATA 1994, Sched. 8, Gp. 5, Item 2).

'Supply in the course of construction' specifically excludes any works of conversion, reconstruction or alteration of an existing building, or the enlargement or extension to an existing building except to the extent that the work creates any additional dwellings (Gp. 5, Note 16). A building only ceases to be an 'existing building' when it is demolished completely to ground level or if the part remaining above ground level consists of no more than a single façade (or where it is a corner site, a double façade) the retention of which is a condition or requirement of statutory planning consent or similar permission (Gp. 5, Note 18). In *McMillan & Anor* (No. 18536) the taxpayer retained the spines of the building to support the façade which had been retained. The VAT tribunal determined that this was sufficient to prevent zero rating applying to the construction services supplied.

The above provisions do not prevent the addition of a separate self-contained flat to an existing building, or for example the addition of a whole new floor comprising new flats, from qualifying as zero-rated construction. The new dwelling, however, must not contain any of the pre-existing accommodation – it must be a wholly new build.

A supply is generally considered to be 'in the course of construction' up until the certificate of practical completion is issued by the architect. Work carried out after this date will be standard rated, unless it is simply a continuation/finalisation of the original contract. In the case of *JM Associates* (No. 18624), deposits were paid prior to completion for the construction of conservatories, but the appellant was not allowed to start work on the conservatories he supplied to purchasers of the new houses being constructed until the new house was complete (subject to snagging). The VAT tribunal decided that creation of a tax point prior to completion, by payment of the deposit, did not make the work carried out zero rated – it was an enlargement or extension of an existing building – the completed new house. Snagging, or the correction of faults, carried out by the builder who has carried out the main construction of the new building, qualify for zero rating even when they are carried out after the certificate of completion has been issued. In cases where a developer completes a building to a shell, and then sells for the buyer to finish, this will be the zero rated supply of a partly completed dwelling, and the remaining work will also qualify as 'in the course of construction' and be zero rated, as would the sale of the completed building by that person.

Work closely connected to the construction of the building may also be zero rated when it allows the construction of the building to take place, or allows the building to be used. For example, demolition of existing buildings on the site, site clearance or ground works (levelling and drainage of the land) which takes place immediately prior to the start of construction of the new dwellings, etc.; provision of access to the site to allow deliveries to be made; provision/connection of water, power or drainage to the nearest existing supply; provision of roads, footpaths, parking areas, etc.; and construction of walls, fences and gates, and basic soft landscaping. If there is a time delay between these works and the construction commencing, or a time delay after construction is complete (unless due to seasonal weather) before these works commence, then they will not qualify for zero rating.

The following conditions must be satisfied to meet the criteria of 'designed as a dwelling' (VATA 1994, Sched. 8, Gp. 5, Note 2):

(a) The dwelling must consist of self-contained living accommodation, including all the facilities necessary for living, cooking, washing and sleeping (see *St Catherine's College (Oxford)* v. *Dorling* [1979] All ER 250).

(b) There must be no direct internal access from the dwelling to any other dwelling or part of a dwelling.

(c) The separate use or disposal of the dwelling must not be prohibited under by the terms of any covenant, statutory planning consent or similar provision. This prevents the typical 'granny annexe' from enjoying zero rating, and can also affect farm cottages where the separate use or disposal is prevented. It will not, however, prevent zero rating if the occupation is simply tied to the agricultural use.

(d) Statutory planning consent must have been granted and the work must be carried out in accordance with it.

In the tribunal decision in *Oldrings Development Kingsclere Ltd* (No 17769), the taxpayer supplied building services to the owner of a substantial property, who had been granted planning permission to build a detached studio room (see condition (d) above). Although it had originally been intended as an artist's studio there was a kitchen and a separate room with a WC and hand-basin, and it was suitable for guests as well, so that it met condition (a) above. The planning permission had no restrictions other than that the new building could not be used for commercial purposes, so that it met condition (c) above. There was no internal access to the existing dwelling – condition (b) above. This meant that it qualified as a dwelling and the building services were zero rated. Note that in such circumstances the planning permission often requires that the new building must be used in conjunction with the existing dwelling, thus preventing condition (c) from being met.

However, it is vital that the appropriate planning consents, etc., are in place prior to the commencement of the work. Although HMRC has in the past allowed zero rating to apply where the planning is gained retrospectively, in the tribunal case of *AE & JM Harris* (No. 18822), at the time of construction the planning restricted the use of the new building as ancillary to the existing dwelling. The planning permission was later amended but this was too late. Many tribunals have ignored what the planning permission describes the new building as and come to their own conclusions as to whether the building meets the conditions for zero rating, unless there is an express provision which is not met such as in the *Harris* case above.

The zero rating also covers the construction of garages constructed at the same time as the qualifying dwelling provided it is intended to be occupied with the dwelling or one of the dwellings.

The case of *Agudas Israel Housing Association Ltd* (No 18798), concerned the construction of eight residential units as a new third floor to an existing building. Each unit consisted of a bed-sitting room with en suite shower room, but there were no cooking facilities, although it would have been practicable to install a microwave oven in each unit. The units were intended to house residents with Alzheimer's disease and safety considerations had to be taken into account, so that some residents ate in the ground floor dining room, some ate 'Meals on Wheels' and some ate meals provided by family. The tribunal found in these circumstances that: 'In our view, in the twenty-first century, premises with their own front door, en suite bathing facilities and the ability to cook with a microwave cooker and a kettle are self-contained living accommodation. The factor of the limited nature of the cooking facilities is outweighed by the factor of the direct access to the Square from a resident's own front door to which he or she has his or her own key.'

The legislation also provides for apportionment (VATA 1994, Sched. 8, Gp. 5, Note 10) where part of the construction services qualify for zero rating and part does not. In recent years, particularly with regard to housing associations, live/work units have been constructed, which consist of a dwelling, but with an area which may or may not be specifically designated for work. Where the area is specifically designated as a work area, then HMRC insists that this part of the construction does not qualify for zero rating, presumably on the basis that this part of the building is not 'designed as a dwelling'.

In respect of communal areas of blocks of apartments, etc., HMRC accepts that zero rating applies to the whole of the construction where such communal parts are to be used only by the residents and their guests. However, where communal areas are to be used by third parties as well, whether or not for a charge, for example where the building includes gym and leisure facilities, then the construction of the communal areas is standard rated.

In addition, where the building contains both residential and non-residential premises, for example a shop with a flat above, the zero rating only applies to the extent that the building is 'designed as a dwelling'. This means that if the access to the flat is solely used by the occupant of the flat, then it will qualify for zero rating, but if there are any shared areas, standard rating will apply.

4.4.2 Relevant residential buildings

The zero rating for construction services is also available for the construction of new 'relevant residential' use buildings, but is restricted to supplies made to the person who will use the building for the qualifying purpose, and must be supported by a certificate given by that person to the supplier of the services (VATA 1994, Sched. 8, Gp. 5, Item 3). For this reason, supplies by sub-contractors will not qualify for zero rating when supplied to the main contractor. The main contractor will, however, be able to recover the VAT charged by sub-contractors against his onward zero rated charge to the qualifying person. Where the main contractor is not working for the person who can provide a certificate, for example if a property investor has commissioned the construction, then the main contractor will also have to standard rate his construction services, but the building owner will be able to zero rate the first grant of a major interest (see **3.3.1**) in the building providing it is to a person who can issue such a certificate. The certificate should be supplied prior to the commencement of the works (VATA 1994, Sched. 8, Gp. 5, Note 12). A form of certificate can be found at *VAT Notice 708, Buildings and Construction*, Appendix A.

Zero rating only applies when the building or a discrete part of a building is to be used 'solely' for the relevant purpose. In cases where the building is for mixed use and the person using the building can identify the parts which will be used solely for qualifying purposes, then an apportionment must be applied so that only the qualifying proportion is charged at zero rate. In cases where the whole of the building will be used for part of the time for qualifying purposes and part of the time for non-qualifying purposes the relief does not apply.

In *Allan Water Developments Ltd* (No. 19131), the company operated a nursing home with room for 81 residents and a new building was constructed to be used for patients with dementia and mental illness. The new building was linked to the existing building by a corridor which was used by staff only, to transport meals across from the existing nursing home. HMRC ruled that the new building was an annexe, and therefore standard rated (not being for charitable non-business use) but the tribunal held that it was a new building so that zero rating applied, applying the dicta in *Cantrell & Cantrell (t/a Foxearth Lodge Nursing Home)* v. *C & E Commrs* [2003] EWHC 404, ChD.

4.4.3 Definition of 'relevant residential'

The term used for a 'relevant residential' purpose is defined in VATA 1994, Sched. 8, Gp. 15, Item 1, Note 4 as use as:

(a) a home or other institution providing residential accommodation for children;

(b) a home or other institution providing residential accommodation with personal care for persons in need of personal care by reason of old age, disablement, past or present dependence on alcohol or drugs or past or present mental disorder;

(c) a hospice;

(d) residential accommodation for students or school pupils;

(e) residential accommodation for members of any or the armed forces;

(f) a monastery, nunnery or similar establishment; or

(g) an institution which is the sole or main residence of at least 90 per cent of its residents.

The Note also specifically excludes use as a hospital, prison or similar institution or a hotel, inn or similar establishment.

In situations where a number of buildings are constructed at the same time on the same site, and are intended to be used together as a unit solely for a relevant residential purpose, then the zero rating applies to the group of buildings as a whole. This would allow zero rating to apply, for example, to a separate dining hall and kitchen constructed at the same time and for use with student accommodation. This provision was specifically introduced in Gp. 15, Note 5 from 1 March 1995 but, in practice, HMRC had allowed the zero rating before this date.

HMRC also accepts that the inclusion of a simple office for a warden, for example, does not prevent zero rating applying to the whole of the construction (see e.g. *Hill Ash Developments* (No. 16747)).

In order for zero rating to apply, the building/building works must be for use 'solely' for the qualifying purpose. For example, in the case of *University Court of the University of St Andrews* (No. 19054), the university constructed a facilities block as part of a new student accommodation complex (zero rated) which also contained a bar and a shop (standard rated). HMRC allowed that the works to the roof, wiring and plumbing should be apportioned under VATA 1994, Sched. 8, Gp. 5, Note 10, which specifically provides for apportionment of the supply in such cases, but refused apportionment in respect of toilets, cupboards, first aid room, corridors, lobbies and other mixed use areas because those areas were not used 'solely' for relevant residential purposes. The tribunal found that the toilets, first aid room and a corridor would have been included in the building whether or not the bar and shop were built and allowed zero rating for these only, agreeing with HMRC as regards the other parts.

In *Fenwood Developments Ltd* (No. 18975), HMRC argued against zero rating for construction of a new nursing home where many of the residents were detained under the Mental Health Act 1983 on grounds that the property was similar to a hospital or a prison (see exclusions above). The tribunal found that there was a difference between 'care' and 'treatment' and that a nursing home provided care and a hospital provided treatment – the nursing home was not therefore similar to a hospital. There was also a difference between a prison and a facility providing care to people in need of care and the facility was not a prison and zero rating applied (see also *Hospital of St John & St Elizabeth* (No. 19141)).

4.5 BUILDING MATERIALS

In addition to the zero rating of the construction services themselves, VATA 1994, Sched. 8, Gp. 5, Item 4 also zero rates the supply of 'building materials' which are to be incorporated into dwellings and relevant residential use buildings, providing they are supplied by the person who is supplying the qualifying building services (i.e. a carpenter supplying the wood, or a bricklayer supplying the bricks and mortar). Group 5, Note 22 defines 'building materials' as goods ordinarily incorporated by builders in a building or its site, including their installation as fittings (Note 23), but specifically excludes the following:

(a) finished or pre-fabricated furniture, other than furniture designed to be fitted in kitchens;

(b) materials for the construction of fitted furniture, other than kitchen furniture;

(c) electrical or gas appliances, unless the appliance is designed to heat space or water (or both) or to provide ventilation, air cooling, air purification or dust extraction; a door-entry system, a waste disposal unit or a machine for compacting waste; a burglar alarm, a fire alarm, or fire safety equipment or designed solely for the purpose of aid to be summoned in an emergency; or a lift or hoist;

(d) carpets or carpeting material.

With regard to (a) and (b) above, HMRC accepts that simply closing off the end of a room, or part of a room to a stud wall, by fitting doors, behind which are a simple hanging rail and shelf, does not constitute a fitted wardrobe. However, if the wardrobe has sides or is more complex in its internal construction (such as having shoe racks or drawers) the restrictions above come into force preventing zero rating from applying. The position of finished and pre-fabricated furniture was considered in the case of *C & E Commrs* v. *McClean Homes (Midlands) Ltd* [1993] STC 335, QB and subsequently in *S H Wade* (No. 13164) the latter which led to HMRC issuing *Business Brief 12/97*, which sets out the above guidance in more detail.

In *Christ's Hospital* (No. 19126), the tribunal considered that the materials used to provide desks and bookcases did not constitute 'furniture' as they were merely planks of wood and furniture would have required more than this (e.g. bookcases would need to have sides to be considered furniture). However, beds with drawers were considered to be furniture.

With regard to (c) above, the Note prevents the zero rating of white goods, such as ovens, hobs, dishwashers, washing machines, etc. incorporated into kitchens, from being zero rated, but does not preclude their fitting as a separate supply from being zero rated.

4.5.1 Examples of 'building materials' qualifying for zero rating

The following are examples of building materials which HMRC states qualify for zero rating in conjunction with construction of new dwellings and relevant residential buildings. These are listed in *VAT Notice 708, Buildings and Construction*, Appendix D and include:

- airing cupboards and other similar basic storage facilities which are formed within part of the fabric of the building;
- shelves formed by box work over pipes, etc.;
- simple bedroom wardrobes;
- window frames and glazing;
- doors, letter boxes;

- fireplaces and surrounds;
- guttering;
- power points;
- outside lights;
- immersion heaters, boilers, hot and cold water tanks, radiators and central heating;
- built-in heating appliances;
- burglar and fire alarms;
- smoke detectors;
- air conditioning;
- ventilation and dust extraction equipment;
- lifts and hoists;
- communal TV aerials in blocks of flats;
- warden call systems;
- work surfaces or fitted cupboards in kitchens and utility rooms including kitchen sinks, baths, basins, lavatory bowls and cisterns, bidets, shower units, fixed towel rails, toilet roll holders, soap dishes, etc.

There is no definition of 'building materials' within the legislation and the usual English meaning is therefore applied – what would normally be expected to be used or installed by builders in the course of construction of a dwelling, etc. The range of materials included within this is therefore constantly widening. For example, in the case of *B Symons* (No. 19174), the goods at issue were air filtration equipment that filtered pesticides and exhaust fumes from the air, which the individual needed due to her allergies. The tribunal accepted that in this modern world the filtration equipment could properly be described as building materials and zero rating applied. See also *VAT Information Sheet 05/00, 'VAT: Construction and Building Materials'*.

4.6 CONVERSION WORKS

4.6.1 Housing associations

Zero rating is provided for the supply to a relevant housing association of services in the course of conversion of a 'non-residential' building or a non-residential part of a building into either a building or part of a building designed as a dwelling or number of dwellings, or into a building or part of a building intended solely for use for a relevant residential purpose (VATA 1994, Sched. 8, Gp. 5, Item 3). The zero rating specifically excludes the services of an architect, surveyor or other person acting as a consultant or in a supervisory capacity (as for construction of new dwellings generally) but otherwise includes any services related to the conversion. The supply of building materials in conjunction with qualifying conversion services is also included in the zero rating, with the same exclusions as for new construction works (see **4.5**). This relief was introduced in recognition that housing associations tend to grant short-term leases and cannot therefore benefit from the zero rating for the grant of a major interest in a newly converted dwelling, etc. (see **3.1**) in the same way that commercial developers can. See also **4.6.4** with regard to bed-sit accommodation.

4.6.1.1   Definition of a 'relevant housing association'

For the purposes of this relief a 'relevant housing association' means:

(a)   a registered social landlord within the meaning of Part 1 of the Housing Act 1996;

(b)   a registered housing association within the meaning of the Housing Associations Act 1985 (Scottish registered housing association);

(c)   a registered housing association within the meaning of Part II of the Housing (Northern Ireland) Order 1992 (Northern Ireland registered housing association).

The construction or conversion of a non-residential part of a building into a garage may also be zero rated if the works are carried out at the same time as the works which result in a new dwelling, etc. However, an existing garage which is occupied with a dwelling is specifically excluded from the definition of a non-residential building for these purposes under Note 8 of the Group. This is to exclude the conversion of a garage into, for example, a 'granny-annexe' and thus qualifying for zero rating.

The works must result in at least one additional dwelling being formed in order to qualify for zero rating (see **3.1.1**) so that if a building already contains an existing dwelling, any dwelling formed as a result of the work carried out will not qualify if it contains part of that pre-existing dwelling (VATA 1994, Sched. 8, Gp. 5, Note 9).

4.6.2   Converting a non-residential building into residential

The 5 per cent reduced rate applies to the works of converting a non-residential building into a house, flats or into bed-sits (VATA 1994, Sched. 7A, Gp. 6, Item 1). It applies to all works to the fabric of the building, including repairs and improvements, and works within the immediate site of the building that are in connection with the means of providing water, power, heat or access to the building; the means of providing drainage or security for the building; or the provision of means of waste disposal for the building. Where a building is part non-residential and part is already residential, the 5 per cent rate will only apply to works where a new dwelling is formed. So, for example, if a property consists of a shop with a flat above and the works are to convert the shop into a flat and renovate the existing flat, the conversion

153

works relating to the shop will qualify, but the works of renovating the flat above will not (unless it has been empty for three or more years, see **4.7**). The relief would apply, for example, to conversion of a barn, hotel, warehouses, church, etc. into residential units.

There is a potential problem with conversions of public houses if they have pre-existing residential accommodation, such as living quarters for the landlord or staff. The zero rate for conversion works only applies if a different number of dwellings result from the works. Therefore, the conversion of the public house containing pre-existing landlord's accommodation into a single house will not qualify for the 5 per cent rate, unless the pre-existing residential accommodation has not been used as a dwelling for at least 10 years (VATA 1994, Sched. 8, Gp. 5, Note 7). If the pub is converted into two or more flats, conversion of the commercial element only will qualify at 5 per cent, but where the second or any other flat contains part of the pre-existing dwelling the works will be at 17.5 per cent.

In the decision in *Jacobs (Ivor)* v. *C & E Commrs* [2005] EWCA Civ 930, the taxpayer had converted a former residential school for boys, comprising classrooms, boarding accommodation, staff bedsits and a headmaster's flat (only one 'dwelling') into one large dwelling for his own occupation plus three flats. None of the four 'dwellings' had been created exclusively from the non-residential part of the school and HMRC refused his DIY housebuilder's claim. The Court of Appeal upheld the High Court's decision that the taxpayer was entitled to recover the VAT incurred on converting the non-residential parts into dwellings. As a result of this decision, HMRC issued *Business Brief 22/05* in which it set out its revised policy, that for the purposes of the DIY scheme only, it is no longer necessary that the additional dwelling be created exclusively from the non-residential part of the existing building. However, it specifically states that it does not consider that this decision impacts on similar projects carried out by builders/developers. Presumably, because it does not consider that a developer would be entitled to make a zero-rated grant of the new dwelling where it incorporates part of the pre-existing residential accommodation.

4.6.3 Changed number of dwellings conversion

With effect from 12 May 2001 a 'changed number of dwellings conversion', for example the works of converting a house into flats, a building comprising flats into a single dwelling or any variation in between, qualifies at the 5 per cent rate (VATA 1994, Sched. 7A, Gp. 6, Item 1). It is vital that there is a change in the number of dwellings in the building (whether up or down in number) or the part of the building concerned, for the relief to apply, and that no one dwelling remains with the same footprint/floor area as before the works, otherwise that dwelling will not qualify and the works will be chargeable at the standard rate. The relief also applies where a building containing flats is converted into a house, again as long as the number of units and the floor area of each unit in the finished project differs from what was there when the project commenced. If, for example, in an existing block of flats, there are three flats on each of three floors, and the works carried out form two flats on one floor (each with an increased floor area) but the other two floors remain with three flats on each, then the 5 per cent rate will only apply to the floor where the number of dwellings has changed from three to two. In the case of *Wellcome Trust* (No. 18417), the appellant converted a building comprising six or seven flats into a building containing four flats so that the 'changed number of dwellings' condition was satisfied, but in respect of the second floor, this was a single flat before the conversion and remained a single flat after the conversion. Therefore, the requirement that the floor area not remain the same was not met and the works for this floor were standard rated, despite there being a small change which the tribunal considered *de minimis*. Conversion of a relevant residential building, such as a nursing home, into flats would also attract the 5 per cent rate. The reasoning behind the 5 per cent rate is to try to bring back into use as many empty properties or disused non-residential properties as possible, particularly in inner city areas – but the rules apply to rural properties in the same way.

There was not much publicity with the introduction of the new rate and many builders still continue to charge standard rate on works which should have been at the 5 per cent rate. If this has happened, a credit note can be raised for the overcharged VAT, as long as the tax point is after 12 May 2001 (that is, the work was not completed before 12 May 2001 and a tax invoice or payment was not received prior to that date) and the adjustment is made within three years of the tax point of the original supply. Many builders were reluctant to apply the 5 per cent rate without some form of certificate. There is no certification required or provided for, except in the case of a special residential conversion, when a certificate similar to that for 'relevant residential' or 'relevant charitable' buildings is required. It is the builder's responsibility to determine the correct rate of VAT applying. The danger of overcharging VAT in these circumstances is that the sale or letting of the completed conversion may well be exempt from VAT and the developer will therefore be unable to recover the additional VAT charged in error. In addition, and in particular in circumstances where the builder becomes insolvent, HMRC could assess the developer for input tax claimed in error (charging VAT in error does not make it a deductible expense) and with the builder being insolvent the developer would have no practical recourse for repayment of the overcharged amount.

4.6.4 Bed-sit accommodation

The work of converting a house, block of flats or, from 1 June 2002, a non-residential or a relevant residential building, into bed-sit accommodation (multiple occupancy dwellings in the terms of the legislation) qualifies for the 5 per cent rate (VATA 1994, Sched. 7A, Gp. 6, Item 1).

With regard to the zero rate under VATA 1994, Sched. 8, Gp. 5, Item 3, for conversions for housing associations, in the tribunal decision of *Amicus Group Ltd* (No. 17693), a building containing bed-sits was converted into self-contained flats and, for the purposes of this legislation, the tribunal determined that bed-sits do constitute 'dwellings'. It relied on the Housing Act case of *Uratemp Ventures Ltd* v. *Collins* [2001] 3 WLR 806 that a 'dwelling' is not the same as a 'separate dwelling' and that VATA 1994, Sched. 8, Gp. 5, Item 3, Note 2, which defines the conditions post-conversion, states that the dwelling must consist of self-contained living accommodation – this pre-supposes that a dwelling can exist without being self-contained. Rather than the zero rate, the reduced rate would therefore apply.

The *Amicus* decision can be contrasted to the earlier tribunal decision of *Look Ahead Housing Association* (No. 16816), in which the tribunal determined that the work of converting a building, split into bed-sits, into flats qualified for zero rating on the grounds that the bed-sits were not dwellings because they did not individually contain all of the facilities for living, having shared bathroom and toilet facilities, neither could all of the building together be described as a single dwelling. It is the *Amicus*, rather than the *Look Ahead* decision which is now followed.

4.6.5 Special residential conversions

The 5 per cent rate also applies to a 'special residential conversion' (VATA 1994, Sched. 7A, Gp. 6, Item 1). This is where a building such as a dwelling, or from 1 June 2002 a non-residential building, or a group of such buildings, is converted into a relevant residential use building such as a nursing home or student accommodation. For the relief to apply, if the intended use is an 'institutional purpose', the buildings converted must form the whole of the institution upon completion. 'Institutional purpose' is defined similarly to 'relevant residential use' but excluding student accommodation and accommodation for armed forces (see **3.3.1**), for example a care home or children's home. This condition was introduced to prevent the relief applying to conversions of outbuildings etc., which extend, for example, nursing homes and similar residential buildings. The relief does not apply to the conversion of any building or part of a building which was used for a relevant residential purpose prior to the conversion works being carried out.

In a similar way as for the zero rate for relevant residential use buildings, the relief only applies when the supply is made to the person who intends to use the building for qualifying purposes and must be supported by a certificate. The certificate must be supplied prior to the commencement of the works. A form of certificate together with further details of the reduced rate for conversions can be found at *VAT Notice 708, Buildings and Construction*, section 18.

4.6.6 What type of works does the 5 per cent rate apply to?

The 5 per cent rate applies to all building works to the fabric of the building and includes works to repair, re-decorate, and works providing water, power, heat, drainage, security, means of waste disposal and access to the dwelling (VATA 1994, Sched. 7A, Gp. 6, Note 11). It also applies to the construction of a garage, or renovation or conversion of a building into a garage, when the work is carried out as part of a project which qualifies for the reduced rate and the garage is to be occupied with the qualifying conversion.

The 5 per cent rate also includes building materials supplied in the course of carrying out the qualifying conversion works, but does not apply to the supply of building materials on their own. It can therefore be cost efficient to have a VAT registered builder carry out the works, all services and materials being chargeable at the reduced rate of 5 per cent, rather than 'doing it yourself' or using a non-registered builder and buying in materials on which VAT at 17.5 per cent is not recoverable. For example, if building materials amounting to £20,000 are going to be purchased, with VAT of £3,500, and the work is planned to be carried out in-house, or by a non-registered contractor, the VAT costs could potentially be reduced if the work is carried out by a third party VAT registered contractor, who also supplies the building materials. As the combined work and materials attracts only 5 per cent VAT, if the labour value is another £20,000, the VAT on the total cost of £40,000 is still only £2,000 at 5 per cent, compared to the 17.5 per cent VAT of £3,500 on the materials alone, when purchased separately. The work could even be carried out by an associated business set up specifically for these purposes. Under *Halifax* principles, setting up the associated business may be 'artificial' but would not seem to be an 'abusive practice' as the purpose of the legislation is to provide this relief from VAT if the work were to be carried out by a third party in this way (see **1.13**).

There is the usual exclusion which applies to 'materials not normally fitted by builders' such as carpets and other soft furnishings, fitted furniture and white goods (see **4.5**). Also excluded is the work of fitting such goods – whereas with the zero rate for new construction these goods are also excluded but the cost of, for example, fitting carpet, is not.

It is also, of course, quite possible that the 5 per cent rate could be combined with zero rating for listed buildings (see **Chapter 6**) so that zero rate applies to the approved alterations and 5 per cent to the rest of the works, including repairs, providing the building has been empty for three years or more or the number of dwellings it contains is changed.

4.7 RENOVATIONS AND ALTERATIONS

The reduced rate of 5 per cent applies to the renovation of dwellings and, from 1 June 2002, bed-sit accommodation and relevant residential buildings, which have been empty for three years or more (VATA 1994, Sched. 7A, Gp. 7).

In the case of relevant residential buildings, in order to qualify under this heading for the reduced rate of VAT, the building must be used solely for qualifying relevant residential purposes after the renovation, and the work must be evidenced by a certificate from the person who will use it for such purposes. Note, however, that the renovation of a relevant residential building and conversion of it into, say, flats, or a single dwelling, at the same time as the renovation works are carried out, would qualify for the reduced rate as a 'conversion' (see **4.6**).

The relief encompasses the building works and builder's materials supplied with the qualifying works and includes all works of renovation, extensions, installing double glazing, etc., including repairs, re-decorations, and works providing water, power, heat, drainage, security, means of waste disposal and access to the dwelling. It also applies to the construction of a garage, or renovation or conversion of a building into a garage, when the work is carried out as part of a project which qualifies for the reduced rate and the garage is to be occupied with the qualifying renovation. There is the usual exclusion which applies to 'materials not normally fitted by builders' such as carpets and other soft furnishings, fitted furniture and white goods and the work of fitting such goods (see **4.5**).

The building must have been completely empty for the three years prior to work commencing, although having squatters in occupation would not count against this. It is not sufficient, for example, for a person to have restricted their use of the property to a few rooms, or even one room, even where the Council Tax has been reduced as a result of this restriction – there is no relief for the part which has not been occupied in such circumstances. The three years is measured from the date of commencement of the works retrospectively. It may be a requirement to provide evidence of the date from which the property has been empty, and the usual source for this is the Council Tax office, providers of utilities, the Empty Property Officers in local authorities or the Electoral Roll. The preferred option of HMRC is a letter from the Empty Property Officer, and in *VAT Notice 708* it states that if you hold a letter from the Empty Property Officer, no other evidence is required.

The 5 per cent rate can be claimed by a DIY renovator as well as by a developer, although special rules apply. In cases where an individual acquires an empty property and moves in, the property must have been empty for three years prior to their acquiring and moving in and the works must be supplied to them in the one year following the date of their acquisition of the property. For further details see *VAT Notice 708*, section 8. Note that with the exception of the owner occupier/DIY renovator of a single household dwelling where the above conditions are met, the premises must not be occupied prior to work commencing, and no renovations or alterations must have taken place in the three-year period prior to work commencing (other than works to keep the building secure and weatherproof) – otherwise the standard rate will apply.

4.8   CIVIL ENGINEERING WORKS

Where civil engineering works are supplied in the course of construction of new dwellings or other qualifying buildings, they are zero rated as long as they relate to work carried out within the perimeter of the development. In cases where connections to mains utilities are outside the perimeter, zero rating is extended to the connection to the nearest existing supply.

Where the site consists partly of dwellings or other qualifying buildings and partly non-qualifying buildings, such as shops, etc., then the supply should be apportioned between the qualifying and non-qualifying works. Any fair and reasonable method of apportionment may be used.

Civil engineering works which are not essential to the construction of the qualifying buildings, such as tennis courts or swimming pools, are standard rated.

Where civil engineering works are supplied to provide the sub-structure for a potential housing estate, but the construction of the houses themselves is not part of the contract, the supply of civil engineering works will be standard rated. This commonly happens when a site is prepared to be sold to DIY housebuilders, for example. In such a case the supply to the DIY housebuilder would need to be apportioned between the exempt land sale and the standard rated civil engineering works, the latter which would form part of the claim for DIY housebuilders.

4.8.1   Permanent residential caravan parks

Civil engineering works necessary for the development of a permanent park for residential caravans also qualifies for zero rating (VATA 1994, Sched. 8, Gp. 5, Item 2(b)) but the zero rating is not available if residence throughout the year is prevented by the terms of any covenant, statutory planning consent or similar condition (Gp. 5, Note 19). The purpose here is to restrict the zero rating so that it does not apply to holiday caravan parks.

Works to upgrade or to provide additional new pitches within an existing site are standard rated, but work which extends the existing site is zero rated – such as extending roads, provision of drainage and utilities and new pitches on previously undeveloped land.

The sale of a residential caravan is zero rated under VATA 1994, Sched. 8, Gp. 9, Item 1, but VAT at standard rate must be accounted for on removable contents.

The zero rate applies only to civil engineering works necessary to the construction of a residential caravan park, such as laying new pitches or bases for the caravans, laying new roads, drives, parking bays and paths, installing water, electricity and gas supplies, and installing drainage and sewerage. It does not cover works which are not necessary for a residential caravan park such as playgrounds and hard landscaping.

The zero rate also does not extend to works which are not 'civil engineering' such as indoor swimming pools, social centres, shops, fitness clubs, a doctor's surgery or a manager's house (although the construction of the latter may qualify for zero rating as a new dwelling (see **4.4.1**)).

4.9 SUB-CONTRACTORS

Sub-contractors can take advantage of all of the zero rates and the lower rates, except in cases where the building is one for use for a relevant residential or relevant charitable purpose. This is because the certificate required can only be issued by the person using the building for qualifying purposes, direct to the person supplying them with services. As the sub-contractor in such cases will be working through a main contractor, his services to the main contractor will be standard rated. The person using the building for qualifying purposes could, of course, directly contract with the sub-contractors instead and issue certificates to them, and as long as they supply their services direct to that person and not through the main contractor, and a separate certificate is supplied, then the works will qualify for zero rate.

4.10 DEMOLITION

Where a contract provides for the demolition of existing buildings and the construction of new buildings that qualify for zero rating, the whole of the contract is zero rated. Demolition services on their own, however, are standard rated. Often the main contractor will be contracted to provide the demolition of the site preparatory to the new construction and his contract with the developer in its entirety will therefore be zero rated. The demolition itself is often sub-contracted and the demolition sub-contractor may zero rate his supplies to the main contractor provided the demolition can be seen as closely related to the new construction works (see *VAT Notice 708*, para. 3.3.4). However, if there is any doubt on whether the demolition services are 'closely related' to zero-rated new construction, for example if there is a time lag between demolition and the commencement of construction, then the demolition contractor should charge VAT at the standard rate.

Where a contract provides for the right to take away materials in the course of demolition, this is a separate supply for VAT purposes chargeable at the standard rate (i.e. it is treated as the supply of second-hand building materials by the site owner) unless there is a single charge for both demolition and removal of materials, in which case it is treated as a single supply chargeable at whichever VAT rate applies. The wording of the contract can therefore be vital in ensuring the zero rate applies.

4.11 PROFESSIONAL SERVICES

The services of professionals such as architects, surveyors, engineers and consultants, together with supervisory or management services, are specifically excluded from the zero and lower rates.

4.12 MANAGEMENT CONTRACTORS

There are generally two ways in which management contractors provide their services. If the management contractor simply provides management of the contract – 'project management' – and does not directly employ the contractors carrying out the qualifying works, the charge made by him is standard rated because it is not supplied 'in the course of construction'. However, if the management contractor employs the contractors carrying out the qualifying works, and re-charges the zero-rated contractors' costs together with the management fee, then the management fee is also zero rated.

In the event that a management contractor is engaged to advise on preliminary matters and the contract does not proceed, then his charges will be standard rated.

4.13 DESIGN AND BUILD

It is usual for a developer to directly contract with an architect to supply the design services, etc., necessary to the construction of the new building, and these services are standard rated. However, a developer may contract with the building contractor carrying out qualifying zero or lower rated services to provide the necessary architectural services in addition to the actual construction work. Where such a contract is for a single lump sum, the total consideration will qualify for zero rating. This applies even if the value of the architectural services is separately identified for the internal purposes of

161

the parties involved in the contract, as long as the contract itself is for a single lump sum.

4.14 BUILDING CONTROL FEES

All building control fees in England and Wales are subject to VAT at standard rate. This is because inspections may be carried out by 'approved inspectors' as well as by the local authority body direct. However, in Scotland and Northern Ireland, the local authorities have the monopoly on planning applications and the building control fees are therefore outside the scope of VAT. Where a building control fee is paid in respect of a regularisation certificate (where prior approval for work had not been granted) this is under the sole ambit of the local authority in England and Wales and these fees are therefore also outside the scope of VAT.

4.15 HIRE OF PLANT

Hire of plant as a separate supply is a standard rated supply of services. However, if the hire of plant is provided together with the services of an operator as a single supply, the whole supply will qualify for zero rating or at the lower rate where qualifying services are provided (e.g. hire of a crane together with an operator on a new housing project would qualify for zero rating).

4.16 SCAFFOLDING

The services of erecting and dismantling scaffolding qualify for zero rating or the lower rate of VAT when the construction work they are supplied in conjunction with qualifies for zero rating or lower rate VAT respectively. Otherwise the services are standard rated. Hire of scaffolding equipment is always standard rated, being the 'hire of goods' rather than a 'supply in the course of construction'. Where scaffolding is used in conjunction with zero-rated work, therefore, zero rating will apply to the erection and dismantling, but the hire of the scaffolding will be standard rated. If there is no separate charge for erection and dismantling, a fair and reasonable apportionment should be made.

In *Peter J Guntert (t/a Abingdon Scaffolding Co)* (No. 10604), the appellant tried to argue that he had charged only for the erection and dismantling of the scaffolding (wholly zero rated) but the tribunal chairman commented that it was agreed by implication that the scaffolding would remain in position for a reasonable time whilst the building work was carried out, and the fact that no separate charge was made for the hire did not mean that the price quoted was not consideration for the hire in addition to the erection and dismantling.

4.17 SITE RESTORATION

Site restoration services supplied as part of a zero-rated or lower-rated project can also be charged at the zero or lower rate respectively. Where site restoration services on their own are supplied, however, the supply is standard rated. Any separate charge for transporting rubbish cleared from the site is also standard rated.

4.18 LANDSCAPING

Services of landscaping are standard rated, except for the laying of topsoil or turf within a housing plot, or construction of simple paths and patios, when they are supplied in the course of, or as work closely related to, zero-rated construction services. Other landscaping, such as planting of trees and shrubs, will qualify for treatment at the zero rate if it is part of a landscaping scheme approved by a planning authority under the terms of a planning consent condition and is shown on the plans of the development.

However, in *Business Brief 07/00*, HMRC states that screening planted along roadside verges or work within a specific plot that is not within an approved scheme, or work performed after completion of construction, such as replacing trees which have died, will not qualify for zero rate.

Landscaping of projects which are at the lower rate of VAT does not qualify at the lower rate, because this relief is restricted to works to the 'fabric of the building' and other specified works.

4.19 WALLS AND FENCES

Walls and fences which are constructed at the same time as the construction services qualifying at zero rate are performed, may also be zero rated. Walls and fences supplied with projects which are at the lower rate of VAT also qualify at the lower rate, provided they are constructed to provide security for the qualifying building, otherwise the work would be standard rated, because the reduced rate is restricted to works to the 'fabric of the building' and certain other specified works.

4.20 INSULATION AND ENERGY-SAVING MATERIALS

The installation of insulation and energy-saving materials will of course qualify for zero rating when supplied in the course of construction of a dwelling or qualifying building (VATA 1994, Sched. 8, Gp. 5) and for reduced rate in the course of a qualifying conversion or renovation (VATA 1994, Sched. 7A, Gps. 6 and 7). However, there is also a provision for the reduced rate of VAT to apply on a more general level outside of these categories (VATA 1994, Sched. 7A, Gp. 2).

The relief applies to the installation of the following in residential accommodation (including dwellings, relevant residential buildings, permanent residential caravans or houseboats) or a building intended for use solely for a relevant charitable purpose:

(a) insulation for walls, floors, ceilings, roofs or lofts or for water tanks, pipes or other plumbing fittings;
(b) draught stripping for windows and doors;
(c) central heating controls, including thermostatic radiator valves;
(d) hot water system controls;
(e) solar panels;
(f) wind turbines;
(g) water turbines;
(h) ground source heat pumps (from 1 June 2004);
(i) air source heat pumps (from 7 April 2005);
(j) micro combined heat and power units (from 7 April 2005);
(k) boilers designed to be fuelled solely by wood, straw or similar vegetal matter (from 1 January 2006).

In addition to the services of installation, the insulation or energy-saving material itself qualifies for the reduced rate when supplied in conjunction with the qualifying services. Insulation or materials purchased on their own are always standard rated. For further information see *VAT Notice 708/6, Energy-saving Materials*, section 2. Note that although carpets and carpeting materials are specifically excluded from the zero rate (see **4.5**) and the reduced rate for conversions and renovations (see **4.6** and **4.7**) there appears to be no restriction on the reduced rate for these items under this heading, providing that the purpose of their installation is insulation.

4.21 GRANT-FUNDED INSTALLATION OF HEATING EQUIPMENT OR SECURITY GOODS OR CONNECTION OF A GAS SUPPLY

Where the following services are funded under a relevant grant scheme and supplied to a qualifying person in their sole or main residence, the 5 per cent rate of VAT applies (VATA 1994, Sched. 7A, Gp. 3):

(a)   installing heating appliances;

(b)   heating appliances when supplied with qualifying installation services;

(c)   connecting or re-connecting a mains gas supply;

(d)   goods supplied in connection with (c) above;

(e)   installing, repairing or maintaining a central heating system;

(f)   necessary goods supplied with (e) above;

(g)   installing, maintaining or repairing a renewable source heating system (such as a heat pump, solar, wind or hydroelectric power system);

(h)   necessary goods supplied with (g) above;

(i)   leasing of goods that comprise a central heating system or part of one;

(j)   sale of goods that qualify under (i) above;

(k)   installing security goods;

(l)   goods supplied in connection with (i) above.

In order for goods to qualify for relief, they must be supplied with the services of fitting/installing them – any goods purchased on their own will be standard rated. If the householder makes a contribution towards the cost, that element of the consideration is standard rated.

A 'relevant grant scheme' is one which has as its objectives the funding of the installation of energy-saving materials into the homes of qualifying persons and is funded by the Secretary of State, the Scottish Ministers, the National Assembly for Wales, by a Minister or a Northern Ireland Department, by the European Community, under an arrangement approved by the Gas and Electricity Markets Authority or the Director General of Electricity Supply for Northern Ireland, or by a local authority.

Heating appliances included in the scheme under Gp. 3, Note 4 includes thermostatically controlled gas-fired room heaters, electric storage heaters, closed solid fuel fire cassettes, electric dual immersion water heaters with factory-insulated (prior to 1 June 2002 'foam insulated') hot water tanks, gas-fired boilers, radiators.

Security goods included in the scheme under Gp. 3, Note 5 are locks or bolts for windows, locks, bolts or security chains for doors, spy holes, smoke alarms.

Qualifying persons include persons over the age of 60 who are in receipt of one of the following benefits: council tax benefit, disability living allowance, disabled person's tax credit, working families tax credit, housing benefit, income support, an income-based job-seeker's allowance, disablement pension, war disablement pension.

4.22   DEDICATION OF ROADS AND SEWERS, ETC.

Where roads and sewers, etc. are dedicated to the local authority for no consideration under the Highways Act 1980, the Roads (Scotland) Act 1984, the Water Industries Act 1991 or the Sewerage (Scotland) Act 1968 then there is no supply for VAT purposes. Input tax incurred on the provisions of the roads, sewers, etc., is recoverable under the normal VAT rules, so that if the disposal of the development is by way of taxable supplies, then such input tax may be recovered in full.

4.23 COMMON AREAS OF ESTATES

Where a developer transfers the common areas of a private housing or industrial estate to a management company which will maintain them, then this is not a supply for VAT purposes if the transfer is effected for nominal consideration. (This includes roads, footpaths, communal parking and open space, etc.) Input tax incurred on the provision of such amenities is recoverable in accordance with the VAT treatment of the disposal of the site.

4.24 PLANNING GAIN AGREEMENTS

Where a developer agrees to provide goods or services (such as amenity land, community centres, etc.) free of charge, or for a nominal consideration, to the local authority under the Town and Country Planning Act 1980, s.106, there is no supply for VAT purposes. The VAT incurred on the provision of such goods or services is, however, recoverable in accordance with the liability of the disposal of the development upon which planning permission has been granted. Where a local authority is paid a sum of money under a s.106 agreement, such as for the future maintenance of land or buildings, this is not a supply for VAT purposes and is therefore outside the scope of VAT.

4.25 HIGHWAY AGENCY AGREEMENTS

Where a developer is required to undertake improvements to roads as a condition of carrying out a development, any VAT incurred is recoverable in accordance with the VAT treatment of the disposal of the development. For example, if the development is a housing estate, the houses of which will be sold as zero rated, then the input tax is fully recoverable.

However, if the developer is not permitted to carry out the works, and these are instead carried out by the Highways Agency, the costs being recovered from the developer, there is no supply and there will be no VAT chargeable by the Highways Agency. The costs will include irrecoverable VAT incurred by the Highways Agency, which is not recoverable by the developer because the supply was not made to them.

4.26 BUILDING SERVICES OUTSIDE THE UK

The place of supply of services for services relating to land, including construction and similar services, is treated as where the land is situated under VAT (Place of Supply of Services) Order 1992, SI 1992/3121, Art. 5. This includes the services of professionals such as estate agents, architects, surveyors, engineers and solicitors when they are directly involved with a specific piece of land, such as conveyancing in the case of solicitors.

Therefore, if the land to which the services are related is in the UK, the services will be subject to the UK VAT regime. If the land is situated in another member state it may be necessary for the supplier to register for VAT in that member state, although in certain cases where the recipient of the supply is registered for VAT it may be possible to avoid registration by use of the reverse charge mechanism depending upon the local rules in the member state concerned (see **1.2.3** and **Appendix E**).

4.27 DIY HOUSEBUILDERS/HOUSE-CONVERTERS

Where an individual or other non-registered person, such as a village hall committee, carries out or organises works which result in the construction of a new dwelling, a new building for relevant residential or relevant charitable use, then they may make a claim for a refund of VAT on the building materials used to carry out the works.

A claim can also be made in the case of a conversion of a non-residential building (or part of a building) into a building designed as a dwelling or number of dwellings, intended solely for relevant residential use. Conversions into a building for relevant charitable use are not included in this relief.

In the case of *C & E Commrs* v. *Lady Blom-Cooper* [2003] STC 669, the Court of Appeal held that VATA 1994, Sched. 8, Gp. 5, Note 9 (the need to create an additional dwelling) applies to VATA 1994, s.35 or s.35A (DIY claims). The case concerned the conversion of a public house to a single dwelling, where the first floor included self-contained living accommodation for the landlord. The part which contained the non-residential elements – the bar and cellar – did not therefore qualify as a non-residential conversion, because there was no additional dwelling created.

However, in the decision in *Jacobs (Ivor)* v. *C & E Commrs* [2005] EWCA Civ 930, the taxpayer had converted a former residential school for boys, comprising classrooms, boarding accommodation, staff bed-sits and a head-master's flat (determined by the court as only one 'dwelling') into one large dwelling for his own occupation plus three flats. None of the four 'dwellings' had been created exclusively from the non-residential part of the school and HMRC refused his DIY housebuilder's claim. The Court of Appeal upheld the High Court's decision that the taxpayer was entitled to recover the VAT incurred on converting the non-residential parts into dwellings. As a result of this decision, HMRC issued *Business Brief 22/05* in which it set out its revised policy, that for the purposes of the DIY scheme only, it is no longer necessary for the additional dwelling to be created exclusively from the non-residential part of the existing building, just that an additional dwelling must be created as a result of the works.

Zero rating will of course apply to the construction of a new dwelling or a relevant residential or charitable building, together with any goods supplied with those services. Therefore, for new build houses, etc., the claim is limited to VAT incurred on the separate purchase of building materials used in the course of construction, whereas for conversions from non-residential buildings the 5 per cent rate will apply and can be included in the claim. It should be noted that professional fees, such as architects and surveyors, are not included in the scheme, and neither can the hire of plant or scaffolding be claimed. 'Design and build' contracts can therefore save VAT in such situations, as can ensuring the builder supplies all plant and scaffolding required, rather than hiring it in separately.

There are conditions which ensure that the work must have been carried out on a lawful basis, and the restrictions which apply to the zero rating for construction of a new dwelling (see **4.4.1**) apply to DIY housebuilders as well, so that claims may not include, for example, white goods such as cookers, washing machines, etc.

In the Tribunal case of *Mr and Mrs Watson* (No. 18675) there was a question as to whether the appellants were eligible for the DIY scheme or whether they were in business. They had originally intended to occupy the barn they converted and let out their existing farmhouse, but the conversion costs were greater than expected and they therefore decided to let the properties for a few years to finance the conversion. The tribunal determined that the time at which the intention of the taxpayer was to be determined was at completion, and they were therefore ineligible for the DIY scheme.

4.27.1 How to make a claim

A claim pack is available from local VAT offices, or may be downloaded from the HMRC website at **www.hmrc.gov.uk**, together with *Notice 719, VAT Refunds for 'Do-It-Yourself' Builders and Converters* which sets out the conditions applying to the scheme. As well as a separate list of VAT inclusive and VAT exclusive invoices (and the original invoices), a list of the quantities of materials used is also required (presumably used to check that the quantity used is credible).

It should be noted that some of the quantities required on the forms are no longer in general use by builder's materials suppliers. The reason for this requirement is so that HMRC can check that the quantity purchased is reasonable for the size of property constructed, and modern quantities are therefore acceptable.

Claims should be made within three months of the date of practical completion of the building, although depending upon the circumstances, longer may be allowed. If a claim is going to take longer than the three months, a letter should be sent to the local VAT office explaining why and requesting more time. In the tribunal decision in *Geoffrey Martin Morris* (No 17860), the taxpayer contracted with a builder to build a bungalow for him. But when all the work except building of paths and a patio had been completed, he decided that the builder's quote for the work was too high and that he would do the work himself. He requested a certificate of completion from the local authority in order that the builder could be removed from the site, and then took some 15 months to complete the patio and paths. He then put in his DIY claim which HMRC rejected as being out of time. The tribunal noted that para. 3.9 of *VAT Notice 719* states that completion occurs when the certificate of completion is issued by the local authority and that the VAT Regulations 1995, reg. 201, prescribes that a claim must be made within three months of completion. The appeal by the taxpayer was therefore dismissed.

In cases where a builder builds a house for his own occupation, HMRC, by concession, allows this to be treated as a zero-rated supply to himself, rather than requiring that the DIY scheme be used to make a claim, providing he has already built houses for sale to third parties. However, where the house for own occupation is the only house built, this is a non-business activity and the DIY scheme applies.

All claims are processed by H M Revenue & Customs, 2 Broadway, Broad Street, Five Ways, Birmingham, West Midlands B15 1BG, telephone 0121 697 4000, fax 0121 697 4002. General enquiries about the scheme should be directed to the National Advice Service, telephone 0845 010 9000.

4.28 CONSTRUCTION SERVICES CARRIED OUT FOR DISABLED PERSONS

As well as the zero-rated construction services to be found in VATA 1994, Shed. 8, Gp. 5, for new buildings, there are additional zero rates available for certain building services carried out on a disabled person's domestic accommodation, contained in VATA 1994, Sched. 8, Gp. 12. These include:

1. The supply to a handicapped person for domestic or his personal use of:

    (a) chair lifts or stair lifts designed for use in connection with invalid wheelchairs (Item 2(d));

    (b) hoists and lifters designed for use by invalids (Item 2(e));

    (c) equipment and appliances not included in Items 2(a)–(f) designed solely for use by a handicapped person;

169

(d) services necessarily performed in the installation of equipment or appliances (including parts and accessories therefore) specified in Item 2 and supplied as described in that Item (Item 7).

As well as the sale of the above goods to handicapped persons, the letting on hire of such goods is also zero rated.

2. The supply to a handicapped person of a service of constructing ramps or widening doorways or passages for the purpose of facilitating his entry of movement within his private residence (Item 8).

3. The supply to a handicapped person of providing, extending or adapting a bathroom, washroom or lavatory in his private residence, where such provision, extension or adaptation is necessary by reason of his condition (Item 10). This relief includes the supply of goods in connection with the qualifying supply of services (Item 13).

4. The supply to a handicapped person of services necessarily performed in the installation of a lift for the purpose of facilitating his movement between floors of his private residence (Item 16).

5. The supply to a handicapped person for domestic or his personal use, or to a charity for making available to handicapped persons by sale or otherwise for domestic or their personal use, of an alarm system designed to be capable of operation by a handicapped person, and to enable him to alert directly a specified person or a control centre (Item 19).

For the purpose of these zero rates, a 'handicapped person' means a person who is chronically sick or disabled, due, for example, to ill health or old age.

In order to take advantage of the zero rates it is necessary for the handicapped person to provide a certificate to the supplier. Draft certificates can be found in *Notice 701/7, Reliefs for People with Disabilities* (available from the HMRC website at **www.hmrc.gov.uk**).

Although there are many building works which may be deserving of zero rating, being specifically for the benefit of disabled persons, the tribunal decision in *Vassal Centre Trust* (No. 17891) demonstrates that, in order for zero rating to apply, the building work must fall specifically within the definitions set out in the legislation. In that case, although colour-coded tapping rails on footpaths, installed for the blind and partially sighted were held to be 'designed solely for use by handicapped persons and for the personal use of handicapped persons (Item 2(g)), the following works did not qualify for zero rating:

*   a front gate with special controls for visual and audible warnings could not be considered to be 'ramps' or 'widening of doorways or passages';
*   colour-contrasted raised cobble bases for columns were not 'goods' within Item 4;

- colouring of paving near the entrance as the paving was not 'goods' within Item 4;
- different coloured strips at the side of internal carpeting denoted walkways and entrances, but these did not come within Item 2 and were not designed solely for use by a handicapped person;
- beading added to the edge of a stage to stop people falling off;
- low surface-temperature radiators were zero rated when fitted as part of a washroom or lavatory adaptation under Item 12, but not elsewhere;
- adaptations to the food preparation area were not designed solely for use by handicapped persons;
- electrical paddle switches, whilst easier for a disabled person to use, were not solely designed for use by handicapped persons;
- glass vision panels on doors would be used by everyone and could not therefore be said to be designed solely for use by handicapped persons;
- car park identification notices could not be fitted into any of the paragraphs of Item 2.

In addition to the above works, HMRC allows, by extra-statutory concession, that works to restore a room which has been subject to any of the above works can also be zero rated. This extra-statutory concession can be found in *VAT Notice 701/7*, para. 6.5:

> Where economy and feasibility dictate that you have constructed or extended in the course of a zero-rated supply, and have occupied space which was previously part of another room then you may also zero rate the service of restoring that room elsewhere in the building to its original size. This is because the work is essential to providing the service to your disabled customer.
>
> Where you provide, extend or adapt a bathroom, washroom or lavatory and, at the same time, construct additional accommodation then you should apportion the supply between its zero-rated and standard-rated parts.

The application of this extra-statutory concession was reviewed in *Lady Nuffield Home* (No. 19123), where HMRC refused to apply it to the new construction of a corridor outside the original external walls where the disabled facilities had been extended into the existing corridor.

There is no specific relief from VAT for alterations carried out in commercial buildings for the purposes of the Disability Discrimination Act 1995.

4.29   FIRST TIME CONNECTION TO MAINS GAS OR ELECTRICITY

As an extra-statutory concession (See *VAT Notice 48*, section 3.16 reproduced below) the first time connection of gas or electricity to a dwelling, relevant residential or relevant charitable building, including houseboats and residential caravans, is zero rated:

3.16   VAT: Connection to the gas or electricity mains supply

Connection to the gas or electricity mains supply, which would have been zero-rated supply before 1 April 1994 by virtue of Group 7 of Schedule 5 to the Value Added Tax [Act] 1983, may continue to be treated as a zero-rated supply provided that:

(a)   It is the first connection to the gas or electricity mains supply (as the case may be) of:

- a building, or part of a building, which consists of a dwelling or number of dwellings;
- a building, or part of a building used soley for a relevant residential purpose (within the meaning of Note 4 to Group 7);
- a building, or part of a building, used by a charity otherwise than in the course or furtherance of a business;
- a residential caravan (that is to say a caravan on a site in respect of which there is no covenant, statutory planning consent or similar permission precluding occupation throughout the year); or
- a houseboat (within the meaning of Group 6 to Note 7); and

(b)   the person receiving the supply does not do so for the purpose of any business carried on by him.

CHAPTER 5

Charitable use property

5.1 INTRODUCTION

The VAT treatment of property used by charities can be extremely complex as it will encompass commercial property (see **Chapter 2**), residential property (see **Chapter 3**) and protected buildings (see **Chapter 6**). There are additional VAT reliefs which can also apply for the construction and sale of new charity buildings which are used for non-business purposes (see **5.2**) including the construction of an annexe (see **5.3**), together with reliefs for certain building works for the benefit of disabled persons (see **5.6**). This chapter is concerned only with those reliefs specifically aimed at charity buildings.

5.2 NEW RELEVANT CHARITABLE USE PROPERTY

The first grant of a major interest (freehold sale or lease of over 21 years) by the person constructing a relevant charitable use property is zero rated for VAT (VATA 1994, Sched. 8, Gp. 5, Item 1(a)(ii)), as is a supply in the course of construction of a building intended for use solely for a 'relevant charitable purpose' (VATA 1994, Sched. 8, Gp. 5, Item 2(a)) provided that the supply is to the person who will use the building for a qualifying purpose and that person provides a certificate that the building will be used for such purposes to the person who directly makes the supply to him.

In respect of construction services, the construction must be of a qualifying charitable use building (see **5.2** and **5.3**) in order to qualify for zero rating, and once again the supply must be directly to a person who will use the building for qualifying purposes, supported by a certificate to that effect. Building materials also qualify for zero rating in the same way as for dwellings and relevant residential buildings (see **Chapter 4**), except that there are additional items of 'building materials' which are accepted by HMRC as qualifying for zero rating (see **5.2.5**).

There is provision for apportionment in cases where part of a building is to be used for qualifying purposes and part is not (VATA 1994, Sched. 8,

Gp. 5, Note 10). Such apportionment must be on a fair and reasonable basis, usually using a floor area based method unless there are specialist requirements in the charitable use building which may make a value basis more attractive.

5.2.1 Definition of 'relevant charitable purpose'

There are two headings under which a building may qualify as being for a 'relevant charitable purpose' (VATA 1994, Sched. 8, Gp. 5, Note 6):

(a) use by a charity otherwise than in the course or furtherance of a business;
(b) use by a charity as a village hall or similarly in providing social or recreational facilities for a local community.

5.2.2 Use by a charity otherwise than in the course or furtherance of a business

This includes all non-business buildings such as, for example, a hospice where services are provided free of charge. If a charge is made for letting the building, or for the provision of facilities, etc., from the building (e.g a hospice where residents are charged for their care) this is a business purpose and the zero rate will not apply (see *C & E Commrs* v. *Morrison's Academy Boarding Houses Association* [1978] STC 1). It is important to appreciate that not all charities will benefit from this legislation as many engage in 'business activities', for example charity shops, private schools, etc.

The tests for whether an activity should be considered 'business' were set down in the early case of *C & E Commrs* v. *Lord Fisher* [1981] STC 238, QBD:

1. Is the activity a serious undertaking earnestly pursued or a serious occupation not necessarily confined to commercial or profit-making undertakings?
2. Is the activity an occupational function which is actively pursued with recognisable or reasonable continuity?
3. Does the activity have a measure of substance to the extent that such measure could be shown in VAT returns?
4. Is the activity conducted in a regular manner and on sound and recognised business principles?
5. Is the activity predominantly concerned with making taxable supplies for a consideration?
6. Are the taxable supplies of a kind which, subject to differences of detail, are commonly made by those who seek to profit by them?

HMRC accepts up to 10 per cent business use as being incidental and therefore zero rating may still apply (see Extra-Statutory Concession 3.29 in *VAT*

Notice 48, Extra-Statutory Concessions). This would allow zero rating in a situation where, for example, a school or college which has at least 90 per cent non-fee paying students, but accepted up to 10 per cent fee-paying students, is having new classrooms, etc., constructed. The 'use' may be calculated in any reasonable way using, for example, time available for use or floor area. In *Business Brief 08/00* HMRC states that the use can be calculated by the time it is available for use, the floor area or the number of people using it.

Recently, the courts have determined that where a charge is made by a charity, provided it is at a discretionary rate and the services are supplied to the socially deprived, or where the activities are wholly funded from government funds, this remains non-business. Case law in this area includes the following.

Yarburgh Children's Trust v. *C & E Commrs* [2002] STC 207, ChD. In this case the High Court ruled that the supplies to the trustees of construction of a day nursery qualified for zero rating in circumstances where the Trust allowed the building to be used by the day nursery operators, an associated Trust, on the basis that in this case the letting was not concerned with the 'exploitation' of property (Sixth Directive on VAT, Art. 4(2)). The playschool was not profit-led and struggled to maintain a balance between remaining affordable and meeting its costs, and the fees charged were fixed on that basis. The court determined that there was no business use of the premises. HMRC issued a Business Brief effectively not accepting the decision and it required the *St Paul's* decision below before it would do so.

St Paul's Community Project Ltd v. *C & E Commrs* [2004] EWHC 2490, ChD. The circumstances were very similar to those of *Yarburgh* above. Nevertheless, the Commissioners appealed to the High Court having again lost the case at tribunal. The Court determined that the services supplied by the nursery were supplied at discretionary prices to a deprived area of the city and, as such, could not be considered to be 'business' (see also *Business Brief 02/05*). HMRC is aggressive in seeking to limit the application of these decisions to circumstances where the services are supplied to a deprived area at prices lower than those set by other local commercial children's nurseries, and may require evidence of pricing to be supplied.

Donaldson's College (No. 19258). The tribunal considered that the College was a non-business charitable organisation, being funded wholly from government sources and for all practical purposes controlled by central government. The College was predominantly concerned with providing a service which was required to be provided by the state (provision of education to deaf and partially hearing children and children with communication difficulties) and the tribunal found that it was not a commercial concern and as such receives no 'consideration', and was not in business.

5.2.3 Use by a charity as a village hall or similar

Under this heading, the use of the building may be charged for at commercial rates without loss of zero rating, such as lettings to scout or guide groups and other groups within the local community. The main beneficiaries are church buildings, most church halls, village halls and community centres. It is important that the services available are for the 'local' rather than for a wider community.

Decisions in this area include the following.

Jubilee Hall Recreation Centre Ltd v. *C & E Commrs* [1999] STC 381. The taxpayer, a registered charity, had lost the decision at tribunal and had won at High Court, with HMRC now appealing to the Court of Appeal. The hall at Covent Garden was run on a commercial basis but the High Court had ruled that the construction qualified for zero rating because the final consumer of the supplies was the local community (VATA 1994, Sched. 8, Gp. 5, Note 6(b)). The Court of Appeal ruled that it was doubtful that the phrase 'local community' could be extended to cover the area envisaged by the appellant – W1, SW1, WC1 and EC4, and that the 'local community' intended by the legislation did not extend to the daily influx of visiting tourists and workers to the area. It ruled that the tribunal was correct in its finding that the use was not similar to a village hall in providing social or recreational facilities to the local community. Similar decisions have been reached in *Southwick Community Association* (No. 16441) and *South Molton Swimming Pool Trustees* (No. 16495).

St Dunstan's Educational Foundation v. *C & E Commrs* [1999] STC 381, CA. This case was heard jointly with the *Jubilee* case above. The appellant is a registered charity owning land and buildings in Lewisham, which were to be used for the purposes of a school free of charge. It constructed a sports hall and swimming pool which was part funded by the National Lottery on the condition that there was 'community use' – use by the community based upon recommendation by the local authority. The hire charges to recommended groups were retained by the school to offset running costs. The Commissioners would not allow zero rating but the Foundation appealed claiming that, insofar as the hall was made available by the charity for no charge, this was 'otherwise than in the course or furtherance of a business' (VATA 1994, Sched. 8, Gp. 5, Note 6(a)). The tribunal rejected that submission on the basis that the charity did not 'use' the hall but simply made it available for use by a third person, the school, but it did accept that it fell under VATA 1994, Sched. 8, Gp. 5, Note 6(b) as a 'village hall or similarly . . .'. The Commissioners appealed directly to the Court of Appeal. The Court of Appeal confirmed that the appellant did not itself 'use' the premises. The school was a fee-paying school and this was not use 'otherwise than in the course or furtherance of a business'. The pupils were not a 'local community' despite the majority being drawn from the local area. The primary purpose of the buildings was use as one of the facilities of a fee-paying school and the Court therefore allowed the Commissioners' appeal.

Ledbury Amateur Dramatic Society (No. 16845). The Society was a members' club and registered charity, and in 1999 constructed the building on land purchased from church trustees at below market value on the basis that it was to provide a community theatre for the town. Finance was substantially from Malvern Hills District Council on terms which included a community benefit agreement and the charges for use or hire of the premises were subject to the approval of the council. The building was run on a voluntary basis by members of the Society. HMRC argued that the building did not qualify for zero rating because it was owned and run by a particular charity which only catered for the social and recreational needs of a limited section of the community, and the supplies were not made to the final consumer as provided for under European legislation. The tribunal decided that the premises had been designed so that the theatre could also be used for other purposes. The supplies were made to the appellant's trustees, rather than the final consumer, but the trustees acted in accordance with the agreement with the council to provide a benefit to the community, and anyone in the community was eligible to be a trustee. The building was therefore similar to a village hall in many respects and the appeal was allowed.

London Federation of Clubs for Young People (No. 17079). In this case a sports centre and swimming pool were ruled not to be similar to a village hall, as it appeared to have a business use, the community would require transport to the premises in view of its location, and the main use of the premises was for children to attend courses run by the appellant. A similar decision was reached in *Beth Johnson Housing Association Ltd* (No. 17095), in respect of a new day centre annexe to a residential care home, on the grounds that the local community was not the final consumer – it was available to the wider community and the day centre was run as a business.

Southwick Community Association (No. 17601). The tribunal had held that a new wing to a community building did not qualify for zero rating (see *Southwick Community Association* (No. 16441)). Southwick appealed the decision to the High Court which determined that the appeal should be remitted for re-hearing by a different tribunal. The Commissioners accepted that the new wing was capable of functioning independently, and the tribunal found that the fact that some members of the Association lived more than six miles away did not prevent the building being regarded as facilities for the local community. Other uses of the new wing (letting to a non-business theatre group for a rent which was limited to an amount to cover overheads)

177

were also non-business, and although the new wing was part of a larger community complex it was used similarly in providing social and recreational facilities to the local community and the tribunal allowed the appeal.

5.2.4 Summary of the case law

- For a 'village hall or similarly' it must be the 'local community' rather than a wider community that the social and recreational facilities are provided for.
- Allowing a third party to use the building without charge does not qualify as 'use otherwise than in the course or furtherance of a business' – it would then be the third party's use that would be considered.
- Use by way of letting is not 'use otherwise than in the course or furtherance of a business'.
- Where charges are made for facilities (e.g. a children's day nursery) this may still qualify as 'use otherwise than in the course or furtherance of a business', providing that the services are supplied to deprived areas at discretionary prices, or an amount to cover costs only. The *St Paul's* decision may have wider ramifications for charities providing other services in similar circumstances.

As for dwellings and other residential property, the provisions do not cover extensions to existing buildings, other than certain approved alterations to listed buildings, but see **5.3** regarding charity annexes. It is not necessary for the 'charity' in question to be a registered charity and the zero rating is allowed widely to non-profit-making organisations.

5.2.5 Building materials

Building materials supplied in conjunction with qualifying services are also zero rated, the same rules applying as for dwellings (see **4.5**).

VAT Notice 708, Buildings and Construction, Appendix E, lists examples of additional items which can be zero rated when incorporated in new relevant charitable buildings:

- General: lighting systems, blinds and shutters, and mirrors.
- Schools: blackboards fixed to or forming part of the walls, gymnasium wall bars, name boards, notice and display boards, and mirrors and barres (in ballet schools).
- Churches: altars, church bells, organs, fonts, lecterns, pulpits, amplification equipment, humidifying plant.

5.3 CHARITABLE ANNEXES

The construction of an annexe (rather than the extension or enlargement of an existing building) for use for a relevant charitable purpose qualifies for zero rating, providing that it is capable of functioning as an independent building and the main access to the annexe is not through the existing building, and the main access to the existing building is not through the annexe (VATA 1994, Sched. 8, Gp. 5, Note 16).

There is no definition provided in the legislation as to what qualifies as an 'annexe', rather than as an extension or enlargement of an existing building, and the ordinary meaning of the word therefore applies. An annexe is a subsidiary building for use in conjunction with a main building, rather than an enlargement or extension of the main building. An annexe would also be expected to have only a limited degree of integration with the main building.

In *Cantrell & Cantrell (t/a Foxearth Lodge Nursing Home)* v. *C & E Commrs* [2003] EWHC 404, ChD, the High Court determined that: 'an "annexe" is an adjunct or accessory to something else and in relation to a building refers to a supplementary structure, be it a room, a wing or a separate building'. In applying the test the High Court stated: 'regard must be had to the physical character of the buildings in course of construction at the date of the relevant supply and that the subjective intentions on the part of the appellants as to their future use are irrelevant, save only in so far as they throw light upon the potential use and functioning of the buildings'.

The High Court has also provided the following guidelines:

(a) the words used in Note 16 are not terms of art;
(b) in applying them it is necessary to adopt a two-stage approach, first identify the existing buildings as they were before the construction work began and, secondly, determine whether the new construction satisfies all or any of the terms in Note 16;
(c) cases decided on the provisions in force before 1 March 1995 are of doubtful help (because of the changes in the relevant legislation from this date);
(d) whether the construction works fall within Note 16 is a question of fact and degree as held in *C & E Commrs* v. *London Diocesan Fund* [1993] STC 369, QBD and *C & E Commrs* v. *Marchday Holdings Ltd* [1997] STC 272, CA;
(e) terms used in the grant of planning permission are not determinative of the nature of the works permitted by the VAT legislation.

Examples of case law in this area include the following.

Colchester Sixth Form College (No. 16252). This concerned the construction of new teaching and communal areas in a gap between the existing buildings. The new structure was bounded on three sides by existing buildings. The

179

point at issue was whether the new structure was an extension or enlargement of the existing buildings, in which case it was standard rated, or if it was an annexe in which case it would be zero rated. There were independent water and heating systems but there was internal access via the old buildings. The tribunal decided that it had to consider the existing buildings before the work was started and then decide whether the work amounted to enlargement, extension or annexe of the existing building. It decided that it was not an enlargement because the size and capacity of the existing buildings was unchanged. The new works provided an additional section to the college buildings and, given the degree of integration of the new structure and its facilities with the old, it concluded that the new structure was an extension. It was too closely integrated with the existing buildings to be considered an annexe.

Grace Baptist Church (No. 16093). In this case the church buildings comprised the original church, built in 1876 as a worship area, a chapel house providing caretaker's accommodation, a church hall, a kitchen and store/boiler room linking the church and the hall, toilet accommodation and a timber-framed building used for youth work. The chapel house was contained within the same building shell as the church. Planning permission was gained for the construction of an extension on the site of the chapel house, which was demolished and a new building constructed filling the site and a former gap between the chapel house and the boundary. HMRC ruled this was an enlargement or extension of the existing buildings, so that zero rating did not apply. The church claimed it as an annexe. The tribunal found that an annexe is a subsidiary building linked to an existing building and to be zero rated it must be capable of operating independently. It considered that the legislation worked as a sieve – if the effect of the new work was to make the existing building larger, it must be an enlargement or an extension, but it was then necessary to consider whether it constituted an annexe. The key issue was the degree of integration with the existing buildings. The tribunal found that the new building was a supplementary building connected to a larger one and was therefore an annexe. It was capable of operating independently and was not for the same use as the church, the existing buildings had their own access, not via the other.

Bryan Thomas Macnamara (No. 16039). This case concerned a free-standing structure, comprising new teaching areas, built in a gap in the existing class-room building. The main access to the new structure was by a door leading into the playground, but the first-floor science laboratories could be reached by internal access from existing science facilities. It was accepted that the internal access prevented the zero rating of the upper floor of the building, but the ground floor was capable of operating separately and its access was not through the existing building. The tribunal considered that in view of the

180

degree of integration with the existing buildings the concept that it was an annexe was tenuous. None of the existing buildings were enlarged, the new work provided an additional section of the school. It was, however, designed as additional teaching space and was not wholly capable of functioning independently. It was therefore an extension and zero rating did not apply.

Wright & Fuller Ltd (No. 15952). The existing site comprised a complex of five buildings used as a nursing home for the elderly. The home provided accommodation for patients requiring 24-hour medical care and for those with severe dementia and it was required by the local authority that each category of patient be housed separately. The works comprised construction of a single story unit to provide accommodation for those patients with severe dementia and was linked to the existing buildings by a corridor. Planning permission described it as an extension but it was designed to be able to operate independently, having its own kitchen, lounge, dining room and laundry, a separate entrance and reception area, separate electricity and water supplies and a separate sewage system. There was only one access door to the existing buildings which could not be used by patients except as an emergency fire door. The tribunal rejected the view that the term 'existing building' in the legislation had to be constricted to one building where a complex was being considered. The result of the work was to link five buildings to form one building or two connected buildings. The tribunal considered that the new building was not separate in every way from the existing ones – it might house patients who were segregated from other patients within the home, but they were still patients of the nursing home. The planning permission made it clear that it was to be used as part of the nursing home and concluded that it was an enlargement and therefore standard rated – it had added to more than one of the existing buildings in the complex and was to be used in conjunction with them as an integral part of the nursing home – an annexe was the least appropriate description.

Torfaen Voluntary Alliance (No. 18797). In this case the new works were held to be an annexe. The new building shared a wall with the existing building but otherwise complied with VATA 1994, Sched. 8, Gp. 5, Note 16(c). The walls of the existing church hall were cream, whereas the new building was brick. The roof continued unbroken onto the new building which comprised offices, kitchen and toilets. The tribunal commented in determining that the works comprised an annexe that:

> Financial and planning constraints would require some form of linking and integration between the buildings in order to create a harmony of appearance but the new building, while connected to the existing building, is not an enlargement (increase in size of an existing building) or an extension (an additional wing or section of an existing building) but an annexe (a supplementary building).

Tests for zero rating of an annexe

1. The degree of integration is the key test – an 'annexe will only be loosely or tenuously integrated with the existing building'.
2. The tribunal must start with what was there before work commenced and then consider what was done.
3. The legislation acts as a sieve, and if the effect of the new work was to make the existing building larger, it must be an enlargement or an extension.
4. Access to the annexe must not be through the existing building and vice versa.
5. For zero rating to apply it must be capable of operating independently – utilities, etc.
6. Terms used in the grant of planning permission are not determinative of the nature of the works permitted by the VAT legislation.

5.4 BUILDINGS CONVERTED FROM NON-RESIDENTIAL

The zero rate available, since 21 July 1994 by concession, and from 1 March 1995 on a statutory basis, for the first grant of a major interest in a non-residential building converted into a dwelling or a relevant residential building, for example a barn conversion (VATA 1994, Sched. 8, Gp. 5, Item 1(b)), does not apply to relevant charitable buildings. However, in its *News Release 13/96* HMRC announced that it would consider refunds to charities which were unable to take advantage of this relief (usually on the basis that they could not sell the building and were ineligible to make a DIY claim). Full details should be sent in writing to:

VAT Construction Branch
H M Revenue & Customs
New King's Beam House
22 Upper Ground
London
SE1 9PJ

5.5 CHANGE OF USE OF A QUALIFYING BUILDING

Where a person who acquires a building or part of a building (whether by purchase, lease or construction) which qualifies for zero rating on relevant charitable grounds, then subsequently uses the building for non-qualifying purposes within 10 years from the date of completion, the legislation (VATA 1994, Sched. 10, para. 1) provides that a self-supply must be accounted for by that person. The value of the self-supply, with effect from 1 June 2002, is 10 per cent of the value of the zero-rated works for each year or part year left in the 10 years since completion, for which non-qualifying use will apply (i.e.

after one complete year of qualifying use only 90 per cent of the self-supply has to be repaid, after two years this reduces to 80 per cent and so on until after nine years only 10 per cent has to be repaid and after 10 years, no self-supply is required). Prior to 1 June 2002 the whole of the VAT benefit of the zero rating was clawed back by HMRC.

In the event that the property owner is not registered for VAT, the self-supply counts towards the registration limits and therefore if the value of the self-supply is over the registration limits in force, registration, if only to account for the self-supply, will be required.

The 10 per cent rule (see **5.2.2**) may also be applied so that minor non-qualifying use will not trigger the self-supply.

The self-supply is also recoverable as input tax if the non-qualifying use is wholly taxable, otherwise in accordance with the partial exemption rules (see **1.9**).

Note that the self-supply may be subject to the Capital Goods Scheme (see **1.10**).

Example

A charity purchases/constructs a new building for £1,000,000 to use for relevant charitable purposes, providing a certificate to the developer, but after five complete years of use for qualifying purposes, changes the use of the building in its entirety to offices for let (a business activity). The charity must account for the self-supply.

If the charity operating the care home had not provided the certificate, VAT of £175,000 would have been payable on the purchase price. As the charity has used the building for five complete years for qualifying purposes and there are five remaining complete or partly complete years, the self-supply is reduced by 50 per cent (£175,000 × 50% = £87,500) and the charity has to pay this amount to HMRC. If the charity is not VAT registered it would still have to account for VAT to HMRC and would be required to register for VAT to do so. The self-supply is declared in Box 1 of the VAT Return.

However, the output tax on the self-supply may then also be recovered as input tax in accordance with the partial exemption rules. If the charity opts to tax and charges VAT on the rent it would be able to recover this VAT on the self-supply in full.

In the event that the building is sold to a person who will not use it for qualifying purposes, then VAT at standard rate must be charged. If the purchaser will continue to use the property for qualifying purposes, then the transaction may qualify as a transfer of a going concern (see **2.15**). If not, the sale will be zero rated if this is the first grant of a major interest and the purchaser provides the requisite certificate, or if it is not the first grant of a major interest the supply will be exempt from VAT.

5.6 CONSTRUCTION SERVICES CARRIED OUT FOR THE BENEFIT OF DISABLED PERSONS

As well as the zero-rated construction services to be found in VATA 1994, Sched. 8, Gp. 5, for new relevant charitable use buildings, there are additional zero rates available for certain building services carried out on charity buildings for the benefit of disabled persons, contained in Gp. 12 of the Schedule.

These include:

1. The supply to a charity for making available to a handicapped person by sale or otherwise, for domestic or their personal use, of:

    (a) Chair lifts or stair lifts designed for use in connection with invalid wheelchairs (VATA 1994, Sched. 8, Gp. 12, Item 2(d)).

    (b) Hoists and lifters designed for use by invalids (VATA 1994, Sched. 8, Gp. 12, Item 2(e)).

    (c) Equipment and appliances not included in Items 2(a)–(f) designed solely for use by a handicapped person (VATA 1994, Sched. 8, Gp. 12, Item 2(g)).

    (d) Installation of qualifying equipment. The supply to a handicapped person or to a charity of services necessarily performed in the installation of equipment or appliances (including parts and accessories therefore) specified in Item 2 and supplied as described in that item (VATA 1994, Sched. 8, Gp. 12, Item 7).

    As well as the sale of the above goods to charities, the letting on hire of such goods is also zero rated (VATA 1994, Sched. 8, Gp. 12, Note 5).

2. Ramps, widening doorways etc. The supply to a charity of a service of constructing ramps or widening doorways or passages for the purpose of facilitating a handicapped person's entry to or movement within any building (VATA 1994, Sched. 8, Gp. 12, Item 9).

3. Bathrooms, washrooms or lavatories (VATA 1994, Sched. 8, Gp. 12, Item 11). The supply to a charity of providing, extending or adapting a bathroom, washroom or lavatory for use by handicapped persons, where such provision, extension or adaptation is necessary by reason of the handicapped person's condition in:

    (a) residential accommodation (a residential home or other self-contained living accommodation provided as a permanent or temporary residence for handicapped persons, but not including accommodation in an inn, hotel, boarding house or similar establishment); or

    (b) a day centre where at least 20 per cent of the individuals using the centre are handicapped persons; or

    (c) another building used principally by a charity for charitable purposes.

184

A 'washroom' is defined as a room containing a lavatory or a washbasin or both but which does not contain a bath or shower or cooking, sleeping or laundry facilities (VATA 1994, Sched. 8, Gp. 12, Note 5K).

This relief includes the supply of goods in connection with the qualifying supply of services (VATA 1994, Sched. 8, Gp. 12, Note 5).

4. Lifts (VATA 1994, Sched. 8, Gp. 12, Item 17). The supply to a charity of services necessarily performed in the installation of a lift for the purpose of facilitating a handicapped person's movement between floors of a temporary or permanent residence or day centre for handicapped persons. This relief includes the supply of goods in connection with the qualifying supply of services.

Following a decision of the High Court in *C & E Commrs* v. *Help the Aged* [1997] STC 406, HMRC reviewed its policy on the installation of lifts to educational institutions which have charitable status, and allowed zero rating on the basis that these could be considered to be 'day-centres'. However, it has now reconsidered this and have reverted to its previous policy that such establishments can only qualify for zero rating for the installation of a lift where it is installed in residential accommodation. Under transitional arrangements, HMRC allows that any contract for the installation of a lift in such an establishment where the contract was entered into before 1 March 2005 retains zero-rated status (provided the other conditions are met) and this also applies to the ongoing maintenance and repair of the lift (see *Business Brief 03/05*).

5. Alarms and control centres (VATA 1994, Sched. 8, Gp. 12, Item 19). The supply to a charity for making available to handicapped persons by sale or otherwise for domestic or their personal use, of an alarm system designed to be capable of operation by a handicapped person, and to enable him to alert directly a specified person or a control centre.

6. The supply of services necessarily performed by a control centre in receiving and responding to calls from an alarm system specified at (5) above (VATA 1994, Sched. 8, Gp. 12, Item 20).

For the purpose of these zero rates, a 'handicapped person' means a person who is chronically sick or disabled, whether due to ill health or old age, for example.

In order to take advantage of the zero rates it is necessary for the charity to provide a certificate to the supplier. Draft certificates can be found in *VAT Notice 701/7, Reliefs for People with Disabilities* for individuals and in *VAT Notice 701/6, Charity Funded Equipment for Medical, Research, Veterinary etc. Uses* for charities (available from the HMRC website at **www.hmrc.gov.uk**).

Although there are many building works which may be deserving of zero rating, being specifically for the benefit of disabled persons, the tribunal decision in *Vassal Centre Trust* (No. 17891) demonstrates that in order for zero rating to apply, the building work must fall specifically within the definitions set out in the legislation. In that case, although colour-coded tapping rails on footpaths, installed for the blind and partially sighted were held to be 'designed solely for use by handicapped persons and for the personal use of handicapped persons' (VATA 1994, Sched. 8, Gp. 12, Item 2(g)) the following works did not qualify for zero rating:

- A front gate with special controls for visual and audible warnings could not be considered to be 'ramps' or 'widening of doorways or passages'.
- Colour-contrasted raised cobble bases for columns were not 'goods' within Item 4.
- Colouring of paving near the entrance as the paving was not 'goods' within Item 4.
- Different coloured strips at the side of internal carpeting denoted walkways and entrances, but these did not come within Item 2 and were not designed solely for use by a handicapped person.
- Beading added to the edge of a stage to stop people falling off was not 'goods' within Item 4.
- Low surface-temperature radiators were zero rated when fitted as part of a washroom or lavatory adaptation under Item 12, but not elsewhere.
- Adaptations to the food preparation area were not designed solely for use by handicapped persons.
- Electrical paddle switches, whilst easier for a disabled person to use, were not solely designed for use by handicapped persons.
- Glass vision panels on doors would be used by everyone and could not therefore be said to be designed solely for use by handicapped persons.
- Car park identification notices could not be fitted into any of the paragraphs of Item 2.

In addition to the above works, HMRC allows by extra-statutory concession, that works to restore a room which has been subject to any of the above works can also be zero rated. This extra-statutory concession can be found at *VAT Notice 701/7*, para.6.5:

> Where economy and feasibility dictate that you have constructed or extended in the course of a zero-rated supply, and have occupied space which was previously part of another room then you may also zero rate the service of restoring that room elsewhere in the building to its original size. This is because the work is essential to providing the service to your disabled customer.
>
> Where you provide, extend or adapt a bathroom, washroom or lavatory and, at the same time, construct additional accommodation then you should apportion the supply between its zero-rated and standard-rated parts.

The application of this extra-statutory concession was reviewed in *Lady Nuffield Home* (No. 19123), where HMRC refused to apply it to the new construction of a corridor outside the original external walls where the disabled facilities had been extended into the existing corridor.

There is no specific relief from VAT for alterations carried out in commercial buildings for the purposes of the Disability Discrimination Act 1995.

CHAPTER 6

Listed and other protected buildings

6.1 INTRODUCTION

Zero rating is available for the grant of a major interest in a 'substantially reconstructed protected building' and for 'approved alterations' to protected buildings. The latter relief may seem peculiar at first glance in that one might expect a relief to be available for the preservation of protected buildings (which is standard rated) rather than for their alteration, but the relief stems from the pre-1984 position when all alterations to buildings were zero rated. In 1984 the government introduced VAT at standard rate on alterations, but due to pressure by the heritage lobby, the relief was retained for protected buildings. The VAT (Protected Buildings) Order 1995, SI 1995/283 substituted a new VATA 1994, Sched. 8, Gp. 6 with effect from 1 March 1995.

6.2 DEFINITION OF A 'PROTECTED BUILDING'

A 'protected building' is defined in the legislation as:

a building which is designed to remain as or become a dwelling or number of dwellings [see 6.2.1] or is intended for use solely for a relevant residential purpose [see 3.3.1] or a relevant charitable purpose [see 5.2.1] after the reconstruction or alteration and which, in either case, is –

(a) a listed building, within the meaning of –

    (i) the Planning (Listed Buildings and Conservation Areas) Act 1990; or
    (ii) the Town and Country Planning (Scotland) Act 1972; or
    (iii) the Planning (Northern Ireland) Order 1991; or

(b) a scheduled monument, within the meaning of –

    (i) the Ancient Monuments and Archaeological Areas Act 1979; or
    (ii) the Historic Monuments Act (Northern Ireland) 1971.

Simply put, therefore, the building must be a Grade I or Grade II listed building (including Grade I* and Grade II*) or a scheduled monument in order to qualify for zero rating. This also includes a building which was constructed before 1 July 1948 (the date listed building control began in its present form) and which is regarded by the planning authority as being within the curtilage of a listed building. It does not include buildings which are within a conservation area but are not listed. In *McMillan & Anor* (No. 18536), the VAT tribunal confirmed that a direction under Art. 4(2) of the Town and Country Planning (General Permitted Development) Order 1995, SI 1995/418 did not amount to 'listing'.

In addition, by extra-statutory concession, any building which is subject to an immunity certificate issued on or before 16 April 1996 is included in this relief if the major interest is to be granted to a person for non-business charitable use. Immunity certificates are issued by the Secretary of State for Culture, Media and Sport and prevent the building being listed for a period of at least five years, thus allowing work to be done outside the constraints of the planning controls for listed buildings.

It does not matter whether the building is of a qualifying description prior to the works commencing, as long as it is within the definition of a dwelling or relevant residential or charitable use building once the work is completed.

6.2.1 Definition of a 'dwelling'

The following definition is found in VATA 1994, Sched. 8, Gp. 6, Note 2, and is similar to the definition for a new dwelling (see **3.2.1**):

> a building is designed to remain as or become a dwelling or number of dwellings where in relation to each dwelling the following conditions are satisfied –
>
> (a) the dwelling consists of self-contained living accommodation;
> (b) there is no provision for direct internal access from the dwelling to any other dwelling or part of a dwelling;
> (c) the separate use, or disposal of the dwelling is not prohibited by the terms of any covenant, statutory planning consent or similar provision,
>
> and includes a garage (occupied together with a dwelling) either constructed at the same time as the building or where the building has been substantially reconstructed at the same time as that reconstruction.

6.3 SUBSTANTIAL RECONSTRUCTION

The relevant legislation for the grant of a major interest in a substantially reconstructed protected building is at VATA 1994, Sched. 8, Gp. 6, Item 1. This confines the relief to the first grant of a major interest by the person substantially reconstructing the building, much in the same way as the grant of a major interest in a new dwelling is restricted to the first grant by the person constructing it (see **3.2**). 'Person reconstructing' includes the person owning the building or who orders/commissions its reconstruction.

There is no legal definition to what amounts to the 'substantial reconstruction' of a building. A two-stage approach is required by HMRC, and this is supported by the tribunal case of *Donald Barraclough* (No. 2529). Before applying the tests set out below (which go to deciding if the work is 'substantial' in nature) one must decide whether the building has been 'reconstructed'. As the legislation does not set out a definition of 'reconstructed' for these purposes, we must therefore turn to the ordinary meaning of the word. The dictionary defines 'reconstruction' as 'having been re-built, re-formed or re-constructed'. HMRC states that a good indication is if there is a radical change of use or a marked increase in the number of units of living accommodation due to the work being carried out.

Once the issue of 'reconstructed' has been decided, Note 4 to the Group does provide the following tests as to whether the building has been 'substantially' reconstructed:

(a)   that at least 60 per cent of the works carried out to effect the reconstruction, measured by reference to cost, qualify for zero rating as an 'approved alteration' or as building materials supplied in the course of an approved alteration;

(b)   that the reconstructed building incorporates no more of the original building (that is to say, the building as it was before the reconstruction began) than the external walls, together with other external features of architectural or historic interest.

In carrying out the first test, services excluded from zero rating such as those of an architect or engineer, or of landscaping, for example, which are always standard rated, must be excluded from the calculation of the 60 per cent. It should be emphasised that simply passing the 60 per cent test on its own does not make the works zero rated – it must be considered to have been 'reconstructed' in accordance with the ordinary definition of the word. In the case of *Southlong East Midlands Ltd* (No. 18943), the works of approved alterations clearly passed the 60 per cent test, but the tribunal determined that the work did not comprise 'reconstruction' and therefore zero rating did not apply.

In applying the test it is not necessary for the person constructing to have employed a VAT registered contractor so that the works are actually received as zero-rated services. It is sufficient that the works themselves would have qualified for zero rating if they had been carried out by a VAT registered person. Therefore, a developer carrying out the works using in-house labour is not prevented from taking advantage of the 'substantial reconstruction' zero rating upon disposal of the project, and thereby recovering VAT in full on the project.

In the case of *Lordsregal Ltd* (No. 18535), the tribunal considered the phrase 'in the course of' to be crucial to the way this test should be considered. Instead of looking at each item of expenditure and categorising it (as argued by HMRC), the tribunal determined that the correct approach was to consider why the expenditure was incurred from a broader perspective. It was therefore not necessary to consider whether each particular job was approved in writing by the planning authority for the purposes of determining whether zero rating applied but whether as a whole the work fell within the parameters of what the consent envisaged.

With regard to the second test, there is no requirement under the VAT legislation that listed building consent, etc., be obtained for the work, it is simply necessary that the building be gutted, with only the external walls and any other parts of architectural interest remaining.

Where a building has been fire damaged and is re-instated to look as it was before the damage was caused, the work is unlikely to qualify for zero rating as an alteration (see **6.4.2–6.4.23**) and the first test outlined above will therefore not be met. However, the grant of a major interest in the building could still qualify for zero rating if the second test is met, and it may therefore be possible to structure a lease of over 21 years or the freehold sale of the building into arrangements (bearing in mind the disclosure rules (see **1.12**) in order to secure recovery of the VAT incurred on the works (see also **1.13** with regard to avoidance of VAT).

6.3.1 Clearance from HMRC

It is often useful to obtain clearance from HMRC in order to avoid any arguments at a later date. Because the treatment as 'substantial reconstruction' often rests upon the 60 per cent rule, and such projects usually involve the repair and maintenance of the existing fabric of the building as well as alterations, it is useful to work from a costed schedule of works/bill of quantities in determining whether the 60 per cent test is passed. This can then be submitted to HMRC and the agreed percentage applied to interim payments, with the usual adjustment for differences which inevitably occur, or any additional work being costed separately at the end of the project.

In the event that the client is the listed building owner, it will probably be necessary to obtain authority from the builder to apply to HMRC on their behalf, because it is the supplier who is responsible for determining the correct VAT treatment.

An example of such an exercise, Whiteacre Hall, is set out below (summary of Bill of Quantities) which involved the conversion of a Grade II listed Hall and outbuildings into flats (the grant of a major interest in the non-residential outbuildings converted into dwellings also qualify for zero rating, as a separate matter (see **3.4**) and the building works to carry out the conversion of the outbuildings (non-residential) qualify for the reduced rate where the zero rate for approved alterations does not apply (see **4.6.2**)). The works of converting the Main Hall and Service Wing also qualify at 5 per cent as a changed number of dwellings conversion, where zero rating for 'approved alterations' does not apply (see **4.6.3**). The 'S/R Other' column is works that are standard rated and excluded from the calculation because, for example, they are not to the fabric of the main building, such as garden works, etc. Preliminary works and Provisionals are apportioned with final adjustment for the latter at the end of the contract.

The author has found that, by presenting the case in such a way to HMRC, agreement can be obtained for the proposed treatment, although in recent years HMRC has been increasingly uncooperative in assisting with such exercises. A covering letter would of course be sent giving further details of certain of the works. As can be seen, in this case, 82.7 per cent of the works were zero rated 'approved alterations' and because the buildings were 'reconstructed' and the 60 per cent test is passed for each part of the project, the disposal of the completed project qualified for zero rating, allowing the developer to recover the VAT charged on all of the standard-rated works carried out. As it is the grant of a major interest in the individual completed units which is zero rated, each unit must effectively qualify under the 60 per cent rule. During the course of the contract, 82.7 per cent of the works would be treated as zero rated, £389,163.91 will be treated as reduced rate, with 3.63 per cent being standard rated, with an adjustment at the end once the final figures are known.

Running down the spreadsheet, the first part is a summary of totals from the costed Bill of Quantities. The 'Calculation of apportionment %' section shows how the External Works, Drainage and Mechanical, Electrical and Lift are apportioned between the Main Hall, Service Wing and Stable Block. The next three sections show each of the parts of the project with the apportionments above being applied, and then Preliminaries and Provisionals are apportioned in accordance with the total of works to the fabric of the buildings, arriving at an overall percentage for each part of the project. The bottom part of the spreadsheet summarises each part of the project to arrive at the overall percentage for the project as a whole.

Of course, one must also take account of fitted wardrobes and other non-deductibles as necessary (see **4.5**).

6.4 APPROVED ALTERATIONS

A supply in the course of an 'approved alteration' to a Grade I or Grade II (including Grade I* and Grade II*) listed building or a scheduled monument, together with the incorporation of qualifying building materials into the building or its site qualifies for zero rating (VATA 1994, Sched. 8, Gp. 6, Items 2 and 3). Specifically excluded from the relief are the services of an architect, surveyor or any person acting as a consultant or in a supervisory capacity, in the same way as for construction of new dwellings and other

Whiteacre Hall – Bill Of Quantities

SUMMARY

	Repair	Alteration	Apportion	S/R Other	Total
Preliminaries			338,991.82		338,991.82
Main Hall	127,014.45	193,200.51		11,460.62	331,675.58
Service Wing	42,915.23	92,545.79		3,279.80	138,740.82
Stable Block (repairs at 5%)	83,172.78	290,442.49		8,974.02	382,589.29
External works	0.00	73,980.91		79,463.70	153,444.61
Drainage		53,921.39			53,921.39
Mechanical, Electrical and Lift		824,041.00			824,041.00
Provisional Sums			622,200.00		622,200.00
TOTAL	**253,102.46**	**1,528,132.09**	**961,191.82**	**103,178.14**	**2,845,604.51**

Total contract value as per Bill Summary					2,845,604.51

Calculation of apportionment %

Main Hall	127,014.45	193,200.51	320,214.96	[38.61%]	
Service Wing	42,915.23	92,545.79	135,461.02	[16.33%]	
Stable Block	83,172.78	290,442.49	373,615.27	[45.05%]	
Total value works to fabric of building	253,102.46	576,188.79	829,291.25	[100.00%]	

Main Hall	**127,014.45**	**193,200.51**			
Apportion External Works		28,566.31		[38.19% of 73,980.91]	
Apportion Drainage Works		20,820.71		[38.19% of 53,921.39]	
Lift		24,511.00		[100% of cost (part mechanical)]	
Other mechanical		308,723.22		[38.19% of Remainder mechanical]	
	127,014.45	575,821.76			
Apportion Preliminaries	23,654.99	107,240.22	130,895.21		
Apportion Provisional sums	43,417.37	196,833.26	240,250.63		
	194,086.81	879,895.25			1,073,982.05
Percentage repairs/alterations	**18.07%**	**81.93%**			

Service Wing	**42,915.23**	**92,545.79**		[16.33% of 73,980.91]	
Apportion External Works		12,084.45		[16.33% of 53,921.39]	
Apportion Drainage Works		8,807.82		[16.33% of Remainder mechanical]	
Other mechanical		130,599.65			
	42,915.23	244,037.71			
Apportion Preliminaries	8,281.28	47,091.52	55,372.80		
Apportion Provisional sums	15,199.81	86,433.78	101,633.59		
	66,396.32	377,563.01			443,959.33
	14.96%	**85.04%**			

Stable Block	**83,172.78**	**290,442.49**			
Apportion External Works		33,330.15		[45.05% of 73,980.91]	
Apportion Drainage Works		24,292.86		[45.05% of 53,921.39]	
Other mechanical		360,207.12		[45.05% or Remainder mechanical]	
	83,172.78	708,272.62			
Apportion Preliminaries	16,049.70	136,674.11	152,723.81		
Apportion Provisional sums	29,458.31	250,857.47	280,315.78		
	128,680.79	1,095,804.20		103,178.14	1,327,663.13

Totals			961,191.82		2,845,604.51
Main Hall	194,086.81	879,895.25			
Service Wing	66,396.32	377,563.01			
Stable Block (repairs at 5%)	128,680.79	1,095,804.20		103,178.14	
	389,163.92	2,353,262.46	0.00	103,178.14	2,845,604.51
Overall contract percentages	**13.68%**	**82.70%**		**3.63%**	

qualifying buildings. For building materials to qualify they must be supplied to the person receiving the supply of qualifying services in the course of carrying out those services – the separate purchase of materials or goods does not qualify for zero rating.

Works to garages physically attached to and for occupation in conjunction with a listed building also qualify for the relief, subject to the conditions below.

There is provision for apportionment of works. For example, although re-decoration is in itself a repair rather than an alteration, if it is necessary for making good where approved alterations have been carried out only, it too will qualify for zero rating. If the total works carried out comprise both approved alterations and repairs and maintenance then the re-decoration works should be apportioned between zero-rated approved alterations and standard-rated repairs or maintenance, usually based on the proportion of works directly qualifying as zero rated to total works.

The relief applies to:

(a)   A listed building within the meaning of:

- the Planning (Listed Buildings and Conservation Areas) Act 1960;
- the Town and Country Planning (Scotland) Act 1972;
- the Planning (Northern Ireland) Order 1991.

(b)   A scheduled monument, within the meaning of:

- the Ancient Monuments and Archaeological Areas Act 1979;
- the Historic Monuments and Archaeological Objects (Northern Ireland) Order 1995.

Essentially this means that the building must be either Grade I or Grade II (or Grade I* or Grade II*) listed or a scheduled monument. Unlisted buildings which are in conservation areas (usually buildings noted by the local authority as being of architectural or other interest) are not included in the relief. Buildings covered by immunity certificates do not qualify for zero rating under this heading, but see **6.3** regarding zero rating for 'substantial reconstruction'.

6.4.1   Qualification for relief

In order to qualify for the relief there are a number of conditions which must be met:

1.   The work must have required *and* received listed building consent under the appropriate legislation, in writing, prior to it being commenced (see *Dart Major Works Ltd* (No. 18781)).

   In the case of a protected building which is an ecclesiastical building to which the Planning (Listed Buildings and Conservation Areas) Act

1990, s.60 applies, listed building consent is not required. Instead, a faculty is obtained from the Church Committee (but this does not include buildings used as a house by a minister of religion, only the church building itself). The ecclesiastical exemption is restricted to the following churches in England and Wales which have all agreed to abide by the guidelines provided by planning authorities: Church of England, Church in Wales, Roman Catholic Church, Methodist Church, Baptist Union of Great Britain and the Baptist Union of Wales, and the United Reformed Church. Ecclesiastical buildings of all denominations in Scotland and Northern Ireland are included in the exemption, providing the building is still used for religious worship.

There is a similar provision for buildings with a Crown or Duchy interest, in which case a qualifying alteration is one which would have required listed building consent.

Where the building is a scheduled monument, approval is required for all alterations from the Secretary of State. In rare cases a building may be both listed and a scheduled monument. In such cases it will be the scheduled monument consent which is required.

2. The work must be to a qualifying building – one designed to remain or become a dwelling, relevant residential or relevant charitable building.
3. The work must comprise an alteration, rather than a repair or work of maintenance (see **6.4.2**) in which case standard rating applies.
4. The everyday definition of 'alteration' applies – there must be a change in the structure (the fabric) of the building. Works to areas which are not the building itself such as to boundary walls, etc., do not qualify, unless the walls are integral to the qualifying building.
5. Where the work is not to a building designed to remain or become a dwelling, in other words a relevant residential or charitable building, a certificate must be supplied to the builder to evidence the qualifying use. A certificate can only be supplied by the person who will be using the building for qualifying use directly to the person supplying services to him. Therefore, any services supplied by sub-contractors to the main contractor will be standard rated, but will be zero rated when charged on by the builder directly to the person constructing.

There have been many tribunal cases in the area of 'approved alterations' to listed buildings. One issue that can disqualify works from zero rating is that if the works did not require listed building consent (even though it has been given). In most cases, however, listed building consent is required for works amounting to the alteration of a protected building, particularly in respect of Grade I*, Grade I and Grade II* buildings. The position of certain internal alterations to Grade II buildings is not as clear, however, and care should therefore be taken when looking at this category of building – see *Tony Castelo* (No. 12787), where the planning officer confirmed that consent for certain works was not required (although in *Mr and Mrs M P Wells* (No. 15169), the tribunal determined that they were not bound by the opinion of the planning officer and substituted its own view on whether the work should have required consent) and *R W Gibbs* (No. 5596) in which the tribunal ruled that the removal of asbestos did not affect the character of the building, and that the work did not therefore require to be authorised.

The main issue, however, is usually whether the works amount to an alteration or not.

6.4.2 Definition of 'alteration' v. 'repair and maintenance'

The definition of an 'alteration' is derived from the case of *C & E Commrs* v. *Viva Gas Appliances* [1983] STC 819, HL, which held that 'alteration' should be construed as including: 'any work upon the fabric of the building except that which is so slight or trivial as to attract the application of the *de minimis* rule'. In addition, following the tribunal's comments in *Lordsregal Ltd* (No. 18535), the chairman commented that rather than looking at each individual item of work in a schedule of works, the project as a whole should be looked at, or at least parts of the project which could be grouped together:

58. In our view the statutory language does not require the sort of analysis for which the commissioners contend. The statute does not require one to ask whether the relevant supplies (broken down into their every element) amounted to an alteration or repair or maintenance. The supplies must be '"in the course of" an approved alteration of a protected building' and we consider that this requires a broader perspective than that of taking each and every item of work in isolation from everything else and seeking to categorise it accordingly. The broader perspective for which Mr Barlow contends is more in keeping with what the statute requires. Note (4)(a) requires us to determine the nature of the supplies that comprised the works of reconstruction and whether they would have fallen within Items 2 and 3 of Group 6. On that basis we think that the great majority of the supplies involved did do so and approaching the supplies from this broader perspective seems more consistent with the type of approach adopted by the Court of Justice in cases such as *Card Protection Plan Ltd v. C & E Commrs* [1999] BVC 155 (HL) (see at para. 27 to 31), in determining the nature of supplies and whether there is a single supply or mixed supplies.

59. In support of the broader perspective Mr Barlow took us to what had been said in *ACT Construction Ltd v C & E Commrs* [1981] 1 BVC 451 (in particular the speech of Lord Roskill at p. 453) and *Windflower Housing Association v C & E Commrs* [1995] BVC 329 (at p. 334) about the expression 'repair or maintenance'. While these cases assist, ultimately we must address the statutory question in the context of the particular facts of this case. Having regard to the evidence, we think that supplies comprising the works of reconstruction, if supplied to the appellant as Note (4)(a) requires, would have been very largely supplies that fell within Items 2 and 3 and certainly as the appellant contends to an extent that exceeds 60 per cent of the relevant costs involved as shown in the schedules. As a particular illustration, the supplies comprising the work on the roof in our view amounted to supplies in the course of an approved alteration even though a number of indi-

vidual elements of that work might be described as repairs to particular parts of the roof and its timbers.

In cases of doubt, one of the key issues raised in tribunal, in order to test whether the work is an 'alteration', is whether the part of the building affected was in need of repair prior to commencement of the work. For example, if a roof is replaced because it leaked prior to the works being carried out then it will likely be considered a work of repair or maintenance even if the work results in an alteration (see *N F Rhodes* (No. 14533) where 65 per cent of the roof area had been in need of repair but the remaining 35 per cent was in good repair and therefore qualified as an alteration). Use of modern building materials and methods in themselves do not constitute an alteration (see *St Petroc Minor Vicar and Parochial Church Council* (No. 16450)). If the roof needed repair but the work also entails substantial alterations, such as the new construction of rooms in the loft space, then it is likely that apportionment will apply.

In cases where there is an alteration as a result of repair or maintenance works being carried out, this does not change the treatment of the supply – it remains standard rated (see *Windflower Housing Association* v. *C & E Commrs* [1995] STC 860, QBD).

Reconstruction of a building was specifically ruled as not being an alteration in the case of *C & E Commrs* v. *C M Morrish* [1998] STC 954, QBD, on the grounds that the work led to a re-instatement of what was there before the fire rather than an alteration of the building which existed prior to the fire. The case concerned a cottage which had been badly damaged by fire and required the rebuilding of exterior walls and re-instatement of the roof. Nevertheless, the building may still qualify for zero rating as a 'substantial reconstruction' under VATA 1994, Sched. 8, Gp. 1 (grant of a major interest) (see **6.3**).

Below are listed some examples drawn from tribunal decisions on the subject of what does or does not constitute an 'alteration'.

6.4.3 Rebuilding of external walls

This was held to be an alteration in the case of *Logmoor Ltd* (No. 14733) on the grounds that the work incorporated the old hayloft stables as part of the house.

6.4.4 Underpinning of foundations

Held to be an alteration in the case of *ACT Construction Co. Ltd* v. *C & E Commrs* [1982] STC 25, on the grounds that it was entirely new work, not work to the existing building. This decision was also followed in *A W Adams* (No. 18054).

6.4.5   New drainage system and sewage treatment plant

In the case of *Walsingham College (Yorkshire Properties) Ltd* (No. 13223), the tribunal ruled that the work went far beyond mere repair or maintenance but the work was apportioned due to it also relating to three unlisted cottages on the estate. The drainage system is generally held to be part of the fabric of the building to the point where it joins the mains services. A similar decision was reached in *A W Adams* (No 18054), and zero rating applied to the extent that the plans showed consent had been given for the works.

6.4.6   Damp proofing

Work to damp proof a building is generally seen as maintenance and therefore standard rated, see *St Petroc Minor Vicar and Parochial Church Council* (No. 16450), where the works were quite extensive. However, in *D H Carr* (No. 19267) the appellant fixed a specialist membrane to the inside of the external walls with drainage channels (not an insertion of a damp proof course in the walls) and this was found to be new works of alteration by the tribunal and therefore zero rated. The floor was also dug out to a depth of 18 inches and a damp proof membrane inserted between the floor screed and concrete.

6.4.7   Garden works

Garden works in the grounds of a listed building do not qualify for zero rating, because the relief is restricted to works of alteration to the fabric of the building (see *Tinsley (AC)* v. *C & E Commrs* [2005] All ER (D) 72 (Jun.), where a garden terrace which abutted the building was determined not be to part of the 'fabric of the building').

6.4.8   Erection of railings

In *R G Powell (t/a Anwick Agricultural Engineers)* (No. 14520) the erection of railings, where the railings actually touched the qualifying building, was held to be an alteration to the qualifying building. However, in view of the High Court's decision in *Tinsley* (see **6.4.7**) this is unlikely to be followed in the future.

6.4.9   Construction of a boundary wall

In the case of *C Mason* (No. 16250) the construction of a boundary wall, where it was attached to the listed building by a 'timber boxing arrangement', was held to be an alteration in part. However, in view of the High Court's decision in *Tinsley* (see **6.4.7**) this is unlikely to be followed in the future.

6.4.10   Construction of a greenhouse

In the case of *C W Mann* (No. 14004) the construction of a greenhouse was held to be an alteration because it was attached to the listed building, but the construction of a swimming pool and stables were held to be standard rated as they were separate buildings and excluded from zero rating.

6.4.11   Garages

The zero rate also applies to works of alteration to a garage occupied with the dwelling, where the garage was either constructed at the same time as the dwelling or, in cases where the dwelling has been substantially reconstructed, at the same time as that reconstruction.

The construction of a separate garage was held not to be an alteration in the case of *J H Bradfield* (No. 5339), because it was separate from the listed building.

In *Sherlock & Neal Ltd* (No. 18793), a chapel stood one foot away from the listed cottage and was incorporated into it. This was accepted as a zero-rated alteration. However, on the other side of the chapel was an agricultural building, which was demolished and a new garage built, which shared a wall with the newly enlarged cottage. The works to construct the garage were standard rated, because VATA 1994, Sched. 8, Gp. 6, Item 2, Note 2 restricts zero rating for garages to when they are constructed at the same time as another building or when another building was substantially reconstructed, neither of which was the case here.

In *Grange Builders (Quainton) Ltd* (No. 18905), a barn which had been constructed at the same time as the main listed dwelling, and had been used as a garage, was held to be a 'garage' for the purposes of VATA 1994, Sched. 8, Gp. 6, Item 2, Note 2, and therefore zero rating applied to the alteration works carried out. HMRC issued *Business Brief 11/05* as a result of this decision, accepting that a barn constructed either at the time of original contruction of the listed dwelling or at a time when it was 'substantially reconstructed', and in use as a garage for a significant period prior to the commencement of the alteration works will qualify for the zero rate.

6.4.12   Outbuildings

VATA 1994, Sched. 8, Gp. 6, Note 10 specifically excludes the construction of a building separate from, but in the curtilage of a protected building, from the definition of an 'alteration' and hence from zero rating. Works to outbuildings does not qualify for zero rating – see *Zielinski Baker & Partners Ltd* [2004] STC 456, HL, in which the court determined that despite the listing covering a number of buildings, which could be construed as a single dwelling, the VAT legislation applied the zero rating for the purposes of the main dwelling only.

In *Lord and Lady Watson of Richmond* (No. 18903), the case concerned a utility room which was attached to a wall which was attached to the house and where the space between the utility room and the house provided access to the garden. Nevertheless, the tribunal followed *Zielinski Baker* in determining that the utility room was a separate building and therefore zero rating could not apply.

6.4.13 Swimming pools

In *C & E Commrs* v. *M Arbib* [1995] STC 490, QBD, the appellant constructed an indoor swimming pool in the grounds of the listed building, which was connected to it by a covered walkway. The High Court upheld the tribunal's decision that zero rating applied because the swimming pool was part of and integral to the protected building.

In *Heijn* (No. 15562), the tribunal considered that a swimming pool built in the grounds of the listed building comprised new construction rather than an approved alteration to the main dwelling, because it was away from the building and not integrated with it.

In *Collins & Beckett Ltd* (No. 19212), the swimming pool was in the grounds of the listed building and in 1988 was covered by a plastic and aluminium greenhouse. In 1998 approval was granted for alterations to the pool building, including a new cover more in keeping with the house, and re-shaping the pool. A window in the main house was also removed and replaced with a door, and this was joined to the pool building with an enclosed passageway. The tribunal found that the work to replace the window with a door and the passageway were approved alterations to the listed dwelling, but the work to the pool building did not constitute an approved alteration because VATA 1994, Sched. 8, Gp. 6, Note 10 excluded the construction of a building separate from, but in the curtilage of, the main dwelling.

6.4.14 Thatching

Replacement of straw thatch with reed thatch on two cottages was held to be an alteration in the case of *Dodson Bros (Thatchers) Ltd* (No. 13734) as the roofs were not in need of repair prior to commencement of the work.

6.4.15 Re-roofing

In *St Dunstan's* (No. 17896) the tribunal considered that re-roofing, even though the roof was in need of repair in certain parts, was an alteration rather than repair or maintenance.

6.4.16 Replacement of a clay pot roof

Replacing a clay pot roof with a lead roof on a church was held to be an alteration in *Parochial Church Council of St Andrew's Church Eakring* (No. 15320) on the grounds that the work was done in accordance with a stipulation of English Heritage in approving the grant, not because it was in need of repair.

6.4.17 Replacement guttering

Replacement guttering laid onto new soles sloping in a different direction and leading to new exit chutes was held to be an alteration in the case of *All Saints Church (Tilsworth) Parochial Church Council* (No. 10490).

6.4.18 Installation of a new lighting system

In the case of *All Saints with St Nicholas Church Icklesham* (No. 16321), installation of new lighting was held to be an alteration on the grounds that it was a one-off in the sense of exceptional expenditure and could not be categorised as a repair or maintenance.

6.4.19 Installation of a different type of sash window

Replacement of single glazed sash windows with double glazed sash windows was ruled to be standard rated in the tribunal decision in *Barry Moore* (No. 18653). The windows were identical in size and appearance and with the addition of fake astragals the outward appearance of the building had not changed, despite the fact that the windows were structurally different – the internal structure of a window is not part of the 'fabric' of the building.

6.4.20 Wardrobes and cupboards

In *E C Owen* (No. 18660), the owner of Devizes Castle had wardrobes with cupboards fitted along one wall of the Grade I listed building, having applied for and been granted listed building consent. This substantial structure included tailor-made coping and skirting. HMRC first argued that the works were pre-fabricated fitted furniture but abandoned this prior to the hearing, instead arguing that the work did not require listed building consent, having received an opinion from a planning officer to this affect. The tribunal, however, allowed the appeal, holding that another planning officer may well have determined that the works, which were substantial, did require consent.

6.4.21 Demolition and replacement of retaining wall

In *A W Adams* (No. 18054), the tribunal held that demolition and replacement of a retaining wall to prevent landslip was a zero-rated alteration. There had been no repair – the wall had been demolished.

6.4.22 Removal of asbestos

In *R W Gibbs* (No. 5596), the removal of asbestos was held to be repair and maintenance on the grounds that it did not affect the character of the building.

6.4.23 Fonts, chancels etc. in churches

In *Holy Trinity Church* (No. 1571), the church chancel was rearranged, including the relocation of the font, holy table, reading desks and pulpit. As these items were not fixed to the church the tribunal determined that they did not comprise an alteration to the fabric of the building.

6.4.24 HMRC guidance

It is usual to try to agree the treatment of works, particularly on large projects, with HMRC, although in recent years they have shown marked reluctance to provide this. Therefore, the best way of dealing with this is to carry out an analysis of a costed schedule of works, preparing a spreadsheet of zero-rated alterations, repairs and maintenance works, works which are always standard rated and works which must be apportioned (see **6.3.1** for an example). This can then be agreed with HMRC and VAT applied on the appropriate proportion of the value of works throughout the contract, with a final adjustment at the end (because the costed schedule will usually be different from the final cost).

HMRC guidance

Typical works of repair or maintenance

- Treatment for woodworm, dry/wet rot etc.
- Cracked and peeling walls filled and repainted.
- Fire damaged buildings restored.
- Internal works to the mechanism of church organs, bell frames and the mechanical systems for ringing bells.

- Re-thatching of thatched roofs, and other roofing work in general.
- Installation of damp proof course or membrane.
- Stripping out and rewiring old electrical circuits.
- Replacing rotten or damaged window frames and doors.
- Repointing frost-damaged brickwork.
- Redecorating.
- Repairing or replacing old or damaged plumbing.
- Rotten or broken roof timbers replaced.
- Broken roof tiles replaced.

Typical works of alteration

General

- New floors constructed at a different level.
- Installation of first time central heating system.
- Additions to electrical, heating and plumbing systems installed within the fabric of a building.
- Converting the internal layout of a building to provide for rooms to be used for specific purposes (e.g. creating/removing bathrooms or kitchens).
- Making new doorways and windows in walls where none existed before.
- Erection/removal of walls of a building (includes substantially altering the structure of a wall).
- Extension/enlargement to the protected building.
- Underpinning.
- The enlargement of window apertures.
- Bricking-up of windows and doors, or providing apertures for new windows and doors.

Churches

- Changing plain to stained glass windows and vice versa.
- Installation of first time lightning conductor.
- Installation of floodlights fixed to the structure of the church.
- Installation of a new bell frame which occupies a different position from the existing bell frame.
- Installation of a new bell frame which differs in size or design from the existing bell frame.
- Alterations to an existing bell frame to carry extra bell(s).

Extract from: HMRC *VAT Guidance Manuals* (Vol. 1–8A. VAT – Construction, ch.3, annex 5C and 5D)

6.5 GRANTS FOR REPAIRS AND MAINTENANCE OF CHURCHES

In addition to the zero rating for alterations there is also a grant available for churches, to fund the VAT chargeable at 17.5 per cent on repairs and maintenance works (prior to 1 April 2004 this grant funded the difference between 17.5 per cent and 5 per cent on such works only). It was introduced with effect from 1 April 2001 and applies to all works of repair or maintenance carried out on or after that date. Claims must be for works amounting to a minimum of £1,000, excluding VAT, although separate projects can be combined over a period of time where each may be under the £1,000 limit.

The scheme was extended to 31 March 2011 in the 2006 budget.

English Heritage's budget for repairs to places of worship for the 2001–02 financial year was £9,049,000, for 2002–03 £10,370,000 and for 2003–04 £12,220,000. HMRC estimates that the scheme could be worth £30 million a year to qualifying places of worship.

The scheme is open to all formally constituted religious organisations, provided that the organisation has charitable status, or is recognised as a charity by the Inland Revenue in Scotland or Northern Ireland, or is covered by a parochial church council.

The sole or main use of the building must be as a public place of worship and services must take place at least six times a year, except in the case of places of worship used by monasteries, nunneries or other similar establishments, and churches owned or vested in certain specific organisations that look after redundant places of worship such as the Historic Chapels Trust, the Friends of Friendless Churches, the Scottish Redundant Churches Trust, the Churches Conservation Trust and the Welsh Religious Buildings Trust.

Ancillary listed buildings are not included unless they fulfil all the same conditions as the principal building, i.e. their sole or main use is as a place of public religious worship. Private chapels in houses or in private schools, not open to the general public, are therefore not included, and neither is a building used or available for use by a minister of religion wholly or mainly as a residence from which to perform the duties of his/her office.

The scheme is administered by the Department of Culture, Media and Sport, and documentation relating to the scheme can be obtained via their hotline on 01845 601 5945, at their website (**www.lpwscheme.org.uk**) or by writing to:

Listed Places of Worship Grants Scheme
PO Box 609
Newport
NP10 8QD

CHAPTER 7

Business sectors

7.1 AGRICULTURAL PROPERTY

Agricultural property, except for the farmhouse, is treated in the same way as any other non-residential property, that is standard rated construction and standard rated on sale of a freehold where the building is less than three years old, otherwise it is VAT exempt.

The option to tax can apply to agricultural land, although it is not often exercised as the land is usually used to make fully taxable supplies of crops or livestock, etc. In cases where farmland is let, and the option to tax may be exercised in order to recover VAT incurred on costs such as fencing or drainage works, etc., it should not be forgotten that all other supplies in relation to the land must also be treated as standard rated. Therefore, if the property is sold, it must be treated as standard rated, unless the transfer of a going concern rules apply (see **2.15**) with apportionment of the value for the residential element as appropriate. Also, where ownership of the property shifts through inheritance or gifting of the property, a VAT charge may arise as a result of the option to tax having been exercised (although with inheritance the transfer of a going concern rules will likely apply if the inheritor is going to take over the running of the farm and providing the other conditions are complied with (see **2.15**)).

7.1.1 Farmhouses

Farmhouses are generally used partly for business purposes as well as for non-business residential use as a family home. As a result of this a proportion of the input tax incurred on the upkeep and maintenance of farmhouses can be recovered, depending upon the proportion of business use the building is put to. This can vary considerably, but HMRC has reached an agreement with the NFU that, in the case of sole proprietorship or partnership farms, 'up to 70 per cent' of the VAT incurred on general repairs and maintenance may be recovered in cases where farming is a full-time business activity. In other cases, recovery of VAT will be much less and will have to be negotiated separately with HMRC. In cases where a specific project such as

205

an extension is constructed, then recovery of the VAT incurred will depend upon whether the new accommodation is to be used for business or for private purposes, rather than applying the 'up to 70 per cent' rule, i.e. if it is to be used as a farm office then 100 per cent recovery will be allowed, but if it is to be used as bedrooms, then no recovery is allowed. Apart from the farm office (which may of course be separate from the house) the kitchen tends to see the most business use (storage of chemicals, drugs, etc., preparation of chickens, warming of lambs, etc.) but this can vary from business to business and it is generally necessary to justify the recovery of input tax and agree a proportion with HMRC.

In the case of farming companies, the rules are different, because VATA 1994, s.24(a) disallows the recovery of input tax in respect of accommodation occupied by a director, or person associated to a director, of the company. In such cases, recovery of input tax is strictly limited to reflect the extent to which the domestic accommodation is put to business use, for example, see *Sangster Group Ltd* (No. 15544), where a 20 per cent recovery was allowed, based on the house being used for business purposes on 64 days in the course of a year.

7.1.2 Share farming

There are various ways that a farm owner can exploit the land he owns: he could farm it and sell the crops or engage a contract farmer to farm the land for him and then sell the crops, in which case he will be making taxable supplies at zero or standard rate; or he could let the farmland to a farmer in which case his income from rent will be exempt from VAT subject to the option to tax. An alternative arrangement is to share farm, an arrangement where a land owner and a farmer get together as a joint venture to exploit the land, in which case the sale of the crops is zero or standard rated and the share of profits is outside the scope of VAT.

In order to be treated as share farming, HMRC will expect to see that both parties are liable for both profits and any losses which may be incurred and are both involved in the farming policy to be adopted and have regular meetings to discuss it. Otherwise, if the farmer simply pays a proportion of the sale proceeds to the land owner as rent, the supply is exempt subject to the option to tax.

7.1.3 Livery

Stabling and livery services were held to be a single supply of an exempt licence to occupy in the tribunal decision in *John Window* (No. 17186), the stabling forming the predominant part of the supply with the livery services being ancillary to this. Similar arguments have been raised in respect of kennelling of cats and dogs, but in *Leander International Pet Foods Ltd* (No. 18870), the tribunal stated:

> Horses, unlike pet cats and dogs, live their lives in stables and fields. On that basis it is understandable that an owner who wants to keep a horse has to obtain a licence to occupy land in order to provide his horse with living space. Pets by contrast inhabit their owners' homes. When they are placed in kennels the object is either to secure a quarantine licence or, in the case of non-quarantine premises, to secure care and safe keeping. Each case has to be decided on its facts and the circumstances of the *Window* decision are, as we have pointed out, significantly different from the present.

7.2 BREWERS' TENANTED PROPERTIES

Where a building consists of both commercial and residential accommodation and the option to tax has been exercised, the commercial element is subject to VAT at standard rate. However, there is provision for exemption of the residential element, and the legislation provides for the value of the supply to be apportioned. HMRC has come to an agreement with the Brewers' Society which deals with the recovery of input tax by Brewers in such situations, which can be found in *VAT Notice 700/57, Administrative Agreements Entered into with Trade Bodies* and is reproduced below.

Agreement with the Brewers' Society about Deduction of Input Tax in Respect of Brewers' Tenanted Estate

1. This agreement, which had effect from 1 August 1989, covers only those brewers who elect to waive exemption of the rents from all their tenanted properties under para.2, Sch.6A VATA 1983 (now para.2, Sch.120 VATA 1994). Brewers who do not elect, or elect from some, but not all, of their tenanted properties, are outside the agreement and should contact their local VAT office if they wish to negotiate special agreements.
2. Under the agreement, the entitlement to deduct input tax in respect of tied tenanted licensed houses containing a residential element is as follows.

    (a) An agreed percentage of the input tax incurred on the maintenance and repair of, and capital expenditure on, tenanted property and of that incurred in selling or leasing such properties, including professional fees shall be deemed to be non-deductible.

    (b) This restriction of an agreed percentage of input tax shall cover the whole matter of the tenanted estate so that no further restriction of input tax shall be required in respect of the exempt supplies made in the form of tenanted rents received and deemed to relate to the domestic accommodation.

    (c) The property expenditure referred to in paragraph 1 above does not include expenditure on tenants' furniture, fittings and equipment, on the costs of cellarage or dispense equipment, advertising and other management expenses.

(d) The method will be used for at least 2 years. However, Customs reserve the right to review the arrangements, should there be a change in brewers' circumstances which affected significantly the amount of input tax they are entitled to deduct.

(e) A brewers' tenanted estate shall be the houses actually tenanted throughout the relevant period. Where this is difficult to ascertain, Customs will accept an average based on the total of houses tenanted at the beginning and end of the appropriate period.

(f) Nothing in the agreement affects the right of any brewer to question the correctness of the apportionment of his input tax in this way, although in such circumstances Customs would also be entitled to propose an alternative basis of apportionment.

The proportion most commonly agreed is 10 per cent, so that in relation to the recovery of input tax this proportion is used to restrict recovery of any costs incurred jointly on the commercial and residential elements and, when rent is charged or a property is sold, VAT is not charged on 10 per cent of the property. It should be borne in mind that this is a special agreement for the Brewers' Society members and in no way reflects commercial apportionments or sets precedent for them.

7.3   CARE HOMES

Nursing and rest homes are exempt from VAT under the provisions for welfare under VATA 1994, Sched. 7, Gp. 7, and are therefore generally unable to register for VAT or recover VAT incurred (see also **3.3.4**). Both nursing and rest homes fall within the category of 'relevant residential' buildings so that the construction of a new nursing/rest home is zero rated.

Following the High Court decision against HMRC in the *Kingscrest Associates Ltd & Montecello Ltd* case) the VAT (Health and Welfare) Order 2002, SI 2002/762 was introduced with effect from 21 March 2002 and amended VATA 1994, Sched. 7, Gp. 7 from that date. The result of the High Court decision would have meant that care provided commercially in residential homes for children and young adults with learning difficulties was not medical in nature and did not therefore qualify for exemption from VAT (*Kingscrest* supplied local authorities which could recover all the VAT they were charged, and wanted their supplies to be standard rated so that they could recover VAT on refurbishments, etc.). The ruling would have affected any residential rest home, but not those providing nursing or convalescent care.

There is also the provision for a self-supply on change of use of a qualifying building within 10 years from the date of its construction. This means that if, for example, a nursing home operator decides to cease trading as a nursing home and instead use the premises as a hotel, that a proportion of the VAT benefit of zero rating of the construction of the nursing home would have to be repaid to HMRC, depending on the number of complete years the building was used as a care home (see **3.3.7**). The same amount would, however, also be recoverable providing that the hotel business has a wholly taxable income (the danger here could be exempt lettings for conferences, etc., but this could be avoided by use of the option to tax).

Work to provide an extension for a nursing home is essentially standard rated. However, in the case of *John Michael Barrie Strowbridge* (No. 16521) the appellant purchased a nursing home (13 beds) and contracted with a builder to carry out alterations and refurbishment of the existing building, and also to construct a new building to provide an extension for about 27 additional patients. When the builder queried the issue of a zero-rate certificate the plans were changed so that the new works became a separate home, with no internal access as had previously been provided. There were already separate supplies of water, gas and electricity. The existing house and the new 'lodge' were registered as nursing homes separately. Due to the sudden death of five patients, and the requirement for staff/patient ratio the homes became unviable to run as separate units and the internal access was re-instated. The appellant ran the home as a single unit for about six months before selling it. HMRC assessed the builder for VAT on the construction. Evidence was available from the local planning authority that, in its view, the creation of two autonomous units did not require planning consent as no material change of use had occurred. The tribunal found that in replacing the internal access the appellant had genuinely changed his original intention, regardless of the fact that the change had occurred in order to avoid VAT. His subsequent decision to revert to the original plan did not alter the fact that upon completion of the work there was a separate nursing home. The construction of the lodge was therefore zero rated.

The partial exemption standard and special method override (see **1.9.4** and **1.9.9**) legislation has brought an end to many of the 'first use' type of schemes which abounded in the 1990s. These relied on the new extension (or other goods and services) being first used for wholly taxable purposes in the first partial exemption year when the input tax was incurred, and providing the extension (or other capital item) was under £250,000 the Capital Goods Scheme was not triggered and no further adjustment in later years, when the asset was used for wholly exempt purposes, was required. For those interested, an example of the scheme, which failed due to use of the extension for exempt purposes in the same VAT year, can be found in the case of *Laurels Nursing Home* (No. 15259), in which planning permission was obtained in 1994 for the extension to provide accommodation for 19 patients, a bathroom, a lavatory, a hairdressing room, a laundry, boiler room and store room, and the construction was carried out between December 1994 and March 1995. During the construction period there were three short lettings of the new extension for demonstration purposes, and on the basis of these taxable supplies the input tax was claimed on the extension. HMRC assessed on the basis that the work was subject to the partial exemption rules and limited to the proportion of taxable to total supplies. Although the appellant contended that his intentions had changed from when the planning permission was obtained, the tribunal could find no documentary evidence to support this. In March 1995, upon issue of the certificate of completion, the extension was brought into use as part of the nursing home. The tribunal decided that the taxable supplies had been made with the intention of recovering the input tax against them, but ruled that during both periods under appeal the input tax had been used in making both taxable and exempt supplies and dismissed the appeal. The standard method for partial exemption, based on proportion of taxable to total income, left the taxpayer with very little recovery.

Disclosure to HMRC for use of this scheme is now required under the VAT avoidance disclosure regulations (see **1.12**), assuming that the turnover requirements for this are met. HMRC would also be likely to challenge the use of the scheme in any case, on grounds that it is an abuse of rights (see *Halifax plc* v. *C & E Commrs* (ECJ, C-255/02) (see **1.13**)) on grounds that it artificially results in a recovery of input tax not intended to be allowable under the purposive application of the legislation.

7.4 ECCLESIASTICAL PROPERTY

The normal VAT rules apply to ecclesiastical property, and the main area for relief from VAT is therefore new construction for relevant charitable purposes, which typically applies to church halls and the like (see **5.2**) and the reliefs for listed buildings and scheduled monuments (see **Chapter 6**). As the use of main church buildings tends to be non-business in nature, there is little chance of recovering input tax related to general repairs and maintenance of the structure, except in the case of larger churches and cathedrals which may have varying degrees of business activity, enabling recovery of some of the VAT incurred. In cases where the church is a listed building or scheduled monument, zero rating will apply to works comprising alterations, as approved by the church diocese via a faculty (see **6.4.1(1)**). There is also a grant system in place for repairs to listed church buildings amounting to the full 17.5 per cent paid at standard rate (see **6.5**). It was announced in the 2006 budget that this scheme will continue until 31 March 2011.

7.4.1 Banding system

HMRC and the Churches Main Committee agreed a banding arrangement in 1994 for the purposes of determining how much VAT could be recovered by cathedrals, and this can also be used as a basis for negotiating recovery for churches with similar activities. Cathedrals do not have to use the banding system and can (and often do) agree their own special method for partial exemption (see *Dean and Chapter of the Cathedral Church of St Peter* (No. 3591) and **1.9.8**).

Use of the banding system must be agreed with HMRC and it will negotiate which band the cathedral falls into (see *Dean and Chapter of Cathedral Church of Christ* (No. 15068)). Once agreed, the banding will continue to be applied unless there are significant changes in activities. The banding arrangements only apply to non-attributable input tax, not input tax that can be directly attributed to a specific business activity:

- Band A – 90 per cent recovery. This applies where there are significant admission charges to all main areas.
- Band B – 65 per cent recovery. This applies where there is no admission charge into the cathedral, but there are large numbers of visitors to which there is associated significant taxable income, for example from admission charges to other areas, lettings for concerts, etc.
- Band C – 45 per cent recovery. This applies where there is no admission charge to the cathedral, and insignificant admission charges to other areas, but there are still a reasonable number of visitors generating taxable income from other sources such as bookshops or tearooms.
- Band D – 25 per cent recovery. This applies where there are no admission charges or insignificant charges, small numbers of visitors with little associated taxable income.

7.4.2   Church housing

Church housing for ministers, etc., is not seen as 'charitable non-business use' and therefore falls within the VAT rules for housing generally (see **Chapters 3** and **4**). See also *Dean and Chapter of Bristol Cathedral* (No. 14591) and *Dean and Chapter of Hereford Cathedral* (No. 11737) in which it was argued successfully that input tax on housing was attributable to the taxable business activities of the cathedral, on the basis that the persons occupying the housing were involved to a greater or lesser extent in those activities.

7.4.3   Church organs

Where the church building is listed or a scheduled monument, and has a pipe organ fitted into the structure of the building (not a free-standing organ), certain works to the organ can comprise 'approved alterations' and therefore qualify for zero rating. Typically this can involve works to the casework, pipework, chests and soundboards and work to the chamber. In order to qualify for the relief, however, the church building must be a relevant charitable use building and if it is hired out for recitals and the like, so that income is derived from it for more than 10 per cent of its use, it will not qualify.

HMRC issued a guidance note on 27 September 1997 which has been agreed with the Institute of British Organ Building.

7.5 EDUCATIONAL PROPERTY

Private schools are generally registered charities and supplies of education are therefore exempt from VAT under VATA 1994, Sched. 9, Gp. 6. State schools, on the other hand, are generally part of the local authority and their supplies are treated as outside the scope of VAT. This means that for state schools the provision under VATA 1994, s.33, to recover VAT incurred on non-business activities applies (see *VAT Notice 749, Local Authorities and Similar Bodies*).

For private schools, construction of new buildings will be standard rated unless the building is for student accommodation (a relevant residential use under VATA 1994, Sched. 8, Gp. 5, Note 4). A certificate of qualifying use will be required by the builder, the form of which can be found in *VAT Notice 708, Buildings and Construction*, Appendix A. The zero rating also covers the construction of dining rooms and kitchens at the same time as student accommodation, if predominantly used by students occupying halls of residence. Insofar as newly constructed buildings are concerned, HMRC generally ignores vacation letting to businesses for 'relevant residential use' qualification where colleges and universities are concerned, but not in respect of schools, where vacation letting must be for qualifying use (i.e. the people occupying the student accommodation must be recipients of a supply of education, whether by the school or a third party such as an English language school or other summer school organisation). However, see the *University of Bath* case below.

HMRC has tried to challenge this zero rating in various ways. In *Urdd Gombraith Cymru* (No. 14881), the issue was whether the short length of time students stayed in the accommodation disqualified it from zero rating, but the tribunal ruled in the appellant's favour.

In *Denman College* (No. 15513), the issue was whether an accommodation block without cooking facilities, again used for short courses, qualified for zero rating and the tribunal again ruled in the appellant's favour.

In *Riverside School (Whasset) Ltd* (No. 13170), the appellant attempted to gain zero rating for the construction of classrooms and workshops on the grounds that they were constructed as part of a group of buildings which were used as a whole for relevant residential purposes. The tribunal ruled against the appellant in this case, and determined that it was the use the particular buildings were put to which qualified them for zero rating.

In *University of Bath* (No. 14235), the university renovated student accommodation and granted a lease to an associated company, claiming zero rating as a grant of a major interest by the person constructing under VATA 1994, Sched. 8, Gp. 5, Item 1, thus recovering input tax on the renovation costs. The tribunal ruled that the buildings were not for use solely for relevant residential purposes, on the grounds that the accommodation was also used for vacation letting for other than educational purposes (e.g. to businesses for conferences in the summer break). The lease was therefore exempt and the input tax was not recoverable. A similar result was arrived at in *University Court of the University of St Andrew* (No. 19054). Note that this type of scheme is now subject to the Disclosure of Avoidance Schemes legislation (see **1.12.1(1)**). These schemes have also been contested with success on *Halifax* grounds by HMRC in recent years (see **1.13**). However, it should be noted that *Halifax* determined that if the 'essential aim' of the arrangements is VAT avoidance this leads to them failing, and therefore if the school has other reasons for making such arrangements, such as using the company rather than the school to generate additional income by summer and other exploitation of the premises, then *Halifax* may not apply.

7.5.1 Higher education properties

It is common for universities and other higher education bodies to have a mixture of fee-paying students and students below the age of 19 who are provided with education on a statutory basis. In such cases there is a mixture of business and non-business activity. HMRC accepts that the VAT treatment of educational buildings can be zero rated if the proportion of fee-paying students is no greater than 10 per cent of the total students attending, calculated on a full-time equivalent basis. From 1 June 2002, apportionment can be applied so that part of the supply can be zero rated if the proportion of fee-paying students is greater than 10 per cent. Prior to this date it was either all zero rated or not at all.

The letting of lecture halls is exempt from VAT subject to the option to tax. However, the supply of a conference organised solely by a university, etc., can qualify for exemption under VATA 1994, Sched. 9, Gp. 6 as a supply of education, and the supply of halls of residence and/or catering together with such a supply would be seen as closely related to education, thus also qualifying for exemption. Generally, supplies of catering or halls of residence to third parties is a taxable supply at standard rate (supplies to students is exempt as closely related to education). Where rooms are let for the purpose of a supply of catering (such as wedding receptions, etc.) together with the supply of bedded accommodation then the supply is standard rated – this is seen as similar to a hotel and therefore within the exceptions from exemption at VATA 1994, Sched. 9, Gp. 1, Item 1(d). However, where there is no bedded accommodation supplied and the supply consists of hire of the room and catering only, the hire of the room is exempt and the catering is standard rated. If a single charge is made, an apportionment on a fair and reasonable basis should be made.

It should also be noted that supplies closely related to education, such as accommodation and catering, can also qualify for exemption from VAT when they are supplied by one qualifying body to another. For example, if a private school provides accommodation and catering to an English language school in the summer break this will be exempt from VAT, even though it is not also supplying the education, because the English language school is a qualifying body to the extent that it supplies courses in English as a foreign language.

With regard to partial exemption, there is a special arrangement agreed between HMRC and the Committee of Vice Chancellors and Principals of the Universities of the United Kingdom (CVCP) known as the Concordat, which deals with the recovery of input tax, known as 'tunnelling' – attributing input tax to each taxable activity rather than using the usual standard method – although apportionment may then be necessary if the activity includes both taxable and exempt supplies. Many universities have in recent years moved away from the use of this agreement, as it ignores potentially large amounts of 'non-attributable' input tax and therefore leads to a lesser recovery, although it may be simpler to use.

For the purposes of zero rating the construction or purchase of student accommodation, the Concordat states the following at para. 37(a):

> Zero rating for the construction or acquisition of a new building for use as student accommodation depends on the higher education institution being able to issue a certificate to the builder or developer as set out in the VAT leaflet on 'Construction: VAT certificates for residential or charity buildings'.
>
> Higher education institutions may, on occasions be in some difficulty with respect to issuing certificates as they know some use is likely to be made of student accommodation for non-qualifying purposes during vacations, e.g. the letting of student accommodation for holiday use or for non-educational conferences, etc., but such use is difficult to quantify. In the circumstances, because in any event tax will be collected in respect of this non-qualifying use and provided that the new building is clearly intended primarily for use as student accommodation for ten years from the date of its completion, then Customs have agreed that higher education institutions may issue a certificate for the construction or acquisition of such a building as a relevant residential building.

7.5.2 Day nurseries

Proprietary children's day nurseries are exempt educational establishments, provided they are registered with the local authority. As such, any construction works are standard rated. In cases where building works for construction of a new building, for example, for use as a day nursery, do not exceed £250,000 (the Capital Goods Scheme threshold) it was common until recent years for a lease/leaseback arrangement to be used. This involves setting up a wholly owned company which is granted a ground lease of the site and through which the building works are carried out. The company registered for VAT and granted a lease back to the trading organisation, also having opted to tax. In this way it recovered the VAT incurred on the capital costs, although the VAT on the rents, which must be at market value, was non-recoverable. If the standard-rated building costs exceeded £250,000 the planning failed because the wholly owned company is prevented from opting to tax (see **2.7.2**).

In the tribunal case of *J E & H L Laurie (t/a Peacock Montessori Nursery)* (No. 17219), a sub-lease and under-lease were granted on a barn being converted for use as a day nursery for children. The standard rated lease was entered into for 'a small tin of baked beans, if demanded', and the tribunal deemed the transactions to have been entered into solely to recover the VAT incurred, and were not in the course or furtherance of a business. The appeal was therefore dismissed.

These arrangements (whether as blatant as the above case or not) have been successfully challenged by HMRC on *Halifax* grounds (see **1.13**), although there remains an argument that has not been voiced – the fact that the £250,000 limit on the Capital Goods Scheme was introduced because HMRC was not concerned with the leakage of revenue where amounts under this limit were concerned. Nevertheless, if the 'essential aim' for the arrangements is the avoidance of VAT, then artificially structuring the arrangements to produce a VAT saving would come within the bounds of the *Halifax* principle.

In respect of children's day nurseries run as a social service, and therefore usually by charitable or other non-profit-making organisations, it is necessary to determine whether the day nursery constitutes a 'business activity' or not. If not, the construction of a new building for use as day nursery premises would be zero rated as a 'relevant charitable use' building. In the case of *St Paul's Community Project Ltd* [2004] STC 95, ChD, the High Court determined that where the day nursery fees were set at a subsidised level and the service was supplied to a socially deprived area, then this is not a business activity and the zero rating may apply (see *Business Brief 02/05* from which it is clear that HMRC are not happy with this, and will restrict use of this decision as far as possible). Until this decision was reached, the policy of HMRC was that any organisation which charged a fee, whether subsidised or not, must be in business. A similar decision was reached in the earlier case of *Yarburgh Children's Trust* [2002] STC 207, ChD but HMRC declined to apply the decision more widely until the release of the *St Paul's* decision.

Following the above two cases, the decision in *Donaldson's College* (No. 19258) was released, in which the tribunal considered that the College was a non-business charitable organisation, being funded wholly from government sources and, for all practical purposes, controlled by central government. The College was predominantly concerned with providing a service which was required to be provided by the state (provision of education to deaf and partially hearing children and children with communication difficulties) and the tribunal found that it was not a commercial concern and as such receives no consideration.

7.5.3 Lifts

Universities, grant-maintained schools and other educational institutions which have charitable status, can purchase lifts to facilitate the movement of disabled staff and pupils between floors of buildings free of VAT (VATA 1994, Sched. 8, Gp. 12, Items 17 and 18). In order to qualify for zero rating, the building in which the lift is installed must be for the provision of a permanent or temporary residence or a day centre for disabled persons. Prior to 1 January 2004, it was the policy of HMRC that educational institutions could be regarded as 'day-centres' and that zero rating could therefore apply to the installation of lifts in non-residential buildings such as classroom blocks, but that policy has now been changed, although HMRC allowed contracts entered into prior to 31 March 2005 (originally 1 January 2004 but amended by *Business Brief 03/05*) to proceed on a zero rated basis. Lifts installed prior to 31 March 2005 which qualified for zero rating remain qualifying for the purposes of future repairs and maintenance.

7.6 EXHIBITIONS

7.6.1 Letting of space

The letting of stands or space at an exhibition is exempt from VAT under VATA 1994, Sched. 9, Gp. 1, Item 1, subject to the option to tax. Interestingly, for European legislation purposes, the 'running of trade fairs and exhibitions' is listed in the Sixth Directive on VAT at Annex H, which cites those items to which member states may apply a lower rate of VAT, but this has not been applied in the UK (and is not required to be).

If an exhibition organiser supplies unallocated space at an exhibition, however, this falls short of a licence to occupy land and is not covered by the exemption. It is therefore a standard rated supply.

7.6.2 Right of admission

Certain cultural services are exempt from VAT under the Sixth Directive, Art. 13(A)(1)(n). It is under this European legislation that the UK introduced an exemption from VAT for the right of admission to exhibitions for certain non-profit making organisations and public bodies under VATA 1994,

Sched. 9, Gp. 13. If the right of admission is supplied by a non-qualifying body, then the supply is standard rated.

Eligible bodies for the purpose of the exemption include local authorities, government departments and non-departmental public bodies listed in the 1995 edition of the publication prepared by the Office of Public Service and known as 'Public Bodies'.

Otherwise an 'eligible body' includes any body which:

(a) is precluded from distributing, and does not distribute, any profit it makes;

(b) applies any profits made from supplies of a description falling within Item 2 to the continuance or improvement of the facilities made available by means of the supplies; and

(c) is managed and administered on a voluntary basis by persons who have no direct or indirect financial interest in its activities.

With regard to condition (c) above, see *Bournemouth Symphony Orchestra* v. *C & E Commrs* [2005] EWHC 1566, ChD, where a trustee was paid a salary as managing director and therefore was determined to have an indirect financial interest in the organisation's activities, so that the exemption did not apply to performance fees.

In respect of a public body, the legislation also specifically excludes any supplies by the above bodies which would cause a distortion of competition if the exemption were applied, so that local authorities, for example, may be required to show that they are not in competition with commercial organisations.

Other commercial bodies charging for entry into a cultural event such as an exhibition are required to account for VAT.

In cases where entry to an exhibition is free to the public and there is no other consideration for putting on the exhibition, this is not a business activity for VAT purposes and the activity is outside the scope of VAT (see *Whitechapel Art Gallery* v. *C & E Commrs* [1986] STC 156, QBD).

7.6.3   Exhibition organisers

To determine the correct treatment of these services we have to examine the place of supply rules, found in the VAT (Place of Supply of Services) Order 1992, SI 1992/3121, where Art. 15 states that:

Where a supply consists of . . .

(b) services relating to exhibitions, conferences or meetings . . .

It shall be treated as made where the services are physically carried out.

The services of organising an exhibition are therefore treated as supplied where the work is carried out. If this is in the UK the supply is standard rated, if it is outside the UK then the supply is outside the scope of UK VAT, although if it is in another member state it may mean that the person must register for VAT in that member state and charge VAT accordingly. Some member states allow the VAT to be accounted for by the customer when the customer is VAT registered.

HMRC guidance is that if an exhibition organiser is required to attend the exhibition to oversee the event, in the course of supplying his services, then the place of supply is where the exhibition takes place. This means that exhibition organisers need to register in the member state where the exhibition is held in order to be eligible to recover VAT on the costs of goods and services bought in locally, as an Eighth Directive refund would not be allowed where taxable supplies are made in the member state concerned.

7.6.4 Construction and installation of exhibition stands

The place of supply of construction services is detailed in the VAT (Place of Supply of Services) Order 1992, SI 1992/3121, Art. 5 as being made 'where the land in connection with which the supply is made is situated'. Therefore, any services of on-site construction of the stand, lighting and power installation, etc., are supplied where the exhibition is held. If this is in the UK the supply is standard rated, if outside the UK it is outside the scope of VAT, but if it is in another member state it may mean that the person must register for VAT in that member state and charge VAT accordingly. Some member states allow the VAT to be accounted for by the customer when the customer is VAT registered.

HMRC states in its guidance that if a UK carpenter is engaged to design, make and install an exhibition stand, the supply takes place where the exhibition stand is installed under Art. 15 of the VAT (Place of Supply of Services) Order 1992, SI 1992/3121.

7.6.5 Design and other consultancy services

Consultancy services generally are treated as supplied where the customer belongs, under the VAT (Place of Supply of Services) Order 1992, SI 1992/3121, Art. 16. Therefore, if the customer is in the UK the supply is standard rated, and if the supplier is outside the UK the UK customer will have to account for the VAT under the reverse charge for imported services. This essentially means accounting for the output tax (Box 1 on the VAT Return) and also claiming the same amount as input tax (Box 4 on the VAT Return) but subject to the partial exemption rules.

7.7 HOTELS AND SIMILAR ACCOMMODATION

Sleeping accommodation, accommodation in rooms in conjunction with sleeping accommodation, or rooms for the purpose of a supply of catering, provided in an hotel, inn, boarding house or similar establishment, is standard rated under VATA 1994, Sched. 9, Gp. 1, Item 1(d) (see also **2.3.3**). This means, for example, that for wedding receptions the hire of rooms is usually standard rated because they are hired primarily for the purpose of a supply of catering.

In the tribunal case of *Blendhome Ltd (t/a Stanhill Court Hotel)* (No. 16048), the hotel was licensed as a venue for civil marriage services and, when it was so used, the reception was often held there as well. Specific rooms were used for the marriage services and the reception respectively, and an exclusivity fee was paid for which the party was given exclusive use of the public rooms and grounds of the hotel. Where that included an evening, the appellant would not let bedrooms to other guests and part of the charge made was to cover this. VAT was accounted for on this charge and on the bar and catering charge only. HMRC argued that there was a single composite supply of the provision of hotel accommodation for sleeping or catering and this was excluded from exemption by VATA 1994, Sched. 9, Gp. 1, Item 1(d). The tribunal found that the reception facilities were the primary consideration for which the appellant paid and the exclusivity merely enhanced that supply – applying *Card Protection Plan Ltd* v. *C & E Commrs* (ECJ, C-349/96) [1999] STC 270, para.30 – and the supply was therefore held as wholly standard rated.

Note 9 to VATA 1994, Sched. 9, Gp. 1 defines 'similar establishment' as any premises in which furnished sleeping accommodation is provided, whether board or facilities for the preparation of food are provided or not, which is used by or held out as being suitable for visitors or travellers.

Where a hotel or guest house only provides accommodation for long-term guests, who have no other place of residence, this does not prevent standard rating from applying, see *McGrath (RI)* v. *C & E Commrs* [1992] STC 371, QBD and also *Namecourt Ltd* (No. 1560) which determined that a 'similar establishment' normally provides accommodation for a transient class of resident.

7.7.1 Conferences

Hire of rooms to third parties for the purpose of a conference or similar meeting is exempt from VAT, subject to whether the hotel has opted to tax. Where tea and coffee are also supplied at minimal additional value for a single inclusive price, this is also wholly exempt from VAT. However, where tea/coffee or other refreshments are separately charged for, these are standard rated.

Hotels usually use a 'delegate rate' in charging for such supplies, the rate depending upon the individual needs of the delegates – conference only, conference plus meal, conference plus meal and sleeping accommodation. Where the rate includes a meal, for a single inclusive price, HMRC has confirmed a change of policy with effect from 18 January 2006 (see *Business Brief 01/06*) that each element of the supply should be treated separately and the consideration apportioned accordingly – conference room hire exempt (subject to the option to tax), meals standard rated, sleeping accommodation standard rated. Prior to this it has viewed any conference including sleeping accommodation as a single standard rated supply.

In cases where the hotel organises and runs its own conference or a similar event, the charge for entry is standard rated.

7.7.2 Long-stay guests

There is a provision within VATA 1994, Sched. 6, para. 9, for the provision to an individual of accommodation in a hotel, etc., for reduction of the value of the supply where the stay is in excess of four weeks. The value is reduced to the value of the supply which is attributable to facilities, which must be treated as at least 20 per cent.

Example

If a person stays in a guest house for six weeks, the final period of two weeks is subject to VAT on 20 per cent of the value of the supply. Food must be dealt with separately, so that if the charges made are £25 per night, including evening meal and breakfast, with the food being £10 of the value, VAT would be chargeable on the reduced amount of £25 – £10 = £15 × 20% = £3.

It should be noted that this only applies when the supply is made to an individual who will occupy the accommodation in question, and therefore the reduced value rule does not apply to commercial organisations providing hotel accommodation for employees (unless the supply is to the employee who received reimbursement from his/her employer).

HMRC has always held that accommodation for asylum seekers or the homeless provided by the local authority cannot therefore qualify for the reduced rate for long stays. However, in the case of *Afro Caribbean Housing Association Ltd* (No. 19450), the appellant had entered into an agreement with the British Refugee Council (BRC) to supply accommodation for asylum seekers and refugees for which BRC would pay. The agreement specified that the supply of accommodation was by way of a licence to occupy to the individual occupant of the room. HMRC argued that the supply was to BRC and that therefore the reduced value for stays of over four weeks did not apply (because this applies only where the supply is to the individual). The tribunal found that there was a tripartite relationship with accommodation being supplied to BRC but the actual accommodation in the room being supplied to the individual (and payment being made by BRC) and that there is no requirement in the legislation that the person who receives the taxable supply of accommodation and the person physically occupying the room be the same person. Therefore, the conditions for the reduced value were met and the appeal was allowed. (Note – at the time of writing this decision has only just been released, and in view of the number of other similar cases where HMRC has assessed tax in similar circumstances, it is quite possible that this decision will be appealed.) The terms of each contract should be reviewed to ensure the supply of the licence to occupy the room is made to the individual as in the above case. In cases where VAT is chargeable, a local authority should be entitled to recover the VAT.

Where there is a break in the stay and an occupant then returns, this will not affect the continuance of the reduced value provided that the guest only leaves for an occasional weekend or holiday, is a student who leaves during vacation but returns the following term, or where they pay a retaining fee.

7.7.3   Supplies of food and accommodation to employees

Under VATA 1994, Sched. 6, para. 10, the value of the provision by an employer of accommodation in a hotel, inn, boarding house or similar estab-lishment for his employees is taken as nil, unless the consideration is wholly or partly in money, in which case it is the value of the money. Similar rules apply to the provision of catering or food and beverages to employees.

7.8   HOLIDAY ACCOMMODATION

The letting of holiday accommodation is essentially standard rated (see also **2.3.4** and **3.7**). In accordance with VATA 1994, Sched. 9, Gp. 1, Note 13, this includes any accommodation which is advertised or held out as holiday accommodation or as suitable for holiday or leisure use. This includes accom-modation in beach huts or chalets, caravans, houseboats or tents. VATA 1994, Sched. 9, Gp. 1, Note 11(a) and Sched. 8, Gp. 5, Note 13 also provide that holiday accommodation includes any property which cannot be occu-pied throughout the year or cannot be used as the person's principal private residence because of a covenant, planning permission or other statutory consent. This effectively prevents zero rating from applying to the grant of a major interest in a new building which may otherwise qualify as a dwelling. However, in *Barbara Ashworth* (No. 12924), this provision was considered to be *ultra vires* the Sixth Directive, Art. 13B(b)(1)–(4) because the European legislation does not allow exclusions to the exemption other than those it specifically cites. Therefore, providing that the dwelling is not held out or advertised as holiday accommodation, standard rating should not apply – see also *Notice 709/3, Hotels and Holiday Accommodation*.

In *Loch Tay Highland Lodges Ltd* (No. 18785), the appellant was granted planning permission to construct holiday chalets, with the restriction that the lodges should be used for holiday use only and 'shall not be occupied as the sole or main residence of any occupant'. The tribunal ruled that VATA 1994, Sched. 8, Gp. 5, Note 13(ii) applied to prevent zero rating of the sale of the chalets:

> (ii) residence there throughout the year, or the use of the building or part as the grantee's principal private residence, is prevented by the terms of a covenant, statutory planning consent or similar permission.

The tribunal contrasted its decision to that in *Livingstone Homes UK Ltd* (No. 16649), which it considered to be wrongly decided.

The freehold sale or premium for a tenancy, lease or licence of 'new' holiday accommodation (that is any sale within three years of completion of the building) is also standard rated. Once the building is over three years old the freehold sale or lease, etc., for a premium, is exempt from VAT.

The sale or letting of land for the purposes of the erection of holiday accommodation is also standard rated under VATA 1994, Sched. 9, Gp. 1, Note 11.

One planning device often employed by developers of holiday homes is to sell the land separately to the construction of the holiday home. The sale of the land is standard rated, because of the right to erect holiday accommodation, but if the holiday home is 'designed as a dwelling' (see **3.2**) then the building work will be zero rated. The key condition which may prevent 'holiday accommodation' being 'designed as a dwelling' is whether there is anything in the planning consents, etc., preventing the separate use or disposal of the property. The fact that occupation of the property throughout the year is restricted does not, however, prevent the building being 'designed as a dwelling'. Note that in using this arrangement, timing is essential – the developer cannot start construction prior to sale of the land, otherwise the sale of the land (standard rated) includes the construction work to the date of sale.

7.8.1 Off-season letting

In places where the holiday trade is clearly seasonal, HMRC allows exemption for the letting of what would otherwise be standard rated holiday accommodation, provided that the letting is for a period of more than four weeks and is for the purpose of residential accommodation.

7.8.2 Timeshares

The sales of timeshares is treated in the same way as the sale of any other holiday accommodation – standard rated if under three years old and exempt if more than three years old. Periodic maintenance and service charges are, however, always standard rated.

7.8.3 Sale of 'holiday accommodation' for residential use

In the tribunal case of *Pembridge Estates Ltd* (No. 9606), the appellant company renovated a flat and let it for holiday purpose for two weeks before selling it to one of the directors for his personal use. As the holiday letting was standard rated (simply by being let or held out as holiday accommodation) the input tax on the renovation was recoverable and the tribunal decided no adjustment was required on the later exempt sale of the property because at the time of completion of the works the appellant had no intention other than holiday letting. This type of arrangement has been used for VAT planning purposes, but care must be taken because if at the time the input tax is incurred and claimed, and the intention is to sell the building after a short period of holiday letting when the VAT is incurred, an adjustment may be required. The Capital Goods Scheme (see **1.10**) would also affect the right to retain the input tax if the taxable cost of the building works is over £250,000. The partial exemption override rules (see **1.9.4** and **1.9.9**) may also affect recovery.

7.9 HOUSING ASSOCIATIONS AND SOCIAL LANDLORDS

Notice 708/5, Registered Social Landlords (Housing Associations, etc.) provides details of the VAT treatment of a number of specialist housing association funding schemes, such as the treatment of grant income from government bodies.

7.9.1 Disapplication of the option to tax

In cases where a 'registered housing association' purchases land there is specific provision that it should be able to purchase the land free of VAT, even where the option to tax has been exercised. This is found at VATA 1994, Sched. 10, para. 2(3)(a) and stipulates that where the housing association has provided a certificate to the vendor that the land will be used for the construction of dwellings, or solely for a relevant residential purpose, then the option to tax is disapplied. Note that the certificate must be supplied prior to the transaction taking place. In the past HMRC has been prepared to allow retrospective issue of certificates, but this is a point which is coming up at tribunal fairly often now and the courts always rule in favour of HMRC on the grounds that the legislation uses the words 'has provided'.

7.9.1.1 Definition of 'registered housing association'

The term 'registered housing association' is defined at VATA 1994, Sched. 10, para. 3(8) as being:

(a) a registered social landlord within the meaning of Part I of the Housing Act 1996;

(b) a registered housing association within the meaning of the Housing Associations Act 1985 (Scottish registered housing associations); or

(c) a registered housing association within the meaning of Part II of the Housing (Northern Ireland) Order 1992 (Northern Irish registered housing associations).

7.9.2 Sales of land by a builder

It is common for builders to acquire land and to supply the land to a housing association together with construction services. This is because housing associations receive separate funding for the purchase of land and construction of the dwellings. This is generally seen as two supplies, one of exempt land, subject to the option to tax (unless the housing association issues a certificate) and a supply of construction services, which presuming they result in new houses or flats, etc., will be zero rated.

If the house builder has incurred a VAT cost on the land this will result in the VAT on the land purchase being irrecoverable as exempt input tax (see *C & E Commrs* v. *Southern Primary Housing Ltd* [2003] EWCA Civ 1662). In this case the company argued that without the sale of the exempt land it would not have entered into the taxable building contract, but the court ruled that the only direct and immediate link between the VAT on the land purchase was with the exempt sale, of which it was a cost component, and the input tax was therefore exempt input tax and irrecoverable.

One way of circumventing the above problems is by what has become known as the 'golden brick' scheme. This involves the builder partly completing the construction to at least above foundation level, and then selling the land with partly completed dwellings on it to the housing association. As partly completed dwellings qualify for zero rating in the same way as new dwellings this supply is zero rated, and the builder can then continue to supply zero rated construction services to complete the construction. The effect of this when opted land is purchased as part of the onward supply is for the builder to gain full recovery of the VAT incurred.

7.9.3 Construction of relevant residential properties to be run by the local authority

Housing associations are often involved in the construction of children's and old people's homes, etc., which will be let to the local authority to be operated by it. Where the housing association contracts with a builder to supply construction services, it is unable to provide a certificate to the builder because it is not the 'person' who will be using the building for the relevant residential purpose. The construction works will therefore be standard rated. However, the housing association will be able to obtain a certificate from the local authority that it will be using the building for the qualifying purpose and therefore as long as the term of the lease is over 21 years, zero rating will apply to the first rent or premium received, allowing the housing association to register for VAT and recover the VAT charged to them.

7.9.4 Conversion services

Services supplied in the course of conversion of a non-residential property into a dwelling or a relevant residential building are zero rated when the recipient of the supply is a relevant housing association, under VATA 1994, Sched. 8, Gp. 5, Item 3. The zero rating also includes builders materials supplied in the course of construction, but excludes the services of an architect, surveyor or any person acting as a consultant or in a supervisory capacity. A certificate must be supplied by the housing association, the form of which is at *VAT Notice 708/5*, Annex B.

7.9.4.1 Definition of 'relevant housing association'

A relevant housing association for these purposes includes (VATA 1994, Sched. 8, Gp. 5, Note 21):

(a) a registered social landlord within the meaning of Part I of the Housing Act 1996;
(b) a registered housing association within the meaning of the Housing Associations Act 1985 (Scottish registered housing associations); or
(c) a registered housing association within the meaning of Part II of the Housing (Northern Ireland) Order 1992 (Northern Irish registered housing associations).

There is also an extra-statutory concession which was published by HMRC in *News Release 15/96* which allows any charity that is in business and is prevented from granting a major interest to take advantage of this relief (see *VAT Notice 708/5, Registered Social Landlords (Housing Associations, etc.)*).

225

7.9.5 'Person constructing' status

In the case of *Peddars Way Housing Association Ltd* (No. 12663), the VAT tribunal ruled that a housing association which had acquired rights and obligations in purchasing the housing stock of a local authority by way of a transfer of a going concern did not acquire the 'person constructing' status – this was not transferable.

Link Housing Association Ltd v. *C & E Commrs* [1992] STC 718, CS, concerned a case where the tenants had a right to purchase the houses which had been built by the association. The association successfully claimed input tax relating to the selling costs, claiming that the sales were zero rated as it was the 'person constructing' under VATA 1994, Sched. 8, Gp. 5, Item 1, even though in most cases the houses had been constructed many years before. The 'person constructing' status therefore remains with the person who constructed the buildings as long as they retain the major interest in the property, although it is only the *first* grant of a major interest by the person constructing a dwelling which qualifies for zero rating (i.e. if the person constructing grants a lease of over 21 years and then later sells the freehold, the lease will be zero rated, but the freehold sale will be exempt).

7.9.6 Construction of own offices

In *Cardiff Community Housing Association* (No. 16481), the tribunal ruled that construction of the housing association's own offices qualified for zero rating on the basis of non-business use. Although the letting of property is generally considered to be an exempt business activity, in this case the tribunal saw the housing association as taking on the role of the local government providing housing needs for the sick and poor on an uneconomic basis.

However, in the decision in *Riverside Housing Association Ltd* (No. 19341), the tribunal determined that despite the provision of housing at a low cost to disadvantaged tenants and an assumption by the appellant of many of the duties of the local housing authority, the high degree of regulation by the Housing Corporation, and high dependence on public funds, this was insufficient to negate the 'business' character of the activities. Therefore, zero rating did not apply to the construction of the housing association's own offices. The tribunal specifically distinguished *Riverside* from *Cardiff Community* on the grounds that the latter was wholly public funded, and the degree of regulation was greater.

7.9.7 Shared ownership schemes

Housing associations often enter into shared ownership arrangements where the ownership of the dwelling is shared between the housing association itself and the occupier. The occupier purchases a share of the dwelling and then pays rent to cover the housing association's retained share, often with the option of the occupier increasing their share of ownership at some time in the future. The initial payment by the occupier for his share in the property is zero rated, with subsequent payments for equity or rent being exempt.

7.9.8   Use of a wholly owned company

A housing association can gain increased VAT recovery in certain circumstances by effectively 'washing' the VAT incurred through a wholly owned company. For example, if instead of contracting for the design and construction of houses directly, the housing association arranges for the professional services and construction to be supplied to its wholly owned company, this company can then grant a zero rated major interest in the dwellings to the housing association, thus gaining recovery of VAT on professional costs associated with the project. (The housing association would of course usually be granting exempt short-term lets and thus be unable to recover this VAT.) This type of arrangement is likely to fall within the disclosure of VAT avoidance schemes legislation (see **1.12**) and HMRC could challenge it on *Halifax* principles (see **1.13**).

7.10   INSOLVENCY PRACTITIONERS

VAT Notice 700/56, Insolvency details HMRC guidance on the treatment of insolvency practitioners. With regard to the position of insolvency practitioners and property, it is vital that they determine the VAT position of the property in question. Issues such as whether the option to tax has been exercised, or when the building was acquired and whether it is still subject to the Capital Goods Scheme are paramount in determining whether a disposal of a property or even rent, should be charged to VAT.

Failure to determine these issues could leave the insolvency practitioner liable to account for VAT which they have not received.

7.10.1   Tax points

Although most insolvency practitioners account for VAT on a cash basis, *Business Brief 04/96*, reproduced below, explains that there are no tax point concessions for insolvency practitioners, whether with regard to the completion of a construction project or other income/activities.

BUSINESS BRIEF 04/96: Insolvency tax points clarified for construction industry

There are no concessions for tax points in the construction industry when a business becomes insolvent. The normal tax point rules apply equally to transactions pre and post the appointment of an insolvency practitioner.

Services, or services and goods in the construction industry are generally provided under contract. The contract need not be in writing and can be made orally, or its existence may be implied by the conduct of the parties. If the contract does not provide for stage payments the normal tax point rules will apply.

Where a contract provides for periodic or stage payments the tax point is the earlier of the date of issue of a VAT invoice or the date that payment is received. Where self billing arrangements are used the effect is to limit the tax point to the date of receipt of payment.

Where the contract is terminated early before the terms have been fulfilled, the supply is considered to have been completed on the day that the work ceased. That date is the basic tax point for those supplies where section 6 of the 1994 VAT Act applies.

The tax point for retentions is restricted to the date of receipt of payment or issue of a VAT invoice, whichever happens first. (Retentions is a term referring to monies which a customer or main contractor withholds from a subcontractor until the contract has been completed to his satisfaction). Where self billing arrangements are used the effect is to limit the tax point to the date of receipt of payment.

7.10.2 Bad debt relief

Where bad debt relief is claimed by a supplier, the customer is required to pay back the input tax previously claimed on the supply. Prior to 1 January 2003, the supplier was required to send a Notice to the customer when making a claim for Bad Debt Relief. This is no longer the case and customers with debts outstanding for more than six months are required to monitor the position themselves and make adjustments to input tax claims as appropriate. In the case of insolvency practitioners, however, there is an extra-statutory concession which relieves them from the requirement of repaying this input tax. It applies to any of the following insolvency procedures, which are to be found at VATA 1994, s.81(4B): Bankruptcy orders, winding-up orders or administration orders, administrative receiverships, voluntary winding-up, voluntary arrangements, deeds of arrangement.

In addition, HMRC has also stated that these arrangements will also apply to the following: Partnership Voluntary Arrangements; Partnership Liquidations; Partnership Administration Orders; Sequestrations; County Court Administration Orders; Schemes of Arrangement; and Deceased Persons Administration Orders.

7.10.3 Law of Property Act Receivers

Law of Property Act (LPA) Receivers are appointed by lenders in cases where borrowers default on the loan. Under the Law of Property Act 1925, s.109, the LPA Receiver is appointed as an agent of the defaulting borrower. This means that for VAT purposes, even though the LPA Receiver is appointed by the lender, any supplies to the LPA Receiver are in fact supplies to the borrower and this affects the right to recover input tax.

In 1994, HMRC agreed special rules for these circumstances which allow the lender to be seen as the agent of the borrower in relation to costs relating to the disposal of the property, and thus such costs are treated as supplied to the lender and supplied on by them under VATA 1994, s.47(3). This allows the lender to recover the VAT incurred and charge on the VAT to the borrower, using the bad debt relief rules to claim back output tax accounted for. These arrangements only apply to the direct costs of disposing of the property such as solicitors' and estate agents' fees, and not to any costs incurred by the lender as principle such as costs in respect of taking possession of the property or securing it, even where they also are charged to the borrower under the terms of the mortgage agreement. In using this facility, LPA Receivers are required to issue a VAT invoice to the borrower for the onward charge of the expenses. The tax point for such charges is the date of the supply to the LPA Receiver (see *Wirral MBC* v. *C & E Commrs* [1995] STC 308).

Since the 1994 agreement by HMRC to the above treatment of input tax in respect of LPA Receiverships, the tribunal has ruled in the case of *Leeds and Holbeck Building Society* (No. 15356), that the costs of obtaining a possession order and securing the property, were recoverable by the mortgager, being incurred in relation to the sale of the property, which was taxable. This supports the treatment outlined above.

LPA Receivers themselves cannot therefore be required to register for VAT, although in practice, HMRC does sometimes accept registrations from an LPA Receiver. It is usually the borrower who accounts for any VAT due in respect of the property under an LPA Receivership, on his normal VAT Return. HMRC can, however, require an LPA Receiver to account for VAT on any property under his control on form VAT 833, if the borrower refuses to do this (see *Sargent* v. *C & E Commrs* [1995] STC 398). LPA Receivers cannot therefore issue tax invoices in respect of rent or other transactions, this is for the borrower to do, and this can cause problems as the tenant or purchaser of the property will require a VAT invoice so that he can recover the VAT paid. In such circumstances it is possible for HMRC to authorise recovery of the input tax on the basis of other evidence.

7.10.4 Sale of repossessed goods

In cases where land or buildings are sold in satisfaction of a debt, a supply takes place by the owner of the land or buildings and VAT must be accounted for accordingly.

7.10.5 Foreclosures

In cases where a person obtains a court order and forecloses on land or property, there is a supply by the owner of the property to the person foreclosing.

In certain cases, this supply could be treated as the transfer of a going concern (see **1.4.15** and **2.15**). Any subsequent disposal of the land or building is made by the person foreclosing and it is their responsibility to correctly account for VAT.

7.11   LOCAL AUTHORITIES

Local authorities enjoy special treatment for VAT purposes under VATA 1994, s.33 (Sixth Directive on VAT, Art. 4(5)) so that in cases where they are carrying out their statutory non-business activities, they are able to recover any VAT incurred in relation to them. HMRC guidance on local authorities can be found in *Notice 749, Local Authorities and Similar Bodies*. However, where they carry out activities which are also carried out by commercial organisations and are therefore in competition with them, these are not treated as non-business and the normal VAT rules apply. There are special partial exemption rules for local authorities which allow most of them to recover all of their input tax as being under the special *de minimis* limits (see *VAT Notice 749*, Appendix F for details). With regard to land and property transactions, these are not treated as 'non-business' and supplies are therefore exempt with the option to tax insofar as commercial property is concerned.

7.11.1   Letting of property

The letting of commercial property by a local authority is generally seen as a business activity (*West Devon District Council* v. *C & E Commrs* [2001] STC 1282, ChD) and is therefore exempt from VAT subject to the option to tax.

With regard to housing stock, where this is provided as 'council housing' under their statutory obligations, this is a non-business activity, but this is not extended to social landlords or housing associations, to which the normal VAT rules apply.

In *Shearing* (No. 16723), the letting of beach huts by Brighton & Hove District Council, was held to be a business activity and therefore standard rated, notwithstanding that the Council had powers under the Public Health Act 1936, s.232 to provide bathing huts.

7.11.2   Option to tax

The statutory block to the option to tax does not apply when the grant is made to a local authority (or to a government department or National Health Service Trust) to the extent that it occupies the property for the purposes of its outside-the-scope s.33 activities (VATA 1994, Sched. 10, para. 10, see also **2.7.2.2**).

7.11.3   Statutory repair work

When a local authority carries out repairs to buildings where owners have failed to comply with statutory notices, this is a non-business activity by the local authority which can therefore recover VAT incurred under the s.33 regime.

7.11.4   Tolls

Road tolls have been treated as a non-business activity by local authorities in the UK and therefore outside the scope of VAT, and otherwise exempt from VAT when provided by commercial operators. However, in *Commission of the European Communities* v. *United Kingdom* (ECJ, C-359/97), [2000] STC 777, it was decided by the European Court that road tolls charged by private commercial operators should be subject to VAT at standard rate, and that only where local authorities operate tolls in their capacity as a public authority should the toll be treated as non-business. Following the decision, HMRC announced that commercially operated tolls would be standard rated from 1 February 2003 (*Business Brief 03/03*).

Following the decision, only the following toll charges remain free of VAT: Cleddau Bridge, Dartford Crossing, Erskine Bridge, Forth Road Bridge, Humber Bridge, Itchen Bridge, Mersey Tunnel, Tamar Bridge, Tay Bridge, Tyne Tunnel.

7.11.5   Congestion charges

Congestion charges levied by local authorities are outside the scope of VAT.

7.11.6   Hostels for the homeless

Following the decision in *City of Westminster* (No. 3667), the provision of accommodation and catering in hostels for the homeless is considered to be a supply of welfare and a non-business activity, providing it is supplied for social reasons in pursuance of the local authority's welfare obligations in the community. The tribunal also decided that it would otherwise fall to be exempt from VAT under the Sixth Directive on VAT, Art. 13A(1)(g) as the provision of welfare services. This decision can be distinguished from that in *Namecourt Ltd* (No. 1560), where although the provision was of hostel accommodation for the homeless, funded mainly from DHSS payments, the organisation supplying the accommodation was not a local authority, etc., and exemption did not therefore apply.

7.11.7 Sports facilities

The provisions at VATA 1994, Sched. 9, Gp. 10, Note 3, exclude local authorities as 'eligible bodies' for the purpose of the exemption under that Group for a grant of sporting facilities to individuals and the right to enter a sports competition.

7.11.8 Burials and cremations

Where a local authority is a 'burial authority' under the provisions of the Local Government Act 1970 its services of the provision and maintenance of cemeteries and crematoria are not considered to be carried out by way of business when they are carried out at less than cost (*Rhondda Cynon Taff County Borough Council* (No. 16496)).

7.11.9 Car parking

Provision of on-street metered car parking by a local authority is outside the scope of VAT, the local authority being the only 'person' which can provide such services. On-street pay and display car parking operated by other than a local authority is a standard rated supply, for example pay and display on-street parking operated by NCP, etc. However, HMRC has always seen the provision of off-street car parking as standard rated. This was challenged in the case of *Isle of Wight Council* (No. 18557), on the grounds that the council was statutorily required to provide car parking facilities as a local authority body. Although the council was initially successful, HMRC appealed to the High Court which directed that the matter be put back before the tribunal to consider whether 'distortion of competition' should not mean that the supplies should be standard rated – the tribunal duly came to this conclusion – see *Business Brief 03/05*. Following this, Isle of Wight Council banded together with three other local authorities to again challenge the treatment of off-street car parking, and in decision No. 19427 the tribunal ruled in their favour in that they had provided sufficient evidence to show that there would be no distortion of competition if VAT were not charged on off-street car parking. The local authorities did have to go to great lengths to provide detailed expert evidence that the removal of VAT from the car parking charges would not distort competition with commercial operators. At the time of writing, this decision has not been challenged by HMRC.

7.11.9.1 Excess charges

Following the VAT tribunal decision in *Bristol City Council* (No. 17665), HMRC confirmed that excess charges in off-street car parks levied under the Road Traffic Regulations 1984 are outside the scope of VAT as penalties, as are penalties levied under the Road Traffic Act 1991. Excess charges in non local authority car parks are subject to VAT arising under the contract between the operator and the car owner/driver (see *J G Leigh (t/a Moor Valley Video)* (No. 5098)).

7.12   SERVICED OFFICE ACCOMMODATION

The VAT treatment of serviced office accommodation depends upon the nature of the supply made and whether this amounts to a licence to occupy land or not. It is primarily seen as an exempt licence to occupy land, subject to the option to tax, providing there is a degree of exclusivity in the rights of the occupier to use the office space provided. Included in the right to occupy land will be such services as reception, telephonist, security, heating, lighting and power (see *Business Enterprises (UK) Ltd* (No. 3161)).

The right to use common areas such as toilets, reception, lifts, cafeteria, and use of a car parking space, also follows the treatment of the supply of accommodation where it is included in the charge for use of the accommodation. The same treatment is also afforded to use of telephones, computers, faxes, photocopiers, etc. where this is included in a single charge for use of the accommodation.

However, where services are separately supplied and charged for, such as photocopying and other secretarial services, and are optional to the right to occupy the land, then these will fall to be treated separately and subject to VAT at standard rate (see *Tower Hamlets Housing Action Trust* (No. 17308) where photocopying was held to be a separate standard rated supply, being paid for per copy, whereas telephone and fax services were held to be part of a single supply of serviced office accommodation as payment was not dependent upon the amount of use).

In cases where the accommodation provided is not specified and simply amounts to shared use of a desk, etc., the supply does not amount to a licence to occupy land, and is therefore standard rated. Similarly, access to office premises to make use of the facilities, such as photocopying, telephone, etc. is a standard rated supply.

In the tribunal case of *United Utilities plc* (No. 17582), the appellant tried to argue that its supplies were the services of acting as a bookmaker's agent (exempt) and the supply of office accommodation (exempt). The tribunal examined the facts of the case and the agreement and determined in commercial reality that there was a single supply of call centre services and information technology support in relation to a telephone betting service and that it would be artificial to split this.

7.13 STORAGE FACILITIES

The VAT treatment of storage facilities depends upon whether the storage provided is a discrete area which the customer has the sole right to store goods in, or whether the facility provider simply stores a customer's goods in his premises, not providing a discrete area for each customer. In the former case the supply amounts to a licence to occupy land and is therefore exempt, subject to the option to tax, but in the latter case it does not and is therefore standard rated.

Separate supplies of packing materials, the value of which depends upon the use of the customer, will be standard rated.

Where the supply of storage facilities is made to the public, it will be in the interests of the supplier to ensure that the income qualifies for exemption from VAT, as this enables them to offer the facilities at a competitive rate and potentially secure a better profit than competitors. This must, however, be balanced against the cost of non-recovery of input tax on related expenditure.

Certain storage facilities, such as facilities for parking a vehicle, housing or storage of an aircraft, or mooring of a boat are specifically excepted from the exemption for a right to occupy land (VATA 1994, Sched. 9, Gp. 1, Items 1(h) and (k)) and these are therefore standard rated. In *Trinity Factoring Services Ltd* v. *C & E Commrs* [1994] STC 504, CS, the Court of Sessions commented in relation to a lease of a garage for storage purposes that: 'If the formal lease had specified that the purpose of the letting was for domestic storage or storage use only, then the supply would have been exempt'. This demonstrates the importance of setting out the terms of the agreement within the formal contract so that it is clear that the 'garage' is not 'facilities for parking a vehicle', etc.

7.14 VILLAGE HALLS

In addition to the VAT relief available on the construction of a new village hall (see **5.2.3**), there are arrangements which can be put into place with a local authority to gain recovery of VAT on village hall construction projects, or indeed other purchases. Local authorities are entitled to recover VAT incurred in relation to their non-business activities under special rules (VATA 1994, s.33) which are explained in detail in *VAT Notice 749, Local Authorities and Similar Bodies* (see also **7.11**). Therefore, in cases where a local authority funds the construction of or works to a village hall, it may recover the VAT incurred to the extent of that funding, subject to certain conditions being met. For example, if the grant funding is of 50 per cent of the cost, then 50 per cent of the VAT incurred may be recovered by the local authority. It is usual in such circumstances for a special fund to be set up to administer the project. In order for the local authority to be able to recover the VAT, it must place the order, receive the supply, receive a VAT invoice addressed to it and make payment from its own funds. Where funds have been raised for the project or trust fund money is utilised, these must be donated to the local authority and cannot be earmarked for a special purpose, otherwise they cannot be treated as the local authority's own funds. The local authority's own funds can, however, include funds derived from other local authorities or government bodies.

Local authorities can also recover VAT on expenditure met from donated funds as long as they retain ownership of the goods concerned and use them for non-business purposes. However, 'donated funds' cannot include funds which have been donated to be used for the benefit of the donor or a specified other party, as this will be seen as consideration for a supply by the local authority, subject to VAT at the appropriate rate.

In cases where the local authority is sole trustee of the village hall, it can therefore recover all of the VAT it incurs on construction work or fitting out costs, as it will retain ownership of these, including any goods purchased with funds donated from any source. The same treatment is afforded to village halls owned by the local authority but let to a voluntary organisation for a peppercorn or other nominal rent.

Where the local authority acts as custodian trustee there is no entitlement to recover VAT.

APPENDIX A

Property VAT liabilities – quick reference table

	VAT treatment	Chapter
FREEHOLD SALES		
First grant of a major interest by the developer in buildings designed as dwellings built or converted from non-residential	Zero	**3**
First grant of a major interest by the developer in communal residential buildings	Zero	**3**
First grant of a major interest by the developer in non-business charitable buildings	Zero	**5**
Other supplies relating to domestic and other non-commercial buildings	Exempt	**3/5**
New commercial buildings (under three years from date of completion)	Standard	**2**
Other supplies relating to commercial buildings	Exempt subject to the option to tax	**2**
LEASES		
New dwellings, communal or residential buildings or non-business charitable buildings or such buildings newly converted from non-residential if for more than 21 years where built by and granted by developer	Zero on premium or first payment rent, exempt thereafter	**3/5**
Other grants in respect of buildings above (existing buildings, lease up to 21 years, not by developer)	Exempt	**3/5**
New commercial buildings	Exempt subject to the option to tax	**2**
Other commercial buildings	Exempt subject to the option to tax	**2**
Assignments (commercial)	Exempt subject to the option to tax	**2**
Assignments (residential, charitable)	Exempt	**3/5**
Surrenders and reverse surrenders (commercial)	Exempt subject to the option to tax	**2**
Surrenders and reverse surrenders (residential, charitable)	Exempt	**3/5**

236

	VAT treatment	Chapter
LISTED AND OTHER PROTECTED BUILDINGS		
Approved alterations to dwellings, communal residential and non-business charitable buildings	Zero	6
Other work on similar buildings (repair, maintenance, etc.)	Standard	6
Freehold sales by developer of substantially reconstructed dwellings, communal residential and non-business charitable buildings	Zero on premium or first payment rent, exempt thereafter	6
Leases of more than 21 years by developer of substantially reconstructed dwellings, communal residential and non-business charitable buildings	Zero on premium or first payment rent, exempt thereafter	6
Works to commercial buildings	Standard	4
Freehold sale of commercial buildings	Exempt subject to the option to tax	2
Lease of commercial buildings	Exempt subject to the option to tax	2
BUILDING LAND		
Sales and leases	Exempt subject to the option to tax, except housing association where certificate for residential development is supplied or DIY housebuilders, when the option to tax is not available	2
REFURBISHED BUILDINGS		
Sales and leases of residential buildings	Exempt, unless the property has been empty for 10 or more years, when the freehold sale or premium or first payment of rent under a lease of over 21 years is zero rated	3
Sales and leases of non-residential buildings	Exempt subject to the option to tax	3

	VAT treatment	Chapter
CONVERSIONS		
Freehold sale by developer of conversion from non-residential into dwelling or communal residential building	Zero	3
As above but grant of lease of over 21 years	Zero on premium or first rental payment, exempt thereafter	3
BUILDING SERVICES		
Construction of new buildings designed as dwellings (including sub-contractors' services)	Zero	4
Construction of communal residential and non-business charitable buildings provided an appropriate certificate is obtained from the customer, and the customer is the person using the building for qualifying purposes	Zero	4
Construction of new commercial buildings	Standard	4
Construction services supplied to registered housing association on conversion of non-residential building into a dwelling or communal residential building	Zero	4
Changed number of dwellings conversion (including conversion from non-residential)	Reduced rate	4
Renovation of dwellings and communal residential buildings which have been empty for three or more years	Reduced rate	4
Repairs and alterations	Standard	4/6
Demolition	Standard	4
Professional services including contract management	Standard	4
CIVIL ENGINEERING WORK		
New work	Standard	
New work as part of a housing or other residential charitable non-business development project under a single contract	Zero	
Repairs, maintenance and alteration	Standard	
OPTIONS		
Option to undertake a transaction which is itself chargeable to VAT	Standard	

APPENDIX B

Table of main changes in land and property VAT law since 1 April 1989

1 April 1989 – Zero rate removed for new or partly completed commercial property. From this date the freehold sale of new commercial property and works of civil engineering became standard rated, with the freehold sale of commercial property over three years old being exempt. The grant of a lease in commercial property became exempt from VAT, whether the property is new or over three years old.

1 April 1989 – The zero rate for the grant of a lease in a new dwelling or other qualifying building is restricted to the first grant.

1 April 1989 – Reaffirmation of standard rate for sales of sporting rights following the result of *C & E Commrs* v. *P J Parkinson and Others* QB March 1988.

1 April 1989 – Reaffirmation of standard rate for the right to occupy a box, seat or other accommodation at a sports ground, theatre, concert hall or other place of entertainment following the result of *C & E Commrs* v. *P Zinn and Others* QB November 1987.

1 April 1989 – Change of use self-supply on relevant residential and relevant charitable property is introduced.

1 August 1989 – The election to waive exemption is introduced, with the provision that any election exercised by 30 November 1989 has effect from 1 April 1989 if so required.

1 August 1989 – The developer's self-supply charge is introduced.

1 April 1990 – Capital Goods Scheme introduced.

1 February 1991 – New holiday accommodation and sites for the development of holiday accommodation are standard rated regardless of the term of the supply.

1 January 1992 – The exemption in land at VATA 1994, Sched. 9, Gp. 1, Item 1 is extended to include 'in relation to land in Scotland, any personal right to call or be granted any such interest or right'.

1 January 1992 – Introduction of mandatory standard rating for a supply of a developmental tenancy, lease or licence.

1 January 1992 – The developer's self-supply is extended to include certain extensions, enlargements and reconstructions of existing buildings.

1 January 1992 – Clarification of the treatment of the right to take game and fish when supplied with freehold land as a single exempt supply.

1 January 1992 – Disallowance of input tax incurred prior to the date of exercising the option to tax, if the person making the election had already received exempt income – permission required to opt to tax in these circumstances.

1 January 1992 – Tenants fitting out costs and other costs incurred by third party specifically excluded from value of self-supply.

1 April 1994 – Extra-statutory concession for service charges to domestic property introduced to provide exemption for all mandatory charges regardless of the interest held.

27 July 1994 – Zero rating for the grant of a major interest in conversions of non-residential buildings into dwellings, and for dwellings not used as such since 1 April 1973, introduced by Extra-statutory concession.

30 November 1994 – Statutory block for the option to tax is introduced where the interest granted is between connected persons, either of which are not fully taxable (at least 80 per cent taxable). This was introduced to block lease/leaseback schemes.

1 March 1995 – Extra-statutory concession for buildings converted from non-residential into dwellings and other qualifying buildings is brought into statute.

1 March 1995 – Zero rating for conversion work into a qualifying building introduced for housing associations.

1 March 1995 – Zero rating for new dwellings and other qualifying buildings restricted to 'first' grant.

1 March 1995 – Zero rating introduced for charity annexes capable of functioning independently.

1 March 1995 – Provision for apportionment in cases of a mixed development is introduced.

1 March 1995 – Definition of an 'existing building' in VATA 1994, Sched. 8, Gp. 5, Note 18 is introduced.

1 March 1995 – Relaxation of block for input tax recovery on items installed by a builder, to include ventilation equipment, burglar alarms, lifts, hoists and, in flats, waste disposal units and door entry systems.

1 March 1995 – Blocking of input tax on items installed by builders extended to include relevant residential and relevant charitable buildings.

1 March 1995 – Zero rating for ecclesiastical buildings restricted to certain named denominations.

1 March 1995 – Definition of 'approved alterations' to protected buildings amended to exclude alterations which are incidental to repairs.

1 March 1995 – Definition of 'building materials' changed re fitted wardrobes as a result of *C & E Commrs* v. *McLean Homes Ltd* [1993] STC 335.

16 April 1996 – Extra-statutory concession allowing treatment of protected buildings to be extended to buildings with immunity from listing certificates is introduced.

26 November 1996 – Statutory block for the option to tax as introduced on 30 November 1994 is repealed due to its ineffectiveness in preventing the avoidance schemes it was introduced to combat.

1 March 1997 – Abolition of developer's self-supply.

19 March 1997 – Statutory block to the option to tax amended to provide the block where the item is a capital item for the purposes of the Capital Goods Scheme, and the intention or expectation of the person developing or financing the development or a person connected with them was that the use would not be for fully taxable purposes.

19 March 1997 – Statutory block to the option to tax amended to allow it to continue to apply to sales of non-residential property to be converted into residential, provided both parties agree and the purchaser will make a zero-rated supply of the completed development. In certain cases the block affects supplies from 26 November 1996, unless the transitional rules apply.

9 December 1997 – Anti-avoidance legislation introduced regarding the tax point on construction services where the intention of expectation is that the building will not be used for fully taxable purposes – the '18-month rule'.

10 March 1999 – Extension of statutory block to the option to tax to cases where the land is intended or expected to become exempt land.

12 May 2001 – 5 per cent rate introduced for conversions of non-residential buildings into dwellings and for conversions involving a change of the number of dwellings in existing housing stock, including conversion of dwellings into bed-sits, and dwellings into relevant residential buildings.

12 May 2001 – 5 per cent rate introduced for renovation of dwellings which have been empty for three years or more.

1 August 2001 – Zero rate introduced for first grant of a major interest in a renovated dwelling which had been empty for 10 years or more.

18 April 2002 – Partial exemption standard method override introduced.

1 June 2002 – Extension of zero rating for conversions to include non-residential and relevant residential into bed-sit accommodation and non-residential into relevant residential.

1 June 2002 – Extension of zero rating for renovations to include relevant residential and bed-sit accommodation.

1 June 2002 – Apportionment allowed where a building is only partly for use as a charitable annexe.

241

1 June 2002 – 5 per cent rate for grant-funded installation of energy-saving equipment extended to include installation of renewable sources of energy, factory insulated hot water tanks and micro-combined heat and power systems.

1 June 2002 – Change of use of relevant residential and relevant charitable buildings – clawback from HMRC makes allowance for time used for qualifying purpose – prior to this the clawback involved 100 per cent of the value of the zero-rated benefit.

10 April 2003 – New rules for treatment of deferred consideration.

1 January 2004 – Partial exemption special method override introduced.

1 January 2004 – Changes to information required on a proper VAT invoice.

1 January 2004 – Changes to VAT treatment of lifts installed in educational buildings, with transitional period to 31 March 2005.

1 January 2004 – Less detailed tax invoice limit increased from £100 to £250.

26 February 2004 – Zero rate for approved alterations no longer applies to outbuildings following the House of Lords' decision in *Zielinski Baker & Partners Ltd* (CA, 15 May 2002).

18 March 2004 – Requirement for purchaser to notify vendor that their option to tax is not subject to the statutory block on transfer of a new or opted property as a going concern.

1 April 2004 – Grants for repairs and maintenance of churches increased to 17.5 per cent of the cost (from 12.5 per cent prior to this date).

1 August 2004 – Introduction of disclosure of avoidance schemes legislation.

1 August 2004 – Changes to VAT grouping conditions.

1 April 2005 – Amendments to the partial exemption rules – rounding up when using standard method removed from businesses with over £400,000 non-attributable input tax – a special method must be in writing – any gap in the treatment of input tax in a special method to be determined according to 'use'.

2 December 2005 – HMRC accepts that for DIY House-converters only where an additional dwelling is formed as part of the conversion the reduced rate applies to all of the works to the parts of the building that were non-residential prior to work commencing.

1 March 2005 – Provision of lifts for charities no longer applies to educational buildings apart from students' residential accommodation.

1 January 2006 – Reduced rate extended to include installation of wood-fuelled boilers.

Draft clause for transfer of a going concern

1. All sums stated in this Agreement are exclusive of VAT and the Buyer shall pay, in addition, any VAT properly payable.
2. The Seller and the Buyer consider that Section 49 of the VAT Act 1994 and Article 5 of the Value Added Tax (Special Provisions) Order 1995 apply to the sale and purchase of the Property so that it is to be treated as neither a supply of goods nor a supply of services for VAT purposes and the Seller and the Buyer intend that VAT will not be payable on the Purchase Price.
3. The Seller warrants to the Buyer that:

    3.1 It is registered for VAT purposes, VAT Registration Number _____ and that it has made a valid election to waive exemption from VAT in respect of the Property pursuant to paragraphs 2–4 of Schedule 10 to the VAT Act, and it will prior to completion provide a copy of such election and the acknowledgement from HM Revenue and Customs to the Buyer.

    3.2 The Property has been and shall be in the period up to Actual Completion used continuously by the Seller as a let, income-producing, investment business.

    3.3 The Seller has demanded, received and accounted for VAT on the rents derived from its interest in the Property.

4. The Buyer warrants to and agrees with the Seller that:

    4.1 It is or will prior to the Completion Date be registered for VAT purposes, and will prior to Completion provide a copy of its VAT registration certificate to the Seller.

    4.2 It will make a valid election to waive exemption from charging VAT in respect of the Property pursuant to the VAT Act 1994, Schedule 10, Paragraphs 2–4 before Actual Completion and will provide to the Seller a copy of such election before the Completion Date (together with a copy of the acknowledgement of such election from HM Revenue and Customs).

    (or if the election is last minute)

    4.3 It will notify HM Revenue and Customs of that election and will produce to the Seller a copy of such notification before the Completion Date (together with proof that such election has been posted to HM Revenue and Customs prior to the Completion Date).

    (Note: In the event that any deposit is held by the Seller's solicitor as agent rather than as stakeholer (see Standard Conditions for Sale) the election must be made and notified prior to the receipt of the deposit.)

    4.4 It will not withdraw or revoke such election.

4.5 It will use the Property to carry on the same kind of business as that carried on by the Seller (that is a let, income-producing, investment business) so that the sale and purchase of the Property under this Agreement constitutes the transfer of a going concern within the meaning of Article 5 of the VAT Order.

4.6 The Buyer notifies the Seller that Article 5(2B) of the Value Added Tax (Special Provisions) Order 1995 as amended does not apply to the Buyer.

5. In the event that at any time HM Revenue and Customs specify in writing that Article 5 of the VAT (Special Provisions) Order 1995 does not apply to the transaction the Buyer will pay to the Seller on demand such VAT provided always that the Seller shall supply the Buyer with a valid VAT invoice relating thereto.

6. Any penalties, interest or fines imposed by HM Revenue and Customs shall, save where due to any fault on the part of the Seller, be the responsibility of the Buyer.

7. The Seller shall preserve all VAT records relating to the Property for such period as may be required by law (*Note: six years*) and the Seller shall:

7.1 Apply for a direction from HM Revenue and Customs for permission under Section 49(1)(b) of the VAT Act 1994 for the Seller to retain all records held by it relating to the Property which would otherwise be required to be handed to and preserved by the Buyer. If HM Revenue and Customs have not issued a direction by Actual Completion the Seller shall retain these records but if HM Revenue and Customs require that they are delivered to the Buyer then the Seller shall immediately deliver them to the Buyer.

7.2 (If the Seller retains the records) Make them available for inspection by the Buyer or its authorised agents on request by the Buyer and shall provide copies (but only one copy of each document) to the Buyer on request.

7.3 (If the records are delivered to the Buyer) Make them available for inspection by the Seller or its authorised agents on request by the Seller and shall provide copies (but only one copy of each document) to the Seller on request.

Extracts from HMRC Business Briefs

BUSINESS BRIEF 01/06

3. VAT: Hotel conference / function facilities – Revised interpretation of law on VAT treatment

This Business Brief article announces changes in HM Revenue and Customs' interpretation of the law on the VAT treatment of hotel conference/function facilities. This change will be incorporated in an update to VAT Notice 709/3, Hotels and Holiday Accommodation, to be issued in due course.

The change being made affects the liability of supplies of rooms by hotels that are to be used for meetings, conferences and similar functions. There is no change to the treatment of supplies of rooms where the primary use will be for the purpose of supplies of catering, such as dinner/dances, wedding receptions, etc. Supplies of rooms for such purposes are always taxable supplies.

Background

Hotels and other establishments often provide rooms for meetings, conferences and similar functions organised by third parties. It is usual for them to make inclusive charges depending on the requirements of individual delegates. It is the general practice for hotels and similar providers to charge organisers on a delegate or attendee basis (referred to as the 'delegate rate'), i.e. the charge will be determined according to the number of delegates requiring:

- Use of conference room only.
- Use of conference room plus meal(s) ('8-hour conference delegate rate').
- Use of conference room plus meals and overnight sleeping accommodation ('24-hour conference delegate rate').

The supply of a conference/function room on its own in these circumstances is exempt from VAT (unless an option to tax has been made). Where, in addition to the use of the conference/function room, a meal is provided to delegates and an inclusive charge made (the 8 hour delegate rate), each element is treated as a separate supply, so whilst the conference room continues to be exempt from VAT (unless an option to tax has been made), the part of the consideration relating to the provision of food is taxable (unless the provision of refreshments is minimal, such as tea and biscuits). However, where the 24-hour conference delegate rate has been applied and an inclusive charge made, HMRC has until now seen the charge as consideration for a single taxable supply of use of the entire hotel's facilities including conference/function facilities, sleeping accommodation and food.

Revised interpretation of the law

Where a room is provided for a meeting, conference or similar function organised by a third party (but not where the primary purpose is for a supply of catering – see above), HMRC now accepts that the provision of conference/function room hire, meals and sleeping accommodation under the 24-hour delegate rate, even where made in return for an inclusive charge, should be treated as separate supplies. These will be taxable supplies, with the exception of the conference/function room hire, which will be an exempt supply, unless the hotel has opted to tax its supplies. In cases where a single consideration is paid for supplies having different liabilities, for example where a charge for room hire is made under the 24-hour delegate rate by a hotel which has not opted to tax its room hire, a fair and reasonable apportionment of the consideration must be made. There is no change to the treatment of 8-hour delegate charges.

Where hotels organise and run conferences or similar events themselves and charge for entry to delegates, their supplies are always taxable supplies.

Making claims or adjustments

Hotels that have made an option to tax will be unaffected by the change and should continue to charge tax on their supplies. For other hotels and businesses, the change described above should be implemented from the date of this Business Brief and there is no requirement to make adjustments in respect of supplies made prior to this date. However, where hotels or other establishments wish to make a claim to HMRC for a repayment of output tax incorrectly paid, they may do so, subject to the conditions set out below, by using one of the following methods (full details are given in VAT Notice 700/45 How to correct VAT errors and make adjustments or claims):

- Where the total of previous errors do not exceed £2,000 net tax, an adjustment may be made to your current VAT return.
- Where the total previous errors exceed £2,000 net tax a separate claim should be submitted to HMRC (in these cases the errors must not be corrected through your VAT returns). Details of where to send your claim can be obtained from the HM Revenue and Customs National Advice Service on 0845 010 9000.

All adjustments or claims are limited to a three-year period and will be subject to the following conditions:

- All claims must take into account input tax that has been claimed, but which under the revised interpretation will not relate to taxable supplies.
- Businesses must be able to produce evidence that they accounted for VAT in the circumstances described above, and must be able to substantiate the amount claimed.

Subject to the three-year limitation period, any claim should be for all prescribed accounting periods in which the liability error occurred.

Should a claim not take into account all errors or all affected accounting periods, then HMRC will seek to set-off amounts owed to us for these periods against amounts claimed in other periods.

HMRC may reject all or part of a claim if repayment would unjustly enrich the claimant. More details on 'unjust enrichment' can be found at part 14 of VAT Notice 700/45 How to correct VAT errors and make adjustments or claims.

A notification to HMRC that a business intends making a claim in the future is not a valid claim.

Future VAT implications for hotels and similar providers

You should treat supplies in the way described above. Some hotels will now be making exempt supplies as a result of these changes. The input tax that they incur will, as a result, be subject to partial exemption rules and some restriction on the amount they can reclaim may follow. Details can be found in VAT Notice 706, Partial Exemption. If hotels prefer, they can continue to treat their supplies as taxable (and thereby be entitled to continue claiming their input tax in full) by opting to tax. Details about how to do this are given in VAT Notice 742A, Opting to tax land and buildings. Hotels that have already made exempt supplies of the meeting room may require permission for an option to tax and they will find further details in Section 5 of Notice 742A.

BUSINESS BRIEF 23/05

1.   Pre-Budget Report – VAT and property developments

This business brief provides details of the VAT and property announcements made at Pre-Budget Report 2005. The Government has announced:

- A new consultation on a re-write of existing law in Schedule 10 to VAT Act 1994 (buildings and land).
- A new consultation on the vat treatment of beneficial ownership of land (Schedule 10, paragraph 8 to VAT Act 1994.
- The outcome of 'The future of the option to tax consultation', announced at PBR 2004.

A new Consultation on a rewrite of existing law in Schedule 10 to VAT Act 1994 (Buildings and Land)

The Government announced a consultation on the re-write of Schedule 10 to the VAT Act 1994 concerning land and buildings. Schedule 10 is the most complex piece of UK VAT legislation. It not only has to reflect the complexities of English and Scottish land law but also contains extensive and complex anti-avoidance legislation.

This consultation includes draft legislation for a new Schedule 10 that retains all the rules and tax treatment of the existing legislation. However, this new draft has amended and re-structured the existing legislation to make it more straightforward and easier to understand. At the same time, the opportunity is being taken to make some minor amendments to the existing rules aimed at improving practical administration of the tax.

A copy of the consultation document containing draft legislation and a draft Regulatory Impact Assessment is available on the HMRC website at www.hmrc.gov.uk. The closing date for contributions is 28 February 2006.

A new Consultation on the VAT treatment of Beneficial Ownership of Land (Schedule 10, paragraph 8 to VAT Act 1994)

The Government also announced the issue of a consultation document looking at the VAT treatment of supplies where the legal and beneficial ownership in land has been separated. HMRC were of the view that Schedule 10, paragraph 8 to the VAT Act 1994 only applied in such situations to treat the beneficial owner as the person who made the supply. However, in the recent case of Abbey National (LON/2003/0303), the Tribunal found that the provision could be applied in situations where little more than an income stream has been assigned, without the other responsibilities that follow with beneficial ownership.

This interpretation goes wider than the explanation of its effect given to Parliament when the measure was introduced and we also believe is wider than EC law permits. However, rather than simply restoring the effect of the legislation back to its original intent, the Government has decided to consult business to see who uses the provision and why, with a view to ensuring that any changes do not inadvertently interfere with normal business practice.

A copy of the consultation document containing draft legislation and a draft Regulatory Impact Assessment is available on the HMRC website at www.hmrc.gov.uk. The closing date for contributions is 28 February 2006.

Outcome of the 'Future of the Option to Tax Consultation' announced at PBR 2004

Following from the consultation announced at PBR 2004, this business brief describes the conditions under which written consent to revoke an option to tax will be granted by the Commissioners once 20 years have elapsed from the date on which an option was made. It also considers certain connected issues that will arise with revocation and which were referred to in the consultation document. A summary of responses received is available on the HMRC website at www.hmrc.gov.uk.

Background

A facility to elect to waive exemption on supplies of commercial property (referred to as 'the option to tax') was introduced from 1 August 1989. Changes in 1995 allowed an option to tax to be revoked after 20 years (or within 3 months of being made), subject to the written consent of the Commissioners being obtained. Options will therefore first become eligible for the 20-year revocation from 1 August 2009.

In order to help businesses plan for the future, HMRC are now announcing the proposed conditions under which written consent to revoke an option to tax will be given (together with changes to the other related issues covered by the consultation). The necessary legislation and guidance will follow in due course.

Revocation

Written consent for revocation will be possible by two routes, either

- Automatic consent or,
- Permission consent.

(i) Automatic consent

The Commissioners will automatically provide written consent once a taxpayer has 'certified' that all the stipulated conditions are met. HMRC intend to make available a draft certificate on their web site although other formats will be acceptable if all the necessary information is provided. The proposed conditions that must be certified as met are that:

- No pre-payment has been made covering any supply of goods or services for more than the next 6 months following the date of revocation.
- No capital item is held (HMRC recognise that many properties may not fulfil this condition and so will be exploring a possible solution).

- Any rents charged have not been under-valued, and no balloon payments fall due at any time after the proposed revocation.
- The taxpayer held an interest in the property at least 20 years prior to revocation and that the property was subject to the option to tax at that time.

These conditions may be amended, deleted or added to with appropriate notice being given.

As well as certifying that the above conditions have been met, business will also be required to provide the following information on their certificate:

- A clear description of the property.
- Evidence of the date of the original option.
- Proposed effective date of revocation.
- A named authorised signature (Sole Proprietor, Partner, Company Secretary, Trustee, Director, or a signed letter of authority from one of these persons).

The effective date of the revocation will be the date of posting of the certificate.

(ii) Permission consent

We would expect the majority of revocations would be by automatic consent. However, HMRC may still grant consent in cases where a business fails to meet one or more of the stipulated conditions of automatic consent, provided that it does not gain a tax advantage other than future supplies of the property being VAT-free. An example might be where a taxpayer meets all the conditions for consent except that they have a pre-payment in place for the next five years cleaning services. If at the time the input tax was incurred on the cleaning services, the taxpayer apportioned the input tax so that only the input tax relating to services used before revocation was recovered, then HMRC would still grant consent. Further examples will be included in guidance in due course.

In any application for permission consent, business will need to provide the following in the form of a certificate:

- A clear description of the property.
- Evidence of the date of the original option.
- Certification of those conditions in (i) above that are met.
- Full details of the conditions in (i) above that are not met and why consent should still be granted.
- A named authorised signature (Sole Proprietor, Partner, Company Secretary, Trustee, Director, or a signed letter of authority from one of these persons).

If HMRC agree to revocation in a permission consent case, the effective date of the revocation of the option will be the date of HMRC's letter agreeing to revocation on completion of their consideration of the individual circumstances and acknowledged acceptance.

(iii) Error correction and penalties

If any information provided on a certificate is subsequently found to be incorrect, HMRC will be able to restore the original option with effect from the date of revocation. They will always take such action where written consent to revoke an option would have been refused if the correct information had been provided. This restoration of the option will make all supplies that have been treated as exempt from the date of revocation taxable and subject to an appropriate VAT assessment plus interest.

249

Where an incorrect certificate is issued, either due to lack of care or deliberately, a penalty will be applied. The development of appropriate forms of penalty is being considered as part of the wider review of HMRC's powers and appeal rights. Further guidance on these penalties will be provided once this work has been completed.

(iv) Re-options

We can foresee situations where, after revocation has taken place, the business wishes to reinstate the option on the property. There will be no cooling-off period allowing the original option to be reinstated, but there will be nothing to prevent the business making a new option on the property. Any new option will be subject to the rules and anti-avoidance provisions in force at that time, and will start a new 20-year period before it can be revoked.

(v) Early revocation

Providing certain conditions have been met, current legislation allows businesses to revoke an option to tax in the first three months after electing. The Government intends to increase this period to 12 months, subject to the same conditions as currently apply.

While HMRC have so far been unable to identify a fair method of early revocation (ability to revoke after 12 months but before 20 years) they will continue to explore options.

(vi) Position of tenants

It is not proposed to impose a condition requiring a landlord to inform a tenant that they have revoked their option.

Other issues

(i) Global options and the 'universal option'

The option to tax legislation requires that an individual opted property is identifiable; however, when the option to tax was introduced, businesses with large property holdings found this extremely onerous. In order to facilitate business, they were allowed to make one option to cover all their property holdings. This was known as a 'global option'. It was originally envisaged that these global options could be phased out, as computerisation of business records increased. However, responses to the consultation document have shown that they are very much appreciated as a facilitation measure by large businesses. HMRC therefore has no plans to phase out existing global options, although new ones will no longer be permitted, once the legislation is changed.

Unfortunately a major disadvantage of a global option is that it is simply a single option, albeit covering all properties. Therefore, it will not be possible to revoke an option on a single property held under a global option. If those with a global option wish to revoke, they can only do so by revoking the entire global option. However, one of the conditions for obtaining consent to revoke is that the taxpayer held an interest in the property at least 20 years prior to revocation and that the property was subject to the option to tax at that time. Therefore it will not be possible to revoke a global option that includes properties that were acquired less than 20 years ago. While this may stop any abuse, it is likely to cause problems for businesses that either wish to revoke in relation to all property held under a global option or to an individual property covered by it.

In order to overcome this difficulty with global options, HMRC intend to introduce a new type of global option, which for ease of identification will be called the 'universal option'. Any taxpayer that chooses the universal option will automatically opt to tax each property as it is acquired and the 20-year revocation clock will therefore run from the date of each property's acquisition. As with global options, properties requiring HMRC's permission to be opted to tax are excluded from the universal option.

In order to assist all those businesses currently holding global options, they will be able, if they so choose, to convert their existing global option to the new universal option. The length of time individual properties have been held under an existing global option will be retained under the new universal option. For example, the option relating to a property held for 12 years under a global option will be capable of being individually revoked after a further 8 years under a new universal option. The universal option will be open to all taxpayers, so that those who have individually notified each option to tax to date can convert their individual options into a single universal option.

However, it is very unlikely that HMRC has a list of the properties that are held or the date they were acquired under a global option but this information will be essential under a universal option. Therefore, as a pre-requisite condition of obtaining the universal option, the applicant will be required to provide a current list of all the opted and unopted properties and interests held and the date they were acquired. There will be no requirement to include properties previously held under the option but since disposed of. However, since these properties will still be covered by the original global option, they may need to be included under the universal option at a later date if an interest in that property is ever re-acquired.

The information required will be as follows:

- Address and identification of each individual property.
- Date the property was first covered by the option to tax for the start of the 20-year clock (this is not necessarily the date of acquisition since it is possible that previous exempt supplies were made or that it was acquired before 1 August 1989 when the option to tax was introduced).
- Price paid or cost of construction.

The effective date of a universal option will be the date on which written acknowledgment of receipt of the above information is sent, after any necessary further information or clarification has been sought. A duly named authorised signatory must sign the request for a universal option. Once a universal option has been accepted, businesses will need to maintain the list of properties by adding new properties as above, or the appropriate following information for subsequent sale or disposals that may occur:

- date of disposal
- date of revocation (if appropriate)
- sale price (net)
- VAT charged.

There will be no prescribed format for businesses to supply the information and we hope that for most businesses this will be relatively easy to compile and maintain. HMRC recognise that in some cases not all this information will be available for properties currently held. In those cases, HMRC will seek to work with the business to try to identify a solution. Once a universal option is in place, it will be the taxpayer's responsibility to keep it up to date and taxpayers will be required to provide an up to date list on demand (after appropriate notice).

The new universal option has the following benefits:

- It will be possible to revoke the option on an individual property, subject to the proposed rules (see above), as the acquisition date of each property will be separately identified.
- Taxpayers will no longer need to notify in advance of an option to tax for a TOGC purchase or a purchase at an auction as currently required, since the universal option will cover every property as it is acquired.
- Rules will be introduced to enable existing global options to be converted to the universal option to ensure that individual properties can continue to be opted without re-starting the 20-year cycle.
- Businesses that have individual options, will be able to convert their current property holdings to a universal option.
- There will be a compliance cost saving for businesses that take up the universal option over individual notifications since much of the information required under the automatic and permission consent condition rules will already be included on the list of property holdings.

Businesses that do not wish to adopt the universal option can continue with an existing global option, or can continue with submitting single notifications. The proposed solution has the advantage of being both a trade facilitation measure and preventing those businesses which have an existing global option from being disadvantaged.

(ii)   VAT groups and the option to tax

Current legislation is designed to ensure that the option to tax is not 'washed out' by a property moving between members of a VAT group. As a result all members of a VAT group are tainted (by being relevant associates) by an option to tax on a property held by another member of the VAT group. This tainting continues even after a member has left the group even if it does not have any interest in the property. Similarly, if the holder of the opted property leaves the VAT group the remaining members continue to be tainted with the option. Indeed, a scenario could arise whereby a VAT group member, who has been tainted by an option to tax in a VAT group, acquires the building some years later after having left the VAT group. Any supply that former member then makes is still covered by the original option to tax.

New legislation is to be introduced to change the current rules. Put simply, where a company is tainted by another's option (a relevant associate), that tainting is revoked as soon as the company no longer is connected with the person that opted and does not have an interest in the property. If a relevant associate acquires an interest in the property, they can revoke that option 20 years after they were first treated as a relevant associate in the same way as any other option to tax.

(iii)   Demolished buildings and options on bare land

Current policy is to allow separate treatment of land and buildings, something that is greatly appreciated by business, as confirmed in responses to the consultation. The current policy is that if a building is opted, the option spreads to the land it stands on while the building exists, but when it is demolished, the option is completely removed from the land. If bare land is opted and a building is subsequently constructed on it, the option on the land does not flow to the building and so goes into suspension, unless the building is opted. However, in the case of *Brigitte Breitsohl* (C-400/98), the ECJ found that that it is not possible to separate freehold supplies of land and buildings under the EC Sixth VAT Directive, Art. 4.

We will therefore be legislating for a new VAT treatment of opting land and buildings. In future, all new options to tax land will also include any buildings that stand on it at the time or are built on it subsequently. However, if a new building is constructed, at the point of practical completion, or on first occupation (whichever comes first) the taxpayer will have the opportunity to revoke the option to tax on the building and the land provided no supplies have already been made of the new building. Conversely, any new option on a building will apply equally to the land on which it stands. If the building is demolished, the option to tax will remain on the land, but there will again be the opportunity to revoke the option when a new building is constructed. This revised system will reduce the compliance cost of business as the number of notifications of an option to tax on a building will be reduced (most new buildings are opted). HMRC believes this solution will largely provide for the same tax treatment that businesses already enjoy, albeit there will be timing and process changes.

These changes will only apply to new options made after the introduction of the legislation. Existing options will continue under the current rules.

(iv) Extensions and linked buildings

Current policy sees an option as flowing into an extension of a building even if the extension goes beyond the original curtilage of the building. To provide certainty and to prevent abuse, we intend to clarify the definition of an 'extension' and that of a 'linked' building. We also intended to clarify that the 20-year revocation period runs from the date the original option was exercised.

BUSINESS BRIEF 22/05

1. VAT: Judgment of the court of appeal in the case of *Ivor Jacobs* ([2005] EWCA Civ 930)

This Business Brief article sets out HM Revenue and Customs' (HMRC) revised policy on the recovery of VAT by those using the 'VAT refunds for DIY builders and converters' scheme in cases where a mixed use building (used for non-residential and residential use) is converted into dwellings in light of the judgment of the Court of Appeal in the case of *Ivor Jacobs* (C3/2004/2457).

Background

Mr Jacobs had converted a former residential school for boys into one large dwelling for his own occupation and three flats. His claim for a VAT refund under the provisions of the 'VAT refunds for DIY builders and converters' scheme was rejected because none of the four resulting dwellings had been created exclusively from the conversion of the non-residential part of the school.

Mr Jacobs appealed against the above decision to a VAT Tribunal. The Tribunal found that, when looked at as a whole ie a 'primary use' test, the school was entirely non-residential and its conversion qualified for the refund scheme.

HMRC appealed the Tribunal's decision to the High Court. The High Court rejected the Tribunal's 'primary use' test and held that the school was in part residential and in part non-residential. However the High Court also rejected HMRC's view that any additional dwelling must be created entirely from the non-residential part. It held that the VAT incurred on converting the non-residential part used in creating the four dwellings was recoverable through the scheme. This is because converting the school had created additional dwellings, the school having contained one dwelling before conversion and four afterwards. The VAT incurred on the conversion of the residential part of the school was not recoverable.

The Court of Appeal unanimously dismissed HMRC's appeal and endorsed the High Court's judgment.

HM Revenue and Customs' revised policy

HMRC now accept that, for the purposes of the DIY Refund Scheme, the conversion of a building that contains both a residential part and a non-residential part comes within the scope of the Scheme so long as the conversion results in an additional dwelling being created. It is no longer necessary for the additional dwelling to be created exclusively from the non-residential part. However, VAT recovery is restricted to the conversion of the non-residential part.

Builders and developers

HMRC do not consider that the Court of Appeal decision has any impact in similar situations where a building, which is part residential/part non-residential, is being converted into a number of dwellings and the number of dwellings present post-conversion is greater than the number of dwellings present pre-conversion.

Items 1(b) and 3(a) of Group 5 to Schedule 8, VAT Act 1994 restrict the zero-rating to the dwelling(s) deriving from the conversion of the non-residential part. Our policy remains that the zero rate will not apply to any dwelling(s) deriving (whether in whole or in part) from the conversion of the residential part.

VAT treatment of past supplies

DIY house builders, who have converted property that was part residential/part non-residential and have increased the number of dwellings in the building overall, are invited to submit claims for VAT incurred on eligible expenditure in converting the non-residential part of the building into a part of the resulting dwellings.

HMRC will only entertain claims in respect of such conversions completed no later than three years prior to the date of this Business Brief.

BUSINESS BRIEF 16/05

1.   VAT ruling – *Abbey National plc* – virtual assignments

This Business Brief article provides guidance on how to treat supplies of virtually assigned property and the use of Schedule 10, paragraph 8 to the VAT Act 1994, following the High Court case of *Abbey National plc* (CH/2004/APP/0496).

Background

(a)   Virtual assignment of property

The main issue in this case concerned property that had been leased to, and occupied by, Abbey National ('Abbey'). Abbey sought to outsource its property holdings, including its lease interests, to a third party, in return for a lump sum. In the case of property leased by Abbey, the leases were not generally legally assigned to the third party, as the landlord's permission had not, or could not, be obtained. However, the intention was to leave the third party in the same economic position as though the leases had been legally assigned to them, so that they could then grant purported leases of those properties back to Abbey. This was referred to as a 'virtual assignment'.

The Tribunal (LON/2003/303) agreed with HM Customs and Excise (now HM Revenue and Customs – HMRC) that a 'virtual assignment' back to Abbey of a property that had originally been virtually assigned to the third party was not a supply that came within Article 13(B)(b) of the Sixth VAT Directive – 'a leasing and letting of immovable property'. The Tribunal therefore agreed that there was a taxable supply of agency and management services to Abbey from the third party, rather than an exempt supply of leasing and letting of immoveable property.

The High Court, in hearing Abbey's appeal, identified a critical issue as being the extent to which Abbey's right of occupation under a virtual assignment (ie where Abbey had not legally transferred its interest to the third party) could still be viewed as a genuine right of occupation granted to it by the third party. The High Court accepted that a genuine right of occupation had been granted by the third party to Abbey even though the third party did not have a right of occupation itself to pass on, as the relevant rights had not initially been created between Abbey and the third party. As a result the virtual assignment back from the third party to Abbey was viewed as coming within Article 13(B)(b) of the Sixth VAT Directive – 'a leasing and letting of immovable property', such a supply being exempt unless an appropriate election to waive exemption had been made. As a result, Abbey were successful in their appeal that a virtual assignment of the relevant properties back to them by a third party was a supply equivalent to 'a leasing and letting of immoveable property'.

The Court of Appeal has given HMRC leave to appeal against this decision of the High Court.

(b)   Schedule 10, paragraph 8 to the VAT Act 1994

A secondary issue in this case was the VAT treatment of those leases that Abbey had virtually assigned to the third party and where the property was occupied by Abbey's sub-tenants. The Tribunal had agreed with Abbey that in these cases there was a deemed supply by virtue of Schedule 10, paragraph 8 to the VAT Act 1994 by the third party to Abbey's sub-tenants, as the consideration for the sub-leases granted by Abbey accrued to that third party, despite the third party not having a legal interest in the property.

HMRC cross-appealed on this issue to the High Court. The view of the Court was that as the agreement between Abbey and the third party incorporated a clear and unambiguous declaration of trust, whereby the rents paid by the sub-tenants accrued in full for the benefit of the third party, Schedule 10, paragraph 8 to the VAT Act 1994 applied and thus the third party should be treated as making the supplies to Abbey's sub-tenants. The Court upheld the Tribunal decision, applying the approach indicated by Lord Slynn in the case of *Nell Gwynn House Maintenance Fund Trustees* [1999] STC 79.

HMRC has not appealed against this aspect of the High Court's decision.

The way forward

(i) Virtual assignments

In HMRC's view, under a virtual assignment agreement (ie where the interest in the property has been assigned to a third party without the landlord's consent and is then purported to be assigned back by the third party) the third party's assignment is not an exempt supply of an interest in land, but a taxable supply of management and agency services. As a result, the third party provider should continue to account for VAT on the taxable supply.

As HMRC is appealing against the decision of the High Court, taxpayers may wish to tax the supplies pending the outcome of that appeal. HMRC will issue assessments to taxpayers who chose to follow the High Court decision and exempt their supplies, but will not enforce these assessments unless it is ultimately successful on appeal. If this is the case, interest and penalties will be applied to the assessments.

If the taxpayer decides to follow the views of HMRC, they may submit voluntary disclosures to protect their position. They need to make it clear on the form or in a covering letter that these claims are not to be repaid until the litigation has concluded. If they do not make such an annotation and the claim is repaid, they will be treated as having followed the decision of the High Court.

Given an option to tax cannot be made retrospectively, whatever course of action taxpayers choose to follow for now, they might like to consider whether to opt to tax in respect of either Abbey or HMRC being ultimately successful before the courts.

(ii) Schedule 10, paragraph 8

Where a legal transfer of an interest in a property is contemplated and:

- the benefit of all of the consideration received from sub-leases accrues to a third party; and
- that consideration is held in a trust for the benefit of the third party,

then Schedule 10, paragraph 8 to the VATA 1994 applies. The third party will be deemed to have made the supply to the sub-lessees as the benefit of the consideration from those sub-leases accrues to the third party. Such a deemed supply will be exempt, unless an option to tax has been exercised by the third party.

Equally, by virtue of Schedule 10, paragraph 8(b) to the VATA 1994, any input tax attributable to the original grant made by the legal owner becomes the input tax of the third party from the time the deemed supply to the sub-lessee is made. The legal owner must not, in these circumstances, claim any of the input tax directly attributable to the legal grant made to the sub-lessee. Thus, where the legal owner remains in occupation of part of the building for the purpose of his business, and

- is still required to make taxable payments to the landlord, or
- carry out repairs to the property,

the third party will only be entitled to recover a portion of the VAT that is directly attributable to the deemed supply made by the third party to the sub-lessee. This is subject to the third party having exercised an option to tax. The legal owner will still be entitled to recover any appropriate input tax incurred in the course of any taxable supplies made by him in relation to any continued occupation of the building, or part of a building, of which he is a legal owner.

Further information can be found in Public Notice 700/45 'How to correct VAT errors or make adjustments or claims' and Business Briefs 25/04 and 28/04. These are available on the HMRC website or by contacting the National Advice Service on 0845 010 9000.

BUSINESS BRIEF 15/05

2. VAT: Supplies of goods and services used by taxable persons for both business and non-business use – ECJ judgement in case 43/03: P Charles, T S Charles-Tijmens

This Business Brief announces changes in HM Revenue and Customs policy on the recovery of VAT incurred on certain goods and services supplied to a business and used for business and non-business (including private) purposes. It also incorporates those parts of Business Brief 22/03 issued on 18 November 2003 which remain relevant. Business Brief 22/03 is cancelled with immediate effect.

Reason for policy change

The change of policy follows the judgment of the European Court in the case of *P Charles, T S Charles-Tijmens* (C-434/03) referred by the Dutch authorities. The Court found that Member States cannot use the derogation under Article 6(2) of the Sixth VAT Directive to deny taxpayers the right to treat all VAT incurred as input tax when they purchase capital goods for mixed business and private use and allocate the goods wholly to their business. It means the UK legislation introduced in 2003 to prevent the Lennartz mechanism being used for certain construction services, combined with the UK rules for input tax deduction, is *ultra vires*.

Details of policy change

HMRC accepts that, where businesses incur VAT on certain construction services or on purchasing land, buildings and civil engineering works for mixed business and non-business use, they can now rely on the direct effect of the Sixth VAT Directive to treat all VAT incurred as input tax and, subject to the normal rules, recover all the tax up front. They must then account for output tax on the non-business use over the economic lifetime of the asset.

The services concerned are those, which result in, or will result in, the construction of a new building or civil engineering work, or a major refurbishment or extension of an existing building.

There is no change to the way that partial exemption operates. If the asset is to be used for both taxable and exempt purposes, input tax can only be deducted in accordance with the partial exemption method in place for the business.

HMRC will challenge any attempts to exploit the Lennartz mechanism to obtain an unfair revenue advantage by introducing artificial arrangements.

Background

In 1991, the ECJ decided in the case of *Lennartz* (C-97/90) that taxpayers making business and private use of goods had, in principle, a right to full and immediate deduction of VAT on their purchase. The private use of goods forming part of the assets of a business is treated as a taxable supply of services (under Article 6(2) of the Sixth VAT Directive) and so liable to output tax. In short, therefore, a business can reclaim the VAT in full 'up front' and then account for the private use of the goods over their economic life (as opposed to apportioning the VAT incurred between business and private use). This is known as the '*Lennartz* mechanism'.

257

In 2002, HMRC became aware that schemes were being proposed to exploit the Lennartz mechanism unfairly. Tax advisers were also increasingly interested in using the Lennartz mechanism for high value capital goods such as buildings purchased by charities and colleges for mainly non-business activities. And the ECJ found in the case of *Seeling* (C-269/00) that the Lennartz mechanism could also be used for construction services, opening it up to those incurring VAT on constructing buildings and not just taxpayers purchasing a major interest in a building.

In order to protect the revenue, changes were made in the Finance Act 2003 to paragraph 5(4A) of Schedule 4 to the VAT Act 1994. These changes provided that where land and buildings and civil engineering works used in the business were put to non-business use, this was not a supply of services for consideration. HMRC considered this meant that where such items were purchased for mixed business and non-business use, there was no right to recover VAT incurred to the extent it was attributable to the non-business use. In making these changes, the UK relied on the derogation in the second paragraph of Article 6(2) of the Sixth VAT Directive.

In the *P Charles, T S Charles-Tijmens* ECJ case, the appellants purchased a holiday bungalow in the Netherlands intending to use it 87.5 per cent for business rental and 12.5 per cent for private purposes. The Dutch tax authorities accepted that there was an entitlement to deduct 87.5 per cent of the VAT incurred but they denied a full deduction under Dutch law. The ECJ found for the appellants – counter to the Advocate General's opinion and to the arguments put forward by both the Commission and other Member States. The ECJ's judgment was that Member States cannot use the derogation under Article 6(2) of the Sixth VAT Directive to deny taxpayers the right to treat all VAT incurred as input tax when they purchase capital goods for mixed business and private use and allocate the goods wholly to their business.

Summary of HMRC's New Policy

The Lennartz mechanism is now available for the purchase of land, buildings and civil engineering works with mixed business and non-business use where those goods are allocated wholly to the business. It can also be used for certain construction services on buildings or civil engineering works. The services concerned are those, which result in, or will result in, the construction of a new building or civil engineering work, or a major refurbishment or extension of an existing building. HMRC will require the output tax charge under the Lennartz mechanism to be calculated over a maximum 20-year period.

The Lennartz mechanism continues to be available for other types of goods, for example, computers, yachts, motor caravans etc. with mixed business and non-business use where those goods are allocated wholly to the business. HMRC will normally require the output tax charge under the Lennartz mechanism to be calculated over a maximum five-year period based on straight-line depreciation.

The Lennartz mechanism also continues to apply in respect of purchases of services where those services are incorporated into goods used in the business and significantly increase the value of the goods to the business.

VAT on services that are consumed in relation to day-to-day activity, such as repair and maintenance, must continue to be apportioned. However, if businesses consider that they should be entitled to use the mechanism for a particular service (such as, say, the major restoration of a business vehicle), they should contact HMRC's National Advice Service on 0845 010 9000 with details.

In all cases where the Lennartz mechanism is available, the business does not have to use it and can instead apportion the VAT paid, treating as input tax the proportion attributable to business use.

Making claims for repayment of tax

Taxpayers who wish to make claims for input tax on the supply of construction services or on purchasing land, buildings, and civil engineering works or past claims for other services may do so by making a voluntary disclosure to their local VAT office, subject to the statutory time limit in Regulation 29(1A) of the VAT Regulations 1995. This restricts late claims of input tax to three years from the due date of the return for the prescribed accounting period in which the input tax was chargeable. Any claims must take into account the output tax due under the mechanism.

Back claims will be accepted in respect of construction services and land, buildings, and civil engineering works purchased after 9 April 2003, provided they are made no later than six months from the date of this Business Brief. Claims will not be accepted for periods prior to 9 April 2003, because businesses already had the option of using the Lennartz mechanism for periods before that date and, having chosen not to use it then, cannot change that choice now.

Calculation of output tax charge under the Lennartz mechanism on land, buildings, and civil engineering works

The calculation of the output tax charge for non-business or private use of a building poses particular problems in arriving at a reasonable value for the annual cost of that use. In the *Seeling* case, reference was made to 'the duration of the economic life' of immoveable property such as land and buildings. HMRC considers that the 20-year period referred to in this context is a fair time frame over which the private/non-business use of immoveable property should be measured. Therefore, HMRC have decided that, when applying the Lennartz mechanism to immoveable property, the output tax charge should be calculated over a maximum 20-year period based on straight line depreciation, unless a shorter period is indicated (e.g. where a taxpayer's leasehold interest in the building has under 20 years to run).

Taxpayers making exempt supplies

Taxpayers who use, or intend to use, goods/services to make exempt supplies as well as taxable supplies and want to apply the Lennartz mechanism to them will also need to consider the impact of their partial exemption method on any claim. If the current partial exemption method does not facilitate the Lennartz mechanism, HMRC will consider proposals for a revised partial exemption method. However, the revised method must result in a fair and reasonable attribution of input tax to taxable supplies for all the trading activities within the VAT registration. Methods that give a good result for the Lennartz sector but do not achieve a fair and reasonable result overall will not be approved.

Example of how to calculate output tax due under the Lennartz mechanism

Goods, such as a yacht, costs £1,000,000 plus £175,000 VAT to construct. The taxpayer chooses to claim the whole £175,000 as input tax on the VAT return for the period in which the yacht was supplied (assuming the taxpayer makes no exempt supplies). Over a five-year period, the baseline figure each year would be £200,000 (£50,000 per VAT period if on quarterly returns).

In the first VAT return period, the yacht is used 50 per cent for non-business use. Output tax will be due on £25,000 in that period (i.e. 50 per cent × £50,000). In the second VAT return period, non-business use increases to 75 per cent. Tax will be due on £37,500 in that period. If non-business use decreases in the next period, the value for the output tax will be lower.

Output tax is payable in each VAT return period in which non-business use occurs over the remaining 17 quarterly tax periods.

Where the yacht remains in the business after the end of the five-year chargeable period and it continues to be used for non-business purposes, it will no longer be necessary to account for output tax. The effect is, therefore, that the non-business use is treated as consumption and taxed over the five-year period.

The same principles apply to land, buildings and civil engineering works but the adjustments will normally be over 20 years.

Treatment of goods at sale or deregistration

Businesses considering whether or not to use the Lennartz mechanism for goods, including land and property, should bear in mind that, under the mechanism, goods are treated as wholly business assets. This means that, on sale of the goods or deregistration of the taxpayer (other than in association with a transfer as a going concern), VAT may be due on their full selling price. However, where apportionment is applied at purchase, VAT need only be accounted for in such circumstances on the proportion treated as business. The mechanism may not, therefore, always be advantageous to taxpayers, particularly where the goods are likely to appreciate in value.

3. VAT: Outcome of consultation: review of Transfer Of a Going Concern (TOGC) rules

Background

In September 2000 HM Customs and Excise (now HMRC) invited comments from businesses and advisers on the practical workings of the TOGC provisions, and common problems. The review was extended to take account of the decision of the ECJ in *Zita Modes Sarl v Administration de l'enregistrement et des domains* (C-497/01) – see Business Brief 09/05, which also announced that we would be publishing a summary of responses to this consultation.

Summary of responses to the consultation

The summary of responses to the consultation is available on our website www.hmrc.gov.uk/consultations. To obtain a hard copy, please contact us as follows:

Email: Colin.Strudwick@hmrc.gsi.gov.uk
Telephone: 020 7147 0567
Fax: 020 7147 0097
Letter: Colin Strudwick
HM Revenue and Customs
Supply of Goods Team, CT and VAT Products and Processes
Room 3E/02
100 Parliament Street
London SW1A 2BQ

BUSINESS BRIEF 14/05

1. VAT – Disclosure of VAT avoidance schemes – changes to the rules

Changes to the VAT disclosure rules announced in the Budget (see Budget Notice CE06/05) will come into force on 1 August 2005.

This Business Brief describes the changes to the rules. It also clarifies the application of the existing 'confidentiality' hallmark.

The existing rules

The existing rules require taxable persons to notify the use of either of two types of VAT scheme to HM Revenue and Customs (HMRC). Taxpayers with an annual turnover exceeding £600,000 must notify the use of certain schemes described in the legislation ('listed schemes'). Taxpayers with an annual turnover exceeding £10 million must notify the use of schemes that contain features associated with avoidance ('hallmarked schemes'), if one of the main purposes of entering the scheme is to gain a VAT advantage. If the taxpayer is part of a corporate group, these turnover figures are those for the whole group.

The changes

There are three main changes to the rules.

First, two new listed schemes are added:

- cross-border face-value voucher schemes involving telecommunications, broadcasting or electronically supplied services. These schemes attempt to avoid paying any VAT on the provision of the services to final retail customers within the UK, and
- the surrender or termination of certain taxable leases of buildings, where the tenant remains in occupation of essentially the same area of the building, but following the surrender or termination pays no or substantially less VAT on the rent. Disclosure is only required if the tenant cannot recover VAT in full on the rent, and the tenant or someone connected to him treats the building as a capital item for the purposes of the capital goods scheme.

This change targets exempt or partially exempt occupiers who have in the past put in place taxable lease structures in order to obtain full VAT recovery on the capital cost of the building, and who now try to obtain further VAT benefits by avoiding irrecoverable VAT on the rent payable for the remainder of the lease term.

Second, a new hallmark is added:

- the issue of face value vouchers with either low expected redemption rates, or those issued to other members of the same corporate group (except members of the same VAT group). Most VAT avoidance schemes involving vouchers in the past have had one or other of these features. Disclosure is only required if the issue is part of a scheme with a main purpose of gaining a VAT advantage.

The new listed schemes and hallmark are described more fully in the VAT (Disclosure of Avoidance Schemes) (Designations) (Amendment) Order 2005 (SI 2005/1724), a copy of which will be available shortly on the HMSO online website.

Third, the Finance (No 2) Act 2005 amends the definition of 'tax advantage' so as to include schemes that are intended to reduce any person's irrecoverable VAT, even when there is no effect on a VAT return (e.g. because none of the VAT being avoided would have been deductible as input tax). However, the disclosure requirement only applies to those taxable persons who are both knowing parties and meet the normal disclosure rules, such as having a turnover in excess of the relevant turnover threshold.

Transitional arrangements

Transitional arrangements will ensure that a taxpayer will not have to notify one of the new listed schemes if they have previously notified it as a hallmarked scheme.

When will the changes apply

All of the above changes will apply to schemes that generate a tax advantage in VAT accounting periods beginning on or after 1 August 2005 (and includes schemes that started before 1 August 2005).

Clarification of the confidentiality hallmark

One of the existing hallmarks is that a confidentiality condition prohibits or limits a person from giving others details of how a scheme gives a tax advantage. It is standard practice for advisers to include a 'general confidentiality condition' within their terms of engagement, prohibiting the client from passing on advice to third parties. Professional advisers have raised concerns that a literal interpretation of the legislation would result in any tax advice that was subject to such a general confidentiality condition falling within the hallmark.

The confidentiality hallmark is aimed at confidentiality conditions that are intended to protect the competitive advantage of a promoter or creator of the scheme over other promoters. That competitive advantage is most likely to arise from the promoter being aware of an opportunity to profit from innovative tax avoidance ideas so that he would want to keep his tax scheme secret from other persons. Such conditions are usually imposed by a promoter on a potential user before explaining the workings of the scheme.

Consistent with this, HMRC's interpretation of the legislation is that a confidentiality condition does not fall within the hallmark if it is simply a general confidentiality condition that is imposed in relation to all advice, not merely the scheme in question. Subject to this, HMRC consider that a scheme will fall within the confidentiality hallmark if either:

- a specific condition of confidentiality is imposed that prohibits or limits a person from revealing details of how a particular scheme gives rise to a tax advantage;
- a general confidentiality condition is introduced specifically in order to prohibit or limit a person from revealing details of how a particular scheme gives rise to a tax advantage;
- a client is required to undertake (either in writing or verbally) not to reveal details of how a particular scheme gives rise to a tax advantage; or
- an adviser specifically draws a client's attention to a pre-existing general confidentiality condition when introducing a scheme to the client, in order to prohibit or limit the client from revealing details of how that particular scheme gives rise to a tax advantage.

VAT Notice 700/8 (August 2004), 'Disclosure of VAT Avoidance Schemes', is being updated and will be re-issued shortly.

BUSINESS BRIEF 13/05

2. VAT: Belated notification of an option to tax land and buildings – clarification of HM Revenue and Customs' policy

This Business Brief clarifies HM Revenue and Customs' (HMRC) policy in relation to the exercise of their discretion to accept a belated notification of an option to tax land and buildings. In particular, it explains the distinction between a belated notification and a retrospective or backdated option. This clarification is given following a rise in the number of attempts to notify options to tax that are retrospective or backdated.

Who is affected?

All those who seek acknowledgement of a decision to opt to tax (sometimes known as an election to waive exemption) outside the 30-day time limit.

Background

There are two distinct stages in the process of opting to tax. The first is making the decision to opt, the 'election'. The second is notifying HMRC of that decision, in writing, within 30 days of the date that the decision was made.

Of course, HMRC must be satisfied that the trader was legally entitled to opt to tax. If a trader has made previous exempt supplies of the property, they may require our prior written permission to opt to tax. If permission is required, the trader cannot make a valid election until our permission has been received. The circumstances when permission is required are detailed in VAT Notice 742A Opting to tax land and buildings, Section 5.

Retrospective or backdated options

The option has effect from the day on which the election is made or any later day specified in the election. This means that no option to tax can take effect from a date prior to the date on which the trader decided to make the election. This would be a backdated or retrospective option and HMRC has no discretion under the law to accept or acknowledge that it is valid.

Belated notification of an option

However, HMRC has discretion to accept a notification of an option to tax later than the prescribed time limit of 30 days after the decision to opt was made. The discretion is designed to cover situations where a trader has genuinely made the decision to opt to tax, but has failed to notify it to HMRC in time. Before considering whether to exercise this discretion, we would need to be satisfied that the decision was made on the date stated in the written notification.

Exercising the discretion

HMRC will usually accept a belated notification if a trader provides evidence, such as the minutes of a Board or management meeting, or correspondence referring to the decision. However, we accept that this is sometimes not available, so in its absence we would normally accept a statement from the responsible person, plus evidence that:

263

- all the relevant facts have been given;
- output tax has been properly charged and accounted for from the date of the supposed election; and
- input tax recovery in respect of the land or building is consistent with the trader having made taxable supplies of it.

There may be other circumstances where we would accept a belated notification, but this would depend on the individual circumstances of the case.

Conversely, HMRC may not accept that a decision to opt was taken, even when the above conditions are met, if for example:

- there has been correspondence concerning or investigation into the liability of supplies of the property in question since the supposed date of the option, and no mention of the option to tax was made;
- the trader or his representative has previously put forward an alternative explanation for the charging of output tax (for example, that the supply was not of land and buildings, or was of a sports facility).

Moreover, HMRC reserves the right to refuse to accept the belated notification if to do so would produce an unfair result, or if the exercise of the discretion was sought in connection with a tax avoidance scheme.

BUSINESS BRIEF 12/05

5.   VAT: Landlord inducements to tenants entering leases

This Business Brief article provides revised guidance on the VAT status of inducement payments by landlords to tenants. It replaces earlier guidance in Business Brief 04/03, dated 27 May 2003.

Business Brief 04/03

Business Brief 04/03 set out Customs' policy following the European Court of Justice (ECJ) and High Court decisions in the case of *Trinity Mirror plc* (formerly Mirror Group plc).

In paragraph 26 of the ECJ's judgment, it was held that a 'tenant who undertakes, even in return for a payment from the landlord, solely to become a tenant and pay the rent does not, so far as that action is concerned, make a supply of services to the landlord'. The High Court subsequently held that paragraph 26 of the ECJ judgment is narrowly drawn, and Business Brief 04/03 sought to give guidance on that.

In line with the High Court ruling, Business Brief 04/03 advised that 'a prospective tenant receiving an inducement payment would make a taxable supply by affording the landlord the advantage of being bound by the lease obligations the tenant has to fulfil'. In effect, this meant any such obligations other than to pay the rent (e.g. to redecorate the demised area every five years) would be sufficient to make the inducement payment consideration for a taxable supply.

Change of policy

Following representations from and detailed discussions with various bodies, HM Revenue and Customs now accept that lease obligations, to which tenants are normally bound, do not constitute supplies for which inducement payments on entering leases are consideration.

HM Revenue and Customs believe that the majority of such payments are therefore likely to be outside the scope of VAT as they are no more than inducements to tenants to take leases and to observe the obligations in them. There will be a taxable supply only where a payment is linked to benefits a tenant provides outside normal lease terms. However, merely putting such a benefit as an obligation in a lease will not mean it ceases to be a taxable transaction.

It is considered that this change of policy now effectively puts inducement payments on a similar VAT footing to rent-free periods, in being mainly outside the scope of VAT and only a taxable consideration when directly linked to a specific benefit supplied by a tenant to a landlord.

Examples of **taxable** benefits by tenants that may be supplied in return for such inducements are:

- Carrying out building works to improve the property by undertaking necessary repairs or upgrading the property.
- Carrying out fitting-out or refurbishment works for which the landlord has responsibility and is paying the tenant to undertake.
- Acting as anchor tenant.

HM Revenue and Customs accept that this is a difficult area where the undertakings of landlords and tenants can change a number of times in the course of negotiating a tenancy. HM Revenue and Customs will therefore seek as much documentation as possible before reaching a decision. HM Revenue and Customs will not assume that there has been a supply and agree that less specific indicators do not determine the issue. For example, publicity indicating that Company X is to take a lease in a development does not, in itself, determine that the company is an anchor tenant.

Equally, undertakings to use improved materials as part of continuous repairs under a tenant repairing lease would not constitute a taxable benefit to the landlord under the first example above.

Past transactions

The policy change referred to above may mean that there have been certain cases where tax has been charged wrongly in respect of landlord inducements under the guidelines in Business Brief 04/03.

Tenants who have wrongly declared output tax on inducements received are not obliged to adjust their VAT position. However, if they choose to, then, subject to the three-year capping provisions, they should proceed in accordance with VAT Notice 700/45 'How to correct errors and make adjustments or claims'.

Option 1

In accordance with paragraph 3.4 of Notice 700/45, where both the tenant and the landlord are registered for VAT, and provided they both agree, tenants may raise credit notes to their landlords and both parties would then adjust their VAT account.

Option 2

Alternatively where the landlord is not registered for VAT, tenants may choose to make a claim under Section 80 of the VAT Act 1994 for overpaid tax. Any such claim would be subject to the three-year capping provisions and the unjust enrichment defence. Sections 5 and 14 of Notice 700/45 refer.

Note that if past transactions are revisited there may be implications as regards deductible input tax – see below.

In all cases where tenants choose to correct past transactions it will be necessary to:

- review the attribution of any input tax incurred on costs, where that attribution was based on those costs being cost components of the taxable supply now being reversed out, and make any resultant adjustments; and
- revisit their partial exemption calculations for the prescribed and longer periods involved as necessary.

Whichever method tenants choose to correct the incorrect treatment of inducements as supplies, landlords must reduce their input tax deductions in respect of the inducements to the extent that they ultimately recovered or were entitled to recover input tax previously. This could also require partial exemption calculations to be revisited if an inputs-based method is used or to determine whether *de minimis* limits are exceeded.

BUSINESS BRIEF 11/05

3. Zero rating for protected buildings – definition of garage

This Business Brief article sets out HM Revenue and Customs' (HMRC) revised policy on what constitutes a 'garage' for the purpose of the zero ratings relating to listed buildings which are dwellings.

It follows a decision of the VAT and Duties Tribunal in the case of *Grange Builders (Quainton) Ltd* (LON/02/982).

Background

The law provides zero rating for approved alterations to a listed building designed to remain as or become a dwelling or number of dwellings and also for the first grant, by the person reconstructing such a building, of a major interest in the building or part of the building, or its site.

For the purpose of the zero rating, such a building can include a garage (occupied together with the dwelling), either constructed at the same time as the building or, where the building has been substantially reconstructed, at the same time as that reconstruction.

HMRC have always considered that in order for the alteration works to a garage to qualify for zero rating, it was necessary for the garage to have been constructed as a garage.

Therefore HMRC would not have seen the zero rate as applying to the alteration of a building (or part of a building) that was in use as a garage if it had not been constructed as a garage at the same time as the dwelling had been constructed (or substantially reconstructed).

The Tribunal decision

The Tribunal found that, for the alteration of a garage to qualify for zero rating, the building does not have to have been constructed as a garage or used as a garage since the time of the construction (or substantial reconstruction) of the dwelling. It held that a small timber-framed barn that was listed as part of the dwelling and in use as a garage was part of the listed dwelling for the purpose of the zero rating because:

- the barn had been constructed at the same time as the listed dwelling;
- it had been used as a garage for a significant period before being altered.

HM Revenue and Customs' revised policy

HMRC now accept that, provided a garage is in use as a garage before the alteration or reconstruction takes place and continues to be used as one afterwards, it is not necessary for the garage to have been constructed as a garage (i.e. as an enclosure for the storage of motor vehicles). It can also have been constructed as something different, e.g. a barn.

The other criteria for zero rating must still be met; these are:

- listing (the garage must be listed, either in its own right or through the deeming provisions of planning law);
- occupation (the garage must be occupied together with the dwelling);
- time of construction (the garage must have been either constructed at the same time as the listed dwelling or, where the dwelling has been substantially reconstructed, at the same time as that reconstruction).

VAT treatment of past supplies

Where a supplier has accounted for VAT on past supplies, they may make a claim for the overpaid VAT, subject to the three-year statutory time limits, in one of the following ways:

(a) If the net value of the total adjustments is £2,000 or less, suppliers may amend their VAT account and include the value of the adjustment on their current VAT return.
(b) If the net value of the total adjustments is more than £2,000, a separate claim for payment should be submitted to the local Business Advice Centre (suppliers cannot make this adjustment on their VAT returns).

Both of the above methods and how to make a claim are explained in VAT Notice 700/45 'How to correct VAT errors and make adjustments or claims'.

NB: HMRC may reject a claim on the grounds that payment would unjustly enrich a supplier. For example, this may happen if the supplier is unable or does not intend to pass on the repayment to his customer. Further details can be found in VAT Notice 700/45.

BUSINESS BRIEF 09/05

3. VAT – Transfer of Going Concern (TOGC) – UK implementation of the European Court of Justice (ECJ) judgment in the case of Zita Modes Sarl

This Business Brief article explains Customs' position following the ECJ judgment of 27 November 2003 in the case of *Zita Modes Sarl* v. *Administration de l'enregistrement et des domains* (C-497/01) (Zita Modes).

Background

The Transfer of a Going Concern (TOGC) rules are intended to simplify accounting for VAT when a business changes hands. They relieve the buyer of a business from the burden of funding any VAT on the purchase. Removing a charge to tax, where the output tax may not be paid to Customs, also protects Government revenue.

The ECJ considered whether the buyer of the business needs to pursue the same type of business as the seller. The ECJ also considered how the rules should operate when only part of a business is transferred.

The ECJ found that for a transfer to benefit from the special treatment:

- the undertaking (or part) transferred must be capable of carrying on an independent economic activity, rather than being the simple transfer of assets, such as the sale of stock; and
- the buyer does not need to pursue the same type of business as the seller **prior** to the transfer, but must intend to continue the business transferred rather than liquidating the assets.

Customs' position

Customs' view is that UK legislation is in line with the *Zita Modes* decision. Therefore, no legislative changes will be made in response to this decision. Customs are considering whether changes to our guidance are needed to ensure the legislation is interpreted consistently with the ECJ decision in *Zita Modes*.

Customs will continue to consider changes to guidance and, where necessary, our legislation to prevent distortion of competition and combat avoidance.

Review of TOGC provisions

Business Brief 13/00 announced a review by Customs seeking businesses' views of the practical workings of the TOGC provisions and common problems. The review was extended to take account of the *Zita Modes* case. Customs have decided not to carry out further consultation, as no legal changes are required. Customs will now complete the review and publish our conclusions shortly.

BUSINESS BRIEF 03/05

2. VAT – Off-street parking provided by local authorities: update

This Business Brief supplements guidance, in Business Brief 18/04, on the VAT treatment of off-street parking provided by local authorities.

Background

Under Article 4(5) of the EC Sixth VAT Directive, bodies such as local authorities are not regarded as engaging in a business when their activities are governed by public law. The exception is when local authorities and businesses provide like services, and to give local authorities more favourable VAT treatment would lead to significant distortions of competition. In the case of the *Isle of Wight Council* (LON/00/653) the VAT and Duties Tribunal ruled that the Council provided off-street parking on the Isle of Wight under a public law regime. The Tribunal also ruled that, in its opinion, the relevant provision in the Sixth Directive (Article 4(5)) is not implemented in national law, concluding that the Commissioners are not in a position to raise any arguments concerning distortions of competition.

In Business Brief 18/04 Customs announced its intention to appeal the Tribunal's ruling that Article 4(5) has not been properly implemented in the UK. The Business Brief also explained that local authorities could either continue accounting for VAT on off-street parking charges or, if they consider that their circumstances are identical to those of the Isle of Wight Council, they could choose not to account for VAT. Customs would, however, issue protective assessments if VAT were not accounted for.

The present position

The High Court has now heard Customs' appeal and has referred the case back to the Tribunal to consider the issues of distortion of competition. This is because the Court has decided that 'the whole of Article 4(5) is directly applicable between (public bodies) and the Commissioners'. Consequently a public body cannot rely on one part of the Directive (special legal regime) without also considering the other part (distortion of competition).

Whether or not significant distortions of competition would arise if a service provided by a public authority were not taxed, whereas the like service provided by a business was taxed, is something that must be assessed on a national basis. Applying that assessment, Customs consider that off-street parking is provided by both the public sector and the private sector, and significant distortions of competition would arise if one sector were afforded more favourable VAT treatment than the other. Consequently, in our opinion the provision of this type of parking in return for consideration is a service that should be taxed at the standard-rate, whether supplied by a public authority or by a VAT-registered business.

Where a local authority has not declared output tax on off-street parking charges and has been issued with a protective assessment, that assessment is now required to be paid.

Where a local authority has not declared output tax on off-street parking charges and has not been assessed by Customs, it should now correct its VAT position by making a voluntary disclosure as explained in VAT Notice 700/45 'How to correct VAT errors and make adjustments or claims'.

Default interest will be charged on all such underdeclared tax.

BUSINESS BRIEF 02/05

3.   VAT – Supplies of nursery and crèche facilities by a charity

This Business Brief article is issued to clarify Customs' position on the business status of supplies of nursery and crèche facilities where those supplies are made by a charity. This issue first arose as a result of the High Court case of *Yarburgh Children's Trust* (see Business Brief 04/03) and has recently been tested again in the High Court case of *St Paul's Community Project Ltd.*

In the earlier case of Yarburgh, the Court decided that the charity was not making supplies by way of business. Despite that decision, Customs' position remained that the provision of nursery and crèche facilities in such circumstances was a business activity for VAT purposes. However, in the more recent case of St Paul's, the Court's decision has again gone in favour of the charity. The Court found that the intrinsic nature of the enterprise was not the carrying on of a business, identifying the distinguishing features as the social concern for the welfare of disadvantaged children, lack of commerciality in setting fees and the overall intention simply to cover costs.

Customs do not agree that these features point to the activities being non-business because we consider that the charity is making supplies of services for consideration in much the same way as a commercial nursery. However, taking into account all the circumstances in this case, Customs have decided not to appeal further.

This means Customs will now accept that the provision of nursery and crèche facilities by charities, along the same lines as those in Yarburgh Children's Trust and St Paul's Community Project Ltd, is not a business activity for VAT purposes.

Background

Both Yarburgh Children's Trust and St Paul's Community Project Ltd are charities which undertake to provide nursery and crèche facilities for pre-school age children as part of their charitable objectives. Both organisations charge fees for their services, which are set at a level designed to ensure that they merely cover their costs. They both undertook construction of new nursery premises. Such supplies would normally be subject to VAT but there are provisions in UK law which allow construction work to be zero-rated where buildings are used by a charity otherwise than in the course of business. Zero-rating can be beneficial to charities, if they undertake exempt activities and the amount of VAT they recover would be heavily restricted. Customs denied zero-rating on the grounds that these charities were making business supplies. The High Court has taken the opposing view that neither charity is in business for VAT purposes.

Customs' policy

It remains Customs' long standing policy that a business activity is possible even in the absence of a profit motive. Customs believe that this approach is consistent with UK and EC legislation and is supported by a number of decisions of the UK and European Courts. Many charities with activities not motivated by profit and whose fees are subsidised by public funds or donations benefit from such activities being business for VAT purposes, because they are able to recover VAT incurred in relation to those activities. It would not be beneficial for the charity sector as a whole if charitable activities were all regarded as non-business, as it would deny them recovery of input tax. In cases that are not broadly in line with *St Paul's* or *Yarburgh*, Customs shall continue to apply the business test, in order to determine whether the supplies concerned are being made by way of business.

What constitutes a business activity for VAT purposes?

As neither UK nor EC legislation has provided an exhaustive definition or test for determining if an activity is business, the meaning of business and economic activity has emerged from a body of case law. This has given rise to the business test, which consists of six elements or indicators that the Courts have seen as being characteristic of a business. These are not a checklist and a business may have some, but not all, of the features indicated. Instead they are a set of tools designed to help compare activities where there is some uncertainty about their nature with features of activities that are clearly business. In most cases, it will be clear that an activity is business but, where difficulties arise, Customs will apply this business test. The elements of this test were set out in Business Brief 04/03 and are reproduced below.

- **Is the activity a serious undertaking earnestly pursued?** (This considers whether the activity is carried on for business or daily work rather than pleasure or daily enjoyment.)
- **Is the activity an occupation or function that is actively pursued with reasonable or recognisable continuity?** (When considering this test one should consider how frequently the supplies will be made.)

- Does the activity have a certain measure of substance in terms of the quarterly or annual value of taxable supplies made?
- Is the activity conducted in a regular manner and on sound and recognised business principles?
- Is the activity predominately concerned with the making of taxable supplies for a consideration? (This has in many instances been seen as the most important and arguably the most problematic indicator. In the appeal of The Institute of Chartered Accountants England and Wales, the House of Lords found that the test must be read as asking 'what is the real nature of the activity' i.e. is the real nature of the activity the making of taxable supplies for consideration or is it something else?)
- Are the taxable supplies that are being made of a kind which, subject to differences of detail, are commonly made by those who seek to profit from them?

BUSINESS BRIEF 15/04

1. VAT – Budget 2004 anti-avoidance: Transfer Of Going Concern (TOGC) involving commercial buildings

In Business Brief 12/04 issued on 21 April 2004, Customs provided further details of the changes announced in Budget 2004 relating to the TOGC involving commercial buildings, effective from 18 March 2004. Included within this Business Brief were details of an interim or transitional measure to allow taxpayers and their advisers to become more familiar with the changes. This interim measure was to have run from 18 March until 31 May 2004.

Customs now announce an extension of this interim period until 30 June 2004. Updates have now been made to VAT Notices 742A 'Opting to tax land and buildings' and 700/9 'Transfer of a business as a going concern' together with respective changes to V1-8 and V1-10 for those with access to Customs internal guidance.

For clarity, the interim measure applies under the following conditions. In cases where the transferee's election to waive exemption is not disapplied by these new changes and all other conditions for the sale to be treated as a TOGC are met, the Commissioners will permit the sale to be treated as a TOGC even if the transferee has not issued a notification for sales of new or elected property (see section 11 of VAT Notice 742A). This interim treatment will apply to sales made between 18 March 2004 and 30 June 2004 and is on condition that both parties agree that it should remain treated as though it were a TOGC, and that they would have met the new TOGC requirements had a correct notification been given.

BUSINESS BRIEF 14/04

2. VAT – partial exemption – attributing input tax to intended supplies of property

This Business Brief article reports a change in policy on evidence of an intention to make taxable supplies of property. It also clarifies policy on attributing input tax to intended supplies of property and when subsequent adjustments need to be made. This takes account of the decision of the VAT and Duties Tribunal in the case of *Beaverbank Properties (Beaverbank)* and of the House of Lords in the case of *Royal & Sun Alliance (RSA)*.

Business Brief

This Business Brief withdraws VAT Information Sheet 08/01 regarding the attribution of input tax on speculative supplies of property.

Background

A taxpayer can deduct VAT on costs attributed to taxable supplies that it intends to make in future. Equally, if the intention is to make exempt supplies, then attributed VAT cannot normally be deducted.

Where an intention changes before costs are used the original VAT attribution may need to be adjusted. If the intention changes from exempt to taxable, then a taxpayer may be entitled to claim the VAT previously attributed to the exempt supply. This is known as a payback claim. Conversely, if the intention changes from taxable to exempt then VAT previously deducted may need to be repaid. This is known as a clawback adjustment. Further information is available in VAT Notice 706 'Partial Exemption'.

Certain supplies of land and property that are exempt can be made taxable by making and notifying an option to tax (option). Doing so can allow VAT on costs to be deducted where it otherwise could not. Further information is available in VAT Notice 742A 'Opting to tax land and buildings'.

Evidence of an intention to make taxable supplies of property

Some land and property supplies are always taxable whereas other supplies are exempt unless an effective option is in place. Prior to the *Beaverbank* case Customs maintained that, where an option was needed to make supplies taxable, then a taxpayer could only have an intention to make taxable supplies once an option was in place.

Customs now accept that a taxpayer can have an intention to make taxable supplies before an option is in place, even though the taxable supplies cannot occur until after the option is made. However, clear documentary evidence of taxable intention is essential.

Suitable evidence includes documents involving third parties that consistently show a firm commitment to make taxable supplies. For example, a document accepting a bank loan on the basis that taxable supplies will be made. However, in most cases, the best evidence of taxable intention remains an effective option to tax.

A firm commitment to make taxable supplies is essential before there can be a taxable intention where the normal liability of planned supplies is exempt. In particular, where property is to be let and the taxpayer is keeping his options open as to whether to opt or not, a taxable intention does not exist.

Customs recognise that property developers often look at many sites in connection with a taxable project and that it may be onerous to immediately opt them all. As projects progress through acquiring an interest in the land and doing necessary work to active marketing, the weight of evidence needed to substantiate a continuing taxable intention without an option will increase. At the same time any commercial reasons to put off opting will decrease. Where a taxpayer is actively marketing a property Customs view the lack of an option as strong evidence that the taxpayer is merely keeping his options open as to whether to opt and that a taxable intention does not exist.

Changes of intention

VAT on costs related to subletting property must be attributed to planned exempt supplies unless there is absolutely no doubt that only taxable supplies will be made. VAT incurred on rents paid (and on other day-to-day costs) that have been attributed to exempt supplies cannot be adjusted once an option is put in place. This is because a payback claim can only be made if costs are put to an alternative taxable use. Costs such as rent for expired periods are not available for use in making taxable supplies because they have effectively been used up in trying to make exempt supplies.

VAT on costs incurred prior to the option that are not used up before the option is made will be available for adjustment assuming all other conditions are met. Equally, VAT on day-to-day costs incurred following the making of an effective option can be attributed to taxable supplies.

Speculative supplies of property (unclear intention)

Some land and property businesses incur VAT on costs without knowing what supplies will be made. For example, costs related to acquiring land for property development when it is not yet clear what type of project, if any, will take place. In these situations it is not possible for VAT to be directly attributed to either taxable or exempt supplies.

Provided the costs are incurred for business purposes, the VAT can be treated as residual VAT relating to the business as a whole. Residual VAT can be deducted to the extent allowed by the taxpayer's partial exemption method.

If a project is aborted, and costs incurred wasted, no adjustments are made to the deduction of VAT on those costs. But, if a project is firmed-up or costs are used in different projects in which taxable or exempt intentions are known, then payback or clawback may apply.

Impact of *RSA*

Following the comments of Lord Hoffmann in *RSA* there has been speculation that the lack of a clear intention of what supplies would eventually be made in speculative property projects prevents the later application of payback or clawback. Customs view the apportionment of residual input tax incurred in speculative projects under partial exemption methods as attribution to taxable and exempt intentions and thus view the input tax as eligible for later adjustment if all other conditions are met.

Claims as a result of the changed policy on intentions

Some taxpayers may consider that they have wrongly attributed input tax in the past based on Customs declared policy. Claims may be submitted for under-claimed input tax subject to the appropriate time limits. For all claims, suitable documentary evidence of intention must be held as discussed above.

(i)   If the net value of adjustments is £2,000 or less, the business may amend its VAT account and include the value of the adjustment on its current VAT return.
(ii) If the net value of adjustments is more than £2,000, a separate claim for payment must be submitted to the local VAT office.

Recovery of over claimed tax as a result of *RSA*

Some taxpayers may have made claims to Customs or prepared their VAT accounts based on the decisions of the High Court or the Court of Appeal in this case. Customs will be seeking to recover any input tax, deducted by taxpayers, which is not now due to the taxpayer. Taxpayers who:

- made claims following the High Court/Court of Appeal decisions; or
- relied on the High Court/Court of Appeal decisions when completing their VAT returns and now know that tax has been over claimed on returns

should make a voluntary disclosure to their local VAT office so that recovery, with interest where appropriate, can be arranged as soon as possible. If a voluntary disclosure is not made and Customs discover the error, the taxpayer may be liable to a mis-declaration penalty.

BUSINESS BRIEF 12/04

2   VAT – Budget 2004 Anti Avoidance: Transfer of Going Concern (TOGC) involving commercial buildings

Budget 2004 announced changes to prevent tax avoidance in supplies of land and property. These changes affect sales of businesses (or qualifying parts of businesses) as a transfer of a going concern (TOGC), where the business includes property on which an election to waive exemption (i.e. 'option to tax') has been exercised, or which is less than three years old. The changes:

- extend the circumstances in which an election to waive exemption for supplies of land will not have effect; and
- restrict the circumstances in which a transaction is treated as a TOGC.

These changes came into effect on 18 March 2004. More details of the changes are contained in Budget Notice CE 30/04.

This Business Brief article explains:

- what supplies of property are covered;
- the purpose of the new notification requirement;
- what to do if a tax point for the initial payment made at exchange of contracts occurred before 18 March 2004 but completion did not take place until on or after 18 March 2004; and
- what to do in cases where the new requirements for a transaction to be treated as a TOGC have not been met.

Supplies of property covered

The new measure applies to all supplies of land and buildings for which an election to waive exemption has been made (freehold, leasehold, licences etc), or where the property is less than three years old.

The purpose of the new notification requirement

Under the pre-Budget rules, for a sale of a business including property on which an election to waive exemption had been exercised (or which was less than three years old) to qualify as a TOGC, the transferee had to make his own election to waive exemption and notify it to Customs before the transaction occurred. Failure to do this meant that the transaction would not qualify as a TOGC, so that the transferor was required to charge VAT on the sale.

Under the new rules from 18 March 2004, for such a business sale to qualify as a TOGC, in addition to electing to waive exemption (as before), the transferee also needs to make an additional notification to the transferor. The notification is that the transferee's election to waive exemption will not be disapplied following these changes. If the transferee cannot make this notification because his election will be disapplied, the transaction cannot be treated as a TOGC.

The reason for the new notification requirement is to provide certainty for the transferor and to allow taxpayers to continue to approach Customs for clearances in complex TOGC cases. In order to treat a sale as a TOGC, a prudent transferor has always needed to be satisfied the transferee has elected to waive exemption. Before the Budget 2004, a copy of the letter from Customs to the transferee acknowledging that their election had been made could evidence this. After the Budget, in addition to being satisfied that the transferee has elected to waive exemption, transferors also need to be sure that the transferee's election will not be disapplied before treating the business sale as a TOGC. If the transferor cannot be certain whether or not the transferee's election will be disapplied, Customs will be in no better position and so will be unable to provide any clearances for TOGC transactions.

Providing all the other TOGC requirements have been met, the Commissioners accept that the transferor who has received a notification confirming the transferee's election has not been disapplied, is entitled to treat the sale of a business as a TOGC. If it subsequently turns out an incorrect notification was given, the Commissioners would not seek to recover any uncharged output tax from the transferor and the supply will remain a TOGC.

In the event of an incorrect notification being given by a transferee, the Commissioners will look closely at the circumstances that led to that event and this, in turn, may lead to further investigations.

What to do if a tax point for the initial payment made at exchange of contracts occurred before 18 March 2004 but completion took place on or after 18 March 2004

In some cases, the deposit payment typically paid at exchange of contracts is actually an initial payment against the sale of the property and creates a tax point. In such cases where exchange occurred before 18 March 2004 and completion on or after 18 March 2004, confusion could arise if the sale is to be treated as a TOGC as different rules now apply to each payment made.

Therefore in these cases, the Commissioners will accept that the payment made at completion can be treated under the same rules as the payment made at exchange of contracts, where that has created a tax point before 18 March 2004. In effect, the pre-Budget TOGC rules will apply providing that both parties to the sale agree that it should be so treated.

Interim measure – cases where notification has not been made

This anti-avoidance measure was introduced without prior notice to prevent fore-stalling. However, the Commissioners recognise that some businesses and their advisers may not have fully understood the implications for them of these changes for transactions they may have made since 18 March 2004.

Therefore, in cases where the transferee's election to waive exemption is not disapplied by these new changes and all other conditions for the sale to be treated as a TOGC are met, the Commissioners will permit the sale to be treated as a

TOGC even if the transferee has not issued a notification for sales of new or elected property.

This interim treatment will apply to sales made between 18 March 2004 and 31 May 2004 and is on condition that both parties agree that it should remain treated as though it were a TOGC, and that they would have met the new TOGC requirements had a correct notification been given.

BUSINESS BRIEF 22/03

VAT: Supplies of goods and services used by taxable persons for both business and non-business use

This Business Brief announces a change in Customs' policy on the VAT treatment of certain services supplied to a business and used for business and non-business (including private) purposes; and the period over which non-business/private use should be considered.

Businesses generally apportion the VAT that they have paid on services with the proportion attributable to business use being treated as input tax. While businesses should, for most services, continue to apportion in this way, Customs now accept that businesses may, in certain limited circumstances, choose to treat all of the VAT on some services as input tax and then account for output tax on the non-business use of the goods to which the services relate.

This option for VAT paid on services may only be used for:

- certain construction services (see below) where a person became entitled to an input tax credit or repayment before 9 April 2003; and
- other services, which are incorporated into goods, used in the business and which significantly increase the value of the goods to the business.

Background and further details are set out below.

Lennartz mechanism

In 1991 the European Court of Justice (ECJ) ruled in the case of *Lennartz* v. *Finanzamt Munchen III* that a taxable person who uses a car partly for business and partly for private purposes has a right to a total and immediate input tax deduction in respect of VAT incurred on purchase of the car. Where a person chose to use this approach (subsequently widely described as the 'Lennartz mechanism'), they were obliged to account for output tax on the private use under Article 6(2) of the Sixth VAT Directive. Although the specific case involved a car, the mechanism was seen as applicable to supplies of goods in general.

News Release 1/92 set out Customs' view of the implications of *Lennartz* in respect of goods. It stated that the ruling did not apply to VAT on services; where there was business/non-business use, apportionment was mandatory.

Seeling ECJ judgment

A recent ECJ case, *Wolfgang Seeling*, involved a German businessman who had constructed a house both as his home and for use in his business. Although the substantive issue was whether the private use was exempt, the decision of the court makes it clear that all the construction costs could be dealt with through the Lennartz mechanism. The court has therefore accepted that VAT on construction services that result in the construction of a building can be dealt with under the mechanism.

Anti-avoidance provisions

In Budget 2003, amendments to Schedule 4, paragraph 5 to the VAT Act 1994 provided that, with effect from 9 April 2003, land, buildings and civil engineering works were removed from the Lennartz mechanism. This was done because Customs had become aware that schemes were being put in place to exploit Lennartz for tax avoidance purposes. As a result, no output tax charge arises on the private or non-business use of such land, and there is no entitlement to recover VAT incurred on either goods or services insofar as the inputs are used for such private or non-business use (i.e. the VAT incurred must be apportioned).

A number of tax advisers have suggested that there is no basis in European law for these changes and say that their conclusion is supported by the *Seeling* judgment. Customs do not agree. The judgment is that when the Lennartz mechanism (Article 6(2)(a) of the Sixth VAT Directive) is applied to a building, it gives rise to taxable deemed supplies, not exempt ones. However, there is a derogation in Article 6(2) that allows Member States to withdraw the Lennartz mechanism altogether for certain assets, so there is no output tax on deemed supplies relating to private use, and no right to full deduction of VAT incurred on those assets. Customs consider that the Budget 2003 changes fall squarely within this derogation.

Customs' new policy

Following the judgment in *Seeling*, Customs have made the following changes in their policy on the Lennartz mechanism:

- While there is a potential argument that the Lennartz mechanism should be seen as a narrow 'private use' mechanism rather than one that is available for wider non-business use, Customs are continuing their policy of not drawing such a distinction.
- The Lennartz mechanism can apply in respect of purchases of services where those services are incorporated into goods used in the business and significantly increase the value of the goods to the business.
- The Lennartz mechanism is not available for land, buildings or civil engineering works (or services related to them such as construction services) where no entitlement for any qualifying input tax arose prior to 9 April 2003.
- The Lennartz mechanism is available for other types of goods, e.g. computers, motor caravans, yachts and aircraft. Services, which improve these goods, e.g. a substantial refurbishment, would also qualify. Customs will normally require the output tax charge under the Lennartz mechanism to be calculated over a maximum five-year period based on straight-line depreciation. Customs' view of how this liability is to be calculated is set out in the example below.
- VAT on services that are consumed in relation to day-to-day activity, such as repair and maintenance, must continue to be apportioned. However, if businesses consider that they should be entitled to use the mechanism for a particular service (such as, say, the major restoration of a business vehicle), they should contact Customs National Advice Service on 0845 010 9000 with details.
- In all cases where the Lennartz mechanism is available for use by a business, the business does not have to use that mechanism and can instead apportion the VAT paid, treating as input tax the proportion attributable to business use.

Buildings, civil engineering works and related services: pre-9 April 2003

Customs now accept that the Lennartz mechanism can be applied to certain construction services on buildings or civil engineering works with mixed use. The services concerned are those, which resulted in, or will result in, the construction of a new building or civil engineering work, or a major refurbishment or extension of an existing building. At least part of the input tax on those services must have been incurred before 9 April 2003.

This means that, where the building works had started and an entitlement to input tax had been established prior to 9 April 2003, the Lennartz mechanism can be applied to any input tax incurred on the services connected with that project after that date. Output tax will then have to be accounted for on private/non-business use of the building. However, for projects where no entitlement to input tax on the services arose prior to 9 April 2003, the Lennartz mechanism is not available and all input VAT must be apportioned between taxable and private/non-business use.

Taxpayers who have incurred input tax after 9 April 2003 but think that they may be entitled to use the Lennartz mechanism under the transitional arrangements detailed above should contact Customs National Advice Service on 0845 010 9000.

The calculation of the Lennartz charge for private use of a building poses particular problems in arriving at a reasonable value for the annual cost of the private or non-business use. In the *Seeling* case, reference was made to 'the duration of the economic life' of immoveable property such as land and buildings. Customs consider that the 20-year period referred to in this context is also a fair time frame over which the private/non-business use of immoveable property should be measured. Therefore, Customs have decided that, when applying the Lennartz mechanism to immoveable property, the output tax charge should be calculated over a maximum 20-year period based on straight line depreciation, unless a shorter period is indicated (e.g. where a taxpayer's leasehold interest in the building has under 20 years to run).

Making claims in respect of pre-9 April 2003 supplies of construction services or past claims for other services

Taxpayers who wish to make claims for input tax on construction services incurred before 9 April 2003 or past claims for other services may do so by making a voluntary disclosure to their local VAT office, subject to the statutory time limit in Regulation 29(1A) of the VAT Regulations 1995. This restricts late claims to input tax to three years from the due date of the return for the prescribed accounting period in which the input tax was chargeable. Any claims must take into account the output tax due under the mechanism. Back claims will not be accepted in respect of goods because businesses already had the option of using the Lennartz mechanism and, having chosen not to use it, cannot change that choice now.

Taxpayers who use, or intend to use, goods/services to make exempt supplies as well as taxable supplies and want to apply the Lennartz mechanism to them will also need to consider the impact of their partial exemption method on any claim. If the current partial exemption method does not facilitate the Lennartz mechanism, Customs will consider proposals for a revised partial exemption method. However, the revised method must result in a fair and reasonable attribution of input tax to taxable supplies for all the trading activities within the VAT registration. Methods that give a good result for the Lennartz sector but do not achieve a fair and reasonable result overall will not be approved.

Example of how to calculate output tax due under the Lennartz mechanism

- Goods, such as a yacht, costs £1,000,000 plus £175,000 VAT to construct. The taxpayer chooses to claim the whole £175,000 as input tax on the VAT return for the period in which the yacht was supplied (assuming the taxpayer makes no exempt supplies). Over a five-year period, the baseline figure each year would be £200,000 (£50,000 per VAT period if on quarterly returns).

- In the first VAT return period, the yacht is used 50 per cent for non-business use. Output tax will be due on £25,000 in that period (i.e. 50 per cent × £50,000). In the second VAT return period, non-business use increases to 75 per cent. Tax will be due on £37,500 in that period. If non-business use decreases in the next period, the value for the output tax will be lower.
- Output tax is payable in each VAT return period in which non-business use occurs over the remaining 17 quarterly tax periods.
- Where the yacht remains in the business after the end of the five-year chargeable period and it continues to be used for non-business purposes, it will no longer be necessary to account for output tax. The effect is, therefore, that the non-business use is treated as consumption and taxed over the five-year period.

Treatment of goods at sale or deregistration

Businesses considering whether or not to use the Lennartz mechanism for goods, including land and property, should bear in mind that, under the mechanism, goods are treated as wholly business assets. This means that, on sale of the goods or deregistration of the taxpayer, other than in association with a transfer as a going concern, VAT will be due on their full selling price. However, where apportionment is applied at purchase, VAT need only be accounted for in such circumstances on the proportion treated as business. The mechanism may not, therefore, always be advantageous to taxpayers, particularly where the goods are likely to appreciate in value.

BUSINESS BRIEF 11/03

VAT: Liability of works to protected buildings – Court of Appeal decision in the case of Zielinski Baker and Partners

This Business Brief article sets out Customs' policy on the VAT liability of works to outbuildings that are within the curtilage of protected buildings and were constructed before 1 July 1948. It follows a judgment by the Court of Appeal in the case of *Zielinski Baker and Partners*.

The Court of Appeal has ruled against Customs that where an outbuilding is treated as part of a listed building under planning law, both buildings together constitute the protected building for VAT purposes.

Customs have been given leave to appeal this decision to the House of Lords.

Customs' interpretation of the law

Certain works ('approved alterations') can be zero-rated when carried out on a 'protected building'. 'Protected building' means a listed building which is designed to remain as or become a dwelling (or intended to be used for a communal residential or charitable purpose) after the works have been carried out.

Customs' long-standing policy is that 'a building' means a single building. Approved alterations carried out to an outbuilding cannot be zero-rated unless the outbuilding is itself designed to remain as or become a dwelling (or intended to be used for a communal residential or charitable purpose) after those works have been carried out.

Customs also argued that zero-rating can only apply to approved alterations to the main listed building, not to an outbuilding or other structure in its curtilage.

279

Implications of the Court of Appeal judgment

The effect of the judgment is to zero-rate approved alterations to a pre-1 July 1948 outbuilding where, on completion of the works, that outbuilding remains or becomes part of the protected building.

Customs consider that the Court of Appeal judgment is limited to cases where the outbuilding shares listing with the protected building and is not applicable where the outbuilding has its own listing. In those circumstances the work will be standard-rated, except where the outbuilding is or becomes a dwelling in its own right or is intended to be used for a communal residential or charitable purpose.

VAT treatment pending Customs' appeal

Pending the outcome of the appeal to the House of Lords, contractors may apply the Court of Appeal judgment and zero-rate approved alterations to outbuildings within the curtilage of protected buildings that were constructed before 1 July 1948. Customs will raise assessments against the contractors for the VAT not declared on returns in order to protect their position should the House of Lords overturn the Court of Appeal judgment. No action will be taken to enforce payment of such assessments until the litigation is concluded. If the final decision is in Customs' favour we will require payment of the tax and interest.

Contractors who have already accounted for VAT on these services in the past can make a claim to their local Business Advice Centre for repayment, as set out in detail in Section 4 of Customs' Notice 700/45 'How to correct errors and make adjustments or claims'. Valid claims will be paid but Customs will make assessments in order to recover the payments, with interest where appropriate, should the Court of Appeal judgment be overturned. All claims are limited to a three-year period and will be subject to unjust enrichment considerations as explained in detail in Notice 700/45.

Alternatively, contractors can continue to standard-rate approved alterations in the above circumstances and wait until the litigation is concluded before deciding what action, if any, to take. Contractors may make protective claims pending the outcome.

VAT: Refunds under the Do-it-yourself Builders and Converters Scheme – Court of Appeal decision in the case of *Lady Jane Blom-Cooper*

The Court of Appeal has unanimously allowed the Commissioners' appeal in this case. This Business Brief article explains the legal position following this decision and what claimants under the Do-it-yourself Builders and Converters Scheme (the Scheme) should do.

This case concerns whether Lady Blom-Cooper may claim a refund of VAT under the Scheme on work to convert a former public house into a single dwelling house. Prior to the conversion the building contained both a non-residential and a residential part. The effect of the work was to extend the residential part of the building into the whole of the building.

The Court of Appeal judgment endorses Customs' long-standing view that conversion of a building that contains both a residential and a non-residential element into a single dwelling house does not qualify for a VAT refund. The Court of Appeal also agreed with Customs that the VAT relief available under the Scheme is designed to reflect the zero-rate relief available to commercial developers. The High Court had previously decided that Lady Blom-Cooper was entitled to a refund of VAT in relation to works on the non-residential part of the building, thereby allowing greater

VAT relief under the Scheme than is available to commercial developers. Lady Blom-Cooper has petitioned the House of Lords for leave to appeal.

Customs will apply the decision of the Court of Appeal to similar claims made under the Scheme. Customs will not re-examine old cases at this stage, whether or not a claim was submitted. New claims where the circumstances are on a par with the *Lady Jane Blom-Cooper* case will be rejected, although claimants may protect their position pending the final outcome of the litigation by submitting their claims within the statutory time limit (three months after completion of the conversion) and appealing to the VAT Tribunal against the decision to reject the claim.

VAT: Building and construction – grants of a major interest by members of VAT groups

The first grant of a major interest in a new dwelling, communal residential building or charitable building is zero-rated. 'Grant of a major interest' means a freehold sale or a long lease in a building. This Business Brief article clarifies Customs' policy in relation to grants of major interest in zero-rated buildings by VAT groups in the rare situation when a group member makes more than one grant of a major interest in a building, the first of which is to another group member.

Where a major interest in a building is granted by one member of a VAT group to another, the grant should not be considered to be the 'first grant of a major interest' in that building by that group member for the purpose of zero-rating.

In effect this means that the first grant of a major interest to a person outside the group can be zero-rated, regardless of the previous activity within the VAT group, so long as the group member making the grant is a person constructing (or converting) the building and it meets all the other criteria.

VAT: Treatment of communal areas in blocks of flats

This Business Brief article announces Customs' new policy on communal areas in new buildings containing two or more dwellings. Typically these buildings are blocks of flats, which consist of individual dwellings and areas for the use of all residents, such as a lounge, laundry and refuse area. The first sale of each flat is zero-rated and the buyer also acquires a right to use the communal areas.

Where the communal areas are only used by residents and their guests, Customs accept that the construction of the whole building is zero-rated. Where the communal areas are partly used by others, for example if they contain leisure or gym facilities, whether or not for a charge, then the construction of the communal areas is standard-rated.

Where a building contains both a non-residential part and a dwelling, such as a shop with a flat above, zero-rating continues to apply only to the extent that the building is designed as a dwelling.

BUSINESS BRIEF 03/03

VAT: The introduction of VAT on privately operated tolls

What has happened?

As announced in news release 108/02, from 1 February 2003 the toll charges payable to use certain bridges, tunnels and roads became subject to 17.5 per cent VAT. This follows a ruling by the European Court of Justice (ECJ case C-359/97, dated 12

September 2000) that while tolls payable to use bridges operated by public authorities are outside the scope of VAT, other tolls are subject to VAT at the standard rate.

What types of toll charge are affected by this ruling?

Under EC VAT legislation, central and local government bodies are not engaged in a business for VAT purposes when they do something in the capacity of a public authority. Government bodies do this when they act under a legal regime that is only applicable to the public sector, as opposed to legal regimes that can equally apply to the business or voluntary sectors.

The European Court of Justice ruled that, in certain circumstances, central and local government bodies act as public authorities when they operate tolled bridges, tunnels or roads. These tolls therefore remain outside the scope of VAT. Individual tolls included in this category, whose operators have not been individually contacted by Customs about the changes covered by this Business Brief, are as follows:

- Cleddau Bridge
- Dartford Crossing
- Erskine Bridge
- Forth Road Bridge
- Humber Bridge
- Itchen Bridge
- Mersey Tunnel
- Tamar Bridge
- Tay Bridge
- Tyne Tunnel.

Where a central or local government body operates a congestion-charging scheme under public statute, these congestion charges are also outside the scope of VAT.

The Court held that in any other circumstances than those described above, a toll charge is consideration for a standard rated supply.

Customs has therefore written to the operators of regulated tolls affected by this ruling to inform them that, from 1 February 2003, their toll charges are subject to VAT, and alerting them to the arrangements which have been put in place by the Department of Transport and Scottish Executive to manage the impact of these changes.

Any operator in any doubt about the VAT status of their toll charges, or any body which is in the process of introducing a toll or similar charge, is invited to contact the National Advice Service.

How does this affect VAT registered businesses using tolled roads?

From 1 February 2003, VAT registered businesses will be able to recover the VAT charged on tolls if they are entitled to do so under the normal rules. Businesses are advised to enquire about the VAT status of toll charges when they pay them.

It will not be necessary to obtain a VAT invoice to support any claim for input tax on a toll paid at the toll booth for a single or return journey costing up to £25. Otherwise, it will be necessary to obtain a VAT invoice or other proof or payment as appropriate.

Any business or tax professional with questions about the implications of this ruling is also welcome to seek advice from the National Advice Service.

BUSINESS BRIEF 08/00

VAT relief on constructing charity buildings

This Business Brief announces a new extra-statutory concession clarifying the rules for charities constructing new buildings. It will come into effect on 1 June 2000.

Background

Charities which construct new buildings can obtain zero-rating on the costs of construction if the building is intended for use solely for non-business purposes. Relief is not available where any non-qualifying use takes place (i.e. when the building is used solely for business use or where business and non-business use take place at the same time).

However, a small amount of non-qualifying use has been allowed in the past under an informal arrangement (often known as the 10 per cent concession) drawn up in 1989.

That arrangement, which measured the use of the building by comparing the amount of time the building was used solely for a non-business purpose to the total time the building was available for use, did not always meet the needs of charities. Customs has now formalised a concession that allows charities to use other methods of calculating the extent of qualifying non-business use.

New methods of calculation

Charities can now calculate the extent of qualifying non-business use by reference to time, floor space or the number of people using the building. The non-qualifying use of the building will be disregarded provided that:

- the building is used solely for non-business activity for 90 per cent or more of the time it is available for use;
- 90 per cent or more of the floor space of the building is used solely for non-business activity; or
- 90 per cent or more of the people using the building are engaged solely on non-business activity.

The above methods can only be applied to the building as a whole, apart from the time-based method which can also be applied to parts of the building. In addition, permission must be sought from Customs to use any of the methods, except the time-based method when applied to the whole building.

The new concession will also apply when determining the use of a listed non-business charitable building when alteration work is carried out.

BUSINESS BRIEF 22/97

VAT: Redrow Group plc – House of Lords' decision

This Business Brief explains Customs' interpretation of the House of Lords' judgment in the *Redrow Group plc* case, and sets out the policy we intend to adopt in cases where the *Redrow* decision is being relied upon. We are issuing the brief in response to a number of enquiries about how Customs view the decision.

The case itself concerned whether Redrow was entitled to deduct as input tax the VAT charged by estate agents as part of a scheme whereby, to encourage the sale of its new houses, Redrow paid the agents' fees for selling prospective purchasers' existing homes. The House of Lords confirmed Redrow's right to deduction of the tax, finding that, in the particular circumstances, Redrow contracted for and received services from the estate agents.

Our view is that the decision only applies where the circumstances are similar to the *Redrow* case. That is, where there is a claim to input tax credit by a taxable person who has commissioned the goods or services and contracted with the supplier for them. The claim would then be allowed to the extent that the goods or services provided by the supplier on which input tax is incurred are used by the taxable person in making taxable supplies.

Specifically, Customs do not consider that the *Redrow* decision supports a broad principle of 'anyone that pays for a supply is its recipient and can deduct the tax on it' or, alternatively, that 'anyone who pays must always be receiving a supply of something in return for the payment'. For example, we consider that it has no relevance to circumstances where a third party is simply meeting the costs of another. Neither do we accept that a taxable person must have paid for a supply in order to be entitled to recover the input tax.

Finally, Customs consider that the broad principles and precedent governing input tax deduction are not affected by the *Redrow* decision.

These principles are explained in Customs Guidance Manual Vol. 1–3, Chapter 2, Section 12(B).

Glossary of terms

Annual accounting scheme a special scheme allowing a taxable person to make a single annual return in accounting for VAT.

Annual adjustment the calculation carried out at the end of March, April or May each year, depending on the VAT period end of the taxable person, with regard to partial exemption, which provides for an adjustment to the VAT recovery made in each of the VAT periods in the year, and is entered in the VAT period after the VAT year end.

Approved alteration an alteration (rather than repair or maintenance) to the fabric/structure of a protected building which required and has received listed-building or scheduled-monument consent.

Bad debt relief the special scheme under which the VAT charged on a debt may be claimed back from Customs after six months have elapsed from the date payment was due.

Beneficial owner the person to whom the beneficial interest in a property accrues.

Building materials materials which are ordinarily supplied and installed by builders in the course of construction.

Capital Goods Scheme the VAT scheme which provides for an adjustment in the VAT recovered on certain items of capital expenditure over a longer period than the VAT year in which they are purchased.

Capital item an item which falls within the terms of the Capital Goods Scheme (certain land or property over £250,000 in value and computers over £50,000 in value).

Cash Accounting Scheme the VAT scheme which allows businesses with a turnover not exceeding £750,000 (£600,000 to commence using the scheme) to account for VAT on a cash basis rather than the usual invoice basis.

Charitable non-business use see 'relevant charitable building'.

Composite supply a supply comprising of one or more elements, where one of the elements is predominant and the other elements are ancillary to this, so that the whole composite supply is treated for VAT purposes in accordance with the predominant element.

Compulsory registration the requirement to register when a business exceeds the turnover limits in force.

Consideration payment for a supply, whether in money terms or in kind, such as with barter transactions.

Curtilage the area of land around a building which is used in conjunction with it. There is no legal definition of curtilage within the VAT legislation.

De minimis **limits** refers to the limit of the amount of exempt input tax under which a partially exempt business may recover all of their input tax.

Deed of rectification a document altering the terms of a contract retrospectively, i.e. altering the term of a lease of up to 21 years in a dwelling or other qualifying building so that it is over 21 years and falls eligible for zero rating.

Deemed supply refers to where the legislation stipulates that a supply is made, for example, private use of business assets.

Default Interest interest charged by Customs on overdue VAT.

Default Surcharge the system which penalises taxable persons who are late in paying tax due on Returns.

Deregistration removal of a taxable person from the VAT register when they cease to make taxable supplies or when taxable supplies fall below the deregistration limits in force.

Directly attributable VAT input tax which is wholly incurred in relation to the making of either taxable or exempt supplies.

Dwelling a house, flat or other self-contained unit for living in. The legislation provides a definition of 'designed as a dwelling' at VATA 1994, Sched.8 Gp.5 Note 2 which applies for zero rating of new construction, etc.

Election to waive exemption see 'option to tax'.

Exempt supplies listed in VAT Act 1994 Sched.9 which are not chargeable to VAT, and carry no right to the recovery of input tax incurred in relation to them – not to be confused with zero-rated supplies, which bear no VAT but do carry the right of input tax deduction.

Exempt input tax input tax which is attributable to the making of exempt supplies, either directly or indirectly.

Exempt land land or buildings which will not be used for at least 80% taxable purposes.

First grant the freehold sale or the premium payable on a lease or the first payment of rent under a lease.

Flat rate scheme a VAT accounting scheme for small businesses with a turnover below £150,000.

Golden brick scheme a planning concept used mainly in conjunction with housing associations which makes use of the zero rating for partly completed dwellings and other qualifying buildings.

Grant of facilities involves the provision or use of the fixtures and fittings in a building rather than a licence to occupy the land or building itself, and therefore falls short of an interest in land for VAT exemption purposes under VATA 1994, Sched.9 Gp.1.

Handicapped person an individual who is chronically sick or disabled.

Input tax VAT incurred on expenditure which the taxable person can recover, subject to the partial exemption rules. The term 'input tax' does not cover VAT incurred on non-business activities, which must be separated from other VAT incurred before input tax can be identified, VAT on private expenditure, or VAT which is statutorily blocked from recovery, such as VAT on cars and certain materials installed by builders.

Input tax recovery the amount of input tax claimable on a taxable person's VAT Return.

In the course of construction usually refers to whether goods are supplied 'in the course of construction', i.e. by the person providing construction services.

Law of Property Act (LPA) Receiver a Receiver appointed under s.109 of the Law of Property Act 1925.

Lease–leaseback an arrangement whereby the owner of a building leases it to a third party and accepts a lease back of the property, used in conjunction with the option to tax to gain recovery of VAT on construction of buildings.

Major interest refers to the grant of the fee simple/freehold interest or a lease of over 21 years, including an assignment or surrender.

Multiple occupancy dwelling a dwelling which is designed for occupation by more than one household (such as bed-sits).

Multiple supply a package of supplies for which a single price is paid, but where one or more of the elements of the supply is not dependent upon another and the consideration should therefore be apportioned between the various elements of the supply in considering their treatment for VAT purposes.

Non-business use use of business goods/services otherwise than in the course or furtherance of a business activity.

Non-recoverable VAT input tax which the taxable person is unable to recover, either because it is statutorily blocked or due to partial exemption.

Novation the contractual release of an original party to a transaction and their replacement by a third party.

Option to tax more technically known as the election to waive exemption, this refers to the provision under Sched.10 to VATA for owners of interests in property to elect to charge VAT at standard rate, rather than leave the supply as exempt from VAT.

Output tax the VAT charged on sales to customers.

Outside the scope activities which are non-business, not carried on by a taxable person, or where the place of supply is outside the UK.

Partial exemption a taxable person who makes both taxable and exempt supplies is said to be 'partially exempt', and the VAT Regulations 1995 provide for a means of determining how much VAT input tax may be recovered.

Partial exemption override the special rules applying to a taxable person who incurs in excess of £50,000 of residual input tax, and requires them to look at the use to which purchases have been put, instead of using the standard method.

Person refers to the legal entity, such as a sole proprietor, partnership, company, trust, co-owners, etc.

Person constructing a 'person' to whom construction services are supplied or who is constructing a building on land in which they own an interest.

Place of supply the country in which a supply takes place as provided for under the VAT legislation.

Protected building a Grade I or II listed building or a building which is listed in the schedule of monuments, that is designed to remain or become a dwelling or number of dwellings, see VATA 1994, Sched.8 Gp.6.

Qualifying person a person who meets the conditions for zero rating to apply, for example, with relevant residential or relevant charitable buildings, the qualifying person is the person who will be using the building for the relevant purpose.

Recoverable percentage refers to the percentage of residual input tax which is claimable under the partial exemption method.

Reduced rate European legislation provides for certain supplies to be taxed at a reduced rate of VAT, which must be between 5 and 15%. In the UK, we have a reduced rate of 5%.

Relevant charitable building refers to a building which will be used for non-business, charitable purposes or which will be a village hall or similar building in providing social or recreational facilities to a local community.

Relevant grant scheme a grant scheme stipulated in the legislation, under which recipients may be charged at the lower rate of VAT for certain supplies, such as security and insulation products.

Relevant residential building a building which is the sole or main residence of at least 90% of its residents, such as student accommodation or a care home.

Residual input tax input tax which is neither directly attributable to exempt activities or to taxable activities and therefore falls to be apportioned between the two in accordance with the partial-exemption method.

Reverse charge the mechanism under which purchasers of certain services from suppliers outside the UK must account for output tax on them and claim it back subject to the partial exemption rules.

Scheduled tax invoice a tax invoice issued annually which stipulates the dates payments are due for the year, where the tax point becomes the date stipulated on the document or receipt of payment, if earlier.

Self-supply where the legislation provides for VAT output tax to be accounted for by the recipient of certain goods or services, for example, the self-supply of construction services, where in-house labour, valued in excess of £100,000, is used by an exempt or partially exempt body to construct a building.

Similar establishment a term used in conjunction with the exception from exemption for accommodation in a hotel, inn, boarding house or 'similar establishment', meaning a building in which serviced accommodation, similar to that in a hotel, etc., is provided.

Single-household dwelling a dwelling which is designed for occupation by a single household.

Special method any partial exemption method other than the 'standard method'. Special methods must be agreed in writing with Customs.

Special residential conversion defines the type of building (other than dwellings) to which the 5% rate of VAT for conversion services applies, under VATA 1994, Sched.7A Gp.6 Note 8.

Standard method the method laid down in the VAT Regulations 1995, which a partially exempt person must use to determine their recoverable input tax if a 'special method' has not been agreed in writing with Customs.

Standard rate European legislation provides that each Member State shall charge VAT at a rate between 15 and 25% on all supplies which are not otherwise relieved (i.e. lower-rated, zero-rated or exempt) under the terms of the legislation.

Substantial reconstruction zero rating is provided for the first grant of a major interest in a substantially reconstructed protected building under VATA 1994, Sched.8 Gp.6. Note 4 to the group provides that a building is substantially reconstructed if it has either been gutted so that only the external walls remain or if at least 60% of the works carried out would qualify for zero rating as an 'alteration' if carried out by a taxable person.

Supply of goods the transfer of ownership of goods.

Supply of services anything which is done in return for consideration which is not a supply of goods.

Tax invoice the document required to be provided by a taxable person making a supply of goods or services to another taxable person under Regulation 13 of the VAT Regulations 1995.

Tax point/Time of supply the time at which VAT is due to be accounted for as provided under the legislation.

Taxable input tax VAT incurred by a taxable person which is directly or indirectly attributable to taxable activities.

Taxable person a person who is or is required to be registered for VAT under the terms of the VAT legislation.

Taxable supplies any supply to which the standard, lower or zero rate of VAT applies. This excludes exempt or non-business income.

Taxable use use of goods or services in carrying out an activity chargeable at the standard, lower or zero rate.

Tunnelling a term use to describe the attribution of input tax under the special method agreed for universities.

VAT fraction the fraction used to multiply a value by to determine how much VAT is included in the value. With VAT at 17.5%, the VAT fraction is 17.5/117.5 or 7/47 in its simplest form. For 5% VAT, the VAT fraction is 1/21.

VAT group corporate bodies under the same control may register as a single VAT registration (a VAT group).

VAT inspection an inspection of the taxable person's VAT and other accounting records carried out periodically by Customs.

VAT period the period covered by a VAT Return, usually quarterly or monthly, or, if the person is using the Annual Accounting Scheme, annually.

VAT planning taking steps wholly within the terms of the legislation in order to minimise the amount of VAT payable or maximise the input tax recovery by the taxable person.

VAT Registration Number the unique identification number assigned to a taxable person when they register for VAT.

VAT Return the document upon which the VAT payable/recoverable in any VAT period is reported to Customs.

VAT year a period of 12 months ending on the 31 March, 30 April or 31 May, depending upon the VAT period end of the taxable person.

Voluntary registration the facility for a person to register for VAT where their taxable supplies do not exceed the compulsory registration limits.

Waive exemption see 'option to tax'/'election to waive exemption'.

Zero rate supplies listed in VATA 1994, Sched.8 which carry VAT at 0%. Zero-rated supplies are taxable supplies and qualify for input tax recovery.

Zero rate certificate a certificate required to be given to evidence that the recipient of the supply will be using it for qualifying purposes, such as for relevant residential or relevant charitable use.

Index